BURY THE CHAINS

BOOKS BY
ADAM HOCHSCHILD

Half the Way Home: A Memoir of Father and Son

The Mirror at Midnight: A South African Journey

The Unquiet Ghost: Russians Remember Stalin

Finding the Trapdoor: Essays, Portraits, Travels

King Leopold's Ghost: A Story of Greed, Terror, and Heroism in Colonial Africa

Bury the Chains: Prophets and Rebels in the Fight to Free an Empire's Slaves

BURY the CHAINS

PROPHETS AND REBELS
IN THE FIGHT TO
FREE AN EMPIRE'S SLAVES

Adam Hochschild

HOUGHTON MIFFLIN COMPANY

BOSTON • NEW YORK

2005

Visit our Web site: www.houghtonmifflinbooks.com.

Library of Congress Cataloging-in-Publication Data

Hochschild, Adam.

Bury the chains : prophets and rebels in the fight to free an empire's slaves / Adam Hochschild.

p. cm.

Includes bibliographical references and index.

ISBN 0-618-10469-0

1. Antislavery movements— Great Britain—History— 18th century. 2. Antislavery movements—Great Britain —History—19th century. I. Title.

HT1163.H63 2004

326'.8'0941—dc22 2004054091

Book design by Melissa Lotfy

Printed in the United States of America

MP 10 9 8 7 6 5 4 3 2 1

Portions of this book previously appeared, in somewhat different form, in *Mother Jones* and the *San Francisco Chronicle Magazine.*

For

Patricia H. Labalme

(1927–2002)

CONTENTS

PART III: "A WHOLE NATION CRYING WITH ONE VOICE"

PART IV: WAR AND REVOLUTION

PART V: BURY THE CHAINS

Note

In quoting letters, newspapers, documents, and other primary sources, I have retained the original spelling and punctuation, including the eighteenth-century habit of scattering about commas, capital letters, and italics far more profligately than we do now.

Giving the equivalents in today's currency to sums of money from two hundred years ago is a matter far from precise, since money then and now bought or buys different things. A Londoner of the 1700s could not buy a computer; one of today cannot buy a stagecoach ticket to Bath. However, to the extent that we can make comparisons, £1 in 1787 had the purchasing power of approximately $140 as this book went to press. My apparent departures from this rule of thumb stem from the decline in the value of the pound over time, and from the fact that the pound used in the various British West Indian islands was worth somewhat less than the British pound.

BURY THE CHAINS

INTRODUCTION: TWELVE MEN IN A PRINTING SHOP

STRANGELY, in a city where it seems that on almost every block a famous event or resident is commemorated by a blue and white glazed plaque, none marks this spot. All you can see today, after you leave the Bank station of the London Underground, walk several blocks, and then take a few steps into a courtyard, are a few low, nondescript office buildings, an ancient pub, and, on the site itself, 2 George Yard, a glass and steel high-rise. Nothing remains of the bookstore and printing shop that once stood here, or recalls the spring day more than two hundred years ago when a dozen people—a somber-looking crew, most of them not removing their high-crowned black hats—filed through its door and sat down for a meeting. Cities build monuments to kings, prime ministers, and generals, not to citizens with no official position who once gathered in a printing shop. Yet what these citizens began rippled across the world and we feel its aftereffects still. It is no wonder that they won the admiration of the first and greatest student of what we now call civil society. The result of the series of events begun that afternoon in London, wrote Alexis de Tocqueville, was "absolutely without precedent. . . . If you pore over the histories of all peoples, I doubt that you will find anything more extraordinary."

To understand how momentous was this beginning, we must picture a world in which the vast majority of people are prisoners. Most of them have known no other way of life. They are not free to live or go where they want. They plant, cultivate, and harvest most of the earth's major crops. They earn no money from their labor. Their work often lasts twelve or fourteen hours a day. Many are subject to cruel whippings or other punishments if they do not work hard enough. They die young. They are not chained or bound most of the time, but they are in bondage, part of a global economy based on forced labor. Such a world would, of course, be unthinkable today.

But this was the world—our world—just two centuries ago, and to most people then, it was unthinkable that it could ever be otherwise. At the end of the eighteenth century, well over three quarters of all people alive were in bondage of one kind or another, not the captivity of striped prison uniforms, but of various systems of slavery or serfdom. The age was a high point in the trade in which close to eighty thousand chained and shackled Africans were loaded onto slave ships and transported to the New World each year. In parts of the Americas, slaves far outnumbered free persons. The same was true in parts of Africa, and it was from these millions of indigenous slaves that African chiefs and slave dealers drew most of the men and women they sold to Europeans and Arabs sailing their ships along the continent's coasts. African slaves were spread throughout the Islamic world, and the Ottoman Empire enslaved other peoples as well. In India and other parts of Asia, tens of millions of farmworkers were in outright slavery, and others were peasants in debt bondage that tied them and their labor to a particular landlord as harshly as any slave was bound to a plantation owner in South Carolina or Georgia. Native Americans turned prisoners of war into slaves and sold them, both to neighboring tribes and to the Europeans now pushing their way across the continent. In Russia the majority of the population were serfs, often bought, sold, whipped, or sent to the army at the will of their owners.

The era was one when, as the historian Seymour Drescher puts it, "freedom, not slavery, was the peculiar institution." This world of bondage seemed all the more normal then, because anyone looking back in time would have seen little but other slave systems. The ancient Greeks had slaves; the Romans had an estimated two to three million of them in Italy alone; the Incas and Aztecs had slaves; the sacred texts of most major religions took slavery for granted. Slavery had existed before money or written law.

One measure of how much slavery pervaded the world of the eighteenth century is the traffic on the Atlantic Ocean. We usually think of the Atlantic of this period as being filled with shiploads of hopeful white immigrants. But they were only a minority of those carried to the New World. So rapidly were slaves worked to death, above all on the brutal sugar plantations of the Caribbean, that between 1660 and 1807, ships brought well over three times as many Africans across the ocean to British colonies as they did Europeans. And, of course, it was not just to British territories that slaves were sent. From Senegal to Virginia, Sierra Leone to Charleston, the Niger delta to Cuba, Angola to Brazil, and on dozens upon dozens of crisscrossing paths taken by thousands of vessels, the Atlantic was a conveyor belt to early death in the fields of an immense swath of plantations that stretched from Baltimore to Rio de Janeiro and beyond.

Looking back today, what is even more astonishing than the pervasiveness of slavery in the late 1700s is how swiftly it died. By the end of the following century, slavery was, at least on paper, outlawed almost everywhere. The antislavery movement had achieved its goal in little more than one lifetime.

This is the story of the first, pioneering wave of that campaign. Every American schoolchild learns how slaves fled Southern plantations, following the North Star on the Underground Railroad. But England is where the story really begins, and for decades it was where American abolitionists looked for inspiration and finally for proof that the colossally difficult task of uprooting slavery could be accomplished. If we were to fix one point when the crusade began, it would be the late afternoon of May 22, 1787, when twelve determined men sat down in the printing shop at 2 George Yard, amid flatbed presses, wooden trays of type, and large sheets of freshly printed book pages, to begin one of the most ambitious and brilliantly organized citizens' movements of all time.

A long chain of events, large and small, led to that meeting. Perhaps the most crucial moment came when Thomas Clarkson, a twenty-five-year-old Englishman on his way to London, paused, dismounted from his horse, and sat down at the roadside, lost in thought. Many months later, he would be the principal organizer of the gathering at George Yard. Red-haired, dressed in black, he was the youngest of those who entered the shop that day, perhaps ducking his head slightly as he came through the doorway, for he was a full six inches taller than the average Englishman of his time. In the years to come, his sixteen-hour-a-day campaigning against slavery would take him by horseback on a thirty-five-thousand-mile odyssey, from waterfront pubs to an audience with an emperor, from the decks of navy ships to parliamentary hearing rooms. More than once people would threaten to kill him, and on a Liverpool pier in the midst of a storm, a group of slave ship officers would nearly succeed. Almost forgotten today, he remains one of the towering figures in the history of human rights. Although we will not meet him until Part II of this book, he is its central character.

There are many others as well, most of whom were not at the meeting that day. John Newton was a slave ship captain who would later write the hymn "Amazing Grace." Olaudah Equiano was a resourceful slave who earned his freedom, spoke out for others in bondage, and reached tens of thousands of readers with his life story. Granville Sharp, a musician, pamphleteer, and all-round eccentric, rescued a succession of blacks in England from being returned to slavery in the Americas. A London dandy named James Stephen fled to the West Indies to escape an intricately tangled love life, and then was transformed when some slaves he saw in a Barbados courtroom were sentenced to a punishment he found almost unimaginable. A colleague of his became the only abolitionist leader who ever crossed the Atlantic on a slave ship, taking notes in Greek letters to disguise them from the eyes of prying crewmen. Later in time, another key figure was a Quaker widow whose passionate stand against all compromise helped reignite a movement in the doldrums. And one was the leader of history's largest slave revolt, which defeated the armies of Europe's two most powerful empires.

The British abolitionists were shocked by what they came to learn about slavery and the slave trade. They were deeply convinced that they lived in a remarkable time that would see both evils swept from the face of the earth. Like anyone who wages such a fight, they discovered that injustice does not vanish so easily. But their passion and optimism are still contagious and still relevant to our times, when, in so many parts of the world, equal rights for all men and women seem far distant.

The movement they forged is a landmark for an additional reason. There is always something mysterious about human empathy, and when we feel it and when we don't. Its sudden upwelling at this particular moment caught everyone by surprise. Slaves and other subjugated people have rebelled throughout history, but the campaign in England was something never seen before: it was the first time a large number of people became outraged, and stayed outraged for many years, over someone *else's* rights. And most startling of all, the rights of people of another color, on another continent. No one was more taken aback by this than Stephen Fuller, the London agent for Jamaica's planters, an absentee plantation owner himself and a central figure in the proslavery lobby. As tens of thousands of protesters signed petitions to Parliament, Fuller was amazed that these were "stating no grievance or injury of any kind or sort, affecting the Petitioners themselves." His bafflement is understandable. He was seeing something new in history.

At times, Britons even seemed to be organizing against their own self-interest. From Sheffield, famous for making scissors, scythes, knives, and razors, 769 metalworkers petitioned Parliament in 1789 against the slave trade. "Cutlery wares . . . being sent in considerable quantities to the Coast of Africa . . . as the price of Slaves—your petitioners may be supposed to be prejudiced in their interests if the said trade in Slaves should be abolished. But your petitioners having always understood that the natives of Africa have the greatest aversion to foreign Slavery . . . consider the case of the nations of Africa as their own."

For fifty years, activists in England worked to end slavery in the British Empire. None of them gained a penny by doing so, and their eventual success meant a huge loss to the imperial economy. Scholars estimate that abolishing the slave trade and then slavery cost the British people 1.8 percent of their annual national income over more than half a century, many times the percentage most wealthy countries today give in foreign aid.

The abolitionists succeeded because they mastered one challenge that still faces anyone who cares about social and economic justice: drawing connections between the near and the distant. We have long lived in a world where everyday objects embody labor in another corner of the earth. Often we do not know where the things we use come from, or the working conditions of those who made them. Were the shoes or shirt you're wearing made by children in an Indonesian sweatshop? Or by prison labor in China? What pesticides were breathed in by the Latin American laborers who picked the fruit on your table? And do you even know in what country the innards of your computer were assembled? The eighteenth century had its own booming version of globalization, and at its core was the Atlantic trade in slaves and in the goods they produced. But in England itself there were no caravans of chained captives, no whip-wielding overseers on horseback stalking the rows of sugar cane. The abolitionists' first job was to make Britons understand what lay behind the sugar they ate, the tobacco they smoked, the coffee they drank.

One thing more makes these men and women from the age of wigs, swords, and stagecoaches seem surprisingly contemporary. This small group of people not only helped to end one of the worst of human injustices in the most powerful empire of its time; they also forged virtually every important tool used by citizens' movements in democratic countries today.

Think of what you're likely to find in your mailbox—or electronic mailbox—over a month or two. An invitation to join the local chapter of a national environmental group. If you say yes, a logo to put on your car bumper. A flier asking you to boycott California grapes or Guatemalan coffee. A poster to put in your window promoting this campaign. A notice that a prominent social activist will be reading from her new book at your local bookstore. A plea that you write your representative in Congress or Parliament, to vote for that Guatemalan coffee boycott bill. A "report card" on how your legislators have voted on these and similar issues. A newsletter from the group organizing support for the grape pickers or the coffee workers.

Each of these tools, from the poster to the political book tour, from the consumer boycott to investigative reporting designed to stir people to action, is part of what we take for granted in a democracy. Two and a half centuries ago, few people assumed this. When we wield any of these tools today, we are using techniques devised or perfected by the campaign that held its first meeting at 2 George Yard in 1787. From their successful crusade we still have much to learn.

If, early that year, you had stood on a London street corner and insisted that slavery was morally wrong and should be stopped, nine out of ten listeners would have laughed you off as a crackpot. The tenth might have agreed with you in principle, but assured you that ending slavery was wildly impractical: the British Empire's economy would collapse. The parliamentarian Edmund Burke, for example, opposed slavery but thought that the prospect of ending even just the Atlantic slave trade was "chimerical." Within a few short years, however, the issue of slavery had moved to center stage in British political life. There was an abolition committee in every major city or town in touch with a central committee in London. More than 300,000 Britons were refusing to eat slave-grown sugar. Parliament was flooded with far more signatures on abolition petitions than it had ever received on any other subject. And in 1792, the House of Commons passed the first law banning the slave trade. For reasons we will see, a ban did not take effect for some years to come, and British slaves were not finally freed until long after that. But there was no mistaking something crucial: in an astonishingly short period of time, public opinion in Europe's most powerful nation had undergone a sea change. From this unexpected transformation there would be no going back.

"Never doubt," said Margaret Mead, "that a small group of thoughtful, committed citizens can change the world. Indeed, it is the only thing that ever has." This book is about one such group. Their story is not a simple one, but a ragged and untidy epic that did not unfold in the orderly way they hoped for. It would sprawl across decades and continents, encompassing not just the long Atlantic traffic in slaves and the British slave colonies of the Caribbean, but also threads that stretched to unexpected places as far off as New York, Nova Scotia, and an improbable Utopian colony on the coast of Africa. It would be filled with dashed hopes and wrong turnings. It would become interwoven with great historical currents which, on that afternoon in the George Yard printing shop in 1787, no one foresaw: above all the dreams of equality unleashed by the French Revolution, and a series of ever-larger slave revolts that shook the British Empire and made clear that if the slaves were not emancipated they might well free themselves. The stage on which British slavery lived and at last died was a vast one. We must begin by visiting—through the eyes of future players in the drama of abolition—several corners of that world of bondage which, to a citizen of the eighteenth century, looked as if it would endure for all time.

I

WORLD OF BONDAGE

1

MANY GOLDEN DREAMS

When people dream of riches, their imaginations follow the shape of the economy. As the twentieth century ended, for instance, dot-com billionaires inspired envy, for it was their private jets that waited on the tarmac at Aspen and Sun Valley. In late-nineteenth-century America, railroads seemed the quickest path to wealth, for it was their robber-baron owners whose luxurious private cars sat on sidings at resorts like Newport. In the England of the eighteenth century, the luxury vehicles were the carriages of Caribbean sugar planters, and the imagined road to riches led through the cane fields of the New World. At his favorite seaside resort of Weymouth, the story goes, King George III once encountered an absentee owner of a Jamaican plantation whose coach and liveried outriders were even more resplendent than his own. "Sugar, sugar, eh?" the King exclaimed. "All *that* sugar!"

The pursuit of wealth from the West Indian plantations, or from the ships that supplied them with slaves and brought their produce back to Britain, shaped the lives of many a young Englishman. Few have left us a more vivid record of this quest than John Newton. Born in London in 1725, he was only eleven years old when his sea captain father first took him on a voyage. As a crewman on his father's ship, Newton made trips to ports in England, Holland, Spain, and Portugal. But Captain Newton had bigger plans for him. When he was seventeen, Newton wrote in his memoirs, "a merchant in Liverpool, an intimate friend of my father's . . . proposed to send me for some years to Jamaica, and to charge himself with the care of my future fortune."

However, a week before he was to embark, while visiting relatives in Kent, Newton fell in love with their daughter, Mary Catlett. "None of the scenes of misery and wickedness I afterwards experienced," he wrote, "ever banished her a single hour . . . from my waking thoughts." He stayed on so long that the ship for Jamaica sailed without him. Newton's father, furious at the opportunity lost, found his son a seaman's berth under a fellow captain, on a voyage to the Mediterranean. Returning to England, Newton again visited Mary in Kent, but this time, soon after departing his beloved's house in a daze, he suffered the fate feared by every young man living near England's seaports: he was seized by a naval press gang. Britain and France, Europe's two most powerful nations, were preparing for one of their periodic wars, five of which they would fight in the eighteenth century. And the Royal Navy, as usual, was manning its ships by sending armed gangs through the streets to kidnap all the sailors they could find.

Newton spent the next year aboard the HMS *Harwich,* braving storms, battling with the French, and writing shy, mournful love letters to Mary. One, dated January 24, 1745, "One in the morning," reads: "I am just now come from performing a Watch of four hours, which I have spent with great satisfaction, by the force of supposing myself in your Company. . . . This Voyage . . . I seriously believe will either make or marr me: Its true I hope to succeed; but . . . I shall not value Riches but for the opportunity of laying them at your feet . . . for I am certain that I could enjoy them with no Relish without you."

To his great dismay, Newton found out that the *Harwich* was scheduled for a five-year patrol in the Far East. While the ship was anchored at Plymouth, the lovesick young man deserted. He was captured two days later, marched back to his ship, and put in irons. Tied to a wooden grating on the deck, he was flogged before all the crew. Then the ship set sail, part of a convoy of more than a hundred vessels. And a grim passage it was, especially for the lowest-ranking sailors, victims of the press gang, whose hammocks were slung in cramped and airless quarters below decks. First a storm blew two ships onto the rocks of the English coast with great loss of life; then one collided with another "and carried away the Foremast while 28 of their best men were furling the Foretopsail who all perished." Added to nature's violence was the navy's: a diary kept by another *Harwich* sailor lists more floggings, including that of one man who was "flogged round the fleet"—given forty lashes for starters, then rowed to receive twenty more in front of each navy ship in sight, as an example to all. Another *Harwich* seaman was forced to run the gauntlet—three circuits of the deck, receiving the blows or lashes of his fellow sailors—"for committing sodomy with a sheep."

When the *Harwich* stopped for supplies at the island of Madeira, Newton spied an unexpected opportunity. "I . . . saw a man putting his clothes into a boat, who told me he was going to leave us." The *Harwich* was exchanging sailors with a "Guineaman," a slave-trading vessel bound for Africa; its captain, as it happened, was a friend of his father. Captains often traded sailors to acquire men with a particular skill or to get rid of troublemakers. Newton begged to be included in the trade, and, to his joy, he was. A half hour later, a seaman from the Guineaman's crew, no doubt horrified, found himself in Newton's place on the way to five years in the Far East. The delighted Newton, who in a single year had been kidnapped, chained, flogged, shot at in battle, and separated from the woman he loved, was now miraculously taking his first step into the flourishing Atlantic slave economy. He was nineteen years old.

Although the expanding British Empire already had outposts in India and its thirteen colonies on the east coast of North America, its greatest wealth lay in the Caribbean sugar plantations. These were supplied with slaves by ships like the one Newton had just boarded, and the chance to be part of this trade seemed to offer riches to even the humblest Englishman. The Atlantic slave trade had first touched British life in 1555, when the mariner John Lok had sailed back from West Africa carrying "certaine blacke slaves, whereof some were tall and strong men." Two centuries later, British ships dominated the insatiable market for slaves in the Americas, supplying African captives to French, Spanish, Dutch, and Portuguese colonies as well as to Britain's own. In peak years, they carried some forty thousand chained men, women, and child slaves across the Atlantic—as many as those carried by the slave ships of all other countries combined. "What a glorious and advantageous trade this is," wrote one man who worked for a firm of slave merchants. ". . . It is the hinge on which all the trade of this globe moves." Another trader believed the transport of slaves was "the foundation of our commerce, the support of our colonies, the life of our navigation, and first cause of our national industry and riches." The thought that anyone might ever want to ban this lucrative business was inconceivable.

Sailors like Newton dreamt of winning their fortunes, but the big money was made by ship owners who often never left England. We have detailed records, for example, of seventy-four slave voyages in which the Liverpool merchant William Davenport invested. His overall rate of profit was 8.1 percent. However, two voyages by his ship *Hawke,* in the dicey war years of 1779 and 1780—when prices soared for slaves who could be slipped past French and American warships to Caribbean buyers—netted returns of 73.5 and 147 percent. Successes are what pass into legend, so the talk of the Liverpool docks and pubs was of bonanza voyages like the *Hawke*'s, not of those where ships went down, or lost their crews to malaria and yellow fever, or were captured by French privateers (the fate of the *Hawke,* as it happened, on its next voyage).

Besides the hope of profits, the slave trade had other allures. To make a slave voyage was to be an entrepreneur. Most officers, the ship's doctor, and sometimes valued senior crewmen like the carpenter got the right to carry a "privilege slave" of their own, whom they could buy in Africa and sell in the New World, pocketing the income. Captains might carry as many as four privilege slaves. Sometimes an officer would bring one home to England as a personal servant, a badge of one's travels to far-off places and a great conversation piece in a country where slaves were rare. Adding to the trade's entrepreneurial flavor, captains thousands of miles away from their home ports had considerable discretion over where in Africa they bought slaves and where in the Americas they sold them, and their fortunes rode on these decisions.

The slave trade promised wealth, independence, and excitement in a way that carrying cargo on a fixed route back and forth across the English Channel never could. To seafaring young Englishmen, it had the aura that their counterparts in the next century would find in a gold rush. The trade was even literally touched with gold, for the guinea coin, in Newton's youth worth about $200 in today's money, took its name from the Guinea coast of Africa and was first minted from African gold; with their stylish cocked hats, slave captains wore laced coats with gold or silver buttons and gold buckles on their shoes.

Finally, the slave economy's profits were a path to respectability. John Gladstone, a member of Parliament and the father of a future prime minister, owned Caribbean sugar and coffee estates with well over a thousand slaves. The cathedral-like library of All Souls College, Oxford, was financed by profits from a slave plantation in Barbados. Family slave estates in Jamaica paid for the elegant house on Wimpole Street where Elizabeth Barrett would be courted by Robert Browning. William Beckford, with a vast fortune based on slave-grown Jamaican sugar, hosted the most sumptuous banquets since Henry VIII and hired Mozart to give his son piano lessons. Edward Colston, M.P., was the best-known philanthropist in Bristol: vestryman of his church, lavish benefactor of schools, poorhouses, hospitals, and retired seamen, creator of an endowment that paid for sermons on specified subjects to be preached annually at several churches and the city jail. Colston proudly declared that "every helpless widow is my wife and her distressed orphans my children." A large bronze statue of him still overlooks Bristol's Colston Avenue, and it was not until one night in 1998 that someone scrawled on its base the name of one of the professions in which he made his fortune: SLAVE TRADER.

In its quest for human cargo, the ship John Newton had joined sailed south, along the great western shoulder of Africa that bulges into the Atlantic. Below the Sahara Desert, where the coast starts to curve inward, slaving territory began. It was on this long expanse, stretching from what is Senegal to Nigeria today, that British ships gathered most of their slaves. The collecting was slow and laborious, for seldom could a captain come anywhere near filling his ship in one spot. Instead, he haggled for two or three slaves here, three or four there, a dozen somewhere else, during what averaged three to four months of sailing back and forth along the coast.

The Atlantic slave trade depended on the fact that most of the societies of Africa—chiefdoms and kingdoms large and small, even groups of nomads—had their own systems of slavery. People were enslaved as punishment for crimes, as payment for a debt, or, most commonly of all, as prisoners of war. Slaves were often less important as labor than as prized status objects. This had its horrific side when they were killed in human sacrifice rituals, but it meant that African slave systems were in other ways sometimes less harsh than those that would come into being in the Americas: some slaves could earn their freedom in a generation or two, and sometimes could intermarry with free people. But they were still slaves. Once European ships started cruising the African coast offering all kinds of tempting goods for slaves, kings and chiefs began selling their human property to African dealers who roamed far into the interior. Groups of captives, ranging from a few dozen to six or eight hundred, were force-marched to the coast, the prisoners' hands bound behind their backs, their necks connected by wooden yokes. Along the coast itself, a scattering of whites, blacks, and mulattos worked as middlemen for the Atlantic trade. They bought slaves from these traveling dealers or nearby African chiefs, held them until a ship appeared, and sold them to a European or American captain. As time went on, ships occasionally tried to cut prices by bypassing the middlemen and sending their own small boats up rivers to buy slaves directly from inland chiefs. Captains paid for slaves with everything from cloth, glass beads, iron bars, and pots and pans, to gunpowder and muskets—the beginning of the long history of the world's North supplying arms to its South.

As his ship filled with slaves, the young Newton quickly took sexual advantage of the women. He does not give us the details, but his diary mentions his "brutish lusts." In the memoirs he wrote twenty years afterwards, he refers to a Bible passage about adultery and then adds, "I was exceedingly vile indeed. . . . I . . . sinned with a high hand." Only still later in his life did he finally admit that sex on slave vessels amounted to rape: "When the women and girls are taken on board a ship, naked, trembling, terrified . . . they are often exposed to the wanton rudeness of white savages. . . . The prey is divided, upon the spot. . . . Resistance or refusal, would be utterly in vain."

Wild and rambunctious, Newton antagonized his fellow crewmen and taunted his new captain: "I made a song, in which I ridiculed his ship, his designs, and his person, and soon taught it to the whole ship's company." Finally, the angry captain threatened to trade him back to the navy, "and this, from what I had known already, was more dreadful to me than death. To avoid it, I determined to remain in Africa; and amused myself with many golden dreams that here I should find an opportunity of improving my fortune."

At this point the ship was most of the way down the West African bulge, off Sierra Leone, a stretch of coastline much frequented by European slave captains. Its slaves, long experienced in cultivating rice in the coastal swampland, fetched good prices from landowners establishing rice plantations in the American South. Newton and his captain were eager to be rid of each other. The ship dropped him on an island where he went to work for a white slave trader whose African concubine was his business partner. With his youthful gift for getting at loggerheads with everyone, Newton quickly fell out with them both. He then became severely ill with what was probably malaria. Setting off on a business trip, the trader left Newton in the care of his concubine, who seemed to relish the rare chance to mistreat a white man. "I had sometimes not a little difficulty to procure a draught of cold water when burning with a fever," he later recalled. "My bed was a mat spread upon a board or chest, and a log of wood my pillow. . . . She lived in plenty herself, but hardly allowed me sufficient to sustain life, except now and then . . . she would send me victuals in her own plate after she had dined. . . . Once, I well remember, I was called to receive this bounty from her own hand; but being exceedingly weak and feeble, I dropped the plate. Those who live in plenty can hardly conceive how this loss touched me; but she had the cruelty to laugh at my disappointment; and though the table was covered with dishes . . . she refused to give me any more." He crept out at night to search for edible roots, which he pulled up and ate raw, though they made him sick. Sometimes "even . . . slaves in the chain . . . secretly brought me victuals (for they durst not be seen to do it) from their own slender pittance."

Later, the trader became convinced Newton was cheating him, and for a time clapped him in irons. Newton always considered this period of humiliation and captivity the low point of his life. But neither at the time nor when he wrote his memoirs nearly twenty years later did he identify in the slightest with the "slaves in the chain" who had risked punishment to share their meager rations with him. His main aim was to find a job with another trading post, in this part of the world where the main commodity sold was human beings. At last he succeeded, and before long he "had a share in the management. . . . Business flourished."

One day in 1747 the sails of a merchant vessel appeared over the horizon. The ship dropped anchor, attracted by the column of smoke from the trading post that indicated goods for sale. The vessel's owner, a Liverpool merchant named Joseph Manesty, was a friend of Newton's father and had told the captain to keep an eye out for young John on the African coast and to try to bring him home. Newton was at first reluctant to leave his promising job, but was eventually convinced to do so by the hope of seeing Mary Catlett again and a story the captain concocted about an unexpected inheritance waiting for him. It was many months, however, before the ship finished trading in Africa and headed back to England. During that time, Newton continued to be, he wrote later, deep in the grip of sin. But the sin that loomed largest in his mind—and nothing says more of how morally invisible was slavery in his world—was that of blasphemy. "My whole life . . . was a course of most horrid impiety and profaneness. I know not that I have ever since met so daring a blasphemer: not content with common oaths and imprecations, I daily invented new ones."

Approaching the British Isles on the final leg of its voyage home, the ship encountered a severe North Atlantic gale. "I . . . was awaked from a sound sleep by the force of a violent sea, which broke on board us. So much of it came down below as filled the cabin I lay in with water. This alarm was followed by a cry from the deck, that the ship was going down." A sailor who went up the ladder to the deck just ahead of Newton was washed overboard. All seemed lost. "I expected that every time the vessel descended into the sea, she would rise no more." The half-frozen, exhausted sailors frantically worked the pumps, bailed with buckets, and jammed clothes and bedding into cracks in the hull. The storm blew most of the sails away, smashed barrels of food to pieces, and swept all of the ship's pigs, sheep, and chickens over the side. Newton pumped for nine hours straight, until he could do no more. Then he cried out, "Lord have mercy on us."

Soon after, the storm abated, as storms will do. When the battered ship limped into the nearest port, its remaining sails stained by seawater, its sailors' rations reduced to small portions of salted cod, Newton remembered his desperate appeal and saw "the hand of God in our danger and deliverance. . . . The Lord had wrought a marvellous thing; I was no longer an infidel; I heartily renounced my former profaneness. . . . I was quite freed from the habit of swearing." On shore, he began going to church, sometimes twice a day. God had saved him, he felt, and his promising career in the slave trade had only just begun.

The following year, 1749, still in search of his fortune, Newton went to sea in another of Joseph Manesty's vessels. This time he was first mate. "My business in this voyage, while upon the Coast, was to sail from place to place in the long-boat to purchase slaves. . . . sometimes venturing in a little canoe thro Seas like Mountains, sometimes traveling thro the woods, often in danger from the wild beasts and much oftner from the more wild Inhabitants." But in a letter home he wrote, "Notwithstanding what I have said in relation to the difficulties I meet with here, I assure you I never was so happy in my life." He abstained from alcohol and meat, feeling that this allowed him to win "mastery over the fleshly appetites."

While on the African coast, Newton helped suppress a shipboard slave rebellion that took the lives of one crew member and several slaves. Then came the ocean crossing. The *Mayflower* had carried 102 passengers on its voyage to New England; Newton's ship was smaller, but held 218 slaves, 62 of whom died at sea. Given the suffocating conditions, the limited and fetid water, and the way sick slaves often had to lie in their own excrement, it is surprising the death rate was not higher. To imagine the slow passage across the Atlantic in a typical square-rigged slave ship, we must picture not only the slaves packed together in rows, each with less floor space than would be taken by a coffin, on a deck dimly lit by a swinging lantern or two at night and forever lurching up and down over the waves, but all of them, plus captain, officers, and crew, jammed for months into a vessel less than one hundred feet long.

When his ship docked at Charleston (then Charles Town), South Carolina, to sell its slaves, Newton walked the brick and cobblestone streets to attend church faithfully, and "almost every day, when business would permit," went into the woods to pray. On his return to England, his good prospects now established, he screwed up his courage and proposed to Mary Catlett. "I sat stupid and speechless for some minutes. . . . My heart was so full, it beat and trembled to that degree, that I knew not how to get a word out." They were married in 1750.

Over the next four years, now promoted to captain, Newton made three more triangle voyages, as they were called, from Liverpool to Africa to the West Indies and back. This route, carrying trading goods to Africa, then slaves to the Caribbean or North America, and then sugar, coffee, cotton, rice, and rum back to Europe, was profitable because vessels could carry cargo on each leg. And the triangle, it seemed, was fatally favored by nature itself, for North Atlantic currents flow clockwise. The Canary Current sped ships from Europe south along Africa's Sahara coast; then the North Equatorial Current carried them and their slave cargoes to the Caribbean; and from there back towards England flowed the Gulf Stream and the North Atlantic Current. The powerful Gulf Stream could add up to 130 miles a day to a ship's speed. For a good part of the year, winds over much of this same route blew clockwise as well.

On his voyages Newton kept a detailed log, punctuated with occasional sketches, that fills 336 pages of a large, leather-bound book; wrote a diary of his spiritual life; and, with every passing ship headed for England, sent voluminous love letters to his wife. He penned everything in a clear script with graceful curls on the capital letters, remarkably neat for being written on a rolling and pitching ship. As significant for what they omit as for what they say, these writings are the widest window we have into the life and mind of a man in the African slave trade.

Much of Newton's journal is the stuff of all eighteenth-century life at sea: the notes of a mariner whose survival depends on wind, calm, storm, the state of rigging, and water supply. He records tides and fathoms, compass courses and speed in knots, and the constant scramble of sending hands aloft to set sails. He labors at the perennial nautical problem of guessing how far east or west he is, since at this time sailors out of sight of land had no accurate way of measuring longitude. Several times, crossing paths with other captains in mid-Atlantic, he stops to hail them, draw up alongside, and compare longitude estimates.

But a slave captain was not just a seafarer; he was also a speculator in a high-risk business. To make money, he had to buy low in Africa and sell high in the West Indies. The part of each triangle voyage along the coast of Africa was really where a captain's fortune was made or lost. Most of what Newton records is the daily business of exchanging muskets, rum, tobacco, and other goods for slaves, all of whom were then branded *JM* with a red-hot iron, to show that they now belonged to Joseph Manesty.

Competition was brisk; there might be well over a hundred ships simultaneously cruising the coast, and demand was always greater than supply. Once it took Newton eight long months to fill his vessel. From the captain's point of view, it was a series of tricky calculations. If it took you too long to assemble a full load of slaves, the earlier batches, imprisoned below decks in the hot, humid climate, would start to die of disease and despair. But if you left for the West Indies before the ship was "fully slaved," you wouldn't turn a profit. If you arrived in the Caribbean in December, as the sugar harvest began, slave prices would be higher—but the last three months of the year had the worst sailing weather for crossing the Atlantic.

In his logbook, Newton constantly weighs these pressures of time, mortality, and profits. When he meets one slave ship with a better supply of trading goods, he vows to avoid its path in the future, because "Captain Ellis gets all the trade that is stirring here. . . . Believe I have lost the purchase of more than 10 slaves for want of the all commanding articles of beer and cyder." When African or mulatto dealers show him slaves, he evaluates them as dispassionately as if they were livestock. "Yellow Will brought me a woman slave, but being long breasted and ill made, refused her, and made him take her on shoar again."

Not long into each stay on the African coast the slaves he has already bought begin to die. "This day buried a fine woman slave, No. 11, having been ailing some time . . . she was taken with a lethargick disorder, which they seldom recover from. Scraped the rooms, then smoked the ship with tar, tobacco and brimstone [sulfur] for 2 hours, afterwards washed with vinegar." Seamen believed "smoking" the ship prevented disease; we can only imagine how the sulfur, tar, and vinegar increased the stench of a poorly ventilated hold jammed with sweating slaves. The smoking was little help against one of the biggest killers, the "bloody flux," or dysentery. "Sent a girl, ill of the flux (No. 92) on shoar . . . not so much in hopes of recovery (for I fear she is past it), as to free the ship of a nuisance. . . . This morning buryed a woman slave (No. 47). Know not what to say she died of for she has not been properly alive since she first came on board."

Death also ravaged Newton's crew, who had no immunities to tropical diseases. It was on these white sailors and officers that Africa took its revenge. In Newton's logbook, slaves, lesser creatures without Christian souls and thus not destined for the next world, "die" or are simply "buryed." But when he speaks of whites, they "depart this life." "A little before midnight, departed this life Mr John Bridson, my chief mate, after sustaining the most violent fever I have ever seen 3 days." On his first trip as captain, Newton left England with a crew of thirty; seven died during the triangle voyage, a higher death rate than among the slaves.

Dozens of entries in Newton's logbook record the meting out of punishments to both crew and slaves. Lovestruck as he might be by his wife, at sea Newton's voice is that of a tough, suspicious man for whom lashing unruly sailors is routine. When one crew-man is caught stealing brandy, Newton "gave him a smart dozen." Sometimes he found that wielding the cat-o'-nine-tails freely was not enough: "In the afternoon while we were off the deck, William Cooney seduced a woman slave down into the room and lay with her brutelike in view of the whole quarter deck, for which I put him in irons." And when a sailor took a swing at another crew member with a sledgehammer,

Newton put him "in hand cuffs and stapled him down to the deck." On another voyage, he discovered "a conspiracy amongst my own people to turn pirates, and take the ship from me." He put the rebels in irons, one in "double irons," and as he so often did, praised God for saving him. "I cannot but acknowledge a visible interposition of Divine Providence."

Every captain had to be constantly on the lookout for uprisings by desperate slaves, particularly when still on the African coast. There were over three hundred documented revolts on Atlantic slave ships, and undoubtedly many more on vessels whose logbooks have been lost or whose captains thought rebellions too commonplace to bother recording. In one famous case some female slaves on the *Thomas,* bound for Barbados, seized muskets, overpowered the crew, and freed the male slaves. But they were unable to sail the ship back to Africa, and a British warship eventually recaptured them. More successful were rebels on a London vessel, the *Industry:* they seized it four days into a voyage to South Carolina, killed all but two of the crew, and managed to run the ship aground in Sierra Leone.

Ever wary, Newton mounted guns on deck and trained muskets on the captives' quarters "to intimidate the slaves." But less than a month after putting down his sailors' abortive conspiracy, Newton, "by the favour of Divine Providence made a timely discovery to day that the slaves were forming a plot for an insurrection. Surprized 2 of them attempting to get off their irons, and upon farther search in their rooms, upon the information of 3 of the boys, found some knives, stones, shot, etc., and a cold chissel [a steel chisel for cutting metal]. Upon enquiry there appeared 8 principally concerned to move in projecting the mischeif and 4 boys in supplying them with the above instruments. Put the boys in irons and slightly in the thumbscrews to urge them to a full confession." A few weeks later, Newton discovered another "intention to rise upon us. Found 4 principally concerned, punished them with the thumb screws and afterwards put them in neck yokes."

In the midst of applying the lash and thumbscrew, Newton kept up an unceasing stream of love letters to Mary. And, much as we might wish otherwise, it is difficult not to be moved by them. "I press to my lips the paper that will be with you in a few days, while I must be kept from you for many months," he writes when leaving on one voyage, imploring her, "Let me know at what hours you usually rise, breakfast, dine, sup and go to bed that I may keep time with you." When some letters of hers reach him, months later, after being transferred through half a dozen ships, Newton is so overjoyed that "I could almost hug every dirty fellow through whose hands they have passed."

"To live without you," he writes Mary from Africa, "constitutes the very essence of Guinea to me . . . I hope and believe I should find myself as much at a loss, and sigh as often for something better, if I lived in the palace of Versailles, and could call it my own, unless you were with me." To make the people around him understand his love for her would be "like describing the rainbow to a man born blind."

In Newton's ceaseless search for slaves to buy, he spent almost all his time in the area he knew best, the Sierra Leone coast. Midway along it lies the estuary of the Sierra Leone River, one of the best natural harbors in Africa. Some eighteen miles upstream rises Bance Island, a rocky outcropping a third of a mile long. Its protected position and abundant fresh water supply made it one of West Africa's most active trading posts, selling slaves and supplies to European and American captains and performing repairs in its small shipyard. Newton moored his ship at Bance Island's stone jetty on several of his voyages. When he arrived there on March 27, 1753, for instance, he traded his longboat for four tons of rice from the island's warehouse. Then he left his vessel, the *African,* at the shipyard to have sixty barrels of water stowed on board and the mollusks scraped off its hull. His logbook does not detail how he spent his spare time while this was being done, but it is possible that he played a round or two of a game just then becoming popular in Europe.

Bance Island's golf course, the only one in Africa, was bordered by mangrove trees and had only two holes, about a quarter of a mile apart. The balls were about the size of today's tennis balls; the clubs were wooden. The players were a motley assortment of the island's traders, slave ship officers, and other white soldiers of fortune. They divided themselves into two teams; members of each took turns driving their team's ball towards the opposite hole. The golfers wore white

Indian cotton. Their caddies, from nearby African villages, were given loincloths of tartan wool woven near Glasgow.

Writing to his wife, Newton says, "I have been very happy this evening, in a solitary ramble round this island. I studiously avoided all company, and chose a retired walk, where I could vent my thoughts aloud, without fear of being overheard." It is not surprising that the now pious Newton declined evening company, for, as one disapproving visitor wrote of the island's traders, "When they get opportunity . . . which is frequent . . . [they] drink away their senses." On his solitary ramble Newton would have seen, on a small hill at one end of the island, a collection of living quarters, offices, and warehouses, most of them inside a protective wall. The side facing the sea was made of brick and stone thirty inches thick, with cannons on the ramparts—a bulwark against French and pirate guns.

Like most such slave posts, the installation was equally fortified against rebellion from within. "Every window had its iron grate," wrote one naval officer, "every door had its iron bar, while the passages were so constructed that only one person could be admitted at a time." From the second floor of the whites' quarters a visitor could look down on holding pens big enough for several hundred chained slaves, the largest one 150 feet on each side and ringed by a 15-foot stone wall. Nearby was a graveyard for the whites, which got a lot of use: between drink and tropical diseases, nearly half the island's white population died each year.

Bance Island had been a British outpost since the 1600s. In 1748, just before Newton began stopping there, it was taken over by an up-and-coming London firm, Grant, Oswald & Co. The holding pens at the fortress meant that ships from Britain or elsewhere willing to pay good prices could take on dozens of slaves at one stop, cutting down on the time they had to cruise the coast. Before long, the island was loading an average of a thousand slaves a year onto ships from many countries. The white staff grew to thirty-five and the African staff, both slave and free, to well over one hundred. Some of them manned the fleet of small vessels, including the ship's longboat Newton had traded for rice, that gathered slaves from the area's network of creeks. The slave depot's largest contract was with a British shipping firm that supplied slaves to French colonies in the Caribbean. When one of the frequent Anglo-French wars threatened to interfere, the firm's ships merely ran up the Spanish flag.

Bance Island's quarters for whites even had a false fireplace, to make the tropics look more like home. To the visitors who have left us their impressions, however, it didn't feel that way. One traveler said he knew when he was "amongst a parcel of Slave traders, for besides their cursing and swearing, they had all on check shirts, a black hankerchief round the neck and another round the waist, all insignia of the bloody trafic in human flesh." Another, Henry Smeathman, a British naturalist who stopped by while collecting insects along the coast, gave a vivid description of the scene at dinner: "The teakettle shall boil, the tea shall be made in it; . . . a piece of old canvas shall contain the sugar, the mate with his tar[r]y dirty fist shall break some into the tea and stir it about with a rusty, dirty, greasy knife, and the dirt and dust which swims on the top, he shall pick out with his fingers & every man shall dip [his cup] in his turn."

After the meal, things only grew worse: "I had the fruits & labours of a long & glorious day totally demolished by the rats whilst I was at dinner. Oh sun & moon & stars! . . . While I am at supper [a candle] is carried and [put] in a quart bottle . . . I return from supper and find the candle fallen, from the softness of the tallow not supporting itself, the table on fire and the tallow floating amongst my books, papers & apparatus. Oh ye Gods! Pity a *poor misfortunate* flycatcher."

Meanwhile, outside, ships were filling their holds with slaves: "Alas! What a scene of misery and distress is a full slaved ship in the rains. The clanking of chains, the groans of the sick and the stench of the whole. . . . Two or three slaves thrown overboard every day dying of fever flux, measles, worms all together. All the day the chains rattling or the sound of the armourer rivetting some poor devil just arrived in galling heavy irons. . . . Here the Doctor dressing sores, wounds and ulcers, or cramming the men with medicines and another standing over them with a cat[-o'-nine-tails] to make them swallow."

The majority shareholder in Bance Island and the dominant figure in Grant, Oswald & Co. was, like the plaid worn by the golf caddies, Scottish. Just as John Newton exemplifies the men who sailed the triangle trade route, so Richard Oswald represents those on its commanding heights. These stretched from the ramparts of whitewashed slave forts in Africa to the sun-baked sugar fields of the Caribbean to the rolling green lawns and formal gardens of country homes in the British Isles. As a young man, much like an executive trainee in a transnational corporation today, Oswald had learned the import-export business in several corners of the empire: Glasgow, Virginia, and Jamaica. In 1746, he settled in London, where, from a modest brick home and office at 17 Philpot Lane, he rapidly built up an international trade in slaves and in a wide range of goods, from horses to wigs. He sold tar and turpentine to the Royal Navy, and wagons, hay, and more than five million loaves of bread to the army. Before long he came to own shares in ships and in slave plantations in South Carolina, Jamaica, and Florida. Oswald's ships could then carry slaves from his depot-fortress at Bance Island to his plantations in the Americas, and return to England loaded with their sugar or tobacco. Although his business ranged as far as India, its core was the triangle trade. With lucrative investments in each corner of the triangle and in the ships that sailed among them, he amassed a fortune of some £500,000, roughly equal to $68 million today.

Oswald, as he appears in portraits, had a long, determined face, intense eyes, and a proudly bowed-out chest. His contemporaries saw him as a wise, thoughtful man who embodied the Scottish virtues of frugality, sobriety, and hard work, and who spent all of his spare time reading, often far into the night. He supervised the construction of a home library with sliding glass panels that contained more than two thousand books of theology, philosophy, literature, and history. His art collection included works by Rubens and Rembrandt, and a friend called him "a Man of Great Knowledge and Ready Conversation." Among those who shared that conversation at his London dinner table, or could hunt pheasants while visiting his 100,000-acre estate in Auchincruive, Scotland, were Benjamin Franklin and the writers Laurence Sterne and James Boswell. Oswald played a major role in Scottish road building, gave to charity, and, as we shall see, would represent his country on a crucial diplomatic mission. Although Bance Island was a cornerstone of his fortune, one way in which he was typical of the Britons who reaped the greatest profits from the Atlantic slave economy was that he never set foot in Africa.

• • •

"No one here can guess, by my looks or behaviour," John Newton wrote Mary from the island, "how much of my heart is in another quarter of the world." For slave captains like him, Bance Island was often the last stop before they headed across the Atlantic. Once wind filled his sails and the ocean currents bore his ship away from the African coast, the "middle passage" had begun. And here we must step back and imagine Newton's tiny ship, dipping and bobbing over the sea, as part of a huge armada spread out in time as well as space, for there were an estimated thirty-five thousand Atlantic slave voyages during more than three and a half centuries of the trade, transporting captives to every destination from Quebec to Chile.

For Newton, pacing the captain's quarterdeck above the slave quarters, the most dangerous and difficult part of the triangle route—buying slaves on the African coast—was over. His logbook entries become cursory, and he seems almost convinced that the slaves are now happy. On a typical Atlantic crossing, he writes: "I shall always take pleasure in ascribing to the helping of the God of peace . . . the remarkable good disposition of the men slaves . . . who seem . . . to have entirely changed their tempers. I was at first continually alarmed with their almost desperate attempts to make insurrections upon us. . . . However from about the end of February they have behaved more like children in one family than slaves in chains and irons and are really upon all accounts more observant, obliging and considerate than our white people."

The end of each middle passage was marked by the sight of the birds and floating seaweed that meant the ship was approaching the West Indies. At this point Newton would order the slaves shaved and their skin given the fake sheen of good health that would attract buyers. "Wash'd the slaves with fresh water and rubd them with Bees wax and Florence [olive] Oil." After selling the slaves on one or more Caribbean islands, he took on cargo—usually sugar—or ballast for the final leg of the triangle, back to England.

When not pressed with trade matters, he spent one to two hours praying and reading the Bible each morning, with another round of prayers at midday, praying especially for "all debauched and profane persons such as I myself too long was." Compared to the seafaring life, with its long spells of solitude between ocean and sky, he knew no "calling that . . . affords greater advantages to an awakened mind, for promoting the life of God in the soul." This was particularly so on slave ships, he felt, because, "excepting the hurry of trade, &c. upon the coast," the extra officers and crew they carried made the captain's job less burdensome. "I never knew sweeter or more frequent hours of divine communion, than in my two last voyages to Guinea, when I was either almost secluded from society on shipboard, or when on shore. . . . I have wandered through the woods reflecting on the singular goodness of the Lord to me."

Whether surviving a storm, defeating a slave rebellion, or marrying Mary Catlett, Newton interpreted all the turning points in his tumultuous life as divine interventions. Always at the last minute, miraculously, it was someone else sent on the mission he had been designated for and who was drowned or came to some other terrible end. God spoke to him at key moments, he felt, by means of portents, blessings, warnings. Yet during the better part of a decade in the slave trade, and for some thirty years afterwards, John Newton seems never to have heard God say a word to him against slavery.

2

ATLANTIC WANDERER

IF JOHN NEWTON saw the world of Atlantic slavery from his captain's cabin, how did it look to someone who survived the slave quarters? The 1740s, the decade in which Newton began his slaving voyages, saw the birth of a man who would leave us an abundant record. Olaudah Equiano grew up, he tells us, "in a charming fruitful vale, named Essaka," in the hinterland of what today would be southeastern Nigeria. His childhood has an idyllic aura, as recollected childhoods so often do in the memories of those who later endure suffering or captivity. His father, Equiano assures us, was a chief, and the Igbo (sometimes spelled Ibo) people of his region lived peacefully "in a country where nature is prodigal of her favours." Swearing was unknown, people were "cleanly," there were no beggars, and women were chaste. Marriage was sacred, and although a man might have several wives, an adulterous woman could be put to death. "We practised circumcision like the Jews," he says, and feasts marked such occasions, for the Igbo were "a nation of dancers, musicians, and poets." A principal drink was palm wine, "though I never saw anyone intoxicated by it." Possibly too good to be fully true (see Appendix), this upbeat description of Equiano's childhood was clearly designed to impress the English readers of the autobiography he wrote late in life. But—unlike many other writers, white and black, in his own time and since—he does not sidestep the fact of African slavery. After a battle with a rival chiefdom, "those prisoners which were not sold or redeemed we kept as slaves." His father owned slaves.

Equiano places his village some days' travel from the ocean, but the reach of the coastal slave trade extended well into the interior. "Generally," he writes, "when the grown people in the neighbourhood were gone far in the fields to labour . . . some of us used to get up a tree to look out for any assailant . . . for they sometimes took those opportunities of our parents' absence, to attack and carry off as many as they could seize." One day he gave the alarm just in time when a kidnapper came to a nearby yard, "there being many stout young people in it."

On another occasion, Equiano was not so lucky. He and his sister were alone in their house when a gang "got over our walls, and in a moment seized us both; and, without giving us time to cry out, or make resistance, they stopped our mouths, tied our hands, and ran off with us." Through a number of intermediaries, one of whom purchased him for 172 cowrie shells, he ended up in the hands of a dealer who supplied the Atlantic ships. Although Equiano did not know it, he had survived the most dangerous portion of a slave's odyssey—not the legendary ocean crossing, but the less recorded forced march in yokes or chains to the coast. That journey might be hundreds of miles and take months, and a Portuguese slave merchant of this era, Raymond Jalamá, estimated that nearly half of newly captured slaves died on the way. Slave dealers preferred to move their caravans in the dry season, and sometimes there was only stagnant water to drink, or none at all. The trails to the coast were littered with skeletons.

We know relatively little about the slave raiders who roamed the West African interior, and can only imagine the terror their raids inflicted. With a mere handful of extraordinary exceptions, which we will come to later, no Africans ever returned to their native villages from the Americas. So if you were captured, you had absolutely no picture of what awaited you. Force-marched down those bone-strewn trails, you were heading into the unknown.

Some six months after his capture, he says, Equiano found himself on board a slave ship. From investigating shipping logs of the time, one scholar believes it may have been a snow—a two-masted vessel with an additional half-mast just behind the mainmast—the *Ogden,* under Captain James Walker of Liverpool. Walker took his cargo of slaves to the Caribbean only about ten days' sail ahead of the *African,* which John Newton was commanding on his third voyage as captain. The ship owners who transported slaves to the New World in snows, brigs, and barkentines kept abundant records, and the best calculation based on them is that just over 11 million slaves were herded onto vessels like these for the middle passage and that some 9.6 million survived to finish it. Equiano's account of this journey is one of the very few by a slave.

"The stench of the hold . . . now that the whole ship's cargo were confined together . . . became absolutely pestilential. The closeness of the place, and the heat of the climate, added to the number in the ship, which was so crowded that each had scarcely room to turn himself, almost suffocated us. This produced copious perspirations, so that the air soon became unfit for respiration, from a variety of loathsome smells, and brought on a sickness among the slaves, of which many died. . . . This wretched situation was again aggravated by the galling of the chains, now become insupportable; and the filth of the necessary tubs [latrine buckets], into which the children often fell, and were almost suffocated. The shrieks of the women, and the groans of the dying, rendered the whole a scene of horror almost inconceivable." It was said that the stench of a slave ship was so strong that other sailors could smell it a mile downwind, and that the odor of the vomit, sweat, and feces of its human cargo worked its way into the very wood and could not be scrubbed away.

As had happened at least once on Newton's voyages, desperate slaves on Equiano's ship tried to kill themselves by jumping overboard. Three managed to leap, and the crew lowered a boat to pursue them. "Two of the wretches were drowned, but they got the other, and afterwards flogged him unmercifully, for thus attempting to prefer death to slavery." When Equiano himself refused to eat, he too was beaten. The ship's officers acted little better towards their own crew: "One white man in particular I saw . . . flogged so unmercifully with a large rope near the foremast, that he died in consequence of it; and they tossed him over the side as they would have done a brute." Legend had it that sharks followed slave vessels, feeding on the bodies in their wake.

• • •

Many slaves died as the small, cramped ship slowly plowed its way across the Atlantic. At last it reached the British colony of Barbados. The easternmost of all the Caribbean islands, it was a frequent first stop for slave vessels from Africa. In the early eighteenth century, Barbados's capital, Bridgetown, was probably the busiest port in the Americas, a maritime crossroads of vessels bringing cargoes from England, Africa, and North and South America. Coconut palms and groves of orange, lemon, and lime trees surrounded its bay, crowded with square-rigged ships at anchor. Gun batteries guarded the harbor entrance, and above the wharves and warehouses of the town, St. John's Church stood on an 850-foot cliff. After an ocean crossing of a month or more, for sailors the first sight of Bridgetown was a welcome relief, but for himself and his fellow slaves, wrote Equiano, "we did not know what to think."

"This island," observed one traveler, ". . . seems to be all in motion," for the hills that rimmed Bridgetown were dotted with dozens of windmills, used to process the crop that determined the fate of most slaves who survived the middle passage: sugar. On his second voyage to the Americas, Christopher Columbus had brought some Canary Islands sugar cane to the Caribbean, where the fertile soil, rainfall, and abundant sun proved ideal for its growth. Europeans had long been looking for tropical land suitable for cane, which yielded its sweetness so much more plentifully than did bees their honey. In the mid-1750s, when Equiano landed in Barbados, it was the sugar-rich British West Indies, not the thirteen colonies on the North American mainland, that had the biggest British slave population in the New World.

Hard hit by smallpox, typhus, and other European diseases, the indigenous Indians of the Caribbean had died off in huge numbers when their new European masters tried to put them to work cultivating cane, and so the colonizers had quickly started importing African slaves. Their labor turned sugar from a rare luxury enjoyed by the wealthy into something found on millions of European dinner tables. Often sugar was used to sweeten another newly fashionable tropical crop harvested by slaves in South America and the West Indies—especially on the high slopes of the more mountainous islands—coffee. But economically sugar loomed above everything else. To feed an insatiable European sweet tooth, some two thirds of all slaves taken anywhere in the Americas ended up on sugar plantations.

Equiano began hearing something of sugar slavery during his first frightening weeks on Barbados, and eventually he would see every grim aspect of it firsthand. Even before he had gotten off the ship, "Many merchants and planters . . . came on board . . . and examined us attentively." When the slaves were taken on shore and divided into wholesale lots called parcels, "we were conducted immediately to the merchant's yard, where we were all pent up together like so many sheep in a fold, without regard to sex or age. . . . On a signal given, (as the beat of a drum), the buyers rush at once into the yard where the slaves are confined, and make choice of that parcel they like best."

Luckily for Equiano, he was to escape the sugar fields themselves. Not yet a teenager, he says, he was weak and sickly from the voyage and no Barbados planter wanted him. So a slave merchant ordered him given "plenty of rice and fat pork" to fatten him up for buyers, and shipped him to Virginia. There, he worked briefly on a plantation, whose owner soon sold him to a Royal Navy officer named Michael Pascal.

Just as in his life he passed through several worlds, so Equiano bore several names. On the ship across the Atlantic, he tells us, the crew dubbed him Michael; on the Virginia plantation he was called Jacob; and now his new master gave him the name by which he would be known for several decades, Gustavus Vasa. As with many slaves named after prime ministers, Roman emperors, and the like, the name was deliberately ironic. The original Gustavus Vasa, a medieval nobleman, became King of Sweden after leading a revolt against Danish rule.

For six years, Equiano was the personal slave of Lieutenant Pascal. At this point his name begins appearing in documents, recorded on navy ships' muster rolls by careless clerks noting down the officer's servant as Gustavus "Vavasa," "Vassor," "Vasser," or "Vassan." Equiano's time as Pascal's slave coincided almost exactly with the Seven Years War (to Americans, the French and Indian War) of 1756–63, one stage of the Anglo-French struggle for global dominance that lasted throughout the eighteenth century and into the next. Equiano followed Pascal from one warship to another, and from one side of the ocean to the other. He visited London, saw snow, survived smallpox, and watched a man hanged. He ran supplies of gunpowder across a deck amid a battle at sea, dodged bullets and shell fragments during fighting on shore in France, and sailed in naval expeditions to Spain and Nova Scotia. Along the way he showed a shrewd entrepreneurial instinct and an eagerness to learn. (Even on the middle passage, a crewman had allowed him to look through a navigational instrument, the quadrant, "to gratify my curiosity.") In the harsh world of the Royal Navy, this bright youngster endeared himself to the people around him. He had a knack for befriending both officers and men, obviously grasping that this was the key to survival. General James Wolfe, for instance, on his way to win a famous victory in Quebec, intervened to save Equiano from a shipboard flogging. He was soon earning pocket money by shaving sailors and cutting their hair.

Pascal sometimes loaned Equiano out, like an exotic toy, to friends or family in England. Fascinated by the young African, some of Pascal's relatives helped him learn to read and write—an opportunity denied to almost all slaves in the Americas. They took him to be baptized at St. Margaret's, Westminster, the venerable church where Sir Walter Raleigh is buried and which is still the official parish of the House of Commons.

On both land and sea Equiano constantly encountered other "countrymen," as he called them. Many Africans, slave and free, were sailors, for the Royal Navy was fighting the French in two hemispheres, and its several hundred ships needed all the strong young men they could muster. Equiano saw the navy's thirst for manpower firsthand when he was put to work under Pascal roaming the streets of London as a member of a naval press gang, a captive black man now putting white men in chains.

He chafed ceaselessly at his own enslavement. His hope of freedom was not without reason, for although slavery was the economic bedrock of the West Indies and the American South, its legal status in England itself was surprisingly uncertain. On one hand, British newspapers of the day carried occasional advertisements such as, "For sale at the Bull and Gate Inn, Holborn: A chestnut gelding, a Tim whiskey [a light carriage] and a well-made good tempered Black Boy." On the other, many slaves were given freedom by their British masters or allowed to earn it; some simply took it themselves, slipping away to small but growing communities of blacks in London and a few other cities. Judging by the many notices offering rewards for information about runaways, their owners recovered them with much difficulty or not at all.

In 1762, Equiano's hopes rose further when he was promoted to Royal Navy able seaman. Sailing back to London with his new rank after another round of fighting at sea, he wondered: Did Pascal have the right to keep him as a slave on British soil? Pascal was clearly starting to worry about this point himself. As soon as their ship dropped anchor in the Thames, he ordered Equiano to leave his books and possessions on board, forced him onto a small boat, and sold him to the captain of the *Charming Sally,* a vessel leaving for the West Indies on the next tide. Equiano was once again transported across the Atlantic in custody, this time to the small Caribbean sugar island of Montserrat. "At the sight of this land of bondage, a fresh horror ran through all my frame, and chilled me to the heart."

On shore, the captain sold him to Robert King, the island's most prominent merchant. Discovering Equiano's fluency in English and experience as a seaman, King realized he was too valuable a piece of property to be wasted in the fields. Equiano was put to work loading and tallying cargo, cutting King's hair, and working as a clerk in his warehouses and as a crewman on his fleet of small vessels that carried slaves and cargo from Montserrat to various West Indian islands—he visited fifteen all told—and to the North American mainland.

Stopping both in major ports and at the small, surf-washed jetties of isolated sugar plantations, he saw the full face of Caribbean slavery. "I have seen a negro beaten till some of his bones were broken, for only letting a pot boil over." He witnessed white sailors on King's vessels "gratify their brutal passion with females not ten years old," and "in Montserrat I have seen a negro-man staked to the ground and cut most shockingly [i.e., castrated], and then his ears cut off bit by bit, because he had been connected with a white woman who was a common prostitute." He saw slaves, "particularly those who were meagre, in different islands, put into scales and weighed, and then sold from three-pence to six-pence, or nine-pence a pound."

Although he is too politic to mention it to the British readers of his memoirs, as he traveled about the Caribbean Equiano surely heard much about another aspect of slavery: rebellions. The largest slave revolt yet seen in the British West Indies had erupted in Jamaica in 1760, only three years before he was purchased by King. With African war cries, thousands of rebel slaves under a leader named Tacky marauded through estates, shooting whites and setting cane fields and sugar works afire. Without enough ammunition for the muskets they had seized, they fired metal fishnet weights. News sent by African drum signals ignited more revolts elsewhere on the island. Jittery whites rounded up sailors from ships loading sugar to help put down the uprising and wondered at possible signs of more trouble: Were shaved heads a symbol of membership in the conspiracy? To protect his estate, one planter armed twenty of the slaves he thought most loyal—who thanked him, raised their hats to him, and headed off to join the rebels.

Tacky, the leader, was soon captured and beheaded, but skirmishes continued for many months. To uneasy planters, the line between loyal and rebel slaves was frustratingly blurred. Many slaves who had disappeared eventually returned to tell their masters they had run away only to avoid being conscripted by the rebels. Owners were suspicious, but to turn these slaves in to the authorities would be to lose their labor force. As soldiers snuffed out the last pockets of rebellion, slaves hiding in the forests hanged themselves rather than surrender, and their bodies were found dangling from trees for months afterwards. In all, more than four hundred rebels died in combat, were executed, or committed suicide. Some five hundred more were transported to penal servitude. Tacky's Rebellion, as it was called, also left roughly sixty whites and at least sixty free blacks and mulattos dead.

No matter how brutally suppressed, revolts continued. Six years later, nineteen whites were killed in one, and ten years after that Jamaican officials discovered a plot among the trusted elite of drivers, craftsmen, and house slaves. Punishment was swift. "So truly unhappy is our situation," wrote one planter, "that my Head-Cook was taken up, while he was dressing dinner, tried, condemned, and executed the day after."

Journeying through this violent world on Robert King's cargo boats, Equiano always had an eye out for how he might escape it. Quietly, he began trading. Spying a market for glassware in Montserrat, he bought glass tumblers when his ship called at the Dutch island of St. Eustatius. On a voyage to St. Croix, he brought along limes and oranges, because he "had heard these fruits sold well in that island." A natural businessman, he remembered years later exactly how much he had made on each sale—300 percent profit, for instance, on four barrels of pork bought in South Carolina and sold in Montserrat. With the money from the pork he bought goods he then sold on a voyage to Philadelphia. And finally, in 1766, he at last had enough to buy his freedom, for the equivalent of more than $6,000 in today's money. "Know ye, that I the aforesaid Robert King, for, and in consideration of the sum of seventy pounds . . . by these presents do manumit, emancipate, enfanchise, and set free, the aforesaid negro man-slave named Gustavus Vasa, for ever; hereby giving, granting, and releasing unto him, the said Gustavus Vasa, all right, title, dominion, sovereignty, and property, which, as lord and master over the aforesaid Gustavus Vasa, I have had . . ."

This prized proof of freedom, however, was no guarantee of safety. Equiano himself once saw a free black man, while brandishing just such a certificate, dragged onto a ship bound for Bermuda. "I was now completely disgusted with the West Indies, and thought I never should be entirely free till I had left them."

After being shipwrecked in a remote part of the Bahamas, Equiano eventually reached London. But he felt himself to be "of a roving disposition, and desirous of seeing as many different parts of the world as I could." And rove, for the next two decades, he did. He worked on ships traveling to the Mediterranean, once seeing Mount Vesuvius erupt, and twice going as far as Turkey, where he was astonished to see that women had their faces veiled, "except when any of them, out of curiosity, uncovered them to look at me." He noted that the Greeks were "kept under by the Turks, as the negroes are in the West-

Indies by the white people." Six times he sailed to the Americas, and once to Portugal. Between voyages he worked in London: as a house servant, a barber, and as an assistant to Dr. Charles Irving, on Pall Mall, an inventor who had been awarded £5,000 by Parliament for devising a still that converted saltwater into fresh—a potentially useful device when ocean voyages took months. He studied the Bible and learned to play the French horn. In Greenwich Park, he ran into his old master Pascal, and, Equiano says, "I told him that he had used me very ill."

One of his many voyages made him, in 1773, among the first African visitors to the Arctic. Royal Navy logs show "Gustavus Weston" on the muster roll of this mission by two small, specially reinforced ships. "I was roused by the sound of fame to seek new adventures," Equiano writes, "and to find, towards the North Pole, what our Creator never intended we should find, a passage to India." Although the navy's hoped-for shortcut to the East proved elusive, in waters off Greenland he saw the midnight sun, plus "many very high and curious mountains of ice; and also a great number of very large whales, which used to come close to our ship." He ate polar bear meat and marveled at the Arctic walruses that approached the ship, making sounds like horses. For eleven days, his vessel was stuck in pack ice: "we were in very great apprehension of having the ships squeezed to pieces." He came within six hundred miles of the North Pole. With his keen eye for influential people, he would have been pleased had he known that a fourteen-year-old member of the expedition who got into trouble for chasing a bear across an ice floe would later become Britain's greatest naval hero, Lord Nelson.

He seized every chance to see something new. "I visited eight counties in Wales, from motives of curiosity." He went down a Shropshire coal mine. He found more adventure than he bargained for, however, when he joined the inventor Dr. Irving in setting up a new plantation in the coastal wilderness near today's Nicaraguan-Honduran border. On the way, they stopped in Jamaica, and Equiano found himself on board a slave vessel once again, this time helping Irving select slaves to be field hands. Curiously, he passes over this reversal of roles in a few quick sentences in his autobiography. It is as if, despite his fierce and successful drive for his own freedom and compassion for those still in bondage, slavery is still such an omnipresent fact of life that he takes it for granted that any plantation in the Americas would be cultivated by slaves.

Once in Central America, he cast an anthropological eye on the Miskito Indians of the coast, observing that they built houses "exactly like the Africans," that they were polygamous, and that their delicacy, roast alligator, "looked like fresh salmon." But he soon tired of the plantation project, resigned, and set off for England, boarding a sloop supposedly bound for Jamaica. However, the captain promptly had him trussed up "and hoisted me up without letting my feet touch or rest upon any thing." The vessel was heading for South America, where the captain "swore he would sell me." With the help of a sympathetic ship's carpenter, Equiano escaped to shore, and finally to London. The experience was only the latest of many reminders that as long as the British Empire permitted slavery, no black person in it could be completely free.

3

INTOXICATED WITH LIBERTY

Among the sounds that defined the world of British slavery were the clatter of chains on slave ships and, on Caribbean plantations, the pistol-like cracks of drivers' whips, marking the start of work in the fields before sunrise, meal breaks, and the workday's end. But people living beside the rivers and canals of southern England in the later part of the eighteenth century often heard a very different kind of sound: chamber music approaching from the distance.

The aquatic concert came from a large barge, towed slowly into view by a pair of horses on a waterside path. Below decks were bedrooms and a dining room; above, an orchestra of a dozen or more musicians performed in the open, or under an awning when it rained. One of their favorite composers was George Frideric Handel, whose *Water Music,* after all, had been written to serenade King George I on the Thames. The musical barge was popular with Britons high and low. "As we passed the Prince of Wales' house," one member of the orchestra noted, "they heard our Musick and all the 4 Princes and Attendance came down to the water side, and stood for near half an hour and sent to request 3 or 4 different songs."

George III, who became King in 1760, was such an enthusiast that when he heard that the barge was moored for the night near Windsor Castle, he and the Queen appeared on the riverbank towpath at seven in the morning, to be invited on board to the strains of "See the Conquering Hero Comes." The famous actor David Garrick came for a musical breakfast as the barge was towed through Hampton, and Lord North, the Prime Minister, wanting to impress a half-dozen ambassadors and visiting foreign ministers, arranged for them to board as the barge approached London. A contemporary painting shows the orchestra with their instruments on deck, the men elegantly got up in tricornered hats, buckled shoes, and waistcoats, the women in long flowing dresses. A dog lies at their feet.

Although musician friends joined them, at the core of the orchestra were eight brothers and sisters, the Sharps. Some of them, and their various spouses and children, lived together; when apart they circulated a "Common Letter" of personal and political happenings, to which each brother or sister added news as it continually made the rounds of all. Their father and grandfather had been prominent Anglican clergymen, but what most united the family, ashore or afloat, was music. William Sharp, whose official post as Surgeon to the King entitled him to a grand uniform, lived on the barge with his wife most of the year; he played the organ and the French horn. Brother James played the bassoon and the jointed serpent, a snake-shaped bass wind instrument. Several sisters sang or played the piano. From the age of four or five, James's daughter Catherine, placed on a table, also sang. His younger brother Granville played the clarinet, oboe, and kettledrums, plus an unusual harp of his own making, with an extra row of strings. At least once, according to an admiring musician witness, the Master of His Majesty's Band, Granville "performed duets upon two flutes, to the delight and conviction of many doubters, who had conceived such an accomplishment to be impracticable." King George III thought Granville had "the best voice in England."

The family's musical expeditions could last for days; one covered 284 miles by water. Granville, who sketched caricatures for the amusement of his friends and sometimes whimsically signed his name as a G-sharp on the treble clef, seems to have been the organizer of these voyages, judging from a memorandum among his papers:

> Things to be thought of for the Barge. . . .
> Sugar, Tea cupps and saucers Butter Bread.

Bed Vinegar Salt honey teaspoons.
4 collars great coats. Hook line. Wine. A glass. Horsegear.

Granville Sharp was able to make no such preparations for his sudden entrance into a world far less placid than England's waterways. It all began one morning in 1765 when a black man named Jonathan Strong, about sixteen or seventeen years old, was seriously injured. Like thousands of others, he had been brought to Britain by a slave owner returning from the Caribbean, David Lisle, a Barbados lawyer. Lisle had beaten Strong "upon his Head with a Pistol till the Barrel and Lock were separated from the Stock," and then abandoned him to the London streets. His head was badly swollen and he had chills and fever. "I could hardly walk, or see my way, where I was going," Strong would later recall. Someone had told him about the King's kindly doctor, William Sharp, who every morning gave free treatment to the poor at his office in Mincing Lane. Granville Sharp happened to be visiting his brother and caught sight of Strong as he approached the door, about to faint.

"The boy seemed ready to die" was Granville's first impression. Strong had "almost lost the use of his Legs and Feet . . . and to compleat his misfortunes [was] afflicted with so violent a disorder in his Eyes that there appeared to be the utmost danger of his becoming totally blind." The brothers gave him money for clothes and food, and Dr. William Sharp, after patching him up as best he could, got Strong admitted to St. Bartholomew's Hospital, where he spent four and a half months recovering. The brothers then found him a job with a pharmacist around the corner from William's office.

Two years later, Strong was serving as a footman on the coach of the pharmacist's wife one day when David Lisle spotted him. Astonished to see his one-time piece of property restored to health and so to commercial value, he followed the coach home to see where Strong lived. He then sold Strong for £30 to a Jamaican planter, hired two men to kidnap him, and arranged for him to be jailed until the next ship sailed for the West Indies.

Strong, his wits about him, managed to get a letter to Granville Sharp, "imploring protection from being sold as a Slave." The indignant Sharp promptly proceeded to the jail, demanded to see Strong, and "charged the master of the prison, *at his own peril, not to deliver him up* to any person . . . until he had been carried before the Lord Mayor . . . to whom [I] immediately went, and gave information that a Jonathan Strong had been confined in prison without any warrant."

The Sharp clan knew everybody, it seemed, and it is likely that the Lord Mayor had been a guest on the musical barge (as at least two of his successors would be). He called a hearing, overrode the objections of Strong's new owner—whose attorney appeared, angrily brandishing the bill of sale—and declared Strong free. Also showing up at the hearing was the captain of the ship in which Strong was to be sent to Jamaica, who immediately seized him. Sharp clapped the captain on the shoulder and declared, "I charge you, in the name of the king, with an assault upon the person of Jonathan Strong, and all these are my witnesses." At this point, Sharp writes, "The Captain . . . withdrew his hand, and all parties retired from the presence of the Lord Mayor, and Jonathan Strong departed also, in the sight of all, in full liberty, nobody daring afterwards to touch him."

Enraged by the triumphant rescue, Strong's original owner challenged Sharp to a duel. Sharp parried with words: "David Lisle, Esq. (a man of the law) called on me . . . to demand *gentlemanlike satisfaction* . . . I told him, that, 'as he had studied the law so many years, he should want no satisfaction that the law could give him.'"

With this case, the thirty-two-year-old Granville Sharp became by default the leading defender of blacks in London, and indeed one of the few people in all of England to speak out against slavery. And speak he would, vehemently, for nearly half a century. The fight against slavery quickly became his dominating passion.

It was far from the only passion, however, for Sharp had strong, contrarian opinions on nearly everything. As a young man, he had been apprenticed to several linen merchants, a trade that bored him, but when a fellow apprentice claimed that Sharp had misunderstood the nature of the Trinity because he could not read the New Testament in its original language, he promptly set about learning Greek and wrote a pamphlet, *Remarks on the Uses of the Definitive Article in the Greek Text of the New Testament.* To better dispute another apprentice, a Jew who questioned Christianity entirely, Sharp studied Hebrew. For years afterwards, neighbors heard his fine singing voice chanting the Psalms in that language the first thing each morning, as he accompanied himself on his doubly stringed harp.

Sharp dashed off tracts and pamphlets by the dozen, on "Land-Carriages, Roads and profitable Labour of Oxen," on whether the Bible's account of Babylon described Rome, on proper pronunciation, on predestination and free will, on the introduction of English liturgy to Prussia. He amassed what was said to be Europe's largest private collection of Bibles, in a score of languages from Hungarian to Mohawk. He taught Scripture to a South Sea Islander who had been brought to England on a Royal Navy ship. When he believed that something was evil, he confidently marched off to confront the evildoer in person, whether it was the captor of an escaped slave or the manager of Covent Garden Theatre, who, to Sharp's disapproval, dressed male actors in women's clothing.

To a modern reader, Sharp's massive outpouring of polemics, strewn with italics and words all in capital letters, appears cranky and nearly unreadable, but scattered through his work are bold flashes of thinking centuries ahead of his time. In one tract, for example, he suggests that "Gentlemen of the Army" are "Men, as well as Soldiers," and voices ideas not applied until the Nuremberg trials: "The Law will not excuse an unlawful Act by a Soldier, even though he commits it by . . . express Command. . . . The time will certainly come, when all . . . military Murderers must be responsible for the innocent blood that is shed in an unjust War."

Running throughout Sharp's screeds was one glorious paradox, which did not bother him in the least. In his passion for human liberty he was very much a man of the Enlightenment, of the age of Locke, Voltaire, and Rousseau. At the same time, in his absolute faith in the Bible as interpreted by the Church of England, he was a man of rigid certainty about all religious doctrine. Thus he was in favor of Irish home rule but had, in the words of an otherwise admiring friend, an "implacable hatred" of Catholicism; he believed in tolerance but was a member of the London Society for Promoting Christianity Among the Jews; he wanted to give the vote to the head of every household—an extremely radical position for the day—but thought the guilty party in a divorce should be banned from remarrying. What to us seems almost contradictory in Sharp's thought he experienced only as strength. When he turned his formidable energy against slavery, he was fully confident that it rested securely on the twin pillars of his faith, the guarantee of freedom in Britain's unwritten constitution and a righteous Anglican God.

Just as he had mastered Hebrew and Greek in order to win earlier disputes, so he now boldly mastered the law to defend himself and his brother against a suit filed by Jonathan Strong's new owner. As the case dragged on, he spent the better part of two years delving into precendents set by British court decisions, other countries' laws, and the history of villeinage, the British form of feudal serfdom. He talked to the solicitor general and other eminent authorities. And, naturally, he wrote a tract, *On the Injustice and dangerous Tendency of tolerating Slavery, or even of admitting the least Claim to private Property in the persons of Men, in England,* which had, he commented proudly, "the desired effect, for it intimidated the Plaintiffs' lawyers from proceeding in their action."

At this point in history, getting slavery abolished in Britain's expanding empire in the Americas was far beyond anyone's powers. But Sharp argued forcefully that the law allowed no one to be a slave in England itself. Slave owners of course felt differently, but case law on the subject was scanty and unclear, and there simply were no statutes allowing, forbidding, or regulating slavery in the British Isles. A definitive case that would decide the question once and for all had yet to be tried.

Ever since King Henry VIII had kept a turbaned African trumpeter two centuries earlier, blacks had worked in England as servants. By now there were at least several thousand in the country, free and slave. A slave named Jack Beef, for example, belonged to a former West Indian colonial official and rode to hounds with his master. The Duchess of Kingston took her black manservant to the opera. The *Times* reported one case where "the wife of a gentleman at Sheerness . . . eloped with a black servant. . . . She said she'd live with no man but the Black." The couple were swiftly caught, and the unlucky servant was press-ganged into the navy.

When blacks from Caribbean islands, where nine out of ten people were slaves, found themselves in an England where almost everyone was free, it was an exhilarating shock. In the words of a disgruntled London magistrate writing in 1768, West Indian landowners would bring their slaves to Britain "as cheap Servants, having no Right to Wages; they no sooner arrive here, than they put themselves on a Footing with other Servants, become intoxicated with Liberty, grow refractory, and either by Persuasion of others, or from their own Inclinations, begin to expect Wages."

Word spread quickly in London's black community that Sharp was prepared to go to court on behalf of slaves wanting freedom, and others soon came to him for help. When an advertisement offered for sale a black girl, "eleven years of age, who is extremely handy, works at her needle tolerably," Sharp dashed off an angry note to the Lord Chancellor (the head of the judiciary), sending his antislavery tract. He had abandoned the linen trade and now held a minor post in the Ordnance Office in the Tower of London, handling supplies for the military. Tedious as he found the job, it required only five or six hours of work a day, leaving time for music, pamphlets, and a string of additional rescues of fugitive slaves.

Soon came the first of several overseas political earthquakes with profound reverberations for the Britain of this era, the American Revolution. This unprecedented colonial revolt put the heady ideas of the Enlightenment philosophers about freedom into concrete form. Some Britons were angry, but Sharp and many others were sympathetic. He had already written a pamphlet insisting that Americans should not be taxed without being represented in Parliament and given 250 copies to his friend Benjamin Franklin, then living in London. Thousands more had been eagerly reprinted in New York, Boston, and Philadelphia. Now he was disturbed to find that his work at the Ordnance Office involved sending cannon and other matériel to British troops fighting the rebels. "I cannot return to my ordnance duty whilst a bloody war is carried on, unjustly as I conceive, against my fellow-subjects," he wrote to his superiors, and resigned.

Several of his brothers and sisters were as unusual as he. James Sharp, a successful engineer and hardware merchant, helped design the family barges, patented an improved coal stove, and invented a "rolling waggon," an ancestor of the steamroller. William, the doctor, shocked conventional medical opinion by preaching the virtues of open windows and fresh air. As Granville parted ways with the Ordnance Office over his beliefs, James wrote him an extraordinarily supportive letter. "We very much approve. . . . I will speak now for my brother William as well as for myself—we are both ready and willing . . . to take care that the loss shall be none to you; and all that we have to ask in return is, that you would continue to live amongst us . . . without imagining that you will . . . be burthensome to us, and also without supposing that it will then be your duty to seek employment in some other way of life; for, if we have the [money] amongst us, it matters not to whom it belongs—the happiness of being together is worth the expense." Granville, who never married, went to live with his brothers, and for the rest of his life he never had to worry about finding a paying job.

He was able to mount his battles in defense of slaves only because a number of them were brave enough to take their destiny in hand and flee their masters. The man whose flight would have the greatest impact had first appeared on his doorstep a few years before he left the Ordnance Office. "James Somerset, a Negro from Virginia, called on me this morning . . . to complain of Mr. Charles Stewart," Sharp noted in his diary on January 13, 1772. Somerset, brought to England by his owner, Stewart, had escaped, but had been recaptured and rushed on board a ship bound for Jamaica. A court order had freed him temporarily, until his case could be decided. His fate now lay in the hands of the Court of King's Bench, Britain's highest criminal court, where Lord Chief Justice Mansfield presided augustly in flowing robe and long white wig.

Mansfield was a man of elegance and wit, with piercing eyes and an aquiline nose, known for reading a newspaper on the bench if he believed a lawyer to be talking more than necessary. A portrait shows him in an ermine cape, with one hand keeping a law book spread open on a reading stand, his hawk's eyes fixing the viewer impatiently, as if he were being detained from important work. He was one of the great parliamentary debaters of the age; a neighbor had once found him practicing oratory in front of a mirror, being coached by his friend the poet Alexander Pope. Deeply conservative, a wealthy investor, creditor, and landowner, Mansfield was the father of modern British commercial law. The prospect of presiding over a case in which the right to property clashed with the right to liberty left him profoundly uneasy, and he did everything possible to avoid having the question be decided by trial. He urged Somerset, Stewart, and their attorneys to negotiate. When that failed, he tried to persuade Stewart to set Somerset free. In vain, also, he urged one of Somerset's supporters to buy him from Stewart and free him.

Sharp had managed several of his earlier legal victories by proving that an owner had freed or abandoned a slave before changing his mind, or that the victim's status as a slave was otherwise unclear; he had not succeeded in getting a judge to rule that slavery itself was unlawful in England. But Somerset had escaped. Whether his recapture was allowed to stand could, in effect, determine whether slavery was legal on English soil. This was the test case Sharp had so eagerly been waiting for. Only three days after Somerset's visit, he had already finished a twenty-eight-page pamphlet designed to put the heat on the judges. He immediately dispatched copies, with key passages marked in red ink, to the Prime Minister and to all the judges on the Court of King's Bench.

Sharp had Lord Mansfield's copy delivered by James Somerset himself.

The trial unfolded in an imposing, high-ceilinged courtroom in Westminster Hall, lit majestically from high windows like a cathedral and with a carved wooden canopy projecting over the judges' bench as if over a throne. Arguing for Somerset, a defense lawyer cited a court ruling about slaves from two centuries earlier, which, he said, affirmed that "the moment they put their foot on English ground, that moment they become free. They are subject to the laws . . . of this country, and so are their masters, thank God!" Lawyers for Stewart spoke of the alarming losses to their owners if the thousands of black slaves now in England—worth an estimated £800,000, or more than $110 million today—were suddenly set free. Moreover, the insane idea that anyone had but to be in England to be free would turn the very world upside down. "It would be a great surprize," said one, ". . . if a foreigner bringing over a servant, as soon as he got hither, must take care of his carriage, his horse, and himself. . . . He tells his servant, Do this; the servant replies, Before I do it, I think fit to inform you, Sir, the first step on this happy land sets all men on a perfect level; you are just as much obliged to obey my commands."

It was high theater, prolonged over several months by recesses when Mansfield vainly kept pushing for an out-of-court settlement. For the first time, the question of slavery, until now something people thought of as existing only on the other side of the Atlantic, caught the eye of the London public. Newspapers and magazines published long articles, and the court was packed. One diarist grumped that he arrived "too late . . . could hear nothing thro' the crowd." Sharp, however, was there, and even hired a shorthand reporter to take down parts of the proceedings. In the end, he triumphantly recorded in his diary, "James Somerset came to tell me that judgement was today given in his favour. . . . Thus ended G. Sharp's long contest with Lord Mansfield." The poet William Cowper hailed the ruling:

> Slaves cannot breathe in England; if their lungs
> Receive our air, that moment they are free.

But the fine print made the air look not so liberating. Mansfield carefully couched his decision in a way that would set Somerset at liberty without automatically freeing other slaves. "The judgement . . . went no further," he later insisted, "than to determine the Master had no right to compel the slave to go into a foreign country." In the end, however, the distinction hardly mattered. Although a handful of slaves were later sold or recaptured in Britain, this was a case in which what people *thought* was decided proved far more important than the actual wording. Almost everyone believed that Mansfield had indeed outlawed slavery in England, including many lower-court judges who subsequently ruled against more than a dozen masters trying to assert ownership over slaves on English soil. Most Britons—though not Granville Sharp—proudly acted as if nothing more needed to be done, overlooking the fact that British ships like those John Newton had captained continued to carry tens of thousands of slaves a year to the expanding British slave plantations in the Americas. Benjamin Franklin wryly noted how the entire country congratulated itself "on its virtue, love of liberty and the equity of its courts, in setting free a single negro."

For Lord Mansfield the contradictions of slavery extended into his own household, where, it turned out, a black woman had lived since infancy. Dido Elizabeth Lindsay was the illegitimate daughter of Mansfield's nephew, a naval officer; her mother had been a slave on board a ship he had captured. Childless themselves, Mansfield and his wife treated Dido as a member of the family. "A Black came in after dinner," one surprised visitor wrote, "and sat with the ladies, and after coffee, walked with the company in the gardens, one of the young ladies having her arm within the other." Another noted disapprovingly, "Lord Mansfield keeps a Black in his house which governs him and the whole family." A portrait of Dido shows a slender and attractive woman with strikingly wide, inquisitive eyes. When grown, she acted as secretary for Mansfield, and on his death he left her £500—more than $65,000 in today's money—plus an annuity of £100 a year for life. Yet, ambivalent to the last about slavery's legality, he thought it necessary to say in his will, "I do confirm to Dido Elizabeth her freedom."

In a London where slaves sometimes had to wear brass or silver collars engraved with a master's name and coat of arms, and where a goldsmith in Duck Lane could advertise "silver padlocks for Blacks or Dogs," the Somerset case galvanized the small black community. A black delegation had attended each session of the court, and when the ruling was given, according to one journalist, "no sight could be more pleasingly affecting to the mind, than the joy which shone at that instant in these poor men's sable countenances." Several days later, more than two hundred blacks paid five shillings each to gather at a Westminster pub to dance and drink Lord Mansfield's health. Word of the decision also swiftly spread across the ocean: it ignited antislavery protests in Massachusetts, and a Virginia newspaper reported slaves trying to stow away on ships for England, "where they imagine they will be free."

One black man who was already free, Olaudah Equiano, was at sea during the Somerset trial. But he knew about Granville Sharp's role in this and other cases and soon sought Sharp's help. In 1774, two years after the Somerset victory, the restless Equiano found a sea captain heading for Turkey. "I shipped myself with him as a steward; at the same time I recommended to him a very clever black man, John Annis, as a cook." Annis had been the slave of William Kirkpatrick, of the Caribbean island of St. Kitts. The two had "parted by consent," Equiano says, but on Easter Monday, Kirkpatrick showed up with six hired men at the Thames wharf where the ship was docked, seized and bound Annis, and put him on another vessel that promptly sailed for the West Indies.

Equiano swung into action. At night, with a bailiff and a court order for Annis's release, he headed for Kirkpatrick's house near St. Paul's Cathedral. Kirkpatrick, alerted, had watchmen looking out for him, but Equiano evaded them brilliantly: "I whitened my face, that they might not know me." Under the direction of Equiano in whiteface, the bailiff managed to serve the order on Kirkpatrick commanding him to come to court.

Then Equiano "proceeded immediately to that well-known philanthropist, Granville Sharp, Esq. who received me with the utmost kindness. . . . I left him in full hopes that I should obtain the unhappy man his liberty." As far as we know, this was the first time the two men met. Equiano had somehow managed to meet General James Edward Oglethorpe, the founder of Georgia (originally a colony without slavery), who had given him an introduction to Sharp.

Despite Sharp's help, there was no way Equiano could get John Annis sent back from the Caribbean. "When the poor man arrived at St. Kitt's," Equiano wrote, "he was, according to custom, staked to the ground . . . was cut and flogged most unmercifully, and afterwards loaded cruelly with irons about his neck. I had two very moving letters from him while he was in this situation; and I made attempts to go after him at a great hazard, but was sadly disappointed: I also was told of it by some very respectable families, now in London, who saw him in St. Kitt's, in the same state, in which he remained till kind death released him out of the hands of his tyrants."

Equiano could paint his face and pass for white, at least in the dark; he could navigate skillfully through the white world's law courts and networks of influential people. But he was powerless to stop a black friend from being plunged back into slavery and tormented to an early death. Only a tiny minority of people in Britain openly opposed slavery, and he and Sharp were almost alone in having actively tried to help its victims. He sank into a despair so bitter that he went to sea again and resolved "never more to return to England."

4

KING SUGAR

THE SLAVE DEPOTS of the African coast, the vessels that took chained captives across the Atlantic, the precarious world of an ex-slave, the courts of London—all this takes us into the triangular world of Atlantic slavery. But not yet deeply enough if we are to understand why it took so long for the antislavery movement to begin. For that had to do with how central were the West Indies to the way Britons saw the world.

Think of them as the Middle East of the late eighteenth century. Just as oil drives the geopolitics of our own time, the most important commodity on European minds then was sugar, and the overseas territories that mattered most were the islands so wonderfully suited for growing it. The riches of the Caribbean, said a prominent French writer of the day, Abbé Guillaume-Thomas de Raynal, were "the principal cause of the rapid movement which stirs the Universe." When the British Parliament set up a large cash prize for the first person to solve the ancient problem that so vexed John Newton and other mariners, of how to determine longitude at sea, the winning technique had to be tested and proved by a Royal Navy ship sailing "over the ocean, from Great Britain to any . . . Port in the West Indies." By the mid-1700s Britain was importing 100,000 hogsheads (sixty-three-gallon casks) of sugar a year. Because of sugar, in 1773 the value of

British imports from Jamaica alone was five times that from the thirteen mainland colonies. In the same year, British imports from tiny Grenada were worth eight times those from all of Canada. Over the course of the century, some 60 percent of all slaves brought anywhere in the Americas were taken to the relatively small area of the Caribbean. Sugar was king.

While slaves labored in the broiling cane fields, whites who owned or managed the large plantations lived in conspicuous comfort, the best off in the legendary "great house" that was the center of every well-established estate. Whenever possible, planters built their great houses on breezy heights overlooking the sea, sometimes at the end of a carriage road lined with cedars or coconut palms. In further search of cooling winds, owners often had their living and dining quarters on the second floor, surrounded by covered porches with rocking chairs. Rooms in the most elegant houses were paneled in hardwood; more wood was shaped into bedposts and banisters for majestically curving staircases; louvers or venetian blinds kept out the sun. Slaves on their knees used coconut husks to polish the dark mahogany floors to a high shine. From chamber pots to wine glasses, many household objects were imported from England.

The planters were renowned for their vast meals. "Such eating and drinking I never saw!" wrote Lady Nugent, wife of the governor of Jamaica and keeper of a revealing diary. ". . . I observed some of the party to-day eat . . . as if they had never eaten before—a dish of tea, another of coffee, a bumper of claret, another large one of hock-negus [wine punch]; then Madeira, sangaree [sangria], hot and cold meat, stews and fries, hot and cold fish pickled and plain, peppers, ginger sweetmeats, acid fruit, sweet jellies." That was breakfast. Dinner, also served by barefoot slaves fanning away flies with palm leaves, was grander.

Wealthy planters spent much of their time paying or receiving visits, which might last several weeks at a time. A traveler to Jamaica described one:

> While we were at breakfast, I saw a column of negroes at some distance coming towards the house, with things upon

their heads, which I could not well distinguish; but the master . . . taking his spy-glass . . . told me that it was only a *trunk-fleet.* . . .

A dozen or more negroes, men and women, are dispatched in the morning, long before day, their heads charged with band-boxes, bundles and heavy trunks, containing the most considerable part of the wardrobe of the visitors:—under this load the poor creatures trudge twelve, fifteen, and sometimes twenty, and five-and-twenty miles, to prepare the toilet for their mistresses, whose arrival they are in time to announce. . . .

An hour after the arrival of the *trunk-fleet,* I perceived something like another fleet, which I soon found to be the lady herself and her family. . . . It was a procession of several horses in a strait line one after the other: it is a rule that the gentlemen should ride before the ladies; so first came young Chewquid, the heir, next Bob Chewquid, then Mrs. Chewquid; after her rode her eldest daughter, then two more daughters on horseback; then three negro boys on mules, then stout negro men a-foot carrying young children.—The ladies wore white and green hats, under which white handkerchiefs were pinned round their faces, meeting over their noses—this is the usual precaution for preventing the sun from blistering the skin. . . .

The eldest son rode a fine stallion, bred in the country, that no English jockey would have been ashamed to mount.

At last the procession arrives before the piazza [the covered porch], all puffing for breath and half stiffled with their handkerchiefs. After the first how-dees were over, the ladies were shewn to their bedchambers, and the gentlemen took chairs in the piazza. . . .

The gentlemen were no sooner seated, than one of them gave a shrill whistle, by the help of his fingers, and immediately a negro boy came running in: as soon as he made his appearance, the gentleman, who had whistled, cried . . . "Fire!"—upon which the boy went out as fast as he had entered, and returned in a minute with a bit of wood burning at one end. By this time the tobacco pouches were all opened, segars prepared, and each with his scissars had clipped the ends: the negro then presented the fire all round [and] the tobacco was lighted.

• • •

Imagine this account read in England, by people living the hard-scrabble lives of clerks or apprentices in crowded London tenements. Promising boundless wealth and slaves to do all the work, the islands dotting the turquoise Caribbean sounded like El Dorado itself. As with many an imagined El Dorado, however, there was somewhat less to the West Indian boom than met the eye: the price of sugar sometimes fell sharply, plunging many of the grand plantations into debt; and the British taxpayer paid dearly for maintaining the soldiers, fortresses, and naval bases that protected the islands against rebellious slaves and the jealous French. But hopes and legends are what drive people to action, not bottom-line calculations by economists of a later age. And in the eighteenth century, no one had the slightest doubt that the British West Indies were, as the writer Bryan Edwards put it in dedicating to the King his history of these islands, "the principle source of national opulence."

With their promise of opportunities, colonies have always been places where people can start over. We think of the Britons who came to the New World as salt-of-the-earth yeoman farmers and religious refugees, and some were. But many others were running away from creditors or scandal. Few of these were fleeing a more complex emotional tangle than a man who would later become a major abolitionist.

Although in old age he would find himself the patriarch of a renowned dynasty, James Stephen was the son of a ne'er-do-well businessman who was sent to a London debtors' prison. Young James himself lived in the prison for a time, because in those days a debtor's family could join him in jail. Eventually his father was released and James returned to school. There he became close friends with a schoolmate named Tom, and fell in love with Tom's sister, Nancy. "Her hair was auburn . . . inclining to red. Her person was pleasing. . . . Her heart was warm and affectionate in a high degree." Dismayed at his family background, however, Nancy's parents forbade her to see James. As in a novel, there were clandestine letters carried back and forth by Tom and a faithful servant, their discovery, confrontations with the angry parents, secret signals, stealthy intermediaries, further prohibitions. Finally, James Stephen went away and began studying law. But he ran out of money, returned to London, found Nancy, and fell in love all over again.

They became engaged. Nancy found him an inexpensive place to live, in a house where a close friend of hers, whom he calls Maria Rivers, was boarding. But ah, Maria. "She was in the full bloom of her beauty. . . . Her features . . . were extremely pleasing, and had an animated playful expression. . . . Her hair was dark brown, and her skin the clearest and softest that I ever saw." Nancy's brother Tom was courting Maria, and now had gone to sea as a Royal Navy officer, hoping to win enough glory and naval prize money to persuade her to marry him. In his absence, James zealously befriended Maria to promote his friend's cause.

Too zealously, it turned out. "It has been said," James Stephen writes, "that no Man can love two women at once; but I am confident this is an error. . . . There was . . . in both cases that which has always with me formed the first charm in a woman; they both loved me, and . . . I thought with equal warmth; and beyond doubt I loved them both, fondly loved them, in return."

Maria had yet another suitor; Stephen challenged him to a duel. "Maddened with admiration of her person, I always forgot in her presence the resolutions with which I met her and [remained] . . . bent on the destruction of her virtue." Before long Maria was pregnant, and Stephen furtively moved her to a different spot in London while they constructed an elaborate ruse that she had gone on a long visit to Scotland. Yet he remained engaged to Nancy, whose "every expression of . . . confidence and tenderness was a dagger plunged into my bosom . . . I feared more than death her discovery of the truth." Nancy soon found out, and threatened to swallow poison. Stephen talked her out of it, still promising to marry her. However, he had also, it seems, promised Maria to marry *her,* and their baby was due.

In the midst of all this, who should arrive but Tom, resplendent in his Royal Navy uniform and more eager than ever to marry Maria. His sister Nancy refused to give him the bad news; that, she told Stephen, was his job. "I wished for death and could have invoked the Earth to open and swallow me up alive to hide my sin and my shame together." He hoped that Tom would demand a duel and kill him.

But the despairing Tom instead drowned his sorrows in drink and asked the navy for a new post at "some distant station, with a resolution if possible to return to England no more."

The autobiography in which Stephen tells this tale was felt so embarrassing by his descendants that it was not published for more than a century after his death. Although he expresses remorse for bringing such heartache to the three people closest to him, Stephen was no John Newton. He believed himself to have been a terrible sinner, but wasn't obsessed with eternal punishment, and seems to have thoroughly enjoyed the sinning itself.

Having promised himself to two women, Stephen earnestly resolved to do the right thing. And this, he solemnly vowed, was to marry the one who could not find another husband. Before he could follow through on this promise, an unexpected family inheritance made it possible for him to resume his interrupted education in law. Then, he decided, he would go to the Caribbean, where lawyers could make far more money, so he could properly support whichever wife he ended up with.

His departure came not a moment too soon. For a new woman had appeared on the scene, with a mysterious past and great "beauty and accomplishments . . . remarkable delicacy and propriety of deportment . . . a tall, graceful woman, with a good face and elegant person; and the Scotch accent, in which she spoke, made her soft voice rather more pleasing." And, he rationalized, "as to the two beloved and injured women who had such strong claims on my heart, the painful dilemma in which I stood towards them would not be made worse . . . by a connection that would neither be permanent nor of an honorary kind. . . . As nobody would be injured, why should I do violence to my own feelings and those perhaps of a woman who had really conceived (so vanity whispered) a personal attachment towards me?"

Meanwhile, as Stephen was juggling Nancy and Maria "it was not easy to satisfy either that she had her fair portion of my time, or that a larger was not given to the other." Maria found another man to marry her, although whether he ever learned of the baby, we do not know. Stephen abandoned the Scotswoman, quickly married Nancy, and they discreetly adopted Maria's baby. Then, to be followed by his wife and child as soon as he got his law practice established, he set off for the West Indies.

It was late 1783 when a ship landed the twenty-five-year-old James Stephen on Barbados. As for Equiano, this fertile island was his first sight of the New World. And here the young man about town juggling his ladyloves found himself plunged abruptly into a different universe. On Broad Street in Bridgetown, for example, were public cages that held captured runaways. Their names were advertised in the newspapers weekly; then, behind hardwood bars and surrounded by their own feces, the slaves waited, in stocks or shackles, to be collected by their owners.

The day after he landed, Stephen was invited to dinner by friends of a London merchant he knew. At the table, the main topic was a trial about to begin, of four plantation slaves charged with the murder of a white doctor. Several of the dinner guests "strongly doubted the guilt of the prisoners" on the basis of evidence that to Stephen "appeared . . . pretty strong"; they thought the real murderer was a white man and that the trial was a cover-up. Many others on the island, black and white, felt the same way.

The budding lawyer eagerly attended the trial. The four accused slaves were led into court in filthy rags, obviously in pain from the tight cords that bound them. The owner of two, in a letter read to the court, declined to pay for a lawyer to defend them: "*God forbid that he should wish in such a case to screen the guilty from punishment.*" To Stephen's amazement, the chief judge "applauded the letter, as honourable to the writer; and the other magistrates concurred." The evidence against the accused was negligible: one supposed witness, a girl slave of about fifteen.* "She was admonished in the most alarming terms, to beware not to conceal any thing that made against the prisoners; and told that if she did, she would involve herself in their

* It was so unusual to have a black witness that several whites wrote alarmed letters to the *Barbados Mercury* that month. A magistrate replied, reassuring readers that a black witness's word could never, of course, count against a white person.

crime, and its punishment. . . . Terror was strongly depicted in her countenance." She was right to be terrified, for the local newspaper reported of this trial that "three negroes" who evidently did not say what they were told to say "were whipped, for giving false evidence." Convinced that the four accused slaves were innocent, Stephen was shocked to hear, soon after, that they had been sentenced to death—by being burned alive.

This form of execution, a common one for blacks in the Caribbean, was a measure of the fear the islands' outnumbered whites felt towards the slaves, for it had been little used in Europe since the medieval burnings of witches and heretics. Two of the Barbados victims won a last-minute reprieve, but on two the sentence was carried out. One, Stephen heard, "in his tortures . . . drew the iron stake to which he was fastened from the ground . . . but they drove the stake into the ground again, and applied more fuel. Both were literally roasted to death."

Stephen's horror was all the greater because he knew that he himself had benefited from slavery. His uncle had been a doctor in the West Indies with an unusual practice: he bought from ship captains low-priced "refuse slaves"—Africans so debilitated from the middle passage that planters didn't want them—then used his medical skills to restore their health and resell them. It was a legacy from his uncle's earnings that had allowed Stephen to finish his law studies.

What he had seen in that Barbados courtroom was to determine the course of James Stephen's life. It would be more than two decades, however, before he would be in a position to strike a crucial, behind-the-scenes blow against British slavery.

The island where Stephen got his first picture of Caribbean slavery in action was one of the earliest British colonies in the region and the first to grow sugar; its plantations pioneered various techniques soon applied elsewhere. We have a detailed picture of slave life there because Barbados, as it happens, was home to an estate that left unusually abundant records, the seaside Codrington plantation.

The land at Codrington totaled 710 acres. The rich red soil and plentiful rain produced a first-rate crop of sugar. There were three wind-powered mills for pressing the juice out of the cane, the largest "boiling house" on the island for turning cane juice into sugar and molasses, and a distillery for making molasses into rum. (The best Caribbean rum was particularly prized; George Washington once shipped a "Rogue & Runaway" slave to the West Indies to be exchanged for, among other things, a hogshead of rum. Finding its way around the triangle, much Caribbean rum also wound up in Africa, as a currency for purchasing slaves.)

Like a steadily increasing number of West Indian plantations—and unlike most of those in the American South—Codrington had absentee owners in England, and so its fine "great house" was occupied by a resident manager, helped by a dozen or so white employees, ranging from a storekeeper to the captain of the plantation's sloop, which carried barrels of sugar and rum around the island to Bridgetown, to be loaded onto ships for England. Nineteen slave servants took care of their every need: cooking meals, doing laundry, and emptying chamber pots. In times of slave rebellions, the white men formed a contingent of Barbados's red-coated militia; the rank of a senior militia officer usually reflected the size of the plantation he owned.

In what little spare time they had, Codrington's slaves built and repaired their own rickety, earth-floored wooden huts, continually repairing the leaky thatch roofs, made of sticks and "trash"—cane after the juice had been squeezed out—held together with thin strands of rope. Hurricanes left the sturdy stone Codrington great house standing but generally blew down the slave quarters.

In a good year, Codrington's profits were more than £2,000—roughly $325,000 in today's money. The plantation's accountants kept a detailed running inventory of all its assets, including the slaves. A headcount in 1781 showed the slave quarters holding 276 men, women, and children. Skilled male workers like the carpenter, the boiler mechanic, and three barrelmakers were valued on the books at £70 apiece, the two children's nurses at only £15 each. Even the names given the slaves reflected their jobs: Sloop Johnny, Cuffy Potter, Quashey Hog, Quashey Boyler.

At Codrington, as throughout the Caribbean, new slaves from Africa were first "seasoned" for three years, receiving extra food and light work assignments. Slaves were vulnerable during this early traumatic period, when they were most liable to die of disease, to run away, or to commit suicide, like Jack Smith, who "hang'd himself" in 1746, only three months after Codrington purchased him. The ordeal of the middle passage, plus the shock of adjusting to new lives, foods, and diseases, was so great that roughly one third of Africans died within three years of disembarking in the West Indies. This merely increased the demand for slaves. If you survived those three years, you were regarded as ready for the hardest labor.

Cultivating and harvesting the crop was brutal work. If you were a field hand, you planted cane shoots in holes or trenches you dug by hand, often in marshland where the air was dense with mosquitoes. At harvest time, you carried huge, heavy bundles of cane to the mill. You then fed each bundle twice through powerful vertical rollers that squeezed out the juice, which flowed into large copper vats in the boiling house, where it was simmered, strained, filtered, and allowed to crystallize into sugar.

The exhausted slaves who worked these vats were "very apt to get scalded," a manual for planters matter-of-factly noted, "especially when they are obliged to continue their labours in the night time." The cane's juice fermented and turned sour within a day or two after cutting, so it had to be rushed to the mill immediately. Profit-hungry planters sometimes recklessly grew more cane than they had mill capacity for, and during the harvest season mills often ran around the clock to try to process it all. Slaves then had to work in the mill or boiling house four to six hours on alternate nights in addition to a full day in the fields. Their clothes soaked with cane juice, they often lay down to sleep wherever they were, too exhausted to walk to their huts, and many caught pneumonia. At night, flames from the boiling house fires were visible to ships at sea.

The fires, the darkness, the agony of scalding: the descriptions of West Indian sugar mills and boiling houses have a satanic ring to them. And there was more. When Lady Nugent visited one plantation, she wrote, "I asked the overseer how often his people were relieved. He said every twelve hours; but how dreadful to think of their standing twelve hours over a boiling cauldron, and doing the same thing; and he owned to me that sometimes they did fall asleep, and get their poor fingers into the mill; and he shewed me a hatchet, that was always ready to sever the whole limb, as the only means of saving the poor sufferer's life!"*

Only small children, the elderly, and invalids escaped work. Most Codrington slaves were field hands, and from the age of seven or eight, old enough to wield a special child-sized hoe, they would be put to work weeding, planting corn, gathering fodder for cattle, or shoveling manure into cane holes. ("How pleasing, how gratifying . . . it is to see a swarm of healthy, active, cheerful, pliant . . . negro boys and girls going to, and returning from the puerile work field," said another manual for planters.) Adults, wearing straw hats or bandanas against the sun, went out to the fields between five and seven A.M., and continued, with meal breaks, until seven P.M., usually six days a week. Sundays, according to a disapproving local minister, the Codrington slaves spent in "vile & vicious Practices . . . either in trafficking with one another, or in dancing, or in other Actions improper to mention." He did not seem to notice that Sundays were often the only time slaves had to cultivate their own meager vegetable gardens.

Discipline was draconian. For a Barbados slave, running away for thirty days or more meant death. An owner who killed a slave, however, was subject only to a £15 fine. Nonetheless, attempts to flee were so common that one expense line in the plantation's annual budget included "rewards for return of runaway slaves." Codrington paid half a dozen such rewards each year, often in the form of a gallon of rum. A woman field hand named Quashebah ran away five times between 1775 and 1784. On some plantations, a long blast on a conch shell was the alarm that signaled a runaway.

As in similar systems the world over, a small number of whites could dominate a far larger number of slaves by enlisting slaves to help them. James Stephen, who with prosecutorial zeal began gathering in-

* The mill rollers had no brakes and sometimes the hatchet did not help. A planter described one incident on Barbados: "Two Negroe Women, being Chained together, by way of punishment for some offence, were employed . . . in a Windmill, one of them unfortunately reaching too near the Rollers, her fingers were caught between them, and her Body was drawn through the Mill. The Iron Chain, being seized by the Rollers, was likewise drawn through & . . . the other Female Negroe, was dragg'd so close to those Cylinders, that her Head was severed from her Body."

formation on all aspects of slavery as soon as he settled on the nearby island of St. Kitts, noticed, for example, how "drivers . . . are intrusted with the power of the whip over their brethren. . . . These men are selected from among the most intelligent and the most athletic of the slaves belonging to the estate, and present in their plump and robust appearance a striking contrast to the . . . poor labourers whom they drive. A long thick and strongly platted whip, with a short handle, is coiled and slung like a sash over their shoulders."

For nearly a decade, Codrington officials tried to reduce escapes by branding all slaves on their chests. In the end, though, the chief deterrent was the lash, plus, at times, an iron collar and a straitjacket. "It's too Notoriously known here how ready Negro's in general are to Joyn in Any Wicked Designe," wrote one manager at Codrington. No "Wicked Designe" ever actually stopped work on the plantation, but its managers, like apprehensive whites on every Caribbean island, always felt that they were at the edge of a cliff. Just a few days' sail away, for instance, authorities on Antigua discovered in 1736 that slaves were plotting to plant gunpowder at the site of a grand ball "to blow up all the Gentry of the Island while they were in the height of their mirth," following which, groups of slaves "were to Enter the Town at Different parts, and to put all the White people there to the Sword." Once the plot was uncovered, seventy-seven slaves were burned to death.

The life of even the most obedient Codrington slave was likely to be short. Careful clerks recorded slave deaths each year, on the same list with those of cattle, hogs, and horses. Causes included "Ulcers," "Suddenly," "a flux," "shot by Accident," "a Fever," "Plague," "debilitated," "convulsed," "Leprosy." In 1743, "three Negro Men, Anning, Yeaboy, & Brumiah were Suffocated to Death by the Steam of a Receiving Cistern in the Distill house."

Caribbean slavery was, by every measure, far more deadly than slavery in the American South. This was not because Southern masters were the kind and gentle ones of *Gone with the Wind,* but because cultivating sugar cane by hand was—and still is—one of the hardest ways of life on earth. Almost everywhere in the Americas where slaves were working other than on sugar plantations, they lived longer. Besides planting the cane, they had to fertilize the soil with cattle manure they carried to the fields on their heads in dripping eighty-pound baskets. The most intense work came during the high-pressure five-month harvesting and processing season. Hour after hour in the hot sun, they had to bend over to slash at the base of the stalks with a heavy machete while clearing aside the cut canes with the other hand. Sugar cane leaves have knife-like edges and sharp points that can jab the eye, cheek, or ear of a tired or unwary cutter. Slaves had none of the protective gear available today: safety boots, aluminum arm and leg guards, canvas gloves with leather palms. Furthermore, in the lush tropics where land was being fertilized, planted, weeded, or harvested for most of the year, there was little winter respite from field work.

The sugar regime was not the only burden. The West Indian climate brought a raft of tropical diseases to both whites and blacks. And with the best arable land on the islands all reserved for cash crops like sugar, the Caribbean slave diet was far worse than that on the North American mainland, causing nutrition-deficiency illnesses like rickets and scurvy. What little protein the slaves were given mostly came from pickled herring or salted cod judged not good enough to sell in Britain. Imported only once or twice a year, the fish often went rotten.* The results of these hardships appeared in a common medical measure of health and nutrition: height. On average, Caribbean male slaves were three inches shorter than those in the American South.

Among the slaves, almost all the skilled jobs, like maintaining mill equipment, building sugar barrels, or doing masonry, went to men. This meant that—contrary to the picture in most Britons' minds, then and now—the majority of slaves in the fields of plantations like Codrington were women. The fact that women did the hardest labor, combined with their abysmal diet, delayed menarche and brought

---

* The famous mutiny on the *Bounty* was connected to the diet of Caribbean slaves. When his men rebelled after leaving Tahiti, the irascible Lieutenant William Bligh was on a mission to fetch specimens of the breadfruit tree for planting in the British West Indies. Plantation owners wanted it as a cheap source of slave food, because once the tree bears fruit, it requires no cultivation, and this, it was hoped, would free even more of the slaves' time for harvesting sugar. The mutiny derailed Bligh's first attempt, but on a second voyage he successfully transported a "floating forest" to the West Indies. The grateful planter-controlled Jamaica legislature awarded him 1,000 guineas. "Breadfruit Bligh," as he became known, also brought from Tahiti a new variety of cane that yielded much more sugar.

an end to a slave woman's fertility by her mid-thirties. In the mid-eighteenth-century British West Indies, fully half of all women sugar slaves never bore a child.

Because of the extraordinarily low birth rate and the early deaths from disease, Caribbean masters depended, far more so than planters in the American South, on a constant flow of new slaves. Without this influx of fresh human cargoes, the slave population of the West Indies would have fallen by as much as 3 percent a year. For most of the 1700s, Codrington's managers regularly bought up to thirty slaves a year off ships arriving from Africa. Plantation owners generally felt, as the saying went, that it was cheaper to buy than to breed. An Antigua planter who bought some slaves from John Newton told him that his policy was "with little relaxation, hard fare, and hard usage, to wear them out before they became useless, and unable to do service; and then, to buy new ones, to fill up their places."

One final set of grim numbers underlines the way slaves on sugar plantations like Codrington were systematically worked to an early death. When slavery ended in the United States, some 400,000 slaves imported over the centuries had grown to a population of nearly four million. When it ended in the British West Indies, total slave imports of two million left a surviving slave population of only about 670,000. The tiny French island of Martinique took in more slave imports over the years than all thirteen North American colonies, later states, put together. The Caribbean was a slaughterhouse.

Codrington's richly detailed records not only portray how a West Indian plantation operated, they also show how the benefits of slavery were enjoyed by the highest reaches of British society—and therefore how difficult it would be to uproot. For the absentee owner for whom all these careful accounts were prepared was not a person, and it was not a family.

It was the Church of England.

Specifically, it was the church's missionary arm, the Society for the Propagation of the Gospel in Foreign Parts, whose governing board included the Regius Professors of Divinity at Oxford and Cambridge and the head of the church, the Archbishop of Canterbury. The estate's brand, burned onto the chests of slaves with a red-hot iron, was

SOCIETY. The clerics on the society's board noticed the plantation's high death rate, but made no move to change how it operated. "I have long wondered & lamented," wrote the Archbishop of Canterbury to a fellow bishop in 1760, "that the Negroes in our plantations decrease, & new Supplies become necessary continually. Surely this proceeds from some Defect, both of Humanity, & even of good policy. But we must take things as they are at present."

5

A TALE OF TWO SHIPS

THE CARIBBEAN COLONIES that were home to plantations such as Codrington, like the rest of Britain's far-flung imperial holdings, ultimately depended on the Royal Navy. This was the force that kept at bay pirates, the French, and other potential rivals who might prey on the long, vulnerable shipping routes that were the sinews of British commerce, above all those of the triangle trade. The red, white, or blue ensigns of naval squadrons—the color indicated the rank of the admiral in command—fluttered in home waters, along the slaving coast of West Africa, and in the Caribbean. Like the Spanish, Portuguese, and Dutch before them, Britain dominated much of the world through sea power. And at the heart of the navy, with a crew that could number eight hundred or more, three towering masts, and fearsome triple rows of gunports, was the battleship. With its immense concentration of firepower, it was the greatest weapon of mass destruction of its day.

During the late eighteenth century, the tallest and heaviest vessel in the Royal Navy was the battleship HMS *Royal George,* bristling with 108 cannons. As Lieutenant Pascal's slave, Equiano had briefly served on this ship, and his first look at it, taking on supplies and filled with hawkers from on shore, awed him: "The Royal George was the largest ship I had ever seen. . . . Here were . . . shops or stalls of every kind of goods, and people crying their different commodities about the ship as in a town. To me it appeared a little world."

One day many years later, the now aging battleship was provisioning in the harbor of the great naval base at Portsmouth, where a dense thicket of masts filled the anchorage while small supply boats swarmed back and forth to shore. Only partly loaded, it was floating high in the water, particularly top-heavy because its heaviest guns were on the upper deck. To make some repairs below the waterline, its captain ordered the guns on the opposite side of the ship run out of their ports into firing position, so their weight would heel the ship over. The crew went below for breakfast. When dockyard shipwrights complained that the spot they needed to work on still wasn't completely clear of the water, the captain ordered more weight shifted to the low side of ship. Just then, a supply barge arrived from shore filled with rum.

If the empire depended on the navy, the navy depended on rum. The sailors' treasured ration of Caribbean rum could reach, in alcohol content, the equivalent of six double whiskies a day. The *Royal George*'s sailors eagerly worked at hoisting the barrels of rum on board, piling them up on the low side of the deck.

A sudden gust of wind added fatally to the weight of rum, guns, and masts. As the ship tipped further, cannonballs broke loose from their racks to thunder across the decks, and water began pouring in the open gunports. In a few moments, rum, guns, the *Royal George,* and most of the officers and sailors on board, from an admiral in his epaulets to many a lowly seaman, all lay many fathoms under water. This was not the most glorious of military deaths, but Britons still wanted to find something noble in it. Church bells tolled throughout the land, memorial services were held, and mourners erected stones and monuments, one in Westminster Abbey. The poet Cowper wrote:

> Toll for the brave—
> The brave! That are no more:
> All sunk beneath the wave,
> Fast by their native shore.

But at the bottom of Portsmouth harbor it was not all men. Among the drowned were some four hundred women, most of them prostitutes, who did just as lively a business as other tradespeople on navy ships in port. Down with the ship also went four hundred Bibles, delivered just the day before as a gift from the Naval and Military Bible Society, of which Granville Sharp was an active member.

Prostitutes and Bibles, rum and sea power, glory and top-heaviness: there is something about the sinking of the *Royal George* that sums up the England of its time. And in no one's life were these themes of the sea, Christianity, and an obsession with sin more closely woven together than John Newton's. Ending his third voyage as a slave ship captain, Newton had safely returned to Liverpool, following the lighthouses that guided mariners up the west coast of England, having lost not a single crewman nor slave at sea—great rarities both. Although he regretted being away so much from his beloved Mary, he was working in what he and everyone around him thought to be, as he put it, a "creditable way of life." Looking back, he wrote: "During the time I was engaged in the slave-trade, I never had the least scruple as to its lawfulness. I was upon the whole satisfied with it, as the appointment Providence had marked out for me. . . . It is indeed accounted a genteel employment, and is usually very profitable."

However, two days before he was again to sail for Africa, while drinking tea with Mary, Newton was "seized with a fit, which deprived me of sense and motion, and left me no other sign of life than that of breathing." Doctors advised him not to go to sea. He took this mysterious seizure as a sign from God that he should take up another calling—a message later confirmed, it seemed, when the captain who replaced him and most of his officers died.

Slave ship owners and suppliers dominated Liverpool's municipal government, and Newton's long-time patron, Joseph Manesty, was a member of its ruling body, the Common Council, living on a street still called Manesty Lane today. Pulling strings on Newton's behalf, he got him a good job in the port's customs service. A year later, in 1756, Britain's imperial rivalry with France once again broke into war, and the Royal Navy needed men. Press gangs roamed the streets of Liverpool. Newton sent an urgent warning to Manesty that the HMS *Vengeance* was out to illegally impress the crew of the *Golden Lion,* a Manesty whaling vessel that had just returned from Greenland. The *Vengeance* sent four boatloads of men to board the *Golden Lion,* whose sixty whalers pulled out their harpoons and blubber knives and fought back. True to its name, the *Vengeance* then opened fire, and stray cannonballs hit parts of Liverpool. The next day, the *Golden Lion*'s whalers and their captain showed up at the Custom House, the headquarters Newton reported to. A magistrate was in the process of confirming their exemption from impressment when the navy's press gang stormed into the building's courtyard, firing pistols. In the melee that followed, five whalers were impressed, exemption or not. Newton had left the slave trade, but violence still swirled around him.

Even though once a victim of it, Newton accepted impressment as part of the natural way of things, just as he did slavery. His mind was focused on changing not the social order of his world but its spiritual life. He was falling more and more under the influence of the Evangelical movement.

Since the Reformation, Britain's official or "established" church had been the Church of England, to which the great majority of the population belonged, especially if they were prominent families like the Sharps. Catholics and Jews had few civil rights and could not vote, and even Protestants of other denominations could not serve as army officers, hold municipal office, or be members of Parliament. To do any of these things, you had to at least go through the motions of following Anglican, or Church of England, ritual. Twenty-six Anglican bishops were ex officio members of Parliament's upper chamber, the House of Lords. The reigning King or Queen, the symbolic head of the church, held the title of Defender of the Faith, although the church was so powerful there was little to defend it against. The main challenge was now emerging from inside.

Part of a larger religious revival touching much of the Western world at this time, Evangelicalism arose among Anglicans who felt that their church was Christian only in form. Like the *Royal George,* the Church of England had grown creaky and top-heavy. The job of parish minister was seen as a sinecure, a "living," in the language of the day. One Archbishop of Canterbury was notorious for dispensing livings and other church posts to his extended family. And Bishop Sparke of Ely handed out so many positions to his relatives that a traveler, it was said, could find his way at night by the light of all the Sparkes shining in their livings. A minister might increase his income by acquiring multiple livings; and to preach to all his congregations on a Sunday, wrote one critic, he "hurries through the service in a manner perfectly indecent; strides from the pulpit to his horse and gallops away as if pursuing a fox."

Many clerics actually were avid fox hunters, and acted in ways the devout found even more shocking: straying from their marriages, playing cards on Sunday, or going to the theater. Lazy ministers simply preached other men's sermons, sometimes helped by the profitable business of Reverend Dr. John Trusler, who specialized in "abridging the Sermons of eminent divines, and printing them in the form of manuscripts, so as not only to save clergymen the trouble of composing their discourses, but even of transcribing them." The great man of letters Samuel Johnson joked to his biographer James Boswell that he had never met a clergyman who was religious.

The Evangelical movement was a reaction against the entire mood of the age: the licentious England of the 1700s preserved for us in Hogarth's exuberant prints and novels like *Tom Jones*. This was the raucous country reflected by such London names as Bladder Street and Codpiece Row (later sanitized to Coppice Row). At a time when even pickpockets got the death penalty, executions were a favorite spectator sport; some took place where Marble Arch now stands. Guarded by redcoats, a man rode to the gallows in the same cart with his coffin and his hangman; people brought him flowers or beer if he was popular, and threw garbage or worse if he was not. When a hanging drew a particularly large crowd, vendors sold gingerbread, liquor, copies of bawdy ballads, and seats with good views.

Prostitutes by the tens of thousands served not only the ill-fated sailors of the *Royal George* but the most elegant Londoners. Some of the higher-priced women worked, to the accompaniment of musicians, in curtained booths on a large boat named the *Folly*, moored near where Waterloo Bridge today reaches the north bank of the Thames. There was even a guidebook, HARRIS'S LIST *of Covent-Garden Ladies . . .* CONTAINING *An exact Description of the most celebrated Ladies of Pleasure. . . .* Such women could be found, wrote a visitor, "got up in any way you like, dressed, bound up, hitched up, tight-laced, loose, painted, done up or raw, scented, in silk or wool, with or without sugar, in short, what a man cannot obtain here, if he have money, upon my word, let him not look for it anywhere in this world of ours." Pimps and madams would assure a customer that the woman he desired was a clergyman's daughter, fallen temporarily on hard times.

This was an England so earthy that a correspondent could write a letter to the London *Morning Chronicle* in 1779 proposing as a topic for a debating society: "Which causes the greatest commotion in the intestines, a purge or a vomit?" Even Parliament lacked dignity: "Sir William spoke a great deal," reported one newspaper the same year, "but a loud *snoring* . . . prevented much of what he said from reaching the ears of the strangers in the Gallery." At county fairs, accompanied by cheering and betting, there were cockfights, cudgel fights, bull-baiting, bear-baiting, bare-fisted boxing, fights between men and dogs, and, for spectators who paid enough, men who would eat live fox cubs.

To the Evangelicals, this was a nation that had lost its moral bearings. Philosophers were too tempted by skepticism, consumption of alcohol was too high, and women's necklines were too low. Everyone, including the clergy, seemed to be carousing in taverns, begetting illegitimate children, and forgetting God. Almost all the Evangelicals were middle or upper class, and they were especially alarmed at sinful behavior by the poor.

We should not, however, dismiss the Evangelicals as mere snobbish spoilsports in the lusty world of Tom Jones and Squire Western. The "ladies of pleasure," for instance, lived in a world of poverty, venereal disease, fatherless children, and early death. Even the author of *Tom Jones,* Henry Fielding, was appalled by Londoners' burgeoning taste for gin, consumed at the average rate of a quart per week per person: "Many of these wretches there are, who swallow pints of this poison within the twenty four hours; the dreadful effects of which I have the misfortune every day to see, and to smell too." On some streets every fifth house sold gin: "In one place not far from East Smithfield," wrote another critic, ". . . a trader has a large empty room . . . where, as his wretched guests get intoxicated, they are laid together in heaps, promiscuously, men, women, and children, till they recover their senses, when they proceed to drink on." Gin ravaged London the way the crack cocaine epidemic hit American inner cities in the late 1980s, until legislation, backed fervently by Evangelicals, abated the "gin craze." The upper classes, however, continued unimpeded to consume vast quantities of their own favorite drink, claret. Based on daily habit, people were known as two-, three-, or four-bottle men. Cabinet members, including William Pitt, Prime Minister for many years starting in 1783, sometimes showed up drunk in Parliament.

Evangelicals, by contrast, advocated close study of the Bible, frequent prayer, and rigorously keeping the Sabbath; they believed one could start a Christian life only with a conscious experience of conversion, as Newton had after the great storm at sea. They disapproved of concerts or balls on Sundays, of plays, gambling, most dancing, and pubs. Sir Richard Hill, the first Evangelical to enter Parliament, unsuccessfully proposed special taxes on corks, dice, horse races, and sheet music. Above all, Evangelicals felt that true Christians had to live every day free of sin. To many, this was a shocking thought: after hearing an Evangelical minister preach, the future Prime Minister Lord Melbourne huffed, "Things are coming to a pretty pass when religion is allowed to invade private life."

The Evangelical John Wesley founded what would eventually become a new denomination, Methodism. Other small Dissenting, or non-Anglican, sects, like the Baptists, gained new strength from the Evangelical movement, which echoed many of their own beliefs. The Church of England stalwart Granville Sharp was basically an Evangelical, although his unusually democratic beliefs about slavery, American independence, and much else put him in a category all his own.

One of the first times John Newton had heard an Evangelical minister preach was when he was delivering slaves to South Carolina. On a later journey, while unloading slaves at St. Kitts, he met an Evangelically minded fellow captain and "for near a month we spent every evening together on board each other's ship alternately, and often prolonged our visits till towards daybreak." A strange scene to imagine: the two captains in their tricornered hats pacing the deck, earnestly talking of God and sin through the night, while slaves lie in shackles below them.

On his voyages, Newton had gathered his crew on deck for prayer, "according to the liturgy, twice every Lord's day, officiating myself." Finally, in 1764, ten years after leaving the sea, he was ordained as an

Anglican clergyman. For the first decade and a half of his ministry, he was curate of a fourteenth-century church in Olney, a market town northwest of London. During his occasional trips away, he still wrote Mary voluminous love letters. His sermons quickly won him a reputation as a leading Evangelical preacher, and his church had to build a new gallery to increase its seating capacity. During these years, working in the third-floor study of his stone vicarage, Newton also became one of the most renowned hymn writers in the English language. His majestic, heartfelt hymns, like "How Sweet the Name of Jesus Sounds" and "Glorious Things of Thee Are Spoken," are still sung throughout the world. In December 1772, he wrote the most famous of all:

> Amazing grace! (how sweet the sound)
> That saved a wretch like me!
> I once was lost, but now am found,
> Was blind, but now I see.

A recent count found more than 1,100 recordings of "Amazing Grace," and its soaring phrases have long had a special resonance for those struggling for justice. The African-American soprano Jessye Norman sang it before seventy thousand people at a London celebration of the imprisoned Nelson Mandela's seventieth birthday; virtually every major black American singer from Paul Robeson to Aretha Franklin has recorded it; it was sung in slave churches before the Civil War; it was an unofficial anthem of the civil rights movement of the 1960s. An occasional songbook even mistakenly classifies it as a Negro spiritual. Periodically, someone rediscovers that this most beloved of all hymns was written by a former slave trader. And then a newspaper column, a sermon, or a Web site celebrates the magic of a change of heart, the miracle of how a man who once trafficked in human beings had the courage to denounce slavery, and to create the great hymn about redemption that has such power to stir us. "Newton wrote the hymn to atone for his early life as a ship's captain in the slave trade," reported the Associated Press not long ago. A well-known modern author of inspirational books tells the tale more dramatically yet: "One day, when he was in his ship's cabin reading a sermon . . . he suddenly saw the evil of what he was doing. He ordered the ship to turn around in mid-ocean, and returning to Africa, he set his human cargo free."

If only this were so. However, for more than thirty years after he left the slave trade, during which time he preached thousands of sermons, published half a dozen books, and wrote "Amazing Grace" and 279 other hymns, John Newton said not a word in public against slavery. Moreover, for many of these years he had his savings invested in the slave ship business of his former employer—an investment that ended only when Manesty went bankrupt. He continued to socialize happily with old slave ship captain friends at their favorite London gathering place, the Jamaica Coffee House, and he owed his position as curate of Olney to an influential slave trade supporter, the Earl of Dartmouth. In 1781, more than a quarter century after he left the trade, Newton preached a sermon summing up all of Britain's sins—for which, he believed, the American Revolution and a chain of disastrous hurricanes in the West Indies were God's punishment. These ranged from adultery to "the magnitude of the national debt" to blasphemy, "which perhaps may eminently be styled *Our* national sin." Slavery did not make the list. Not until years later, when forces burst into life around him that made it impossible for him to remain silent, would he finally speak about it.

Only a single small religious denomination, with fewer than twenty thousand members in all of Britain, had officially come out against slavery. Pacifist and democratically minded, the Quakers believed that the "Inner Light" of God's revelation shone equally on human beings of any race or class. The British Quakers' history as a persecuted minority sect also disposed them against slavery; in the previous, less tolerant century, when many were jailed for their beliefs, some five hundred Quakers had died in prison or soon after their release. Many more had immigrated to the United States. There, Quakers who owned slaves had not only freed them; some took a step more far-reaching than anything before or since, of paying the slaves compensation. In Pennsylvania, the center of American Quakerism, as in England, Quakers who did not free slaves they owned were expelled from the church.

In 1783, British Quakers formed a committee of six people to agitate against slavery and the slave trade. They worked valiantly, sending articles to a dozen newspapers and distributing a fifteen-page pamphlet to the royal family and hundreds of other notables. Ten thousand more copies were sent throughout the country. The committee even quietly paid the doorkeepers of both houses of Parliament to give pamphlets to all members. Quaker antislavery delegations also visited Eton, Harrow, and other elite schools, some of whose students were the sons of wealthy West Indian planters.

No one paid much attention. In a country highly attuned to the markers of caste and class, Quakers were conspicuously different. They addressed people as "thee" and "thou" because they believed that using the originally more formal "you" was flattery. In deference to God, Quaker men would uncover their heads when preaching or praying, but would never doff their hats to a mere mortal, even to royalty. The early Quaker leader William Penn had been thrown out of the house by his father (ironically, the admiral who captured from Spain what would become Britain's largest slave colony, Jamaica) for refusing to take off his hat before the King. Quaker men wore neither ruffles nor swords, and women neither lace nor jewelry; both dressed in clothes of undyed wool. Quakers refused to play music, read novels, or erect tombstones. Not only did Quaker habits make them objects of mockery, but the laws that reserved all elected and civil service posts for Anglicans left them politically marginalized. Almost everyone laughed off the Quakers as powerless oddballs who would not remove their peculiar hats, and their bold and prescient attempt to turn their fellow Britons against slavery had no impact. The only people who seemed to notice were former slaves: Equiano and seven other Africans went to London's Quaker meetinghouse and presented an "address of thanks" in Equiano's flowery language. But not a single member of Parliament was persuaded to take up the cause. After much effort, it was clear to the disappointed Quakers that they needed a new approach.

Equiano, too, was discouraged about ever seeing slavery's end. He considered living in Turkey, but its allure soon paled—perhaps because he realized it was full of slaves. Despite his vow to stay away from England forever, he had returned, for it was where he knew he was safest from reenslavement. He spent much of the late 1770s and early 1780s in London, working as a house servant.

On March 18, 1783, some seven months after the *Royal George* went to its grave, his eye was caught by the mention of another ship. That day's *Morning Chronicle and London Advertiser* carried ads for "singular Combs, on an entire new construction" just arrived from Paris, for "Olympian Dew, or Grecian Bloom Water" to remove freckles, and for a new play called *The Mysterious Husband.* The news included reports that thieves had tried to rob two coaches in Grosvenor Square, and that "a mad bullock tossed four men in Oxford Road . . . and then made his way into a pastry cook's shop, and did much damage." But what Equiano noticed was a letter to the editor. A case being heard in a London courtroom, the writer said, "seemed to make every person present shudder." The following day Granville Sharp recorded in his diary that Equiano "called on me, with an account of one hundred and thirty Negroes being thrown alive into the sea, from on board an English slave ship."

More than a year earlier, the *Zong,* under Captain Luke Collingwood, had sailed from Africa for Jamaica loaded with some 440 slaves, many of whom had already been on board for weeks. Headwinds and spells of calm stretched the transatlantic voyage to more than twice its usual length. The inexperienced captain (his previous job had been as a ship's doctor), who had more than the usual mariner's trouble with longitude, mistook Jamaica for another island and overshot his destination. Not until nearly four months after leaving Africa would he finally put into the Jamaican port of Black River.

Jammed tightly into a vessel of only 107 tons, the slaves had long before begun to die. After some three months' sailing, more than sixty were dead, and many of the rest looked as if they would not make it. Like John Newton, Collingwood was paid the customary slave captain's salary of £5 a month, plus a share of the owner's profits. But dead slaves brought no profits. A way out, however, occurred to him. Because the shipping business treated slaves as cargo, they were insured—at £30 apiece, or more than $4,000 in today's money. A competent captain was expected, of course, to keep his slaves properly shackled and chained, and insurance paid nothing if he had to kill some in suppressing a rebellion. But the standard maritime insurance policy covered all "Perils . . . of the Seas." If slaves died because of "Perils" beyond the captain's control, insurance covered the loss.

Captain Collingwood called his officers together and ordered them to throw the sickest slaves into the ocean. He told them to say, if they were later asked, that because of unfavorable winds, the ship's water supply was running out. If the ship *had* been running out of water, the loss would indeed have been covered by insurance under the principle of "jettison" in maritime law: a captain was allowed to throw overboard some of his cargo—in this case, slaves—if necessary to save the remainder.

Chief Mate James Kelsal at first opposed the captain's plan, but then gave in. Fifty-four of the sickest slaves were "jettisoned" the first day, and forty-two a day or two later. By the time the third group's turn came, the slaves were fighting back, and as a result, twenty-six of them were tossed over the side with their arms still shackled. The remaining ten, as a contemporary account put it, "sprang disdainfully from the grasp of their tyrants, defied their power, and, leaping into the sea, felt a momentary triumph in the embrace of death." Altogether, 133 slaves had gone over the side, although amazingly, wrote Sharp later, "*one* man . . . escaped, it seems, by laying hold of a rope which hung from the ship into the water, and thereby, without being perceived, regained the ship, secreted himself, and was saved."*

A few months afterwards, the *Zong*'s owners filed an insurance claim for the value of the dead slaves. At £30 apiece, this added up to the equivalent of more than half a million dollars today, and the insurers disputed the claim. When the case came to trial, they had the support of the chief mate, apparently now guilt-ridden for his part in the deaths. The ship had had plenty of water, he testified: no one had been on short water rations, rain replenished the supply, and the *Zong* had arrived in Jamaica with 420 gallons to spare. The court none-

* Echoing down through the years, this mass murder inspired a famous painting, J.M.W. Turner's *Slave Ship*, today in the Boston Museum of Fine Arts. Shackled black hands protrude from the ocean, a ship rocks on the swells, and the red clouds of sunset cast an accusing, blood-colored glow over the whole scene.

theless found in favor of Captain Collingwood and the owners. The angry insurers appealed.

The moment Equiano pointed out the newspaper article to him, Sharp leapt into action. As with the Somerset case, he hoped this new trial might be a defining moment in which he could turn the full majesty of British law against slave owners. He consulted an Oxford law don, called on two bishops, and fired off letters to the Prime Minister, the Lords of the Admiralty, and the newspapers. He hired lawyers, personally interviewed at least one member of the *Zong*'s crew, and found a passenger, a colonial official, who "told me himself, that he saw several of the poor creatures plunging in the sea that had been cast overboard."

By this point in his life there are portraits of Sharp, and so it is easy to picture his disapproving face in the front row of the spectators' benches: thin lips, a long nose, a fierce, determined gaze accentuated by an outward jut of the chin. Presiding over the appeal, the white-wigged Lord Mansfield must have wondered: Why is this insufferable crank in my courtroom again? According to Sharp, at one point the ship owners' lawyer "violently exclaimed to the Judges, that a person was in Court (at the same time turning round and looking at me) who intended to bring on a criminal prosecution for murder against the parties concerned: 'but,' said he, '*it would be madness: the Blacks were property.*' "

Mansfield did his usual waffling. He insisted that murder was not the issue and that it was "just as if horses were killed." He conceded only that for "the throwing overboard of the negroes . . . upon the evidence, there appears to have been no necessity." He and his fellow judges ordered another trial, merely on the question of whether the insurers should pay the claim. But what outraged Equiano and Sharp was that after 132 human beings had been flung alive to their deaths, this was not a homicide trial. It was a civil insurance dispute.

Sharp failed to get anyone prosecuted for murder. And in striking contrast with the nationwide mourning for the victims of the *Royal George,* Britons totally ignored the fate of those thrown overboard from the *Zong.* There were no inquests, no memorial services, no ballads, and, except for the one short newspaper item Equiano had seen, virtually no press coverage. But a passionate salvo of letters Sharp wrote spread the word of what had happened on board the ship, and several prominent clergymen later mentioned the case in sermons, essays, and letters. It was as if, at the moment when Equiano had raced to see Sharp, a fuse had been lit, although it would be several years before it ignited any tinder. And then, oddly, the language in which a great movement would flame into life would be Latin.

II

FROM TINDER TO FLAME

6

A MORAL STEAM ENGINE

THE YEAR OF the *Zong* trial, 1783, marked the beginning of a boom in the British slave trade, for with the end of the American Revolutionary War, slave ships could sail unimpeded once again. British slave traffic, dominating the business, surged towards new heights. Slavery seemed as entrenched as ever. If pressed, some Britons might have conceded that the institution was unpleasant—but where else would sugar for your tea come from? Where would Royal Navy sailors get their rum? The slave trade "was not an amiable trade," as a member of Parliament once commented, "but neither was the trade of a butcher an amiable trade, and yet a mutton chop was, nevertheless, a very good thing." John Newton had written that he was relieved to have left the trade because "I considered myself as a sort of *gaoler* or *turnkey* . . . perpetually conversant with chains, bolts, and shackles." But to leave behind a career as a prison guard is one thing; to call for closing all prisons entirely another.

There were voices advocating an end to slavery, but they were scattered and few. Several American states had passed emancipation laws, but they were mostly ones like Vermont and Connecticut, where few slaves lived. Slavery opponents in France included such intellectuals as Rousseau and Diderot, and, in America, Benjamin Franklin and a fellow signer of the Declaration of Independence, the physician and chemist Benjamin Rush. In Scotland, a legal philosopher named

George Wallace had made a forceful attack on the institution, and a pseudonymous and little-noticed British pamphleteer argued not only that slaves have the right to revolt, but that "it is the duty of others, white as well as blacks, to assist those miserable creatures . . . and to rescue them out of the hands of their cruel tyrants." Another anonymous tract writer proposed a settlement of freed slaves in Florida, which, he claimed, would demonstrate productivity far superior to that of the Caribbean plantations. No major thinker defended slavery, but few spent real effort attacking it. Samuel Johnson once scandalized an Oxford dinner party by toasting "the next insurrection of the negroes in the West-Indies," but he never went much further in devoting his formidable literary energy to slavery. The plight of the poor slave—often an African nobleman whose true status was unknown to his master—was a theme in sentimental poetry and an occasional play.

A latent feeling was in the air, but an intellectual undercurrent disapproving of slavery was something very different from the belief that anything could ever be done about it. An analogy today might be how some people think about automobiles. For reasons of global warming, air quality, traffic, noise, and dependence on oil, one can argue, the world might be better off without cars. And what happens when India and China have as many cars per capita as the United States? Even if you depend on driving to work, it's possible to agree there's a problem. A handful of dedicated environmentalists try to practice what they preach, and travel only by train, bus, bicycle, or foot. Yet does anyone advocate a movement to ban automobiles from the face of the earth?

Similarly, despite the uneasiness some people in late-eighteenth-century England clearly had about slavery, to actually abandon it seemed a laughable dream. Persuading white people to bend at the waist all day cutting sugar cane under a tropical sun would be unthinkable. "It is as impossible for a Man to make Sugar without the assistance of Negroes," wrote the planter John Pinney of the island of Nevis, "as to make Bricks without Straw." Slavery was a fact of the past—Aristotle had written, "Humanity is divided into two: the masters and the slaves"—and surely would be so in the future. Sir Thomas More had included it in his *Utopia.* "Slavery . . . has hardly any possibility of being abolished," Adam Smith had declared in 1763. ". . . [It] has been universall in the beginnings of society, and the love of dominion and authority over others will probably make it perpetuall."

The 1700s were, of course, the century of the Enlightenment, the upwelling of ideas about human rights that eventually led to the American and French revolutions, expanded suffrage, and much more. Yet surprisingly few people saw a contradiction between freedom for whites and bondage for slaves. Among political figures, the slave-owning Thomas Jefferson was almost alone in revealing any discomfort over this. The philosopher John Locke, whose ideas about governments arising from the consent of the governed had done so much to lay the foundation for this century of revolutions, invested £600 in the Royal African Company, whose RAC brand was seared onto the breasts of thousands of slaves. In France, Voltaire mocked slaveholders in *Candide* and other works, yet when a leading French slave ship owner offered to name a vessel after him, he accepted with pleasure. Once the French Revolution erupted, merchants would promptly christen slave ships *Liberté, Égalité,* and *Fraternité.* Nor was the Church of England's slave plantation anything out of the ordinary: Countess Huntingdon, the leading patron of the Methodists, also owned one, and George Whitefield, the most influential Evangelical minister of his day—both Newton and Equiano heard him preach—owned more than fifty Georgia slaves and believed firmly that "hot countries cannot be cultivated without Negroes."

This, then, was the world into which Granville Sharp sent his fusillade of outraged letters about the slaves thrown overboard from the *Zong.* Most were ignored. But directly or indirectly the news reached a prominent Anglican clergyman, Dr. Peter Peckard, and it deeply disturbed him. In 1784, the year after the case was heard in court, he preached a sermon condemning the slave trade as a "most barbarous and cruel traffick." Soon afterwards, Peckard became vice-chancellor—the equivalent of an American university president—of Cambridge University, and there, in 1785, he put to use one of the most powerful tools the head of a university had at his command. He set as a topic for Cambridge's most prestigious Latin essay contest the question *Anne liceat invitos in servitutem dare?*—Is it lawful to make slaves of others against their will?

Latin and Greek competitions were a centerpiece of British university life. As with the Heisman trophy or a Rhodes scholarship today, to win one was to gain an honor that would be bracketed with your name for a lifetime. Decades later, for example, people still remembered that Lord Mansfield had won a major Latin poetry prize at Oxford, defeating his lifelong rival and a future prime minister, the elder William Pitt, who made a fatal spelling error.

One entrant in Peckard's Latin contest was a twenty-five-year-old divinity student, Thomas Clarkson, attending Cambridge on a special scholarship for the sons of deceased clergymen. One of the few things we know about Clarkson's background that offers any clue to his character is that his father, who died when Thomas was six, was known for his concern for the poorest members of his congregation. "It was on one of these visits to the sick poor of his parish," a family member wrote, "that he caught a fever which deprived him of his life." Throughout his own life, Thomas kept in his home the lantern his father carried on such missions.

In 1784, Thomas Clarkson had won a lower-ranking Latin prize and now, in 1785, he was competing for the big one; no student had ever managed to take them both. He had two months to research and write the essay. With the thoroughness and energy that would characterize his life, Clarkson read all he could find, managed to get access to the papers of a slave merchant who had recently died, and sought out several British officers returned from the American war, where they had seen slavery firsthand. One of these was his younger brother, John, a lieutenant who had served on ships in the West Indies, where many slaves worked as Royal Navy stevedores and dockyard laborers.

Clarkson had entered the essay competition with only a student's ambitions. "I had no motive but that which other young men in the University had on such occasions; namely, the wish of . . . obtaining literary honour." Unexpectedly, as he marshaled his evidence, he found himself overwhelmed with horror. "In the day-time I was uneasy. In the night I had little rest. I sometimes never closed my eye-lids for grief. . . . I always slept with a candle in my room, that I might rise out of bed and put down such thoughts as might occur to me in the night . . . conceiving that no arguments of any moment should be lost in so great a cause."

His essay won first prize. Clarkson read it aloud in Latin to an audience at the university's majestic Senate House, where such ceremonies are still held today. His studies finished, already a deacon in the Church of England, he mounted the horse he owned to head for London and for what seemed a promising career.

Over six feet tall, Clarkson had thick red hair and large, intense blue eyes that looked whomever he spoke to directly in the face. Riding to the capital in the black garb of a clergyman-to-be, he found himself, to his surprise, thinking neither of his prospects in the church nor of the pleasure of winning the prize. It was slavery itself that "wholly engrossed my thoughts. I became at times very seriously affected while upon the road. I stopped my horse occasionally, and dismounted and walked. I frequently tried to persuade myself in these intervals that the contents of my Essay could not be true. The more however I reflected upon them, or rather upon the authorities on which they were founded, the more I gave them credit." These feelings grew more intense at the midpoint of his journey, as he was riding down a long hill towards a coach station where the road crossed the River Lea. "Coming in sight of Wades Mill in Hertfordshire, I sat down disconsolate on the turf by the roadside and held my horse. Here a thought came into my mind, that if the contents of the Essay were true, it was time some person should see these calamities to their end."

Some person should see these calamities to their end. If there is a single moment at which the antislavery movement became inevitable, it was the day in June 1785 when Thomas Clarkson sat down by the side of the road at Wades Mill. That moment would reverberate through the remaining sixty-one years of his life and beyond. For his Bible-conscious colleagues, it held echoes of Saul's conversion on the road to Damascus. For us today, it is a landmark on the long, tortuous path to the modern conception of universal human rights.

If there had been no Clarkson, there would still have been a movement in Britain, but perhaps not for some time to come. On that early summer day when he got off his horse, the Quakers' antislavery committee had been unsuccessfully trying to ignite such a movement for two years, and Granville Sharp for two decades. It would take Clarkson to bring it into being, and his contemporaries recognized him for this. Samuel Taylor Coleridge called him a "moral Steam-Engine . . . how very highly I revere him. He shall be my Friend, Exemplar, Saint." Praising another writer, Jane Austen wrote to her sister that "I am as much in love with the author as ever I was with Clarkson." "An institution is the lengthened shadow of one man," wrote Ralph Waldo Emerson, ". . . the Reformation, of Luther; Quakerism, of Fox; Methodism, of Wesley; Abolition, of Clarkson. . . . All history resolves itself very easily into the biography of a few stout and earnest persons." There are many stout and earnest persons in this story, but Thomas Clarkson's fiery resolve is at its very center.

Long months of doubt followed his roadside moment of revelation. Could a lone, inexperienced young man have "that solid judgment . . . to qualify him to undertake a task of such magnitude and importance;—and with whom was I to unite?" But each time he doubted, the result was the same: "I walked frequently into the woods, that I might think on the subject in solitude, and find relief to my mind there. But there the question still recurred, 'Are these things true?'—Still the answer followed as instantaneously 'They are.' — Still the result accompanied it, 'Then surely some person should interfere.'" Only gradually, it seems, did it dawn on him that he was that person.

With the help of his brother, he translated his Latin essay into English, expanded it, and decided to publish it. Visiting one well-known London publisher, he was disappointed to find that the man wanted to print the essay only because it had won the prize and would therefore be read by "persons of taste." Clarkson, however, was already thinking like an activist. "I was not much pleased with his opinion. I wished the Essay to find its way . . . among such as would think and act with me." Turning down the offer, he left the publisher's office and was walking to a friend's house when, in the street outside the Royal Exchange, he ran into a Quaker friend of his family. The man greeted him warmly and said Clarkson was just the person he was looking for. Why hadn't he published that antislavery essay of his?

Together they walked to the printing shop and bookstore of James Phillips, in George Yard, just a few blocks away in the warren of narrow, curving streets of London's business district. In those days, publishing, printing, and bookselling often happened under the same roof (with the printer and his family likely to be living upstairs and a cow and a few hens out back), and this was the work that the forty-year-old Phillips did for his fellow Quakers. Clarkson took an immediate liking to him, and on the spot he agreed to let Phillips publish the essay. This was the day that Clarkson discovered he was not alone.

Soon after, Phillips took him to meet a small group of other Quakers. It was here, it appears, that Clarkson first learned the details of how Quakers on both sides of the Atlantic had long been working against slavery. His new friends may have told Clarkson about Benjamin Lay, for example, who had used what today we would call guerrilla theater to dramatize the living conditions of slaves. To show what slave families endured, Lay once stood outside an American Quaker meetinghouse with one leg bared, deep in snow; another time, it is said, he kidnapped a slave owner's child for a few hours. He publicly smashed teacups in which slave-grown sugar was consumed. He was finally rewarded when, in 1754, the Philadelphia Quakers came out against slavery. It was not only about Quakers that Clarkson learned: "How surprised was I to hear in the course of our conversation of the labours of Granville Sharp . . . of all which I had hitherto known nothing!" Phillips then introduced the two men to each other. Clarkson, the impassioned twenty-five-year-old, and Sharp, more than twice his age, discovered that they were distant cousins. Clarkson also met Equiano, as he sought out Africans, "the most intelligent . . . [I] could meet with in London."

Phillips edited the essay carefully, recommending changes that Clarkson gratefully accepted. It was the length of a book when published in June 1786 as *An Essay on the Slavery and Commerce of the Human Species, particularly the African, translated from a Latin Dissertation, which was honoured with the First Prize in the University of Cambridge for the year 1785, with Additions.*

The *Essay* is a curious document. Heartfelt outrage about slavery glimmers through a certain mustiness of style, as if, in this first of the many pieces of writing that would flow from his pen, Clarkson had not quite shaken off the century in which he was living. Many footnotes citing classical authors are still in Latin; an "Imaginary scene in Africa" and an "Imaginary conversation with an African" are mixed with factual accounts of the torture and abuse of slaves. And these are often attributed to people unnamed—a "friend, who had resided twenty years in the West Indies," or someone who "was a long time on the African coast," or "a gentleman, eminent in the medical line."

Like many white abolitionists to come, Clarkson shared some of the ideas of his time about race. For example, to refute those who claimed that their skin color meant God destined Africans to be "hewers of wood and drawers of water," he argued not that color doesn't matter, but rather that Africans might not be permanently black after all. Skin color, he claimed, must be linked to climate, for are not children of African slaves in the New World often lighter-skinned than their parents? Apparently it didn't occur to him that there might be another reason for this lighter skin, a point on which any slave or Englishman in the Caribbean could have enlightened him. "I have known 350 women sup and sleep on board on a Sunday evening, and return at daybreak to their different plantations," wrote one naval officer. On shore, white men had black concubines—"no man here is without one," noted Lady Nugent. One governor of Barbados openly took his mulatto mistress along on his official travels.

(Clarkson could have learned even more on this score had he been able to read the revealing ten-thousand-page diary kept by the Jamaican planter Thomas Thistlewood, who died the year Clarkson's *Essay* appeared. Besides describing the sadistic punishments he meted out, Thistlewood systematically recorded his sexual encounters with well over one hundred slave women: with Congo Flora "among the canes" at 10:30 A.M.; with "unknown Negroe girl" on "floor, at north bed foot, in the east parlor" at 2 A.M.; with "Susanah in the curing house" in the evening; with "Phoebe, the cook . . . in North Room" at 7 P.M.; with "Warsoe, in the boiling house" at 3 P.M.; and so on. Thistlewood seems to have been single-handedly responsible for lightening the complexion of whole plantations. White men like him had a weapon as powerful as any rapist's gun: the ability to assign women who refused them to twelve-hour days in the sugar fields.)

The Quakers introduced Clarkson to two important antislavery books James Phillips had published, by James Ramsay, an Evangelical Anglican minister recently returned from the West Indies. Almost everything else written against slavery was, like Clarkson's *Essay,* a mixture of biblical citations, philosophical argument, and second-hand accounts. Ramsay, by contrast, offered a searing eyewitness picture. He vividly described beatings he had seen; he told of weary slaves carrying cane to the mill by moonlight, and how new mothers had to bring their babies to the fields, leaving them in furrows exposed to the sun and rain. Responding to planters who claimed that blacks were inferior and animal-like by nature, Ramsay wrote, "Had nature intended negroes for slavery . . . they would have been born without any sentiment for liberty."

When he heard that Clarkson was trying to visit everyone who might join a fight against slavery, the minister was, Clarkson writes, "almost overpowered with joy." Ramsay himself had come face to face with the institution for the first time as a young doctor serving on the twenty-four-gun HMS *Arundel* in West Indian waters. A slave ship arriving from Africa approached the naval fleet and asked for help: an epidemic of dysentery had killed many slaves and crew, including the physician. Ramsay was the only navy doctor who volunteered to go on board. Shocked by the feces and blood that covered the slave decks, Ramsay treated the hundred or so victims still living. Soon after, he resigned from the navy and entered the church. As a clergyman on St. Kitts for fourteen years, he preached to the slaves, taught them the Bible in his home, and made enemies of the island's sugar planters. One angry white man stood at the communion table in Ramsay's own church and showered him with curses; others walked out when Ramsay prayed for the conversion of the slaves. The attacks continued after he returned to England; his books enraged the planters and provoked a string of vituperative pamphlets denouncing him.

Spending a month with Ramsay at his rectory in Kent made Clarkson realize how much more he needed to learn about slavery. He didn't have far to look, for many ships sailed for Africa from the docks along the Thames. He boarded one called the *Fly,* a 143-ton vessel built in Newbury, Massachusetts, which regularly carried slaves from the Gold Coast—today's Ghana—to Jamaica. "Here I found myself for the first time on the deck of a slave-vessel.—the sight of the rooms below and of the gratings above . . . filled me with melancholy and horror. I found soon afterwards a fire of indignation kindling within me."

He hounded everyone who could supply him with information:

"My object was to see all who [had] been in Africa"; these included merchants, captains, army and navy officers—and John Newton. With the instincts of a good reporter, "I made it a rule to put down in writing, after every conversation, what had taken place." Simultaneously, Clarkson threw his energy into lining up influential recruits for his cause—lords and ladies, bishops, and members of Parliament. One potential convert, a young nobleman, "seemed to doubt some of the facts in my book, from a belief that human nature was not capable of proceeding to such a pitch of wickedness. I asked him to name his facts. He selected the case of the hundred-and-thirty-two slaves who were thrown alive into the sea to defraud the underwriters. I promised to satisfy him fully upon this point, and went immediately to Granville Sharp, who lent me his account of the trial." The doubter, now convinced, "took a part in the distribution of my books."

During this period, Clarkson "was seldom engaged less than sixteen hours in the day." He found lodgings at the Baptist Head Coffee House in Chancery Lane in order to be close to the law offices of a new friend, Richard Phillips, a cousin of his publisher. In his voracious quest for every scrap of useful data, Clarkson had stumbled onto an unexpected treasure. Records at the Custom House included muster rolls of men who had left London in the crews of slave ships. Clarkson and Richard Phillips "looked over them together. We usually met for this purpose at nine in the evening, and we seldom parted till one, and sometimes not till three in the morning. When our eyes were inflamed by the candle, or tired by fatigue, we used to relieve ourselves by walking . . . when all seemed to be fast asleep."

In these ships' records, the two men found something that astonished them: on average, about 20 percent of each slave ship's crew had died by the time the ship returned to England. Scholarly studies today bear out their findings. A seaman's ditty went:

> Beware and take care of the Bight of Benin
> Few come out, though many go in.

The biggest killers were the malaria and yellow fever of the African coast, for which Europeans had little resistance and no cure. Furthermore, a ruthless captain had no incentive to keep a sick sailor alive on the final leg of the triangle voyage, for then he had to be paid. These statistics would not have surprised Newton, whose logbooks were filled with the names of officers and seamen who "departed this life." But for Clarkson and Phillips they were potential ammunition. That the trade was killing not only slaves but also British sailors could prove a strong political argument in a cause where moral exhortation alone, Clarkson sensed, would never carry the day.

He knew his major allies would be the Quakers: they were rock-firm in their convictions and had a strong tradition of supporting their beliefs with generous donations. As organizers, they had a national network—an international one, in fact, because of their close ties to American Quakers: one of the people in Clarkson's new circle, for instance, was William Dillwyn, a plump, ruddy-cheeked Quaker businessman from Pennsylvania who had gone to the American South to study slavery firsthand, lobbied the New Jersey legislature for slave freedom, then moved to London. For the Quakers, Clarkson was a godsend: young, brimming with enthusiasm, skilled at persuading people to join the cause—and, above all, an Anglican. Their strenuous pleas against slavery had been ignored, they knew, simply because they were Quakers. To influence public opinion they needed a talented Anglican willing to devote all his time and energy to the movement, and now at last they had one.

At James Phillips's house, a group of Quakers told Clarkson "that from the time they had first heard of the Prize Essay, they . . . had had their eyes upon me, and, from the time they had first seen me, had conceived a desire of making the same use of me as I had now expressed a wish of making of them." The ultimate success of the movement would be grounded in a series of brilliant alliances. This, between Clarkson and the Quakers, was the first. Together they decided to form a new organization that no one could write off as being controlled by a fringe sect. After much careful planning a committee of a dozen men was agreed on—nine Quakers, including James and Richard Phillips and the American-born Dillwyn, and three Anglicans, including Clarkson and Granville Sharp, who, as the elder statesman of antislavery efforts, would be titular chairman.

"Went to town on my mare to attend a committee of the Slave Trade now instituted," confided Dillwyn to his diary as he headed for the first meeting, on the afternoon of May 22, 1787, at James

Phillips's bookstore and printing shop. Phillips's neighbors in George Yard included a Mr. Mussard, who gave dancing and fencing lessons, and a pub, the George and Vulture. From descriptions of similar establishments at this time we can imagine the printing shop itself. Type would be sitting in slanted wooden trays with compartments for the different letters; the compositors who lined it up into rows, letter by letter, would be working, as the day ended, by the light of tallow candles whose smoke, over the decades, would blacken the ceiling. The printers, operating a flatbed press by hand, would take the large sheets from the press, each with many pages printed on it, and use a special pole-like instrument to hang them up on dozens of overhead lines for the ink to dry. Around the sides of the room, stacks of dried sheets, the latest antislavery book or Quaker tract, would await folding and binding. And finally, the most distinctive thing about an eighteenth-century printing shop was its smell. To ink the type as it sat on the bed of the press, printers used a wool-stuffed leather pad with a wooden handle. Because of its high ammonia content, the most convenient solvent to rinse off the ink residue that built up on these pads was printers' urine. The pads were soaked in buckets of this, then strewn on the slightly sloping floor, where printers stepped on them as they worked, to wring them out and let the liquid drain away.

These were the unlikely surroundings in which the twelve men gathered, the Quakers in their broad-brimmed, high-crowned black hats. The minutes of the occasion, only one page long, are in Clarkson's clear and flowing handwriting. They begin with a simple declaration: "At a Meeting held for the Purpose of taking the Slave Trade into Consideration, it was resolved that the said Trade was both impolitick and unjust." Perhaps most remarkable, for it showed how much the twelve were of one mind, they promptly resolved that for conducting committee business, only three members would be needed for a quorum.

We can only imagine how the committee members felt as they dispersed to their homes that night. The task they had taken on was so monumental as to have seemed to anyone else impossible. They had to ignite their crusade in a country where the great majority of people, from farmhands to bishops, accepted slavery as completely normal. It was also a country where profits from West Indian plantations gave a large boost to the economy, where customs duties on slave-grown sugar were an important source of government revenue, and where the livelihoods of tens of thousands of seamen, merchants, and shipbuilders depended on the slave trade. The trade itself had increased to almost unparalleled levels, bringing prosperity to key ports, including London itself. How even to begin the massive job of changing public opinion? Furthermore, nineteen out of twenty Englishmen, and all Englishwomen, were not even allowed to vote. Without this most basic of rights themselves, could they be roused to care about the rights of other people, of a different skin color, an ocean away?

In all of human experience, there was no precedent for such a campaign.

7

THE FIRST EMANCIPATION

CURIOUSLY, when Clarkson, Sharp, and the Quakers came together in May 1787 to take their bold step into the unknown, the first mass emancipation of British slaves had already taken place. And most of the people sitting in James Phillips's printing shop that afternoon probably knew nothing about it. Yet the long odyssey of these freed slaves, an epic journey through uncertainty, despair, and hope on two continents, would eventually intersect with the efforts of the abolitionists. Both groups would face a difficult challenge: In an Atlantic world still in slavery's grip, was it possible to build a free black community? If so, where?

To pick up this new thread of our story, we must first jump a dozen years back in time, to the event that inaugurated this era of upheaval, the American Revolution. When the first stirrings of rebellion came in 1775, the British were desperate to do anything they could to cause trouble for the rebels. So they promised freedom to any American slave who deserted a rebel master and joined the British Army. The first three hundred blacks who arrived were enlisted as the Royal Ethiopian Regiment and given British uniforms emblazoned with the provocative words LIBERTY TO SLAVES. Many blacks worked as low-paid laborers for the army; others, under British officers, saw combat.

This promise by the British did not come from wanting to end slavery, of course; it was merely a strategic maneuver to deprive the enemy of property. (They promised no freedom to slaves of masters who remained loyal to the crown.) The move hit the rebel colonists where it hurt. "Hell itself could not have vomitted anything more black than this design of emancipating our slaves," wrote one. And a dismayed George Washington feared that, with freed slaves joining their army, British "strength will increase as a snow ball by rolling: and faster, if some expedient cannot be hit upon." Several of Washington's own slaves ran away to join the British, as did some belonging to his fellow Virginians Patrick Henry and James Madison.

A later British proclamation broadened the promise, pledging freedom to any slave, male or female, who deserted a rebel owner by crossing into British-held territory. Many thousands did so, sometimes taking their masters' clothing and possessions with them. South Carolina planter Rawlins Lowndes lost seventy-five slaves, who apparently took his horses. "Consider one moment, Sir," he complained to the British authorities, "the feelings of a man in this condition, used hitherto to all the Comforts and Conveniences of Life, and now divested in the most pressing Exigency even of the use of a Horse." In Williamsburg, Virginia, a resident wrote, "Poor Mr. Cocke was deserted by his favorite man Clem; and Mrs. Cocke, by the loss of her cook, and is obliged to have resource to her neighbors to dress her dinner for her." The runaway slaves were not just from Southern masters; more than five hundred came from New Jersey and New York.

The British authorities gave no thought to the question, What would happen to all these ex-slaves once the war was over? When that time came, some slaves were recaptured by their owners, others left North America with the British troops for England, others found jobs on Royal Navy or merchant ships, and some were sent to the West Indies, where they often found themselves reenslaved. However, the biggest single group, some three thousand former slaves, remained in New York City, which the British had occupied for most of the war. Would they be evacuated along with the white British troops also stranded in New York—or returned to their owners?

This was a key question on the table when representatives of Britain and the victorious Americans sat down in Paris in late 1782 to start peace talks. Then, as now, when important agreements were to be negotiated, governments sometimes turned to people with a vested interest—or, as these men themselves might have preferred to put it, a special expertise—in the matters at hand. And so it was only natural that the chief British negotiator at Paris should be Richard Oswald, the immensely wealthy Atlantic merchant and owner of the Bance Island slave depot, golf course and all. Similarly, one of the American negotiators turned out to be Oswald's close friend and fellow slave dealer Henry Laurens, former president of the Continental Congress.

Laurens was an owlish-looking, hard-working man, short and stocky, who prided himself on sleeping no more than four hours a night, and rose well before dawn to do his business correspondence by candlelight. A South Carolina rice planter and the owner of some three hundred slaves, he was at one point the biggest slave merchant in the thirteen colonies, doing much business with John Newton's employer Joseph Manesty as well as with Oswald. British ships had long dominated the South Carolina slave trade, and for years Laurens received a 10 percent commission from Oswald on cargoes of Bance Island slaves sold there.

"Just now our visiting Doctor is come up from the vessel and tells us the men are a very fine parcell of Slaves . . . ," Laurens had written Oswald's firm in a typical letter in 1756. "We shall hope to rend you an agreeable sale." Many letters later (the methodical Laurens sometimes sent several copies of an important message, in case the first went down with a ship), he wrote Oswald, "I make no doubt that this will be the best Market for Africans all the next [year], of any in America. . . . If I am on the spot when any of your Vessels arrive here you may command and depend upon my best advice and assistance."

Like other slave owners, Laurens had been shocked by the British promise of freedom, and he had personally ordered a raid to recapture some South Carolina slaves who had taken advantage of it.* Later in the war, while traveling to Europe on a diplomatic mission for the Americans, Laurens was captured at sea by the British and imprisoned in the Tower of London. Oswald visited him there several times, even-

* Surprisingly, Laurens's son John was a passionate abolitionist—almost unheard of for a white Southerner at this time. He urged his father to free his slaves, and repeatedly proposed freeing any slaves who joined the American forces. Appalled legislators rejected the plan in both Georgia and South Carolina—the latter was actually offering slaves to white soldiers as enlistment bonuses. Fighting the British, John Laurens was killed in combat in 1782 at the age of twenty-seven.

tually arranging his release by posting £2,000 bail before Lord Mansfield in court.

When the war ended, Laurens proceeded to Paris to join Benjamin Franklin's team of American peace negotiators, arriving after talks were under way, but "in time to offer suggestions which my colleagues were pleased to accept." These suggestions concerned the fugitive slaves, and someone also happy to accept them was his fellow slave dealer Oswald, across the table representing Britain in the final negotiating session, held at the Grand Hôtel Muscovite on the Rue des Petits Augustins. "Mr. Laurens said there ought to be a stipulation that the British troops should carry off no negroes or other American property," wrote John Adams, another American delegate. "We all agreed. Mr. Oswald consented. Then the treaties were signed, sealed, and delivered, and we all went out to Passy to dine with Dr. Franklin." Either because his mind was on dinner or out of eagerness to get the treaty signed, Franklin apparently did not notice or object. The one surviving copy of the treaty shows Laurens's last-minute clause about returning "Negroes or other Property" inserted with a caret. When the two delegations dined together that night at the elegant headquarters of the American mission, they assumed that the three thousand ex-slaves with the British forces in New York would soon be returned to their owners.

General George Washington, the American commander, made the same assumption. When news of the Paris peace agreement reached him, British troops still occupied New York City, and camped with them were the former slaves. Washington forwarded to his representative in New York a long list of runaway slaves and asked for help in "securing them . . . if they are to be found in the City. . . . Some of my own slaves . . . may probably be in N York. . . . If by Chance you should come at the knowledge of any of them, I will be much obliged by your securing them."

A week later, on May 6, 1783, in his temporary headquarters in Tappan, New York, a small brick and sandstone house with steep gables which still stands today, ten miles north of Manhattan, Washington awaited the arrival of his British counterpart for talks. The ex-slaves were at the top of the agenda.

General Sir Guy Carleton, the British commander, sailing up the Hudson in the frigate *Perseverance,* was no armchair soldier. A six-footer with a hawk-like nose, prominent eyebrows, and an erect, military bearing, he had at one point early in the war avoided capture by disguising himself as a fisherman and slipping past American ships in a whaleboat. An incorruptible military reformer, he had swept hundreds of sinecured bureaucrats out of office. As his ship approached Tappan, Carleton sent an officer ahead in a small boat to announce his arrival. Washington met him at the shore and brought Carleton to his headquarters by carriage, the other officers following on foot or horseback. After "an Hour was spent in Congratulations, and seperate Chat in and before the Door," in the words of one of Carleton's aides, the generals sat down in the parlor of the house, a pleasant room with small-paned windows, thick ceiling beams, blue and white Delft tiles above the fireplace, and wide floorboards of virgin timber.

According to the aide, Washington "delivered himself without Animation, with great Slowness, and a low Tone of Voice." Item one, Washington told Carleton, was "the Preservation of Property from being carried off, and especially the Negroes." Carleton replied that some had already left New York on British ships. "Here Washington [was] startled—'Already imbarked!' says he." His conscience as an officer, Carleton maintained, required him to respect the promise of freedom made to the slaves. "The National Honor . . . must be kept with all Colours."

Though a deeply conservative man who had no objection to slavery, Carleton did have a powerful sense of honor. Knowing he was talking to a slave owner, he shrewdly hinted that *he* might not have made this rash promise of freedom—but a promise by the British crown had to be kept.

Carleton's determination carried the day. Washington claimed Carleton was violating the peace treaty. Carleton countered cleverly: the slaves were not "property" covered by the treaty because the British proclamation had already freed them. Furthermore, he promised, the British would compensate their former owners, as one should when taking property. To that end, he was keeping a careful register of the slaves, including the names and addresses of their former masters. When Washington responded that slaves might give false names,

Carleton refused to budge and the conversation came to a halt. "Washington pulled out his Watch, and observing that it was near Dinner Time, offered Wine and Bitters. . . . We all walked out, and soon after were called to [a] plentiful Repast under a Tent"—a lunch prepared by a well-known New York tavern owner, which, under the circumstances, must have been rather strained. Carleton then sailed back downriver to Manhattan.

Washington fired off disgruntled messages to Carleton and diplomatic protests to Britain, but Carleton was uncompromising. Washington should be ashamed, he wrote—with an audacity astonishing for the representative of a defeated power who was violating a treaty his country had signed—even to suggest that the British give back the slaves; Carleton would not agree to a "notorious breach of the public faith towards people of any complection." Faced with this steely resolve, Washington grew fatalistic, and it is easy to imagine him looking as grim as he does in his portraits. "I have discovered enough," he wrote a friend, ". . . to convince me that the Slaves which have absconded from their Masters will never be restored to them."

Several years after he became President, Washington stopped asking for the return of the New York slaves and instead began demanding the promised compensation. A dispute over this would continue, through peace and war and peace again, for some four decades, until it was finally arbitrated by the Tsar of Russia, of all people. In 1826, Britain agreed to pay the American slave owners or their heirs half the market value of their former slaves.

When Carleton returned to New York after his contentious meeting, it was to a chaotic, overcrowded city, which then occupied only the southern tip of Manhattan, today's financial district. Muddy streets were packed with refugees, redcoated British troops impatient to go home, and the ex-slaves. Entire neighborhoods had been swept by a fire at the beginning of the Revolution, and thousands of people, black and white, were living in "Canvas Town"—a collection of temporary huts with roofs of sailcloth. Provisions were short, and during the winter people had burned fences and church pews to fend off the cold. The ex-slaves eked out livings as best they could, as house servants, laundresses, or low-paid laborers for the British Army.

Many slaves had braved great hardships escaping to freedom, among them a young carpenter named Boston King, who later wrote his life story. Born on a South Carolina plantation, the teenaged King fled to British territory when the war began, working as a seaman and servant to army officers. Recaptured, he escaped a second time, from Perth Amboy, New Jersey, crossing creeks, marshland, and then the Hudson, to reach the British troops in New York. "About one o'clock in the morning I . . . found the guards were either asleep or in the tavern. I instantly entered into the river, but when I was a little distance from the opposite shore, I heard the sentinels disputing among themselves: One said, 'I am sure I saw a man cross the river.' Another replied, 'There is no such thing'. It seems they were afraid to fire at me, or make an alarm, lest they should be punished for their negligence. . . . I travelled till about five in the morning, and then concealed myself till seven o'clock at night, when I proceeded forward, thro' bushes and marshes. . . . When I came to the [Hudson] river, opposite Staten-Island, I found a boat; . . . I ventured into it, and cutting the rope, got safe over."

As soon as news of the Paris peace accord was published, word swept through New York's community of ex-slaves, King wrote, that they "were to be delivered up to their masters, altho' some of them had been three or four years among the English. This dreadful rumour filled us all with inexpressible anguish and terror, especially when we saw our old masters coming from Virginia, North-Carolina, and other parts, and seizing upon their slaves in the streets of New-York, or even dragging them out of their beds. . . . For some days we lost our appetite for food, and sleep departed from our eyes." General Carleton, to his credit, did his best to put a stop to these raids and to mistreatment of blacks. When a young white refugee kicked a black cart-driver, British troops arrested him and forced him to apologize. "Such cruelties did his majesty's loyal subjects suffer," wrote a fellow colonist, shocked that a white man would have to be so humiliated.

To Carleton, it was clear that to keep the British promise of freedom to the ex-slaves, they would have to be evacuated. The nearest convenient British territory, one to two weeks away by sail, depending on the winds, was Nova Scotia. "Boston King, 23, stout fellow, formerly the property of Rich. Waring of Charleston, South Carolina . . .

left him 4 years ago" was how King went into Carleton's roster as he boarded a ship for Canada. (One column in the roster of slaves was for "Description," and included such phrases as "snug little wench," "an idiot," "fine boy," "likely rascal," and "nearly worn out.") Those boarding the ships sang:

> Now, farewell, my Massa, my Missy, adieu,
> More blows and more stripes will I ne'er take from you . . .
> And if I return to the Life that I had,
> You can put me in chains, 'cause I surely be mad.

As they disembarked from Carleton's fleet in Nova Scotia, the three thousand former slaves had no idea what fate awaited them. But they knew that the new lives they managed to build here could hold out hope for those still in slavery elsewhere in the empire, for they were now the largest community of free blacks in one spot anywhere in British territory in the Americas.

8

"I QUESTIONED WHETHER I SHOULD EVEN GET OUT OF IT ALIVE"

TODAY WE TAKE for granted the practice of forming a committee to agitate for a humanitarian cause, but when Clarkson and his colleagues gathered to do so in James Phillips's printing shop, it was far from usual. In Britain, as one scholar puts it, "National extraparliamentary associations . . . were unknown in 1750, novel in 1780, commonplace in 1830." What little lobbying there was had traditionally been done by religious sects or tradesmen: Baptists or weavers or tinsmiths might band together to petition the authorities about their grievances. But an entity like the new committee was far less familiar. The abolitionists were pioneers in forging a central tool of modern civil society.

The committee recorded its minutes in leather-bound books today preserved at the British Library, and it is deeply moving to look at page after page of graceful, almost calligraphic handwriting from this age before typewriters. At times the minutes seem quaintly formal: "Dr. Baker of Lower Grosvenor Street has been very active. . . . RESOLVED that the thanks of this Committee be communicated by Thomas Clarkson to the said Dr. Baker for his zealous Exertions in the Cause of Humanity and Freedom." Then you turn the page and it's all business, the record of determined men who knew they had a huge job to do. They opened a bank account, hired a lawyer, and drew up long lists, page after page of names from all over Great Britain, and beside each person the name of the committee member assigned to contact him. They were mobilizing the Quaker network.

For £25 a year, the committee found a room at 18 Old Jewry, a street then and now in the heart of the City, London's financial district, whose name comes from the medieval synagogue that once stood there. A servant had a fire and candles burning when the members arrived for each meeting. There were no recorded votes, decisions being made Quaker style, by consensus. For the first few meetings Clarkson himself kept the minutes. The other members helped with the letter-writing—and this posed a problem. In addition to their firm beliefs about such matters as not taking off one's hat except before God, Quakers spoke and wrote differently. And it was not just a question of saying "thee" and "thou." On principle they refused to address a nobleman or bishop as "My Lord," because there was only one Lord. They would not address a commoner as "Mr.," because it derived from "master." And they refused to sign letters with the customary "your humble and obedient servant," because one should be a humble and obedient servant only to God. Furthermore, they did not use the names of the days of the week or of the months, because these derived from Roman or pagan names.* In these practices, Quakers were unbending. Even the pamphlet they had unsuccessfully used to lobby Parliament a few years earlier had been dated simply "the 28th day of the eleventh month, 1783." (Days of the week were simply First day, Second day, Third day . . .) No wonder M.P.s ignored them.

So how was the committee to get non-Quakers to take its letters seriously? Very simple: Granville Sharp, the figurehead chairman, would sign them. This meant that letters could be written, as the bemused Sharp put it, "in the *ordinary stile.*" Sharp signing letters and Clarkson

* Instead of the rhyme "Thirty days hath September . . . ," Quaker children learned:

The fourth, eleventh, ninth, and sixth,
We thirty days to each affix;
All the rest have thirty-one
Except the second month alone;
To it we twenty-eight assign;
But leap year makes it twenty-nine.

as the committee's main face to the world: for all their strict adherence to their religion, these Quaker businessmen were shrewdly practical.

Although Anglicans like Sharp and Clarkson received more public attention, it was the Quakers who really shaped the campaign. Their church had no bishops or ordained ministers, and their form of worship was the most open imaginable: any man—or woman—in a Quaker meeting could stand up and speak. The spirit of this most democratic and nonhierarchical of Western religions would infuse the antislavery movement, where local chapters, time and again, would push for goals and tactics far bolder than anything contemplated by national headquarters.

The movement reflected another part of the Quaker heritage as well—a century's experience as a pressure group. To read the abolition committee's minutes, with their careful listings of jobs to be done, is to feel in the presence of confident, experienced activists. The Quakers had long dissented on certain political issues, refusing to pay taxes and tithes that supported the Church of England, to do military service, and—following a biblical injunction—to swear oaths. From battles over tithes and oaths, they had learned to send deputations to call on government officials and members of the royal family; to publish pamphlets and place articles in newspapers; and to mobilize the faithful to send petitions to Parliament. All these tools and more would be needed as they set out to challenge slavery.

How large the system they planned to take on, yet in how small a space this whole drama seemed to be taking place. On Old Jewry also lived Granville Sharp's surgeon brother William, in whose house the family orchestra gathered to play sacred music every Sunday evening. James Phillips's bookstore was only half a dozen short blocks away, along busy streets whose cobblestones tended to sink into the mud whenever it rained. Around the corner from it was the principal London Quaker meetinghouse. Philpot Lane, home of the trading firm of Bance Island owner Richard Oswald, was some two minutes' walk farther; Oswald himself had just died, but other triangle trade merchants and ship owners prospered on the same street and often gathered nearby at the Jamaica Coffee House on St. Michael's Alley, said to have the best rum in London. Slave ship captains collected their mail there. Another two minutes would take you to the bank of the

Thames, near London Bridge, which barred tall-masted oceangoing ships from proceeding farther upriver; dozens of them would be docked or anchored there, including many slaving vessels outfitting for the voyage to Africa. On the riverbank was the Custom House, where Clarkson had dug up statistics on the death rate of British sailors in the trade. Equiano was living on Baldwin's Gardens, Holborn, only some fifteen minutes' walk away. This corner of London was steeped in history; just two years earlier, workers excavating for a new sewer a few hundred feet from Phillips's bookstore had uncovered a huge trove of Roman coins and pottery—artifacts of another empire founded on slavery.

With nearly a million people living under its grimy haze of coal smoke, London was the biggest city in Europe—and one that seemed to move at a faster tempo than the rest of the world. "I happened to go into a pastrycook's shop one morning," wrote the poet Robert Southey, "and inquired of the mistress why she kept her window open during this severe weather. . . . She told me, that were she to close it, her receipts would be lessened forty or fifty shillings a day—so many were the persons who took up buns or biscuits as they passed by and threw their pence in, not allowing themselves time to enter."

Foreigners were always stunned by the city's pace. As one German visitor put it:

> In the road itself chaise after chaise, coach after coach, cart after cart. Through all this din and clamour, and the noise of thousands of tongues and feet, you hear the bells from the church-steeples, postmen's bells, the street-organs, fiddles and tambourines of itinerant musicians, and the cries of the vendors of hot and cold food at the street corners. A rocket blazes up stories high amidst a yelling crowd of beggars, sailors and urchins. Some one shouts, "Stop, thief," his handkerchief is gone. . . . Before you are aware of it a young, well-dressed girl has seized your hand. "Come, my lord, come along, let us drink a glass together. . . ." An accident happens not forty paces away. "God bless me," calls one. "Poor fellow," cries another. . . . Every one is intent on helping the victim. Then there is laughter again: some one has fallen into the gutter. . . . Next comes a yell from a hundred throats as if fire had broken out, or a house was

> falling. . . . You are lucky to escape with a whole skin down a side alley until the tumult is over. Even in the wider streets all the world rushes headlong without looking, as if summoned to the bedside of the dying.

The abolitionists must have felt they were living in the center of the universe.

It was a universe that took slavery for granted, and so the committee members faced a central decision: What, exactly, were they taking on? Were they going to agitate only for abolition of the slave trade, or for emancipation of all slaves? On June 7, 1787, only two weeks after the committee's formation, the issue was on the table. Granville Sharp alone spoke out in favor of demanding full emancipation, with, in Clarkson's words, "a loud voice, a powerful emphasis, and both hands uplifted towards Heaven." The others prevailed, however, because abolishing the slave trade looked possible, while the immediate freeing of all slaves did not. For emancipation, Parliament would have to override the lawmaking powers of the West Indian colonial legislatures. Even more daunting, in a country where property rights were deeply sanctified by tradition and law, the committee feared that emancipation would be seen, Clarkson said, as "meddling with the property of the planters."

Nonetheless, everyone knew the high death rates on the West Indian plantations, and knew that the labor force was kept up only by constant new shipments of slaves. If that supply was cut off—the calculation seemed so simple—either the slave population would eventually die out or planters would be forced to treat their slaves so much better that it would be only a few more easy steps to freedom. Both abolitionists and planters took this for granted. Abolishing the trade, Clarkson was certain, was "laying the axe at the very root" of Caribbean slavery itself. And so the committee officially became the Society for Effecting the Abolition of the Slave Trade.*

Accomplishing even that, of course, required changing the minds

* Unlike American usage, in Britain the words "abolition" and "abolitionist" referred to abolishing the slave trade, not slavery itself. But the abolitionists' enemies suspected, correctly, that almost all of them favored emancipation of the slaves as well.

of people not just in bustling and sophisticated London, but throughout the country. Equally important, the committee would need eyewitnesses willing to testify before Parliament, to shock legislators into doing something. In late June, Clarkson prepared for a trip of several months to find witnesses, organize sympathizers, and gather more information from the "fountain head," as he called it: the big slave ports of Bristol and Liverpool. For many years to come, Clarkson would be the movement's sole full-time organizer.

As he set off on this first journey, it was already clear that speaking out against slavery might not be a safe or peaceful business. The ordeal of Reverend James Ramsay, now a close friend of Clarkson's, showed this painfully. Because Ramsay had actually lived in the Caribbean, West Indian plantation owners—many of them living in England—loathed him as a traitor. He had responded to their attacks in kind. Ramsay had neither wealth nor a government post to fall back on, and as their fierce pamphleteering got under his skin, the planters clearly sensed some personal vulnerability in him as well. The attacks increased, both in the West Indies and in England: Ramsay was a charlatan Presbyterian disguised as an Anglican minister; he had mistreated slaves of his own, had been the terror of all the slaves in his district, had illicitly gotten a pension from a fund intended for the relief of poor seamen. His enemies sent him packages of stones from the West Indies, because under the prevailing postal system, charges were paid by the recipient.

It is never easy to be the object of deliberate slander, but Ramsay tried vainly to answer every charge and the effort was destroying him. One planter from the island of Nevis challenged him to a duel and wrote three vituperative pamphlets, to each of which Ramsay issued an angry rebuttal, in one case hinting at the planter's known penchant for black mistresses. Works by Ramsay poured from the presses, with titles like *A Reply to Personal Invectives and Objections contained in Two Answers published by certain Anonymous Persons, to an Essay on the Treatment and Conversion of African Slaves in the British Sugar Colonies.* The movement hadn't even begun and already Ramsay was beleaguered and exhausted.

This ominous example may have been on his mind as Clarkson rode his horse westward, through intermittent rain, to Bristol. The city he was heading for had warehouses full of slave-grown products just arrived from the Americas: tobacco, cocoa, and sugar for Bristol's numerous refineries. Its huge new docks were packed with ships, thirty-one of which would sail to gather slaves in Africa this year alone, guided by pilots and small towboats down the winding Avon River. It was a city tradition that the owner of the first ship of the season to bring sugar back from the Caribbean celebrated by buying wine for all his friends. Local factories produced copper sheathing, whose use slave vessels were now pioneering, to protect ships' hulls. They also made the bottles and glass ornaments, pots and pans and wire, brandy and gunpowder that were among the goods traded for slaves on the African coast. For several decades, plantation and triangle trade wealth had helped finance a wave of new building in Bristol, and the slave trade was reflected in names like Guinea Street and the African House tavern. In the suburb of Clifton and the surrounding countryside lived one of Britain's largest concentrations of absentee West Indian landowners. Eleven of the city's mayors had owned shares in slave ships.

It took Clarkson three days to reach Bristol, and his diary for most of that time is filled with a tourist's descriptions of weather, pleasant views, and "the best Rolls I ever tasted in my Life" at a roadside inn. The magnitude and danger of his mission dawned on him only as he reached the edge of the city.

"On turning a corner . . . at about eight in the evening, I came within sight of it. The weather was rather hazy, which occasioned it to look of unusual dimensions. The bells of some of the churches were then ringing; the sound . . . filled me, almost directly, with a melancholy for which I could not account. I began now to tremble, for the first time, at the arduous task I had undertaken, of attempting to subvert one of the branches of the commerce of the great place which was then before me. . . . I questioned whether I should even get out of it alive." This was not, it would turn out, an unreasonable fear.

In the autobiographical history of abolition he later wrote, Clarkson left an unforgettable record of this summer. If there is a single period of the antislavery crusade that a modern reader might most want to experience, it is these few months in 1787 when we can see through one man's eyes the birth of the greatest of all human rights movements. The very paper seems to smoke and burn with his outrage. As he stalks purposefully through the streets of Bristol, we can sense him fully discovering his skills as an investigator, as a propagandist, and as an organizer who has found his life's calling. "I began now to think that the day was not long enough for me to labour in. I regretted often the approach of night, which suspended my work, and I often welcomed that of the morning, which restored me to it. . . . I lived in hope that every day's labour would furnish me with that knowledge, which would bring this evil nearer to its end." At the city's Custom House, he carefully copied ships' muster rolls, finding that Bristol slave ship sailors, like London's, perished in shockingly high numbers. He prowled the docks and haunted taverns, collecting stories of sailors who had died at sea or been brutally treated. We must imagine this determined red-haired man, dressed in the somber black of a deacon, striding along cobblestone streets filled with drunken seamen, prostitutes, beggars, and street musicians. At a time when the average English male was only about five feet six inches tall, Clarkson, at more than six feet, would have towered over almost everyone.

He tracked down a slave ship in the harbor that was having trouble recruiting sailors because the captain had lost thirty-two seamen on his previous voyage—a number larger than many a ship's entire crew. The treatment of one sailor, a free black man named John Dean, "exceeded all belief. . . . The captain had fastened him with his belly to the deck, and . . . poured hot pitch upon his back, and made incisions in it with hot tongs." Dean had disappeared from Bristol, but Clarkson found witnesses, among them Dean's former landlord, who "had often looked at his scarred and mutilated back." He then tracked down documents about a massacre of some three hundred Africans by British slave traders on the coast of what is today Nigeria.

Hearing of the particularly cruel captain of the *Alfred,* which had just returned from a triangle voyage, he managed to find a crewman who had been chained to the deck for days on end. The victim was now on shore, in bed, delirious and heavily bandaged. "I was greatly affected by the situation of this poor man, whose image haunted me both night and day, and I was meditating how most effectually to assist him, when I heard that he was dead." He met another sailor so brutally treated by the same captain that he had tried to commit suicide by jumping overboard. Carefully studying sailors' contracts, Clarkson discovered how captains routinely cheated them out of much of their wages. "On whatever branch of the system I turned my eyes, I found it equally barbarous. The trade was, in short, one mass of iniquity from the beginning to the end."

Clarkson wanted to see everything for himself. When he heard that two small sloops were being fitted out to make slaving voyages and then be sold as pleasure yachts in the West Indies, he went on board. The slaves would be packed in rows into a space that was, he found, only two feet eight inches high. This was the first time on record that anyone not in the trade took measurements on a slave ship.

Each discovery led to another. If slave vessels were so notoriously brutal and the death rate so high, why did Bristol seamen continue to sail on them? Clarkson put the question to a man named Thompson, the owner of a pub, the Seven Stars, near the Bristol waterfront. Thompson offered to show him exactly how officers recruited their crews. For nearly three weeks, the two men went out late every night, visiting a series of pubs on Marsh Street. "The young mariner, if a stranger to the port, and unacquainted with the nature of the Slave-trade, was sure to be picked up." He would be told wages were high and women plentiful. "If these prospects did not attract him, he was plied with liquor till he became intoxicated. . . . Seamen also were boarded in these houses, who, when the slave-ships were going out, but at no other time, were encouraged to spend more than they had money to pay for." The pub owner then demanded payment, and only "one alternative was given, namely a slave-vessel, or a gaol. These distressing scenes I found myself obliged frequently to witness." At the end of each evening Clarkson wrote up his notes. "I seldom got home till two, and into bed till three. My clothes, also, were frequently wet through with the rains. The cruel accounts I was daily in the habit of hearing . . . often broke my sleep in the night, and occasioned me to awake in an agitated state."

Unwilling to risk their livelihoods, captains and mates wouldn't talk to him. One day in the street, however, he noticed a well-dressed stranger in conversation; an overheard fragment made him follow the man, a doctor, as it turned out, named James Arnold, who had made two slave voyages and was embarking in several days on a third. (Slave ships often carried doctors, lest too many slaves die and profits drop. The doctors also advised captains which captives on the African coast were healthy enough to buy.) Although "cautioned about falling-in with me," Arnold poured out to Clarkson the story of a slave uprising that had been suppressed on his previous voyage: one rebel holdout remained barricaded below decks until boiling water and fat were poured down on him. Clarkson asked why, having seen all this and more, had Arnold signed on for another slave voyage? The doctor replied that he was "quite pennyless. . . . But if he survived this voyage he would never go [on] another." Would Arnold be willing "to keep a journal of facts, and to give his evidence, if called upon, on his return"? The answer was yes. Another slave ship doctor agreed to do the same, and Clarkson felt, triumphantly, "that I had procured two sentinels to be stationed in the enemy's camp."

One sentinel would return at a crucial moment.

Clarkson had good luck with doctors. He soon found another, Alexander Falconbridge, who had made four slave voyages and proved a fount of information. Would he, too, be willing to talk about his experiences at a parliamentary hearing? "He answered me boldly, and at once, that he had left the trade upon principle, and that he would state all he knew concerning it, either publicly or privately, and at any time when he should be called upon. . . . The joy I felt rendered me quite useless, as to business, for the remainder of the day."

Besides witnesses, Clarkson was also collecting objects. From Bristol ships he eagerly gathered samples of African ivory, gum, rice, two kinds of pepper, rare and beautiful woods, and "small pieces of cloth made and dyed by the natives"—probably the brightly colored and intricately patterned kente cloth still used in West African dress. He was starting to think not just like an organizer but also like a performer: when he spoke in public, he would need to dramatize how Britain could carry on a profitable trade with Africa in goods other than human beings. What he called "my little collection of African productions" would become something he carried everywhere.

One day the pubkeeper Thompson came to Clarkson with news of a mate trapped on the *Africa,* anchored off Bristol and about to sail, who had changed his mind because he had not been allowed to read the "articles," or contract, he had signed. "Thompson entreated me to extricate him, if I could. He was sure, he said, if he went to the Coast . . . that he would never return alive." In a small boat, Clarkson and a Quaker friend headed out to the *Africa,* where they found the mate eager to escape. As he was climbing into the boat, "there was a general cry of 'Will you take me too?' from the deck; and such a sudden movement appeared there, that we were obliged to push off directly from the side, fearing that many would jump into our boat and go with us."

Experiences like this only increased Clarkson's rage against the trade, and his desire to act on it. In the eighteenth century it was virtually never the government that filed criminal charges in court, but rather the victim or the victim's representative. Clarkson daringly brought charges against the chief mate of the slave ship *Thomas,* who had killed a sailor. But in the weeks it took to bring the murderer to trial, two witnesses had gone off to work in a Welsh coal mine, and despite a strenuous journey through the night by boat and horseback, Clarkson couldn't fetch them in time. Two others were "bribed by the slave-merchants, and sent to sea." The case was dismissed. "After this time the slave-captains and mates . . . used . . . to start from me, indeed to the other side of the pavement, as if I had been a wolf, or tiger, or some dangerous beast of prey."

Word of Clarkson's combativeness filtered back to London, where the abolition committee had not expected its traveling investigator to pluck sailors off ships or bring murder charges in court. Now, as he prepared his assault on Liverpool, the world's largest slave ship port, they were no less startled when he asked to take his new ally Dr. Alexander Falconbridge with him at the committee's expense. Speaking for the group, a Quaker member wrote, "With respect to the employment of Mr. Falconbridge, to give thee assistance . . . I think there will be no objection, provided he is really a man of good character, and deserving confidence. But the little experience I have already had of mankind has excited much caution . . . and I hope the zeal and animation with which thou hast taken up the cause will be accompanied with temper and moderation."

Clarkson showed no moderation, however, as he rode onwards. It

John Newton: slave ship captain, writer of "Amazing Grace" and 279 other hymns, and belated abolitionist.

Olaudah Equiano, in a portrait made for the best-selling autobiography that introduced tens of thousands of Britons to the life of a slave who earned his freedom.

An African dealer marching slaves to the coast for sale.

Cape Coast Castle, Ghana. The ship that transported Quobna Ottobah Cugoano on the middle passage left from here.

Granville Sharp: musician, eccentric, pamphleteer, and pioneer antislavery crusader.

Sailors, at right, remove a dead slave from below decks. More than 1.4 million slaves died on the middle passage across the Atlantic.

Slaves in a sugar boiling house, Antigua.

Feeding the boiling house furnace with crushed and dried cane.

Although photographed after emancipation, huts like these in Jamaica housed British slaves throughout the Caribbean. Hurricanes blew away their thatch roofs.

Slaves cutting sugar cane, Antigua.

Slaves thrown overboard at sea. One hundred thirty-two such murders on the ship *Zong* set in motion the chain of events that ignited a movement.

Thomas Clarkson and his box of woods, spices, cloth, and other "African productions," which he hoped would show that the continent could be a trading partner in something other than slaves. At left are busts of William Wilberforce (left) and Granville Sharp.

TO BE SOLD, on board the Ship *Bance-Iſland*, on tueſday the 6th of *May* next, at *Aſhley-Ferry*; a choice cargo of about 250 fine healthy

NEGROES,

juſt arrived from the Windward & Rice Coaſt. —The utmoſt care has already been taken, and ſhall be continued, to keep them free from the leaſt danger of being infected with the SMALL-POX, no boat having been on board, and all other communication with people from *Charles-Town* prevented.

Auſtin, Laurens, & Appleby.

N. B. Full one Half of the above Negroes have had the SMALL-POX in their own Country.

Ships co-owned by Richard Oswald brought slaves from Sierra Leone to his friend the South Carolina slave dealer Henry Laurens. Forty slaves died on this 1760 voyage.

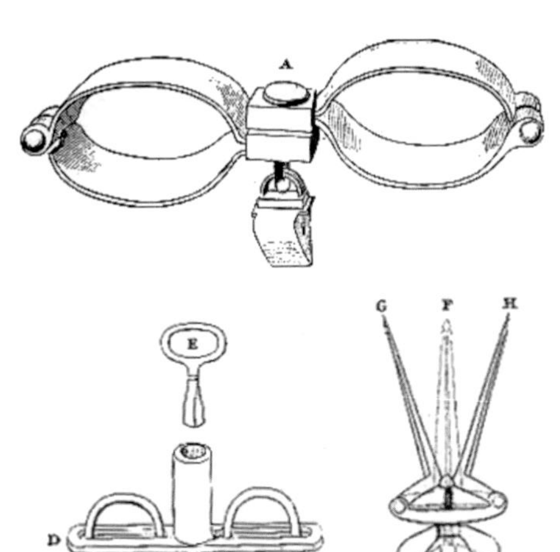

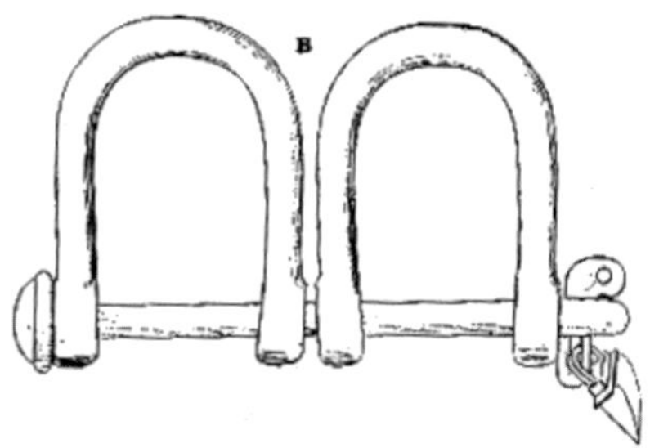

Handcuffs, thumbscrew, leg shackles, and an instrument for prying open slaves' mouths for force-feeding. An outraged Clarkson purchased these in Liverpool in 1787.

William Wilberforce, for nearly four decades the movement's chief voice in Parliament.

Designed by one of Josiah Wedgwood's craftsmen and emblazoned on such things as cufflinks and hatpins, this logo was the forerunner of the political campaign buttons we wear today.

was late summer when he reached Liverpool, a city of narrow streets and great wharves, its skyline filled with domes, steeples, and hundreds of ships' masts, and there he moved with the same fierce energy he had shown in Bristol. His mind was totally on the work to be done: "I had never had time to read a newspaper since I left London." At the wharfside Custom House, which faced the bowsprits of a long row of docked sailing vessels, he again copied out names of sailors who had never returned from slave voyages. He wanted to destroy for good the myth that the trade was a useful nursery for British seamen. By the time he was done, "in London, Bristol and Liverpool, I had already obtained the names of more than 20,000 seamen . . . knowing what had become of each."

Liverpool—John Newton's home port on each of his voyages—this year would be sending a total of eighty-one slave ships to Africa from its six miles of docks. From 1783 to 1793, a thriving between-wars decade for the trade, Liverpool ships would carry more than 300,000 Africans into slavery. Its shipyards built many of these vessels, and some were among the largest of their day, holding up to a thousand slaves each. Carved heads of African elephants and slaves decorated the town hall. When a visiting actor, George F. Cooke, was hissed for appearing drunk on a Liverpool stage, he retorted, "I have not come here to be insulted by a set of wretches, every brick in whose infernal town is cemented with an African's blood." Most people in Liverpool were proud of that cement. At the time of Clarkson's visit, thirty-seven of the forty-one members of the city's governing body, the Common Council, were directly or indirectly involved in the slave trade, including the two co-owners of the notorious *Zong,* both of them former mayors. The trade also helped pay the salaries of everyone from coopers and gunsmiths and sailmakers to workers in the city's fifteen rope factories.

Slave voyage profits were widely shared as well, for a ship owner was less the sole proprietor of a business than the manager of a venture capital syndicate. Triangle voyages were chancy propositions, and, as with a Broadway production or a dot-com start-up today, risk and gain were shared. Commonly each voyage was a separate partnership, in which anywhere from two to eight people or families might together invest the £7,000 or more it could cost to outfit and insure a ship for the yearlong voyage and fill it with the goods to be traded for slaves in Africa. Even shopkeepers, carpenters, and tradesmen bought shares in the voyages of some smaller ships, thereby participating, as a local writer put it, in a trade that "may be said to pervade the whole town."

Liverpool's handful of Quakers and other opponents of slavery kept a low profile, and none of them dared invite Clarkson and Falconbridge to stay. One local doctor would treat an abolitionist patient only if he came after dark, so that his carriage could not be easily recognized outside the doctor's house. Abolitionists in Liverpool were soon to receive threats that if they spoke out against the trade their houses would be torn down. They did not trust the mail; when in months ahead they would correspond with the committee in London, it would be through the mailing addresses of friends not known for antislavery views.

One day, as he was walking past the window of a Liverpool ship chandler's shop, Clarkson was shocked to see on display handcuffs, leg shackles, thumbscrews, and a surgical instrument with a screw device, called a speculum oris, used by doctors in cases of lockjaw. He asked why it was there, and the shopkeeper explained: it was for prying open the mouths of any slaves on shipboard who tried to commit suicide by not eating. Clarkson bought samples of each, and described them in an angry letter to the London *Times.*

At the King's Arms hotel, where he stayed, a group of slave traders went to the owner to try to get him evicted. Men pointed him out in the dining room. "Some gave as a toast, Success to the Trade, and then laughed immoderately, and watched me when I took my glass to see if I would drink it." Clarkson again seethed with indignation at the way the trade dehumanized sailors as well as slaves. If sailors abandoned the trade after one voyage, "they usually escaped the disease of a hardened heart. But if they went a second and a third time . . . it was impossible for them to . . . carry away men and women by force, to keep them in chains, to see their tears . . . without contracting those habits of moroseness and cruelty, which would brutalize their nature."

Once again, he got embroiled in trying to prosecute a sailor's murderers, and an abolitionist in Liverpool wrote to one in London complaining that Clarkson was spending too much time with the "lower class of seamen." Was he right to pursue cases like this? The strenuous weeks of effort he put into these failed prosecutions was probably not the best use of his time, but he seems to have been a man simply unable to witness a crime without trying to see justice done. The stories of "the ill treatment of the seamen in this wicked trade," he wrote, ". . . were in my thoughts on my pillow after I retired to rest, and I found them before my eyes when I awoke."

Before long he was receiving anonymous death threats. Falconbridge—"an athletic and resolute-looking man," as Clarkson described him—now accompanied him as a bodyguard. (Only later did Falconbridge reveal to Clarkson that he always carried a gun.) One day, however, without Falconbridge in tow, Clarkson stopped at the end of a Liverpool pier to watch how some small boats were riding out a heavy gale. Suddenly, "I noticed eight or nine persons making towards me." The group included one of the slave ship officers he was trying to prosecute for murder. "I was then only about eight or nine yards from the precipice of the pier. . . . They closed upon me and bore me back." His tall, strong build saved him from harm—and possibly from death if, like most Britons of his day, he did not know how to swim. "It instantly struck me that they had a design to throw me over the pier-head; which they might have done at this time, and yet have pleaded that I had been killed by accident. There was not a moment to lose. . . . I darted forward. One of them, against whom I pushed myself, fell down. Their ranks were broken. And I escaped, not without blows, amidst their imprecations and abuse."

Alarmed that Clarkson's combativeness seemed "deficient in caution and prudence," as one member wrote confidentially, the committee ordered their traveling organizer back to London—ostensibly because they needed him to write another book. By now it was the autumn of 1787 and he had been away some five months. But after Clarkson got on his horse again, he couldn't resist stopping on the way home, most notably in the weaving and manufacturing city of Manchester. All sorts of new ideas were stirring in this center of the early Industrial Revolution. Tripling in size in the last quarter of the eighteenth century, it was about to become England's second-largest city.

Manchester sold some £200,000 worth of goods each year to slave ships—some $28 million in today's money—chiefly cloth that was traded for slaves. In addition, the very cotton woven in the local mills was grown by slaves, and so the city might be expected to be hostile territory for Clarkson. But he found the opposite. On his first morning in town, he had several visitors, including Thomas Walker and Thomas Cooper. This may have been Clarkson's first encounter with a type of activist with whom he would soon feel a strong bond: those who saw the crusade against slavery as only one facet of a larger movement for human rights.

Walker, a cotton merchant, was a crusader for electoral reform, full rights for people of all religions, and universal public education. Significantly, he had just run a campaign to mobilize public opinion, organizing tens of thousands of people to sign a petition that made the government withdraw a new tax on cotton cloth. Cooper, who had recently published a series of articles against the slave trade in a local newspaper, was a doctor who provided free service for the poor; a few years later, he would move to the United States in search of a site for a Utopian colony of democratically minded Britons. Clarkson was "overpowered with joy" when his visitors told him that antislavery spirit was so strong in Manchester that people wanted to petition Parliament, on the model of their successful defeat of the cloth tax. This is just what Clarkson and the committee had long had in mind as the opening stage of a national campaign.

Clarkson felt so caught up in his work that "I had given up all thoughts of my profession." But when his Manchester visitors discovered "that I had been educated as a clergyman, they came upon me with one voice, as if it had been before agreed upon, to deliver a discourse the next day, which was Sunday, on the subject of the Slave-trade." And so, for one of the first times in his life and less than forty-eight hours after arriving in the city, Clarkson found himself in the pulpit delivering a sermon. The church was "so full that I could scarcely get to my place." No longer an unknown divinity student, he was, exhilaratingly, the representative of a cause in a crowd of fervent supporters. He took his text from Exodus: "Thou shalt not oppress a stranger: for ye know the heart of a stranger, seeing ye were strangers in the land of Egypt." Manchester may have been so receptive to abolition because its tens of thousands of workers, flooding into this new "town of the uprooted" from an impoverished countryside, knew what it was like to be strangers. And among the listeners he saw before him that morning were some who knew that experience even more strongly: "a great crowd of black people standing round the pulpit . . . forty or fifty of them." Neither blacks nor whites among his audience needed much persuading. When Clarkson's new Manchester friends sent their petition off to Parliament some weeks later, it contained more than ten thousand names, one out of every five people in the city. A movement was under way.

9

AM I NOT A MAN AND A BROTHER?

THE ABOLITION COMMITTEE needed eyewitnesses and activists, but it also needed another kind of help. In the spring of 1787, some weeks before Clarkson set off on the journey that would take him to the seedy waterfront pubs of Bristol and Liverpool, he had gone on a recruiting mission in very different surroundings. The occasion was an elegant London dinner party at the mansion of Bennet Langton. In the words of a contemporary, Langton was "one of the worthiest, as well as the tallest, men in the kingdom." At six feet six inches, he was a "long-visaged man, much resembling . . . a stork standing on one leg." The scion of a wealthy, ancient family, Langton was a close friend of James Boswell and Samuel Johnson. Clarkson found that his *Essay* "had made a deep impression" on him, and Langton had volunteered to aid the cause as host of this gathering. Johnson was by then dead, but Boswell paused in his labors of writing the great man's biography to come for dinner, as did the famous portrait painter Sir Joshua Reynolds—and as did the person Clarkson really wanted to talk to, a diminutive, wraith-thin young man, a good two heads shorter than the host.

Despite his side whiskers, the blue-eyed William Wilberforce, at less than five feet four inches tall, looked more like an earnest choirboy than the member of Parliament he was. One contemporary described him as "all soul and no body." Clarkson and his Quaker friends thought Wilberforce would be the ideal voice of the anti–slave trade campaign in the House of Commons. He had a reputation for integrity, he was a political independent, he was wealthy, and—as all M.P.s had to be—he was an Anglican. Most important of all, he was a close friend of William Pitt (sometimes known as Pitt the Younger, for his father had held the same post), who four years earlier had become Britain's youngest Prime Minister. Pitt had great respect for his friend's abilities; as a speaker, he thought, Wilberforce had "the greatest natural eloquence in England."

Wilberforce had recently become an ardent Evangelical. He sometimes slipped a pebble into his shoe to remind himself that his thoughts should be on loftier things. Later in his life he would spend the winter in Brighton in order to try—unsuccessfully—to convert to Evangelicalism another of the town's residents, the future King George IV. A conversation about religion with John Newton had been a spiritual turning point for Wilberforce—although, typically, on that occasion, Newton seems to have said nothing to him about slavery. He had also come to know Reverend James Ramsay and some supporters of his, who, seeing a well-connected young M.P. casting about for a worthy cause, *had* talked slavery with him, urging him to take up the issue in Parliament. And this same spring a similar suggestion came from Pitt, as the two were talking beneath an old oak tree on Pitt's estate outside London. With a shrewd politician's sense that this issue lay just beneath the surface of British life and could define his friend's career, the Prime Minister encouraged him: "Do not lose time, or the ground may be occupied by another."

Wilberforce and Clarkson had already met. Clarkson's *Essay*, Wilberforce later said, was crucial to making him think about slavery. Clarkson had promised his Quaker colleagues that he would try to enlist Wilberforce in their cause, but on visiting him alone, Clarkson had found himself uncharacteristically tongue-tied. "I had a feeling within me for which I could not account, and which seemed to hinder me from proceeding. And I actually went away without informing him of my errand." Perhaps he felt intimidated by someone less than a year older but already an M.P.; perhaps he sensed that in the subtle calibrations of Britain's class system, Wilberforce was of higher rank; perhaps he was simply afraid that Wilberforce would say no. And so he had asked Bennet Langton to set up this dinner, where the question could be put to Wilberforce in company and surroundings where he would be likely to say yes.

After the meal, according to Clarkson, "the subject of the Slave-trade was purposely introduced." He then displayed his samples of African cloth and spoke at length about the sufferings of the slaves. Even the crotchety Boswell (who was later to change his mind) expressed backhanded support: "After saying the planters would urge that the Africans were made happier by being carried from their own country to the West Indies, [he] observed, 'Be it so. But we have no right to make people happy against their will.' "

At last, Clarkson recalled, "Mr. Langton put the question, about . . . which I had been so diffident, to Mr. Wilberforce." He replied that "provided no person more proper could be found," he would raise the issue in Parliament.

Within a few years of Bennet Langton's dinner party, West Indian planters would be burning Wilberforce in effigy; later, it was reported, runaway slaves in the Jamaican backcountry would be praying to Saint Wilberforce. It was a most unlikely fate for a gentle, impractical man who, on almost every other major issue, was profoundly conservative. He was against increasing the tiny number of Britons with the right to vote, fearful of any attempt to mobilize public opinion, and dismayed by members of the lower classes or women who questioned their assigned places in the social order. He wrote to one woman friend to scold her for "a certain quickness of reply which is unbecoming the submissive obedient demeanour which certainly should distinguish the wife towards her husband." Like many Evangelicals, he believed that popular amusements were a path to sin. The year of Langton's dinner party, for instance, he admonished his sister for going to plays, because "I think the tendency of the theatre most pernicious." Later in his life, when he referred to the "greatest of all causes" he had served, it was not the antislavery movement. It was the introduction of Christian missionaries to India.

Whatever their differences of belief and temperament, Clarkson, the agitator, needed Wilberforce, the insider. Absent revolution, the usual purpose of building a movement, after all, is to get legislators to change laws. Clarkson would not have been an effective agitator had he not shared the dreams of change and freedom in the air during this pregnant interlude between the American and French revolutions. Wilberforce would not have been an effective member of Parliament had he not shared the worldview of his fellow M.P.s, who were mostly reactionary landowners. Despite occasional strains, their friendship would last for nearly fifty years.

Wilberforce was twenty-seven on the evening of the Langton dinner. He had been born in a spacious brick home in the port of Hull, to a prosperous merchant family, one of the few in England capable of tracing its ancestry to before the Norman conquest. Once he decided to enter the House of Commons, election was assured. On his twenty-first birthday, he threw a huge feast in one of his family's fields —an ox roasted whole, a bonfire, many barrels of ale—then passed out over £8,000 (more than $1.2 million in today's money) among the voters in his Hull constituency, as was the custom of the day, and took his seat a few weeks later. Since Hull was not a slave port, taking a stand against the trade would never pose a political risk for Wilberforce. Nor, in elections in which he was seldom opposed, would much else. Nonetheless, he and his supporters kept a record book listing each voter with an income of £100 or more a year, and information such as "whether he likes the leg or wing of a fowl best, that when one dines with him one may win his heart by helping him."

Although at one point in life, weakened by illness, Wilberforce would weigh a mere seventy-six pounds, he had an unexpectedly strong, almost mesmerizing public speaking voice, a great advantage in this unamplified age. "I saw what seemed a mere shrimp mount upon the table," wrote Boswell of one of his election speeches, "but, as I listened, he grew, and grew, until the shrimp became a whale." Madame de Staël, no bore herself, described him as "the wittiest man in England." The Prince of Wales reportedly said that he would go anywhere to hear Wilberforce sing. "His mirth was as irresistible," a friend wrote, "as the first laughter of childhood." He was renowned for his charm and his ability to mimic anyone. Of all the people in this story, he is the one who might have been most enjoyable to spend an evening with.

At his conversion to Evangelicalism, Wilberforce felt shaken to the core by "a sense of my great sinfulness in having so long neglected the unspeakable mercies of my God and Saviour." He resolved to read the Bible and to do good. His sense of sin seems puzzling, however, for unlike such Evangelical converts as John Newton and James Stephen, his youth yields no record of debauchery. One searches in vain for any offense worse than falling asleep in church.

Wilberforce did not, in 1787, bring up slavery in Parliament. The committee had not yet sufficiently laid the groundwork, and in any case he had much else on his mind, especially the suppression of sin. Given the enormous symbolic power of the British monarchy, Wilberforce felt, the King must be persuaded to issue a royal proclamation against vice. George III readily obliged, ordering prosecution of "excessive drinking, blasphemy, profane swearing and cursing, lewdness, profanation of the Lord's Day, or other dissolute, immoral, or disorderly practices." Wilberforce then founded the Society for Carrying into Effect His Majesty's Proclamation Against Vice and Immorality. Many felt the proclamation should really have been directed at the King's large, unruly brood of sons and daughters, who eventually produced among them, it is estimated, an impressive fifty-six illegitimate children.*

In November 1787, Clarkson finally finished his long trip to the slave ports, riding his horse back to London. Activists in Manchester were getting up their petition; the influential Wilberforce was now in abolitionist ranks; articles against slavery were starting to appear in newspapers. The up-and-coming artist George Morland was about to exhibit the first antislavery painting, at the Royal Academy no less: *Execrable Human Traffick* showed a protesting African being hustled

---

* One cause of this was the Royal Marriages Act, passed at the urging of the King. It prevented members of his family from marrying without his consent before the age of twenty-five and limited their right to do so thereafter. By promoting arranged marriages, the act was intended to elevate the dynasty's prestige; it accomplished just the opposite.

into a ship's longboat by white traders. Even a new children's book, *Little Truths better than great Fables,* included a description of slaves in a ship "pressed together like herrings in a barrel, which caused an intolerable heat and stench." Clarkson revised his own *Essay* for a new edition, and then holed up at his mother's home near Cambridge to work on another book, dedicated to Wilberforce. Having made the moral case against slavery, he now made the practical one, using his copious notes about British seamen's deaths and African products. As a present from the country he sent a turkey by mail coach to his publisher, Phillips, whose presses were "kept almost constantly going."

The committee had been working hard from the moment of its founding, with an eye to both home and abroad. Its members knew it was not enough to flood Britain with antislavery material; they had to think internationally. Although Britain was the maritime superpower of the day, to fully stop the slave trade they would also have to change minds in continental Europe and the United States. And so they arranged for some of the books and pamphlets now pouring off the presses, as 1788 began, to be translated into the languages of the other slave-trading powers: French, Portuguese, Danish, Dutch, and Spanish. They sent letters to the King of Sweden and the King of Spain. The transatlantic conversation with American activists was particularly spirited: Quakers were constantly going back and forth; Clarkson had relied heavily on the writings of an American Quaker, Anthony Benezet, for his *Essay,* and when that was published the American abolitionist sympathizer Benjamin Rush sent a copy to the governor of every state.

From the beginning, the committee's minutes show an organization that is methodically thorough. If a job is assigned to someone—to gather the names of sympathetic M.P.s or send material to abolitionists in Boston or Philadelphia—the person and task are listed again, every week, until the job is done. In its meticulous efficiency, as in so much else, the committee reflected its predominantly Quaker membership. As with Europe's Jews, who long faced similar prohibitions, the laws excluding Quakers from so much of public life had helped turn many of them into a merchant caste. This was the first great social reform movement run mainly by businessmen—indeed, almost all the committee's meetings took place only after the closing of the Royal Exchange and the end of the business day. These careful lists of uncompleted tasks are like so many liabilities on a company's balance sheet.

This well-organized group also pioneered several tools used by civic organizations ever since. First, they periodically printed five hundred to a thousand copies of what the minutes referred to as "a Letter to our Friends in the Country, to inform them of the state of the Business." What activist group today does not publish such a newsletter, print or electronic? Then the committee agreed on a piece of text, signed by Granville Sharp, that was to be hand-delivered to every donor living in greater London, appealing for another contribution at least as big as the last. This may have been history's first direct-mail fund-raising letter.

Before long, nearly two thousand people had contributed, and there were contacts—most though not all of them Quakers—in thirty-nine counties. One new member of the committee was Josiah Wedgwood, the famous pottery designer and manufacturer, who had had a leg amputated in his youth. (He kept a large array of spare wooden legs on hand and was said to use one to smash pots that didn't meet his exacting standards.) Besides money, he had something every movement needs: a flair for publicity and marketing. When Wedgwood was made Potter to the Queen, he promptly sold a line of china as Queensware; after Catherine the Great of Russia ordered a 952-piece set of table service, he marketed his "Russian pattern." He produced the first printed catalogue of ceramics and gave each new line of products an aura of desirability through a by-invitation-only opening in his London showroom. Nearly two centuries before Hollywood discovered "product placement," he arranged for his vases to appear in works by well-known painters.

Wedgwood asked one of his craftsmen to design a seal for stamping the wax used to close envelopes. It showed a kneeling African in chains, lifting his hands beseechingly, encircled by the words "Am I Not a Man and a Brother?" Reproduced everywhere from books and leaflets to snuffboxes and cufflinks, the image was an instant hit. Wedgwood's kneeling African, the equivalent of the lapel buttons we wear for electoral campaigns, was probably the first widespread use of a logo designed for a political cause. Antislavery sympathizer Benjamin Franklin knew a good piece of propaganda when he saw it and declared the impact of the image "equal to that of the best written Pamphlet." Clarkson gave out five hundred medallions with this figure to people he met. "Of the ladies, several wore them in bracelets, and others had them fitted up in an ornamental manner as pins for their hair." In this way women could show their antislavery feelings at a time when the law barred them from voting, and tradition from participating in political groups.

How much effect did all this agitation have? There were no opinion polls in the London of 1788, but one group of businessmen depended for their livelihood on gauging the public mood: the proprietors of the city's several dozen debating societies. These forums, which bore colorful names like the Ciceronian School of Eloquence and the University of Rational Amusements, were commercial enterprises. Just like rock concert promoters today, their owners had to cover the expenses of renting a hall and buying newspaper advertisements and wanted to attract the largest possible crowd. Admission was usually sixpence, only half the price of the cheapest lecture or theater ticket, and so the audience—for a popular topic, perhaps six or seven hundred—ranged across the class spectrum. The subjects for verbal battle reflected a shrewd entrepreneur's sense of what the public wanted. Sex was always a sure thing; good crowds always turned out for topics such as "Whether Vice or Virtue affords superior pleasures?" or "Whether the fashionable infidelities of married couples are more owing to the depravity of the Gentlemen or the inconstancy of the Ladies?" Politics drew a good audience as well. After many years in which slavery was hardly ever a topic, abruptly, in February 1788, a Londoner would have been able to attend seven debates on the abolition of the slave trade, half of *all* public debates on record in the city's daily newspapers that month.

Another sign of sudden public interest comes from the *Gentleman's Magazine,* a bellwether journal of news and gossip with no love for the abolitionist cause. In 1787, its index lists not a single item about slavery or the slave trade; for 1788, there are sixty-eight references. At the start of this pivotal year, Joseph Woods, a Quaker wool merchant and one of the abolition committee's founding members, wrote that the British people were like "Tinder which has immediately caught fire from the spark of Information which has been struck upon it."

There are many reasons why Britons of this era might have been predisposed to question slavery, from the "spark of Information" in books by Clarkson and Ramsay to the news of arguments over slavery as the fledgling United States drew up its new constitution in 1787. And, after the disgrace of losing the American Revolutionary War, Britons were perhaps in the mood for a national crusade in which they could feel morally superior. But James Phillips had been printing antislavery books for several years now, the American war had ended half a decade earlier, and Enlightenment ideas about human freedom were older still. Why did the antislavery cause so suddenly catch the eye of the London public at the beginning of 1788?

One group that helped tip the balance were the energetic abolitionists Clarkson had met in Manchester several months earlier. Not only did they gather an impressive ten thousand names on their petition to Parliament, but they then resolved, reported a Manchester newspaper on January 1, 1788, that a "letter be addressed . . . to the mayor or other chief magistrate of every principal town throughout Great Britain" urging similar anti–slave trade petitions. They also wrote to "respectable individuals" around the country. And the Manchester activists didn't stop there; they paid a man named William Taylor £129, 4 shillings, 1 penny (about $18,000 today) to place notices of their unprecedented petition in newspapers in the capital and throughout the British Isles, advertisements that appeared in mid-January.

Something else happened the same month: a man long silent at last spoke. Indeed, no one had been more conspicuously quiet about slavery than John Newton, now retired from the slave trade for nearly thirty-four years. His fame as an Evangelical preacher had won him a prestigious pulpit in the heart of London: St. Mary Woolnoth, a majestic baroque church just two blocks from Phillips's printing shop. The Lord Mayor was one of his parishioners. Now in his sixties, Newton had grown extremely stout. In portraits his benign, almost dreamy face, topped by white curls, sits above a white clerical cravat and a body whose bulk even his black robe cannot hide. With a vocal movement coming to life around him, Newton now published a forceful pamphlet, *Thoughts Upon the African Slave Trade.* He begins by apologizing for a "confession, which . . . comes too late. . . . It will always be a subject of humiliating reflection to me, that I was once an active instrument in a business at which my heart now shudders."

The curious thing, of course, is that for so long the slave trade apparently wasn't a subject of humiliating reflection for him at all. That Newton shuddered now is testimony to the way a strong social movement can awaken a conscience—even in a clergyman, whose very business is the awakening of consciences. In his pamphlet, he lets out what had been dammed up in him all those years: his knowledge of the slave trade's cruelty and of how it brutalized those who practiced it. "I know of no method of getting money, not even that of robbing for it upon the highway, which has so direct a tendency to . . . rob the heart of every gentle and humane disposition, and to harden it, like steel." He describes the rows of slaves, shackled together and fighting seasickness, forced into tight spaces too low for someone to stand. Speaking of slave rebellions on shipboard, he refers, with startling openness, to one slave who leaked word of a conspiracy as a "traitor to the cause of liberty," and to those who conspired for their freedom as "patriots."

Of these rebels, he says, "I have seen them sentenced to unmerciful whippings, continued till the poor creatures have not had power to groan under their misery, and hardly a sign of life has remained. I have seen them agonizing for hours, I believe for days together, under the torture of the thumbscrews; a dreadful engine, which, if the screw be turned by an unrelenting hand, can give intolerable anguish." He recalls a ship's mate, annoyed by the crying of a child, who tore the baby from its mother's arms and threw it overboard, and slave traders who cheated the Africans with every sale of goods: kegs of watered-down liquor, barrels of gunpowder with false bottoms, bolts of textiles with cloth removed from the middle. "When I have charged a black [trader] with unfairness and dishonesty, he has answered . . . with an air of disdain, 'What! do you think I am a white man?'"

Having a prominent Anglican clergyman like Newton on record was a coup for the committee. The first edition of his pamphlet immediately sold out; it was swiftly reprinted and sent to every member of Parliament. But he, after all, had left the trade more than three decades earlier. Fortunately, for testimony no less vivid and far more recent, Clarkson could call on his burly ally from Bristol, Alexander Falconbridge. In a series of interviews Falconbridge told his story to committee member Richard Phillips, who shaped it into a short, grisly, and unforgettable book that appeared over Falconbridge's name in February 1788. His searing descriptions came from his experience as a ship's doctor:

> The place allotted for the sick negroes is under the half deck, where they lie on the bare planks. By this means, those who are emaciated, frequently have their skin, and even their flesh, entirely rubbed off, by the motion of the ship, from the prominent parts of the shoulders, elbows, and hips, so as to render the bones in those parts quite bare. . . . The utmost skill of the surgeon is here ineffectual. . . . The surgeon, upon going between decks, in the morning, to examine the situation of the slaves, frequently finds several dead; and among the men, sometimes a dead and living negroe fastened by their irons together.

And then there were the latrine buckets:

> It often happens, that those who are placed at a distance from the buckets, in endeavouring to get to them, tumble over their companions, in consequence of being shackled. . . . Unable to proceed, and prevented from getting to the tubs, they desist from the attempt; and, as the necessities of nature are not to be repelled, ease themselves as they lie. . . . The nuisance arising from these circumstances, is not infrequently increased by the tubs being much too small for the purpose intended, and their being usually emptied but once every day. . . . The deck, that is, the floor of their rooms, was so covered with the blood and mucus which had proceeded from them in consequence of the flux [dysentery], that it resembled a slaughterhouse. It is not in the power of the human imagination, to picture to itself a situation more dreadful.

At a slave market in the West Indies, said Falconbridge, one Liverpool captain disguised his slaves' dysentery by ordering the ship's doctor to plug up their anuses with rope fiber.

Finally, he depicted the treatment of British sailors in the trade: the miserable food, the salt water and pepper poured on the raw wounds from a flogging, the clothing and tobacco sold them by rapacious captains at high prices, and the way, when the ship was filled with slaves, sailors had to sleep on deck, protected against wind and rain only by a tarpaulin thrown over a spar. At the harbor at Bonny, in what is today Nigeria, dead British sailors were buried, he wrote, on a low, sandy peninsula covered at high tide; the rest of the time the air was filled with the stench of decaying bodies. As for dead slaves, they were merely thrown to the sharks.

The combined effect of such testimony, of the committee's torrent of additional propaganda, and of the Manchester petition rippled through the country. The metaphor of flame again leapt to mind when a touring actor wrote in April 1788 that many British cities he had passed through had "caught fire" over slavery. Several months later, in the biggest slave port, the editor of the *Liverpool General Advertiser* bemoaned "the infatuation of our country, running headlong into ruin."

Eager as they were to mobilize witnesses, Clarkson and his colleagues had strikingly little interest in the testimony of any of the thousands of former slaves in Britain, some with whip scars on their backs. There are no records of any of them appearing on speakers' platforms with abolitionists at this time, and the committee made no effort to record their stories, although Clarkson, Ramsay, and Sharp all knew Equiano and other ex-slaves in London.

The abolitionist attitude towards blacks was perhaps summed up best by Wedgwood's design. The African may have been "a man and a brother," but he was definitely a younger and grateful brother, a kneeling one, not a rebellious one. At a time when members of the British upper class did not kneel even for prayer in church, the image of the pleading slave victim reflected a crusade whose leaders saw themselves as uplifting the downtrodden, not fighting for equal rights for all. To our eyes, it is curious to see an instinctive democrat like Clarkson, with his burning outrage against injustice, as part of a movement whose rhetoric was so paternalistic. But the committee's campaign was ultimately aimed at one target: Parliament. The upper-class Britons comprising that body might be moved by pity, but certainly not by a passion for equality.

In valuing British voices over African ones, the all-white committee was loath to challenge the racial attitudes of its time. It is not so simple, however, to define just what these were. Most eighteenth-century Britons, their heads filled with a jumble of images that ranged from the noble savage to the blackness of Satan, had no very coherent ideas about race; the vast majority, after all, had never seen a black person. Whites who had lived in the West Indies, on the other hand, knew exactly what they thought: they regarded slaves as cattle breeders might their animals, discussing whether Igbos were more unruly than Coromantees, Congos stronger field hands than Krumen. Edward Long, a Jamaica planter and historian of the island, spoke of blacks as subhuman, no better than apes or oxen, and, like many a race theorist to come, was particularly aghast at sex between black men and white women: "The lower classes of women in *England,* are remarkably fond of the blacks, for reasons too brutal to mention; they would connect themselves with horses and asses, if the laws permitted them." Although not similarly bothered about interracial sex, even Clarkson believed that blacks bred more rapidly than whites, being, as he put it, "peculiarly prolifick in their nature."

However, the hysterical railing against black-white liaisons by Long and others only emphasizes how many of these there were. The former slaves living in England were overwhelmingly male, and memoirs, paintings, and parish marriage records give ample evidence that hundreds of Englishwomen of the 1700s had no fear of what Long called the "malignancy" of sex with black men. Antiblack racism in Britain was by no means universal. The best testimony to this is that over five long decades of defending slavery in Parliament, the West Indian lobby virtually never argued that blacks were innately inferior; instead they talked of how vital were the Caribbean plantations to the imperial economy. Autobiographies, letters, and other fragments of evidence show blacks both being insulted on London streets and being warmly welcomed into white homes. Eighteenth-century British attitudes ranged from scorn to condescension to kindness to—

perhaps predominantly—a naïve, puzzled curiosity about people who looked so different.

In their interest in listening to black voices, the public was notably more open-minded than the abolitionists, and one such voice helped stimulate the public concern about slavery that became so dramatically visible in early 1788. In the summer of the previous year, but with little apparent help from the abolition committee, a black man made himself heard. He was an African in London named Quobna Ottobah Cugoano, who published a book, *Thoughts and Sentiments on the Evil and Wicked Traffic of the Slavery and Commerce of the Human Species.* Kidnapped in Africa at about the age of thirteen and enslaved for two years in the West Indies, he was brought to England in 1772 by his master. There, he eventually found a job as a house servant for a husband-and-wife team of high-society portrait painters. He and Equiano knew each other, and there are signs that Equiano may have helped him write the book. Cugoano was said to have married an Englishwoman, and announced plans to open a school for blacks in Britain. But no written trace of either the marriage or the school survives.

Surprisingly to modern eyes that so value victims' life stories, only 5 of the 102 pages of Cugoano's book deal with his own experience. He describes being captured as he was playing in a field near his home. "I must own, to the shame of my own countrymen, that I was first kidnapped and betrayed by some of my own complexion." Taken to the coast by an African slave dealer, he was able to observe the exact price he fetched: "I saw him take a gun, a piece of cloth, and some lead for me, and then he told me that he must now leave me there, and went off." His ship for the West Indies sailed from the great, thick-walled castle, with room for more than a thousand slaves and a chapel atop the dungeons for its British staff, that still stands at Cape Coast, Ghana. On shipboard, the slaves conspired to set fire to the vessel, "to perish all together in the flames; but we were betrayed by one of our own countrywomen, who slept with some of the head men of the ship."

Very quickly, however, Cugoano moves on to the larger question of the morality of slavery, letting go a barrage of biblical quotations, praising Sharp and Clarkson, and defending James Ramsay against the malicious attacks on him. Implicitly, he challenges the abolitionists for advocating only the ending of the slave trade. "I would propose that . . . universal emancipation of slaves should begin." He calls for a proclamation against slavery, like the royal proclamation against vice, with a penalty of £1,000 for anyone who bought or sold another human being.

More radical than his white peers in another way, Cugoano attacks the colonial conquest of the Americas, although he safely limits his examples to Spanish possessions. "Led on by the treacherous Cortes, the fate of the great Montezuma was dreadful and shocking; how that American monarch was treated, betrayed and destroyed . . . no man of sensibility and feeling can read the history without pity and resentment." He identifies wholeheartedly with the indigenous Aztecs and Incas, whom the Spanish treated as cruelly as slaves.

Cugoano's book attracted enough readers to go through at least three printings in 1787, to be translated into French, and to be revised for a new edition four years later. At that point he apparently traveled the country promoting it, for in a letter to Granville Sharp—with whom he had worked a few years earlier in rescuing a black man about to be shipped to the West Indies—he remarks, "I have, within this last three months b[een] . . . upwards of fifty places but, Complexion is a Predominant Prejudice." And then Cugoano drops from sight. Frustratingly, we know nothing of what happened to him, or of how Britons in "upwards of fifty places" felt about this rare, bold African voice in their midst.

African voices also rang out in the London debating societies. At one, during the tipping-point month of February 1788, an advertisement promised that "a NATIVE OF AFRICA, many years a Slave in the West-Indies, will attend . . . and communicate to the audience a number of very remarkable circumstances respecting the treatment of the Negroe Slaves . . . together with several interesting circumstances relative to the conduct of the Slave-holders towards the African women." At another, reported the *Morning Post,* "an ingenious African . . . contributed much information on the subject." One or both of these Africans were almost certainly Cugoano or Equiano, who that month published several antislavery letters in London newspapers. An impressed correspondent of a provincial paper wrote about Equiano that "the zeal of this worthy African, in favour of his brethren, would do honor to any colour or to any cause." These seem to be the first recorded instances of black Britons speaking in public.

They were not the only ones who spoke for the first time. At another debate the same month ("Can the Slave Trade be justified on the principles of Justice, Christianity, Policy or Humanity?"), a newspaper reported excitedly that the audience was "honoured by a circumstance never before witnessed in a Debating Society. A lady spoke to the subject with that dignity, energy, and information, which astonished every one present, and justly merited what she obtained, repeated and uncommon bursts of applause from an intelligent and enraptured auditory. The question was carried against the Slave Trade." A rival proprietor seeing a chance for profit quickly advertised a new debate on the subject at which "a LADY, whose intellectual accomplishments, and wonderful powers of eloquence, delighted a public audience on Wednesday last . . . is expected to honor the Society with her sentiments." Meanwhile, a "Lady of distinguished ability" addressed a women-only gathering on the question of whether women whose husbands were members of Parliament should urge them to support abolition. These are, one scholar says, "among the earliest examples of public speaking by women in Britain outside the context of religion." The "ladies," like the Africans, did not merit having their names recorded. There is no clue who they were.

What Clarkson referred to as "ferment in the public mind" bubbled up in other forms as well. The most important expression of feeling came on great, stiff rolls of parchment. Manchester's petition set a pattern copied around the country. By the time the 1788 session of Parliament adjourned, 103 petitions for abolition or reform of the slave trade had been signed by between 60,000 and 100,000 people. (The numbers are estimated because most petitions were later lost in a fire.) Throughout Britain, petitions were left for signature at town halls, printing shops, hotels, banks, coffeehouses, and pubs. Often Quaker volunteers organized this; a tobacconist named William Rawes and two other Quakers toured Dorset and Somerset gathering names, for instance. Individual sheets of parchment, once covered with signatures, were sewn together into long scrolls; the bigger the scroll, the more dramatic the moment when it was carried into the chamber of the House of Commons and ceremoniously placed on a wooden table. As the rolls of parchment flowed to London, the abolition committee wrote to the mayor of every town that had not yet sent one, trying to stimulate more.

Petitions were a time-honored means of pressure in a country where voters had no control whatever over the House of Lords, and where fewer than one adult man in ten could vote for the House of Commons. They were the nearest thing to a referendum. The right to petition was recognized in the Magna Carta, the charter of liberties demanded from a resentful King John in 1215, restated forcefully in the Bill of Rights won by Britons in 1689, and was considered important enough to be enshrined in the First Amendment to the U.S. Constitution. A final spark for the American Revolution, after all, had been King George III's refusal to accept a petition about the colonists' grievances. The British Parliament took the subject seriously enough to pass an Act Against Tumultuous Petitioning (no more than ten people may present one), still on the books today. The 1788 abolition petitions outnumbered those on all other subjects combined.

In other campaigns over the years, most petitions had come from groups touting their status: nobles, magistrates, clergy, Oxford or Cambridge professors. Seventy percent of the sudden wave of abolition petitions, however, came simply from the "inhabitants" of a city or town, a figure that would eventually approach 100 percent as the campaign went on. The movement was rapidly taking on a highly democratic flavor. At least two dozen of the petitions had their start at public meetings against the slave trade, and one at Leeds explicitly invited signatures from "the rough sons of lowest labour." Something new and subversive was making its first appearance: the systematic mobilization of public opinion across the class spectrum.

"Even those who have no vote, are nevertheless comprehended in our idea of the public mind," declared one of the abolition committee's pamphlets. "Nor is any man of sense and virtue . . . to be deemed of no account. Upon his judgment, his voice (if not his vote), his example, much may depend." But if any man's judgment mattered, people might ask, why couldn't any man vote? And if the voice of any man counted, why not that of any woman? Without ever intending to do so, the abolitionists helped put these questions in the air.

Gathering signatures was one thing, but getting the political establishment to change course quite another. Landowners and merchants alike were intricately tied to slavery. William Beckford, the famously hot-tempered Lord Mayor of London known as "Alderman Sugar-Cane," was the richest absentee plantation owner of his time; his dozen properties in Jamaica, where Beckford had spent his boyhood, were worked by more than two thousand slaves. Most daunting was the strong West Indian influence in Parliament itself. Even though London was the abolitionists' base, the city was also a slave ship port and the headquarters for the bankers and brokers who financed the sugar plantations. All four of its representatives in the House of Commons were proslavery. All told, several dozen M.P.s owned West Indian plantation land.

The eighteenth-century Parliament, soon to become the battleground on the issue of slavery, was long used to polite duels of wit among landed gentry discussing game laws and the like. An exclusive club, it had only recently and grudgingly begun to tolerate newspaper reporters taking notes on its debates. Members were not accustomed to feeling the pressure of public opinion on issues framed as burning moral questions. It was said that a bird could nest in the wig of the speaker of the House of Commons and never be roused from slumber. Such a bird, it appeared, would soon sleep no longer.

Wilberforce was ready to raise the issue of the slave trade in Parliament's 1788 session. But before he could do so, he fell ill. His diary and letters are filled with cryptic references: "very unwell," "great langour, total loss of appetite, flushings, &c.," "head utterly unfit for business." He was, his two sons recorded enigmatically, suffering from "an entire decay of all the vital functions." Fearing for his life, his doctors ordered him rushed to Bath by coach. Eventually he was restored to fragile health, by drinking the waters of Bath, the passage of time, or the doctors' insistence that he take a favorite eighteenth-century medicine, opium, which he would continue to do for the rest of his life. With Wilberforce out of action, his friend Prime Minister Pitt moved that the slave trade debate be postponed.

One slavery-related bill did pass Parliament that year. Sir William Dolben, a friend of Wilberforce, led a group of M.P.s to visit a slave ship being outfitted in the Thames. Horrified by its cramped quarters, Dolben introduced a bill limiting, according to a ship's tonnage, the number of slaves it could carry, and requiring every ship to have a doctor as well as to keep a register of slave and crew deaths. The abolition committee feared Dolben's bill would establish, as one member put it, "the Principle that the Trade was in itself just but had been abused." Nonetheless, this was the first British legislation of any kind to regulate the trade; its vocal supporters included one M.P. with the notable name of John P. Bastard. They also included Equiano, who evidently figured that a regulatory bill was better than none. He led a black delegation to Commons and was received by Dolben, Pitt, and other M.P.s.

Angry Liverpool ship owners sent a rival group to lobby against the bill. "God knows what will be the consequence if the present Bill is passed! . . . It may end in the destruction of all the whites in Jamaica," wrote Stephen Fuller, London agent for the island's planters. The Lord High Chancellor scorned the measure as the product of a "five days fit of philanthropy." An exasperated Dolben mocked the Liverpool ship owners who claimed that "the ships most crowded were the most healthy" and that "the time passed on board a ship, while transporting from Africa to the colonies, was the happiest part of a negro's life." If this were so, he challenged them, why not take the voyage themselves, in "dangerous storms and perilous gales, rolling about with shackles upon them, in their own sickness and its consequences," and then come and address the House "after experiencing these extraordinary proofs of happiness"? Weakened by amendments and often to be evaded in practice, the Dolben bill finally passed.

Mild as the bill was, abolition agitation spread horror in the slave ports. "To abandon [the trade] to our rivals the French would be to stab the vitals of this nation, as a trading people," one resident of Bristol wrote to a newspaper, "and leave our posterity to be in time Slaves themselves." Equally alarmed were the West Indian planters, who had long known that they were sitting on a powder keg. On every island, there were vastly more slaves than whites; on Tobago, for example, the ratio was twenty to one. On remote plantations it might be fifty or sixty to one. The planter lobby in London felt helpless to stem the outbreak of antislavery fever. "The Press teems with pamphlets upon this subject, and my table is covered with them. . . . The stream of popularity runs against us," Fuller reported to his Jamaican employers. And to a proslavery M.P. he voiced the fear in the minds of all West Indian whites: "Your Lordship may depend upon it, that during the time this business is agitated in parliament, the slaves will be minutely acquainted with all the proceedings. . . . They will . . . strike while the iron is hot, and by a sudden blow finish the business themselves."

With Wilberforce recovering, the abolitionists hoped to bring banning the slave trade before Parliament at last, but their plans were again derailed by illness. King George III went mad. He had been behaving oddly for weeks before leaping from his chair at dinner one evening, grabbing the Prince of Wales, and smashing his head against the wall.

This unexpected turn of events raised the prospect of the King's removal from power. The Prince of Wales was a drunkard and womanizer transparently eager to be made Regent in place of his mad father. Parliament began a contentious months-long debate over whether the Prince should become Regent, and with what powers. All legislation was put on hold, because no bill passed by Parliament became law until signed by King or Regent.

The King's illness riveted the country. Reports circulated of how he talked for nineteen hours nonstop, or believed that he could see Germany through a telescope. He issued orders to people who were dead and gave promotions and honors to servants who happened to enter the room. His limbs shook in violent fits, and he turned so thin that the palace staff removed mirrors lest he be shocked by what he would see.

Eminent doctors authoritatively diagnosed the King's illness as "the flying gout," prescribed mustard plasters and purges, and ordered that the royal scalp be shaved and blistered to draw the poisonous "humours" from his brain. His Majesty was given a large dose of a popular nostrum, Dr. James's Powder, a powerful laxative advertised as suitable for "all Inflammatory and Epidemical Disorders, as well as for those which are called Nervous, Hypochondriac and Hysteric." The King, reported to be making "a new noise in imitation of the howling of a dog," was tied to his bed at night and put in a straitjacket by day. Not surprisingly, he cursed his physicians. He believed he was the King of Persia, foamed at the mouth, turned red in the face, planned the building of new palaces, and talked incessantly of bedding the Earl of Pembroke's wife (which may not have been such a mad idea, for she was a great beauty). British political life remained at a standstill, for no major question could be settled until the King's situation was resolved.

10

A PLACE BEYOND THE SEAS

AT THE SAME MOMENT in history that Britons began paying attention to the plight of slaves in the West Indies, more also started to notice the free blacks in London itself. The number of these grew throughout the 1780s as some of the slaves freed by the British proclamation during the American Revolutionary War made their way to England. There were now at least five thousand black men and women in the capital, and perhaps twice that number in Britain. No one in London could miss them. Blacks played in the bands of the Royal Artillery and of many fashionable regiments, which vied with one another in outfitting their musicians with ever-fancier bearskin hats, turbans, sashes, scimitars, or coats with silver buttons and fur trim. The black writer, composer, and shopkeeper Ignatius Sancho, born on a slave ship, had his portrait painted by Gainsborough. Samuel Johnson left much of his estate to his beloved valet-butler-secretary, Francis Barber, originally brought to England from Jamaica as a slave. The mulatto child prodigy George Bridgetower played the violin on the London stage; Beethoven later wrote the "Kreutzer" Sonata for him. Billy Waters, a former Royal Navy sailor who had lost a leg after falling from a topsail yardarm, wore a red vest and feathered hat and played the violin outside the Adelphi Theatre in the Strand. (He and his companion, African Sal, briefly moved inside the theater to play themselves in a show called *Life in London.*) One black prostitute claimed twenty members of the House of Lords as customers.

But freedom alone was hardly enough; of the capital's blacks, one observer noted, "those who are not in livery are in rags." A petition to the government from six black veterans said that their discharge at the end of the American war "leaves us, dark coloured Men, the unemployed, unprotected, & homeless Objects of Poverty, Want & Wretchedness." Except for house servants, blacks mostly lived in the slums of the city's East End. Many had trouble finding work, and few had skilled jobs. Some sang on the street or begged. Some ended up in the workhouse; three, only in their thirties, died in one at Wapping. Landlords' "enclosures" of what had once been commonly used grazing and cropland caused the jobless rural poor to flock to London from all over the British Isles, and, as whites, they were first in line for any available menial work. In petitioning for help, one black man wrote, "I endeavour'd to get Work but cannot get Any I am Thirty Nine Years of Age & am ready & willing to serve His Britinack Majesty While I am Able But I am realy starvin about the Streets Having Nobody to give me A Morsel of bread & dare not go home to my Own Country again."

This was, however, the dawn of the great age of British charitable groups, whose very names weave a tapestry of imperial confidence that for every problem there is a solution. As a later description put it, "Ours is the age of societies. For the redress of every oppression that is done under the sun, there is a public meeting. For the cure of every sorrow by which our land or our race can be visited, there are patrons, vice-presidents, and secretaries. For the diffusion of every blessing of which mankind can partake in common, there is a committee." A myriad of associations were springing up, from the Humane Society for the Recovery of Drowned and Suffocated Persons to the Ladies Association for the Benefit of Gentlewomen of Good Family, Reduced in Fortune below the State of Comfort to Which They Have Been Accustomed. There were committees for converting Gypsies to Christianity, for the relief of clergymen's widows, and for rescuing "Forlorn Females," foreign visitors, and seamen in distress. So perhaps it was only natural that there should have appeared, the year before the first meeting of the abolition committee (a few people would be members of both), a Committee for the Relief of the Black Poor. With it begins another strand of our story, but one that will soon intersect with the others.

No philanthropic venture ever included more oddballs. First among them was Henry Smeathman, the naturalist we briefly met spending a memorable evening with the slave traders of Bance Island (see page 26), who had studied plants and insects on the Sierra Leone coast, where he took two African wives. Smeathman read a paper on African termites to the Royal Society, and, in a letter to a friend, painted a glorious picture of Sierra Leone: "Pleasant scenes of vernal beauty, a tropical luxuriance, where fruit and flowers lavish their fragrance together on the same bough! . . . I contemplate the years which I passed in that terrestrial Elysium, as the happiest of my life."

Smeathman's dream was to create a colonial settlement of emancipated slaves in this tropical paradise. Products of his Elysium, he claimed, could successfully compete with both "the riches of the East" and the slave-grown produce of the Americas. "Nothing is wanted but encouragement, to procure great quantities of cotton, as fine as the E. Indian, and tobacco as the Brazilian; also sugar and a species of indigo infinitely superior to that of the west." Fleeing creditors, Smeathman went to France, where he pushed his idea on everyone, including the representative of the newly independent American states. "Master Termites is gone to Paris," a friend wrote, "to tell Dr. Franklin of his plan for civilising Africa."

Benjamin Franklin had other priorities, however. Smeathman, a man of many enthusiasms, turned to hot-air balloons and invented one that, he claimed, could be steered in flight, "a vessel to represent a mixed form of a fish, a bird and a bat." The balloon, he hoped, would finance his "African Plan," about which he swore he could not think "without a sort of . . . delirium. . . . This fit is too often followed by a great depression of spirits; you may call one the hot and the other the cold fit."

Smeathman's hot-fit African Plan, as it happened, came along at just the right moment for Granville Sharp, who received black paupers and gave them money for food every Monday morning. When they heard about Smeathman's idea, he writes, "Many of them came to consult me about the proposal." For Sharp and other Britons opposed to slavery, the idea of a settlement of free blacks in Africa had great appeal. It would help former slaves to prosper, and would prove that Africa could be the source of something other than endless raw material for the slave trade. It was abolition in practice.

Sharp, too, had his hot fits. The temperature clearly rose, for example, whenever he thought of an ancient system of government called frankpledge, and in a Sierra Leone settlement, he saw a God-given chance to satisfy his passion for it and to smite slavery at the same time. The origin of frankpledge lay in the ill-documented and romanticized Anglo-Saxon past. As Sharp grandly resurrected frankpledge for use in Sierra Leone, families would be divided into groups of ten households, called "tithings," ten of these making up a "hundred." Each tithing would elect a "headborough," and each hundred a "hundreder." "The most essential branch of it," he declared, was "a constant watch and ward, by regular rotation, of all the males from sixteen to sixty, with their own arms in their own hands," protecting the community from violent or "morose" individuals. He claimed that frankpledge in some form had been practiced by the ancient Israelites, the early Christians, and even "savage and heathen nations," and he therefore had boundless confidence in "this glorious Patriarchal system; which is the only effectual antidote to unlimited or illegal government of any kind." Sharp urged Benjamin Franklin—who seems to have been at the receiving end of many suggestions—to adopt frankpledge for "your States."

A portrait of Sharp at this stage in his life shows his hair in a pigtail, a prominent nose, and a stern, thin visage, very much the face of a man with absolute certainty that he has the correct answer to any question. On hearing about Smeathman's plan, Sharp rushed out a pamphlet. The titles of his works, one scholar observes, are sometimes essays in themselves, and this one was no exception: *Memorandum on a late Proposal for a New Settlement to be made on the Coast of* AFRICA*; recommending to the Author of that Proposal, several Alterations in his Plan, and more especially the Adoption of the ancient Mode of Government by Tithings (or Decenaries) and Hundreds, as being the most useful and effectual Mode of Government for all Nations and Countries.*

Rigid as were Sharp's prescriptions, there is still in them something far ahead of his time. No one else in the 1700s, after all, was talking about a community of black people governing themselves according to the will of "the majority of the settlers . . . because they themselves will certainly be the most competent judges of their own situation and affairs." Fines for criminal offenses would be levied "in due proportion to the wealth and possessions of the delinquent," while in the settlement's prison there would be conjugal visits. Finally, the settlement must be established with "the consent (and association, if possible) of the *native inhabitants.*" All this was far more idealistic than many later Utopian communities: Brook Farm in Massachusetts, for instance, never invited American Indians to join.

Meanwhile, there remained the black poor on Sharp's doorstep, whom, during the particularly harsh winter of 1785–86, a group of prominent Londoners had begun to feed and clothe. The first sign of this work was a newspaper notice: "A Gentleman, commiserating these unhappy People has made a Beginning to this Charitable Work by authorising Mr. Brown, Baker, in Wigmore Street, Cavendish-square, to give a Quartern Loaf [of bread] to every Black in Distress." Before long, nearly a thousand blacks were on relief.

The "Gentleman" involved, Jonas Hanway, was the third in this trio of eccentrics. A philanthropist and pamphleteer, he had strong feelings about the proper paving of streets, good ventilation, and prison reform. He vigorously denounced the keeping of pets and the use of ostrich plumes in women's dress—why not use the feathers of good British birds like the goldfinch and the peacock? Wearing a sword at all times, he opposed dueling. Hanway is best remembered for being one of the first men to walk the streets of London under an umbrella—"derided but dry," as one writer has put it—and for condemning the "pernicious custom" of drinking tea.

Tea, Hanway was certain, led to insomnia, scurvy, "lassitudes," "melancholy," "feminine disorders," rotting of the teeth, early death, and the dangerous export of British gold to the Orient in payment. Furthermore, "the loss of time taken in . . . washing the dishes, sweetening the tea, spreading the bread and butter, the necessary pause which defamation and malicious tea-table chat afford . . . largely account[s] for half a day . . . spent in . . . worse than doing nothing."

When Hanway founded the Magdalen House for Penitent Prostitutes, its inmates were to be rescued from sin by means of gray woolen clothes, Bible readings, knitting, and a tea-free diet.

Hanway's Committee for the Relief of the Black Poor quickly attracted donations from various notables, including the Duchess of Devonshire and Prime Minister Pitt, who sent 5 guineas. Because so many blacks were military veterans, people felt that Britain owed them something. (Indeed, public sympathy was so strong, one newspaper reported, that white beggars sometimes wore blackface to increase their take.) But the committee's most generous supporters were members of the nascent antislavery movement who saw helping London's black poor as part of the same cause. Before long, the committee was giving out soup, meat, and bread daily from rented rooms at two pubs; it also provided bare-bones housing, an infirmary, and free clothing.

But blacks needed jobs that London didn't have. Could they be helped to emigrate somewhere? One letter to a newspaper suggested Nova Scotia as a destination, because of the three thousand ex-slaves who had gone there from New York in 1783. But in that community—to which we will return—all was not well, and the idea of sending more free blacks there was dropped.

For some white Londoners racism clearly was a motive for wanting to resettle the poor blacks abroad; Britons had had such impulses ever since, nearly two hundred years earlier, Queen Elizabeth I, alarmed at the presence of "divers blackamores brought into this realm, of which kinde of people there are already to manie," had ordered them "sent forth from the land." Hanway himself felt that emigration would "prevent the unnatural connections between black persons and white." However, many of the poor blacks themselves were eager to leave England to find a better life. Their hopes rose when, in 1786, the House of Commons asked the King to provide for sending "distressed Black Persons . . . to such Place beyond the Seas as shall by His Majesty be thought best."

Exactly where beyond the seas? Enter termite expert Henry Smeathman, who enthusiastically declared Sierra Leone the ideal spot. "Such are the mildness and fertility of the climate and country, that a man possessed of a change of clothing, an axe, a hoe, and a pocket knife, may soon place himself in an easy and comfortable situation. . . . The earth turned up . . . 2 or 3 inches, with a light hoe, produces any kind of grain." The land was so rich, he swore, that even enslaved blacks—it was a bit foggy just how they would get to Sierra Leone—could, with merely a year's work, "pay for their redemption."

Smeathman's assurance that crops virtually cultivated themselves in this part of Africa was convincing, since not only had he lived there, but he was also volunteering to lead this expedition to Eden himself. The Committee for the Relief of the Black Poor happily accepted his proposal. The British government promised to supply the necessary transport ships and three months' worth of supplies. After that, in the verdant, fertile land Smeathman had described, the settlement would be self-supporting. Strangely, neither the government nor any of the earnest philanthropists involved paused to consider Sierra Leone's role as a major center of the slave trade.

Some of the black poor, however, were all too aware of this. Meeting at one of the pubs where relief was handed out, a group of them refused to sign on unless the government promised they would not be sold as slaves on reaching Africa. Jonas Hanway appealed to them "as an old man on the Confines of Eternity, who had no worldly Interest to serve, [that] he must be the worst of all the wicked on Earth to deceive them." Still uneasy, the blacks demanded a written guarantee, plus arms for hunting and self-defense.

In the summer of 1786, in the midst of plans for the expedition's departure, Henry Smeathman most inconveniently, in the words of a contemporary, "was taken ill of a fever, and died in about three days." Subsequently, the committee discovered that he had been embezzling their money to pay his debts. Only two months later, Jonas Hanway crossed over the "Confines of Eternity" as well.

With Smeathman and Hanway gone, Granville Sharp became the leading figure in the project, and his strong antislavery credentials relieved many blacks of their anxieties. He now turned his attention to finding a suitable clergyman to accompany the settlers, finally accepting one supplied by the Society for the Propagation of the Gospel (the same group that owned the Codrington slave plantation in Barbados). Fervent as ever about the Church of England, Sharp felt strongly that

"*Pagans, Papists, Mohametans, Infidels &c.*" should not be allowed in the new colony. The relief committee also purchased copies of a tract called *Christian Doctrines and Instructions for Negroes,* for, besides helping freed slaves, the Sierra Leone project was very much about bringing Christianity and British influence to Africa. The tension between the democratic and the imperial sides of this enterprise would only deepen over the years.

Sharp was still as active as ever in defending blacks in distress; in July 1786, for instance, he helped save an ex-slave named Henry Demane from being forced onto a ship for the West Indies, and persuaded him to sign up for the Sierra Leone expedition. He reached into his pocket to redeem from pawnshops the possessions of several prospective settlers. As the first group boarded ships for Sierra Leone in November, they took with them a 226-page book of Sharp's rules and regulations for frankpledge. Each group of a hundred households was to mount a nightly "watch and ward" patrol of three people while two other patrols were "stationed at the gate-house, or watchtower," the patrols changing places at two-hour intervals. A weekly court for every forty households was to meet each Saturday afternoon, except for the last Saturday of the first and second months of the quarter, when there was a court for each hundred-household unit, and the last Saturday of the third month of the quarter, when there was a court for the whole settlement. Bewilderingly, Sharp used old Anglo-Saxon terms: the hundred-household court was a Wappentac, a council meeting was a Folkmote, and so on. In an appendix of more than fifty pages he gave prayers to be used at every conceivable occasion.

As preparations mounted, the navy, whose ships were to carry the settlers, needed a "commissary"—a supervisor of stores and supplies for the expedition. It turned to Olaudah Equiano. As a literate African respected by London's blacks, who knew English ways, basic accounting, and ships and the sea, he was the obvious man for the job. It was the highest position a black person had ever held under the British government, and he was among the 459 passengers who finally boarded the ships.

Besides the black poor, the group included seventy of their white wives or common-law wives, plus several dozen other whites, from gardeners to doctors, recruited for their skills. The ships pulled away from the London docks and headed down the Thames in February 1787, only to find themselves caught in a series of winter storms that tore part of the foremast off one vessel and caused another to spring leaks. While the convoy was anchored at Portsmouth for lengthy repairs, Equiano and the expedition's white superintendent, with confusingly overlapping responsibilities, fell into a furious row. Equiano, vocally supported by many blacks, accused the other man of pocketing expedition funds. Both sides took their accusations to the newspapers, which printed a jumble of fact and rumor. Since the ships did have to unexpectedly take on substantial additional supplies at the last minute, Equiano's charge may have been true. His friend James Ramsay felt that the authorities were simply not willing to tolerate a black man this strong and independent in the job.

The third top official of the venture, an abolitionist Royal Navy officer named Thomas Boulden Thompson, captain of the escort vessel, the *Nautilus,* complained to his superiors that the settlers were "troublesome and discontented," that Equiano had taken "every means to actuate the minds of the Blacks to discord," and that the white superintendent was not suited "to conduct this business." In the end, however, it was Equiano who lost his job, even though the Navy Board declared him to have "acted with great propriety and been very regular in his information." More than two dozen other "discontented persons," white and black, were also sent ashore at the last minute. Finally, on April 9, the fleet of four ships hoisted their anchors and sailed for Sierra Leone, to begin an unprecedented experiment in establishing an interracial free community on a continent racked by slavery.

11

"RAMSAY IS DEAD— I HAVE KILLED HIM"

GEORGE III's madness, which had brought British political life to a virtual halt towards the end of 1788, continued into the next year. One newspaper reported that the King walked up to an oak tree outside Windsor Palace, took a branch, and shook it, convinced he was talking with the King of Prussia. A duchess claimed that the King pulled off his doctor's wig and picked the pocket of his page. It was said that he planted some beef in his garden, to grow a herd of cattle.

A bill to install the eager Prince of Wales as Regent passed the House of Commons. Just before Lords could vote on the bill, however, encouraging news arrived. The King had sung "Rule, Britannia" to his Queen and daughters, and this was considered by all a sign of returning sanity. And he himself thought he had no more need of a physician, for when he came upon his chief gardener filling a basket with fruit, he said, "Get another basket, Eaton, and pack up the doctor in it and send him off at the same time." At the beginning of March, King and Queen slept in the same bed for the first time in months, and soon afterwards a "Prayer of Thanksgiving upon the King's Recovery" was distributed to churches throughout the realm. At fetes and balls women wore headbands with "God Save the King" spelled out in diamonds. Throughout London, celebratory lanterns burned in windows (except those of Quakers, who did not believe in such extravagance). Fireworks filled the sky, and even the lowliest cobblers' stalls were decorated with farthing candles.

Modern medical historians believe the King to have suffered from porphyria, a rare blood disease that can cause hysteria. Whatever the case, the King would, later in life, again experience baffled doctors, straitjackets, and the delusion that he was married to the beautiful Lady Pembroke. But for now he was sane, and the news spread far and wide. When it reached Naples, the British envoy summoned all his compatriots in the city for a party where, he wrote to a friend, "there shall be such a sirloin of Beef on my table as I am sure never appear'd before . . . in this country where nobody seems to give themselves any trouble to be well served." The Prince of Wales was in disgrace, his carriage jeered in the London streets. Pitt, who had stayed loyal to the King, was cheered by crowds, and his authority as Prime Minister was enhanced. Political life resumed, and at last the stage was set for Wilberforce to introduce an abolition bill in the 1789 session of Parliament.

The way to the debate was paved by ongoing hearings on the slave trade, begun under abolitionist pressure the previous year. These were being held before one of those ancient and near-powerless bodies that have long festooned British political life: the Committee on Trade and Plantations of the Privy Council. Nonetheless, the hearings were vital, for through them the abolitionists were able to put a huge amount of material on the public record. This was the first time in any country that the slave trade had been subject to an official investigation, and the resulting testimony is a crucial source of information to us still.

Proslavery forces were relieved that a reliable supporter, Lord Hawkesbury, was president of the Committee on Trade and Plantations. Hawkesbury owned land in the West Indies and his chief clerk was the London representative of the planters of the Bahamas. There was even a slave ship named in his honor. However, he turned out to be hard-working and surprisingly fair. He requested statistics and reports from slave traders, missionaries, colonial legislatures, and other slave-trading countries. He inquired how much space was allocated to soldiers in troopships, to see how this compared to conditions for slaves. He asked the British envoy in Warsaw what had been the results when the serfs in the Austrian-controlled parts of Poland were freed several years earlier.

Still off balance from the upwelling of public feeling against the trade, proslavery forces for the first time sensed that making their usual case that British prosperity rested on the West Indies might not be enough. Some ship owners now threatened to take their business—and its thousands of jobs—overseas. A manifesto from one group of traders claimed that several "British merchants . . . have lately moved a considerable share of their capital to France." To the abolitionists, this underlined how urgent it was to make their movement international.

Answering questions about conditions on the slave ships, one proslavery witness at the hearings swore that slaves were so relieved at escaping Africa's barbarism that "Nine out of Ten rejoice at falling into our Hands." Lord Rodney, a famous admiral, declared that he had never seen a Negro flogged half as severely as an English schoolboy. James Penny, a former captain, made the slaves on the Atlantic crossing sound almost like cruise passengers: "If the Weather is sultry, and there appears the least Perspiration upon their Skins, when they come upon Deck, there are Two Men attending with Cloths to rub them perfectly dry, and another to give them a little Cordial. . . . They are then supplied with Pipes and Tobacco . . . they are amused with Instruments of Music peculiar to their own country . . . and when tired of Music and Dancing, they then go to Games of Chance."

Clarkson took charge of organizing abolition witnesses. He produced Ramsay, Falconbridge, and many others. John Newton, with the added authority of his fame as an Evangelical preacher, was a witness no one dared impugn. Clarkson himself testified, covering his mop of red hair with a curled, powdered wig. "Monstrous calumnies," thundered an angry proslavery spokesman in response. "I do not believe that a series of more abominable falsehoods ever blotted a page in the wide history of human depravity!" To the hearings Clarkson brought his box of African trading goods (without ever stopping to think, it seems, that most African products were made or harvested by indigenous slave labor). Like a traveling salesman's sample case, it was divided into sections. One held four-inch squares of a dozen kinds of mahogany and other woods; another, ivory, pepper, cinnamon, rice, cotton, and dried fruits; a third, a small African loom and spindle, cloth, pipe bowls, and ornaments; and a fourth, the slave trader's instruments he had bought in Liverpool: thumbscrew, iron punishment collar, chains, shackles, the speculum oris for prying slaves' mouths open, plus a rope's end knotted into a large ball to show how British sailors were beaten to death. The Privy Council called no ex-slaves to testify, but this did not stop Equiano from writing a long letter to Lord Hawkesbury, which he also published in a London newspaper.

When the Privy Council took a break, Clarkson rode 1,600 miles in two months, scouring the country for more witnesses. All too often, he complained, "when I took out my pen and ink to put down the information, which a person was giving me, he became . . . embarrassed and frightened." For a seaman to testify, of course, meant that he could never find work in the slave trade again.

Incapable of not organizing, Clarkson founded local offshoots of the abolition committee while on the road. The chairman of one new branch he set up, in the port city of Plymouth, soon produced something that immediately spread excitement in antislavery circles. Equiano, always eager to celebrate whatever could advance the cause, quickly wrote to the Plymouth committee: "Having seen a plate . . . which you are pleased to send to the Rev. Mr. Clarkson, a worthy friend of mine, I was filled with love and gratitude." The "plate" was a diagram, with top, side, and end views, of a fully loaded slave ship, the *Brookes,* owned by a Liverpool family of that name, which carried slaves from the Gold Coast to Jamaica.

With the help of James Phillips and other committee members, Clarkson reworked and expanded the diagram. It gave measurements in feet and inches while showing the slaves closely lined up in rows, lying flat, bodies touching one another or the ship's hull. As in all its work, the committee took great care not to exaggerate: the diagram showed 482 slaves, although on several earlier voyages, under "tight-packing" captains, the *Brookes* had carried anywhere from 609 to 740. The diagram began appearing in newspapers, magazines, books, and pamphlets; realizing what a powerful new weapon it had, the committee also promptly printed up more than seven thousand copies as posters, which were hung on the walls of homes and pubs throughout the country.

Iconic images have power because they allow us to see what previously we could barely imagine. Today we are accustomed to photographs: the emaciated faces staring out of the bunks at a Nazi concentration camp, the napalmed naked Vietnamese girl running down a road, the lone Chinese man facing down a tank near Tiananmen Square. In an era before photography, the *Brookes* diagram "seemed to make an instantaneous impression of horror upon all who saw it," wrote Clarkson. Long afterwards, the daughter of abolition committee charter member Samuel Hoare recalled how "horrible engravings of the interior of a slave ship were pinned against the walls of our dining room." In this highly religious age, the image carried additional force because it seemed a sinister echo of a scene familiar to all: detailed drawings of the animals in Noah's Ark.

You have seen this diagram. Rare is the illustrated schoolbook of world history, or book or television documentary about the slave trade, that does not show the famous top-down schematic view of the *Brookes,* with the slaves' bodies as close together as anchovies in a can. Part of its brilliance was that it was unanswerable. What could the slave interests do, make a poster of happy slaves celebrating on shipboard? Precise, understated, and eloquent in its starkness, it remains one of the most widely reproduced political graphics of all time.

Through means like this, the committee's impact was now reverberating around the Atlantic world. On the French sugar island of Martinique, an official reported a wave of runaway slaves: "the reason they give is that as all the English Negros are to be made free they have a right to be the same." The Marquis de Lafayette, recently returned from helping the American colonists fight for liberty, sent word that he was starting an abolition group in Paris, the Société des Amis des Noirs. Clarkson thought Lafayette "as uncompromising an enemy of the slave-trade and slavery, as any man I ever knew." Several years before, Lafayette had bought a clove plantation with forty-eight slaves in what was later known as French Guiana, started schools, paid the slaves for work done, and begun emancipating them. (He once told Clarkson, "I would never have drawn my sword in the cause of

America if I could have conceived that thereby I was founding a land of slavery.") The committee rushed to translate more of its literature into French. A powerful movement across the Channel would answer the objection that, if British ships stopped carrying slaves, the French would simply pick up the business. France, however, was under the authoritarian monarchy of Louis XVI, and there was no legislature resembling the British Parliament that could hold hearings or respond to public opinion. The British abolitionists dared not let their hopes soar.

One visitor to London in early 1789 was James Stephen, the young lawyer who had been so shocked, some five years earlier, when a Barbados court sentenced several slaves to be burned alive. Now a family man, he had put his complex tangle of love affairs behind him. His West Indies law practice was thriving, although he refused to own slaves himself and had purchased the freedom of some who belonged to others. Eager to put his legal skills to work on behalf of slaves, he had helped prosecute a white man from St. Kitts who had repeatedly beaten two slave children. (When neighbors complained of their cries, the man had tied pieces of wood into their mouths as gags. To Stephen's outrage, the slave owner was merely fined £2.) "Mr. Stephen breakfasted—slave business," Wilberforce noted in his diary. It was the beginning of a forty-year collaboration over the "slave business." When Stephen returned to the West Indies some months later, he began quietly sending the committee information.

Meanwhile, Clarkson, Ramsay, and their allies continued to organize witnesses for the hearings. Clarkson later declared that this was the most exhausting work he did in his life: he was up past midnight sorting, editing, and copying evidence, firing off ten or twelve letters a day to supporters throughout the British Isles, sometimes riding hundreds of miles to persuade a recalcitrant witness to appear. The most dramatic testimony came as the hearings were drawing to a close. A year and a half earlier, Clarkson had asked two Bristol doctors to keep journals on slave voyages to Africa. Now, when he was in despair—the Privy Council had sharply limited the number of witnesses he could present, and the last of them was finishing his testimony—"who should come up to me but Mr. Arnold!"

The other doctor had died in Africa, and his journal had been buried with him. But the Privy Council decided to allow James Arnold to testify, and he poured out a torrent of names, dates, and details from the voyage he had just returned from, under a particularly brutal Bristol captain. His testimony was a passionate reprise of all the themes the abolitionist witnesses had emphasized. Arnold told of how he had treated British sailors injured by the captain's beatings, and of slaves flogged and tortured; of how the captain kidnapped and enslaved African traders who came on board to sell ivory; and of how the trade corrupted everyone it touched. "A Woman was one Day brought to us to be sold; she came with a Child in her Arms. The Captain refused to purchase her on that Account, not wishing to be plagued with a Child on board; in consequence of this she was taken back to the Shore. On the following Morning, however, she was again brought to us, but without the Child, and she was apparently in great Sorrow. The Black Trader who brought her on board [said] that the Child had been killed in the Night to accommodate us in the Sale."

Following hearings that stretched, with interruptions, for a year, in late April 1789, the Privy Council finally issued an 850-page report, the size of a modern telephone book, which laid out the testimony from both sides. There were less than three weeks remaining for Wilberforce to digest it all before beginning the first parliamentary debate on abolishing the trade. In the meantime, other committee members systematically lobbied both houses of Parliament. London was abuzz. Of a dinner party he attended, the young barrister Samuel Romilly wrote to a friend, "The abolition of the slave trade was the subject of conversation, as it is indeed of almost all conversations."

From James Phillips's presses came another new tool in the abolition arsenal—poetry. The committee mobilized poets much as backers of a cause might today enlist authors to produce op-ed pieces. They urged John Newton, for instance, to ask his friend the well-known poet William Cowper to write some verses, and Cowper responded with "The Negro's Complaint," which, as Clarkson commented, "spread . . . almost over the whole island. . . . It was set to music; and it then found its way into the streets . . . where it was sung as a ballad." It began:

Forc'd from home, and all its pleasures,
Afric's coast I left forlorn;
To increase a stranger's treasures,
O'er the raging billows borne,
Men from England bought and sold me,
Paid my price in paltry gold;
But, though theirs they have enroll'd me,
Minds are never to be sold.

With less success, the other side launched a counterattack. A musical play, *The Benevolent Planters,* opened in 1789 at the Theatre Royal in Haymarket; two black lovers, separated from each other in Africa, end up living on adjoining plantations in the West Indies, reunited, Christianized, and saved from African darkness by their kindly owners.

Literary salvos were but part of the escalating political war, for by this point the proslavery forces had awakened to the danger they faced. Already the furor had depressed Caribbean land prices and discouraged the opening of new sugar plantations. The main proslavery lobby, informally known as the West India Committee, sometimes met at the London Tavern on Bishopsgate, just a few minutes' walk from abolition headquarters on Old Jewry. It brought together two overlapping interest groups. One was composed of the merchants and ship owners who transported slaves to the Americas and West Indian produce to England; the other, more influential, of plantation owners. Some of these landowners had now lived in England all their lives—indeed, many "West Indians" who sat in the House of Commons had never set foot in the islands.

The West India Committee's propaganda campaign, now gearing up, was a lavish affair, paid for by a levy on the members for each barrel of sugar or rum or bag of cotton imported. The fee would vary over the years, a gauge of how embattled the proslavery interests felt. In April 1789, when copies of the slave ship diagram were spreading around the country and Wilberforce was preparing to introduce his abolition bill, the fee shot up from a penny a barrel to sixpence. As the abolition pressures grew still stronger a few years later, that sum would be doubled. We do not know how much money the lobby spent all told, but the amount was substantial. By one estimate the city authorities of Liverpool alone dispensed more than £10,000—the equivalent of some $1.4 million today—and we know that the West India Committee paid £4,400 to a single lobbyist for three years' work. Just as the abolitionists were the prototype of modern citizen activism, so the West India lobby was the prototype of an industry under attack. One of its first impulses was to consider cosmetic changes.* "The vulgar are influenced by names and titles," suggested one proslavery writer that year. "Instead of SLAVES, let the Negroes be called ASSISTANT-PLANTERS; and we shall not then hear such violent outcries against the slave-trade by pious divines, tender-hearted poetesses, and short-sighted politicians."

On May 12, 1789, Wilberforce rose to make his first speech against slavery, in the famous voice that, as one observer noted, was "so distinct and melodious that . . . if he talked nonsense you would feel obliged to hear him." He spoke from notes for three and a half hours. His fellow parliamentarian Edmund Burke, himself one of history's great speakers, claimed that Wilberforce's speech was "equal to any thing . . . ever heard . . . in modern oratory; and perhaps . . . not excelled by any thing to be met with in Demosthenes."

What strikes the reader of this speech today, however, is less its eloquence than its extreme politeness. Wilberforce attacked no one in Britain for the evils of the slave trade. "We ought all to plead guilty," he declared. Appalled as he was by the dreadful conditions on the slave ships, he was no less sure that the ship owners would be as well. "I . . . believe them to be men of humanity. . . . If the wretchedness of any *one* of the many hundred negroes stowed in each ship could be brought before their view . . . there is no one among them, whose heart would bear it." He knew that plantation slaves suffered terribly, but often this was because cruel managers ignored the enlightened in-

* The planters were also developing public relations skills on the West Indian islands themselves. James Stephen noticed how they gave Potemkin village tours to naïve visitors. If a traveler asked to see the slave quarters, he or she was ushered through homes of the elite "drivers, carpenters, masons . . . [or] chiefs of the gang," who usually lived only one family to a hut, not the far more crowded homes of common field hands.

structions of owners in England (who of course included many M.P.s listening to his speech). He reserved especially harsh words for something neither the owners of ships nor of plantations were directly involved in: the incentive the trade gave African chiefs and kings to wage war. "In Africa, it is the personal *avarice* and *sensuality* of their kings . . . we depend upon . . . for the very maintenance of the Slave Trade. Does the king of Barbessin want brandy? He has only to send his troops, in the night-time, to burn and desolate a village; the captives will serve as commodities, that may be bartered with the British trader."

Wilberforce assured the merchants and planters that, with the slave trade ended, they could still prosper. Ships could carry other cargoes, and slave plantations would only become more profitable: "When the manager shall know, that a fresh importation is not to be had from Africa . . . humanity must be introduced . . . an assiduous care of [the slaves'] health . . . will take place. . . . Births will thus encrease naturally . . . each generation will then improve upon the former, and thus will the West Indies themselves eventually profit by the abolition of the Slave Trade." He never mentioned the abolitionist hope that this nebulous process would cause slavery itself to wither away.

If Britain were to give up the trade, he asked, addressing a question on all minds, wouldn't France simply take over the business? At this point, "a cry of assent being heard from several parts of the House," Wilberforce declared that the same could be said of any evil. "For those who argue thus may argue equally, that we may rob, murder, and commit any crime, which any one else would have committed, if we did not."

Wilberforce's appeal to British virtue moved many, but he failed to assuage fears of French competition and he proved a poor legislative strategist. The slave interests deftly outmaneuvered him. They insisted that the massive Privy Council report—which most members of Parliament had, of course, not even read—was not enough; on such an important subject, the House of Commons must exercise its historic right to hold its own hearings. A convenient excuse for uncertain M.P.s to delay taking a stand, this argument carried the day. Without protest, the gentlemanly Wilberforce, who always acted as if his opponents had only the best of intentions, consented. As Clarkson put it, the whole question was thereby, maddeningly, "by the intrigue of our opponents deferred to another year."

In preparing Wilberforce for the debate in the House, no one had worked harder than Reverend James Ramsay. But the relentless, scurrilous attacks on him continued;* a newspaper article claimed that he sold church artifacts for personal profit. And now came more assaults on the floor of Parliament itself, where Crisp Molyneux, an M.P. who owned a plantation on St. Kitts, where Ramsay had worked, let loose a venomous blast accusing Ramsay of shirking his duties and ignoring sick slaves under his care. Wilberforce, always uncomfortable with personal invective, remained silent, which could only have left Ramsay feeling hurt.

Equiano, by contrast, never hesitated to speak up in the clergyman's defense. "I have known him well both here and in the West Indies for many years," said the former slave in one of several newspaper articles he wrote defending Ramsay. "Many of the facts he relates I know to be true." Equiano's vigorous backing of his friend brought down the wrath of proslavery writers on him in return. To allow a black man like Equiano credit for his arguments, someone wrote under the pen name of "Civis" in the *Morning Chronicle and London Advertiser,* "would not prove equality more, than a pig having been taught to fetch a card, letters, &c., would shew it not to be a pig."

Ramsay, not as resilient as Equiano, felt the toll. He wrote to Clarkson, "The whole of this business I think now to be in such a train, as to enable me to bid farewell to the present scene with the satisfaction of not having lived in vain, and of having done something towards the improvement of our common nature." A few days later, at the age of fifty-five, he died of a massive gastric hemorrhage. Soon after, the lawyer James Stephen reported from St. Kitts that Molyneux had triumphantly written to his son on the island, "Ramsay is dead—I have killed him."

---

* The way his attackers defended slavery could be strange indeed. One dismissed as irrelevant Ramsay's horror that slaves were burned to death by saying that "Negroes condemned to be burnt alive . . . are previously strangled."

The abolitionists' spirits were down: Ramsay was a martyr; the bill in Commons was postponed; and a full-fledged new round of hearings had to be prepared for. Clarkson once again climbed on his horse and set off to organize supporters and look for new witnesses. But soon he received a message calling him back to London. Extraordinary news had just arrived from France. A crowd in Paris had stormed the Bastille, the ancient prison that was a symbol of tyrannical rule. Louis XVI no longer had absolute power. A constitutional monarchy like Britain's seemed to be in the making. Talk of democracy was in the air.

Furthermore, the abolitionist Lafayette, one of the rebels, had been appointed mayor of Paris. Surely he and other French antislavery activists would put banning the slave trade at the top of the new regime's agenda. And if they succeeded, it would make the job in Britain immeasurably easier. Even the cautious Wilberforce felt the "commotions" in France might be good for the cause. Suddenly the committee felt a surge of hope, and decided it was urgent to send someone to coordinate efforts with the French abolitionists.

Clarkson headed for Paris.

III

"A WHOLE NATION CRYING WITH ONE VOICE"

12

AN EIGHTEENTH-CENTURY BOOK TOUR

IN THE SAME MONTH that the abolition committee sent Clarkson to France, Olaudah Equiano set off on a mission of his own. Calling on a clergyman named Jones at Trinity College, Cambridge, he handed him a letter:

> Dear Sir,
>
> I take the Liberty of introducing to your Notice Gustavus Vasa, the Bearer, a very honest, ingenious, and industrious African, who wishes to visit Cambridge. He takes with him a few Histories containing his own life written by himself, of which he means to dispose to defray his Journey. Would you be so good as to recommend the Sale of a few and you will confer a favour on your already obliged and obedient Servant
>
> Thomas Clarkson.

Still known by his slave name, Equiano had written his autobiography, and he was at the beginning of what would be an epic-length book tour.

He was no stranger to the printed word. In the preceding two years he had written some dozen forceful letters to London newspapers, praising new antislavery books, defending abolitionist friends, and protesting a proslavery speech he had heard from the House of Lords visitors' gallery. Knowing that George III was hostile to abolition, he wrote instead to the Queen. He also signed—and probably organized and drafted—more than half a dozen joint letters about slavery from groups of black men in London, who once or twice referred to themselves as the "Sons of Africa."

So familiar a public figure was he that when one London newspaper described a debate at Coachmakers Hall, it reported that a proslavery speaker "was replied to by an African (not Gustavus Vassa)." He did not shy from controversy, and even strongly praised intermarriage—something never endorsed by white abolitionists. For well over a century to come, it would be almost unheard of for anyone to speak as Equiano did in one open letter to a West Indian plantation owner: "A more foolish prejudice than this [against interracial marriage] never warped a cultivated mind. . . . Why not establish intermarriages at home, and in our Colonies? and encourage open, free, and generous love upon Nature's own wide and extensive plan . . . without distinction of the colour of a skin?"

In this stream of letters to the press, he at least once subtly touted the autobiography he was preparing, and when it appeared its two volumes totaled 530 pages: *The Interesting Narrative of the Life of Olaudah Equiano, or Gustavus Vassa the African.* At seven shillings—about $48 today—it became a bestseller. The *Interesting Narrative* was quickly translated into German, Dutch, and Russian, and during the three years after publication was the sole new literary work from England reprinted in the United States.

Its timing could not have been better. As the book appeared in the spring of 1789, the Privy Council was winding up its hearings, the abolition committee was plastering the country with slave ship diagrams, and Wilberforce was arguing for abolition in the House of Commons. Equiano, who clearly saw his writing as part of the campaign, began the book with a petition addressed to Parliament and ended it with his antislavery letter to the Queen. His was the first great political book tour, and never was one undertaken with more determination. He began in London, then went on to other cities, later writing to a sympathetic clergyman in Nottingham: "I trust that my going about has been of much use to the Cause of the abolition of the accu[r]sed Slave Trade—a Gentleman of the Committee the Revd. Dr. Baker has said that I am more use to the Cause than half the People in the Country—I wish to God, I could be so."

Nothing is of more use to a cause than a person who seems to embody it, as, in our own time, the cause of freedom in Tibet has seemed embodied by the Dalai Lama or in apartheid-era South Africa by Nelson Mandela. The tens of thousands of Britons who read Equiano's book or heard him speak got to see slavery through the eyes of a former slave.

Wherever he went Equiano demonstrated his skills of promotion and diplomacy. He offered a discount to readers who bought six copies or more of his book; there was also a deluxe edition "on Fine Paper, at a moderate advance of price." After a particularly friendly welcome in Birmingham, one of the new manufacturing cities now becoming antislavery strongholds, he wrote the local newspaper, thanking by name more than thirty people whose "Acts of Kindness and Hospitality have filled me with a longing desire to see these worthy Friends on my own Estate in Africa, when the richest Produce of it should be devoted to their Entertainment; they should there partake of the luxuriant Pine-apples and the well-flavoured virgin Palm Wine, and to heighten the Bliss, I would burn a certain kind of Tree, that would afford us a Light, as clear and brilliant as the Virtues of my Guests."

In the midst of his book tour, a newspaper reported that Equiano, "well known in England as the champion and advocate for procuring a suppression of the Slave Trade, was married at Soham, in Cambridgeshire to Miss Cullen daughter of Mr. Cullen of Ely, in the same County, in the presence of a vast number of people assembled on the occasion." Equiano did not know his year of birth, but was probably in his mid-forties. Except that he was putting his belief in intermarriage into practice, we know next to nothing about his new wife, whom he may have met through his friendship with Reverend Peter Peckard, the abolitionist vice-chancellor of Cambridge. But his focus on selling his book pushed even his marriage into the background, for he wrote his Nottingham friend shortly before the wedding, "I now mean . . . to . . . take me a Wife . . . & when I have given her about 8 or 10 Days Comfort, I mean Directly to go [to] Scotland—and sell my 5th. Editions."

Susanna Cullen was not the first or last writer's spouse whose marital comfort took second place to book promotion. At least Equiano brought her along for part of his travels. "GUSTAVUS VASSA, with his *white* wife, is at Edinburgh," reported another newspaper. On his honeymoon, however, his mind still seemed to be on sales. "I . . . have sold books at Glasgow & Paisley," he reported to a friend. ". . . I hope next month to go to Dunde[e], Perth & Aberdeen." And to the *Edinburgh Evening Courant* he dashed off an antislavery letter signed with his name and his temporary address on High Street, "where my Narrative is to be had."

Any publisher would be delighted to have such an energetic salesman as an author. Equiano, however, was his own publisher, something more common then than it is today. Self-publishing promised him more profit. Unlike many white abolitionists, he had no family wealth or connections to fall back on, and in his early years he had had bitter experience of white people cheating him out of money due him. Publishing his own book was a successful business move, just like the trading deals he had made while still a slave earning money to buy his freedom.

The book caught on quickly and the first edition of more than seven hundred copies was soon sold out. He issued eight more editions of the *Interesting Narrative* during his lifetime, each prefaced by an ever-lengthening list of "subscribers"—people who had ordered copies and paid half the book's price in advance, thereby financing the printing costs.* The number and rank of an author's sub-

---

* Selling book subscriptions was not for the faint of heart. When another eighteenth-century writer, John Morgan, sought subscribers for his two-volume *Complete History of Algiers,* he complained bitterly that some of the people he approached said, "What care we whether there is any such rascally place as Algiers existing upon God's earth?" He was asking three half-crowns for his first volume, but found buyers "would not give half of three half crowns for the whole Ottoman dominions. . . . Before I would think of again undergoing such fatigue, such scurvy base treatment in hawking about with any work of mine . . . I would sooner choose to be a hackney horse. . . . Nothing in nature would set afloat this book of mine but a war with the Algerines."

scribers were themselves a form of advertising; its nearest equivalent today might be an invitation to a charity banquet listing a "dinner committee" of prominent people who have already bought tables.

The subscriber list at the front of Equiano's first edition included Clarkson (two copies), Sharp (two copies), the Bishop of London, plus an impressive roster of M.P.s, earls, dukes, and even the proslavery Prince of Wales—how Equiano got to him we do not know. He would round up similar lists of notables from the provincial cities where several later editions appeared: 211 people in Hull, 248 in Norwich, and the majority of the professors at the University of Edinburgh. Eventually his subscriber list totaled well over a thousand, some of them buying multiple copies. There are no records of how many copies Equiano sold in all, but it was clearly many times that number.

Being his own publisher gave Equiano control over every aspect of his book. For the frontispiece to the first volume, for instance, he chose an engraving of himself. The image is one of only a handful from the England of this time that show black men or women whose identities we know. Gazing straight at the viewer, Equiano holds an open Bible and wears the gentlemanly attire of the day: ruffled cravat, waistcoat, elegant jacket, lace cuffs. The artist has made no attempt to Europeanize his features; his curly hair, dark skin, and thick lips mark him as a proud African. The frontispiece to the second volume shows a scene from his adventurous life, of Equiano rescuing some white fellow sailors after a shipwreck.

In any town he visited, he immediately looked up local abolitionists for help in making sales, but he also sold copies directly to stores—the *Interesting Narrative* was available at some fifteen bookshops in London alone, all of which he must have visited, books in hand. He sold the copies as well at public lectures he gave, where he had no need to share profits with a bookstore owner. The book reached a wide audience. The pioneer feminist Mary Wollstonecraft reviewed it, and Methodism's founder, John Wesley, read it on his deathbed. Although he had long before taken a strong stand against slavery, he was still shocked to learn from the *Interesting Narrative* that "a man who has a black skin, being wronged or outraged by a white man, can have no redress; it being a *law* in all our Colonies that the *oath* of a black against a white goes for nothing. What villany is this!"

Equiano essentially spent the rest of his working life on a book tour. For more than five years he crisscrossed the British Isles. In Ireland, where activists were agitating for better representation in Parliament and against their status as second-class citizens, he met an especially receptive audience, selling 1,900 copies during an eight-and-a-half-month stay. He found that the Irish, too, felt themselves to be victims of oppression. He was in Ireland when a procession wound through the streets of Belfast to celebrate the second anniversary of the fall of the Bastille. On one side of a great banner was a scene of a crowd storming the prison; on the other was a chained figure representing Ireland; the next banner in the parade denounced the slave trade. This was a heady mix, a sign of rising democratic hopes in a world where up until now hierarchy and domination had been the order of the day.

Irish patriots warmly welcomed him. One of his Belfast supporters introduced him to a friend, writing, "The bearer of this, Mr. GUSTAVUS VASSA, an enlightened African . . . goes to-morrow for your town, for the purpose of vending some books. . . . [He] was a principal instrument in bringing about the motion for the repeal of the Slave-Act." Each time Equiano got such a recommendation, he added it to the lengthening array of endorsement letters that prefaced every new edition of his book. And some stops on the tour allowed him to reinforce his ties with the influential. On his way to sell books in Bristol, he wrote to Josiah Wedgwood, reminding him of an offer of help Wedgwood had once made, should Equiano ever be seized by a press gang. This was not an unreasonable fear, for it was bold and defiant for a black abolitionist to appear in public in a slave ship port. Wedgwood promised to contact the right person at the Admiralty if need be.

The *Interesting Narrative* said much that abolitionist literature by whites could not. Although Equiano's pages on the middle passage and the horrors of West Indian slavery are searing, he knew that most of his audience had by now heard such stories. Nor does he devote much space to the familiar argument that Britain's businessmen had much more to gain from legitimate trade with Africa ("except," he wryly noted, "those persons concerned in the manufacturing [of] neck-yokes, collars, chains, hand-cuffs, leg-bolts . . . thumb-screws, iron-muzzles . . ."). Instead, most of the book is the tale of his own redemptive passage from freedom in Africa through slavery to precarious freedom in England. Equiano wrote with a modern, personal sensibility; he had obviously noticed the huge impact on readers of Newton's and Falconbridge's eyewitness accounts and the similar effect on audiences when he spoke of his experiences. He knew that the most powerful argument against slavery was his own life story.

When Equiano brought his book into the world in 1789, most Britons thought of Africans as heathen illiterates, with minds and bodies alike scorched into strangeness by the intense heat of the tropics. Now suddenly here was a man who was Christian, who could wield the English language well, who had *earned* his freedom by his skill in trading, who had learned to navigate and to play the French horn. Could any reader imagine a more impressive tale of rising in the world through the hard work that the British prized so dearly? "I . . . embraced every occasion of improvement," wrote Equiano of his early days in England, "and every new thing that I observed I treasured up in my memory." He presented himself, in short, as an estimable black Englishman.

Other aspects of his story that obviously appealed to his audience included his curiosity about the world, his acts of patriotic derring-do in the Royal Navy, and his compassion for the British sailors he saw flogged as cruelly as slaves. Further, there was his dislike of the Catholicism he had encountered in Portugal, and the love he declared for the country he made his home, the place "where my heart had always been." He subtly cast some of his antislavery remarks as compliments, as when, on first arriving in England, he found the British "did not sell one another, as we did. . . . I was astonished at the wisdom of the white people in all things I saw."

Equiano had noticed the most popular forms of literature around him—the adventure travelogue, the riches-to-rags-to-riches tale, the religious convert's testimony—and skillfully combined elements of them all. But, more important and lasting, the *Interesting Narrative* is the voice of a brave, resourceful, and compassionate man who on occasion risked much to help those still trapped in slavery. Equiano put on paper a story matched by none of his contemporaries, and one that has lasted. Of the hundreds of books that argued for freedom for the British Empire's slaves, his is the only one a reader can easily find in a British or American bookstore today. Each year more people read it than did so during his entire lifetime.

Equiano must have often wondered what his life would have been like if he had not lost his job with the Sierra Leone venture just before he was scheduled to sail there. He followed news of the settlement closely.

When the little fleet carrying the black and white settlers from London reached its destination, the passengers were awed by the dramatic landfall at Sierra Leone. The name comes from Serra Lyoa, or Lion Mountain, as early Portuguese sailors called the forested range of hills that rise sharply from an otherwise flat coastline to dominate a broad estuary. As the ships dropped anchor on May 10, 1787, it happened to be the very same month, in this age of new beginnings, that another group of people gathered, an ocean away, to begin constructing another new society. But where the law involved women's suffrage, capital punishment, and above all slavery, the Constitutional Convention in Philadelphia would be far less bold.

The Royal Navy escort vessel *Nautilus* fired a thirteen-gun salute to the African ruler on shore, and negotiations for land began. After a few weeks of talk and the payment of various goods, including 130 gallons of rum and two dozen lace-trimmed hats, the settlers acquired a vaguely defined stretch of land at the mouth of the Sierra Leone River for their "Province of Freedom." The European notion of a land purchase lasting in perpetuity was unknown in most of Africa, where political fealty was more to a ruler than to a defined piece of territory. But local leaders, like many Africans in decades to come, were faced with a well-armed Royal Navy ship and agreed to what the white chiefs wanted.

When the news reached Granville Sharp in London, he was jubilant, convinced more than ever that successfully settling free blacks in Sierra Leone would help turn Britain away from the slave trade and towards a more benign relationship with Africa. "They have . . . purchased twenty miles square of the finest and most beautiful country . . . that was ever seen!" he wrote one of his brothers. ". . . Fine streams of fresh water run down the hill on each side of the new township; and in the front is a noble bay." However, the settlers who came ashore could not find what they had been told awaited them in this tropical paradise: neither the supposedly plentiful oyster shells and limestone for making mortar nor the abundance of fruits, ripe for the picking. All they had were Sharp's extremely detailed plans for everything from public holidays to the tax system, which included a somewhat mysterious "*tax on pride and indolence.*" Sharp had also provided bundles of currency, based on the idea that human labor is the source of prosperity. These elaborately printed paper notes, fringed with biblical quotations, could be redeemed not for gold but for a certain number of days of labor.

Following Sharp's frankpledge plans, the black settlers elected one of their number as leader, but the whites seem not to have recognized this. A greater problem was that the expedition's delayed departure from England meant that it had arrived on the African coast in the midst of the malarial rainy season. Soon "fevers, fluxes and bilious complaints" began felling people. In the first four months alone, 122 died. One white settler wrote Sharp, "I am . . . very sorry indeed, to inform you, dear Sir, that . . . I do not think there will be one of us left at the end of a twelvemonth. . . . There is not a thing, which is put into the ground, will grow more than a foot out of it. . . . What is more surprising, the *Natives* die very fast; it is quite a plague seems to reign here among us." Some months later, a black settler informed Sharp that "we came too late to plant any rice, or anything else, for the heavy rains washes all out of the ground," while a newly chosen supervisor, John Reid, had "made away with the chiefest part of the stores, and sold them; and . . . took the opportunity of running away by night, and has been away ever since." But Reid reappeared and soon after wrote to Sharp to complain that "the rain was so heavy it beat the tents down." The settlers sheltered under old sails, donated by the navy. When they managed to coax a few English vegetables out of the ground, ants promptly devoured the leaves.

The ground, in fact, was another major problem: steep, forested slopes with thin topsoil. "When they make a hogshead of sugar there," an English visitor would comment later, "I will engage to do the same at Charing Cross." And it was no simple matter to clear the forest: "Some trees in the country have the peculiar property of letting down from their top branches very straight shoots without leaves, which take root upon reaching the ground. . . . This renders the woods impenetrable."

In honor of Sharp, the settlers named their collection of tents and gardens Granville Town. But the bedraggled settlement's shoreline bordered the deep-water shipping channel in the Sierra Leone River used by slave ships sailing a dozen miles upstream to collect their cargoes at Bance Island. Its former owner, Richard Oswald, was dead, but two of his nephews had inherited control and operated their own slave vessels as well as selling slaves to others. Their agent in charge was outraged when an abolitionist Utopia run by a "very dangerous bad set of people" suddenly appeared next door. The colonists, he declared, had "intermixed with the Natives and have by telling them a number of Falsehoods given them a great many bad Notions of White Men in general that has made them more saucy and troublesome than ever they were known before."

As supplies at Granville Town dwindled and crops failed, the increasingly frustrated settlers turned to the long-time mainstay of the local economy, the slave trade. Ever more of them, white and black, became clerks, carpenters, or shipyard workers at Bance Island, where there were always jobs for experienced and literate workers, whatever their color. Three white doctors from Granville Town ended up at the thriving slave depot also. When the frustrated white chaplain of the settlement could not persuade his parishioners to build him a church or a house, he conducted worship under a tree; then, falling sick, he too sought shelter at Bance Island.

From London, a fuming Sharp wrote an open letter to "the worthy Inhabitants of the Province of Freedom, in the Mountains of Sierra Leone": "I could not have conceived that men who were well aware of the wickedness of slave-dealing, and had themselves been sufferers . . . under the galling yoke of bondage . . . should become so basely depraved as to yield themselves instruments to promote and extend the same detestable oppression over their brethren." He fervently urged that the houses of these "deserters" be seized in punishment, not realizing that many of them had deserted to Bance Island mainly to get a roof over their heads. His horror knew no bounds when he learned that one of those tempted into the slave trade was an ex-slave he had recently rescued from being shipped back to the Caribbean. "Remind Mr. Henry Demane of *his own feelings* under the *horrors of slavery* . . . he is now in danger of *eternal slavery!*"

Looking for an explanation for these defections, Sharp could point only to a traditional villain: rum. Stubbornly insisting that Sierra Leone was "the most eligible spot for . . . settlement on the whole coast of Africa," he dispatched another shipload of black and white settlers and supplies—which included, strangely, twelve hogsheads of porter donated by the brewer Samuel Whitbread. But many settlers on this ship were also "wicked enough to go into the service of the Slave Trade," Sharp later discovered.

The Committee for the Relief of the Black Poor had closed its books after the first convoy departed from London, and the British government's role in the project ended when the navy ships that had carried the settlers to Africa hoisted their sails to return home. Sharp had already contributed more than £1,700 to the venture out of his own pocket. Knowing that finding further charitable contributions would be difficult, he raised more money by founding a private corporation to carry on trade with the colony. Wilberforce, Clarkson, James Phillips, and many other abolitionists bought shares in the new Sierra Leone Company. For all of them, it was an article of faith that Africa had a grand future as a peaceful trading partner for Britain, and that the settlement was a potential cornucopia.

However, no riches flowed back to London, only news of yet another disaster. In 1789, a Royal Navy warship making its way down the coast fired a shot that set a Sierra Leone village on fire. The local chief took revenge by giving the settlers three days to depart, and then burning Granville Town to the ground. Two and a half years after they arrived with such high hopes, the settlers were evacuated. Most humiliatingly, the canoes that came to rescue them were sent by the slave traders of Bance Island.

• • •

Still obsessed with frankpledge, Sharp had recently dispatched to Sierra Leone "six stout watch-coats for the night-watch," although it is unclear how useful thick English overcoats would be a few hundred miles from the equator. Frankpledge or not, he and his fellow investors now felt they urgently needed someone to help get the settlers off Bance Island and back onto land of their own, and to make the whole venture profitable. For this mission they chose Clarkson's friend and one-time bodyguard, Alexander Falconbridge. Clarkson convinced him to take the job. The former doctor seemed a good choice: a staunch abolitionist who, from his four slave voyages, knew the African coast. Accordingly, Falconbridge, his young wife, Anna Maria, and his brother, William, who was to be his assistant, headed for Africa, traveling, ironically, on a slave ship owned by Richard Oswald's nephews. Throughout the eighteen-day voyage the captain and the hot-tempered Falconbridge argued furiously.

With this journey, a new voice enters the Sierra Leone story—neither settler nor abolitionist nor slave trader. Like the voice of an unreliable narrator in a novel, however, it cannot always be taken at face value, for its owner was settling scores with various people in writing. The daughter of a Bristol watchmaker and goldsmith, Anna Maria Falconbridge was a spirited, opinionated young woman and sharp-eyed observer, who at the age of nineteen had recently married the antislavery physician over the opposition of her family. Her book about her experiences in Sierra Leone would be one of the first travel narratives by an Englishwoman.

Naturally, everything went wrong from the start. William Falconbridge had a row with his brother and, lured by the promise of riches to be made at Bance Island, promptly quit the mission. With many gifts, Alexander Falconbridge managed to persuade local chiefs to let the shrunken band of settlers reoccupy their now overgrown land. But he and his wife did not get on. He drank too much, and was, she complains, "of an irritable disposition." When they first arrived, a Bance Island trader invited them to stay in one of the depot's buildings, instead of living on the colony's small cutter. She would gladly have accepted, finding the island's traders "gentlemen," who "received me with every mark of attention and civility." But her husband refused to let her, "for he would not subject himself to any obligation to men possessing such *diabolical* sentiments. It was not proper for me to contradict him at that moment, as the heat of argument and the influence of an over portion of wine had *quickened* and *disconcerted* his temper; I therefore submitted . . . to come on board this tub of a vessel, which in point of size and cleanliness, comes nigher a hog-trough than anything else you can imagine."

A day or two later, the quarreling couple were back at Bance Island for a meal with the traders. The dining room window looked out on the slave yard; indeed, the room had musket firing ports—put to use on at least one occasion on record—for suppressing slave uprisings. "Judge then what my astonishment and feelings were," Anna Maria Falconbridge wrote, "at the sight of between two and three hundred wretched victims, chained and parcelled out in circles, just satisfying the cravings of nature from a trough of rice placed in the centre of each circle." Nevertheless, the sight in no way deterred her from future visits; she simply "avoided the prospects from this side of the house." Anything was better than the quarters of her tiny "floating prison," where the only food supplies were "salt beef, so hard, we were obliged to chop it with an axe, and some mouldy, rotten biscuits."

The longer she spent in Sierra Leone, the more dim her view of the whole enterprise. For taking her husband away from a good medical practice near Bristol she blamed Clarkson, "at whose instance Falconbridge . . . enlist[ed] in the present (though I fear chimerical) cause of freedom and humanity." And as for the Sierra Leone settlement itself, she wrote, "It was surely a premature, hair-brained, and ill digested scheme, to think of sending such a number of people all at once, to a rude, barbarous and unhealthy country, before they were certain of possessing an acre of land."

She did, however, hit it off wonderfully with the slave traders. This rough, unkempt crew, kerchiefs around their necks and pent up on their fortified island for months on end, were clearly delighted to be distracted from their usual round of shackles and chains by the laughter of a lively young Englishwoman. They became co-conspirators in her battles with her husband. One day, she "feigned sickness, and begged to be excused from attending Falconbridge; he therefore set out, reluctantly leaving me behind: when he was gone, I went on shore, and spent the day in comfort and pleasantry, under the hospitable roof of Bance Island house; where I related the adventures of the preceeding day, which afforded much mirth and glee to the company. . . . Before Falconbridge returned . . . I had not only got on board, but in bed, and as he did not ask how I had spent the day, I did not inform him."

13

THE BLOOD-SWEETENED BEVERAGE

WHEN THOMAS CLARKSON arrived in France in the summer of 1789, it was one of those rare moments in history when all dreams seem within reach. In Calais, where he got off the boat, he found citizens and soldiers jubilantly sporting in their hats the tricolor cockade, the rose-shaped badge of ribbon loops worn by supporters of the Revolution. In the contrast between the hundreds of peasant famine victims who swarmed around travelers at every stop to beg and the three-hundred-horse stables of the Prince de Condé, which he toured at Chantilly, he saw the stark disparities that had triggered the nation's upheaval. When he reached Paris by fast coach, he found its boulevards full of street theater, dancing bears, and "People whose Hearts appear'd light & happy beyond Description." At the Bastille, crowds wandered through the old prison, helping workers tear it down. Clarkson found a cell wall still standing where a prisoner had scratched in Latin that he "wrote this Line in the anguish of his heart." Deeply moved, he paid laborers to pry the stone loose so he could bring it home to England.

French abolitionists gave him a warm welcome, and he was swept up by their contagious hope that France was on the verge not just of freeing its slaves, but also of granting full human rights to its own citizens. Indeed, only two weeks after his arrival, the new National Assembly adopted the Declaration of the Rights of Man and Citizen, a stirring, prophetic document asserting that "men are born and remain free." Surely the slave trade could not last, he reported to London. "I should not be surprised if the French were to do themselves the honour of voting away this diabolical traffic in a night."

Soon, however, there were signs the night might be long. France had some 675,000 slaves on its lucrative Caribbean islands, which produced more sugar than the British West Indies. Suddenly Clarkson began getting letters with death threats. Newspapers published his Paris address, and accused him of being a British spy and the Société des Amis des Noirs of sending arms to West Indian blacks. A gang of soldiers arrived to search the group's offices. Two members of the organization were discovered to be police spies and were barred from future meetings. Behind these shadowy doings, it appeared, was the powerful French planter lobby. Alarmed by Clarkson's visit, it dispatched an agent to London, to reconnoiter the abolitionist movement there.

Clarkson still had hope. Over dinner at Lafayette's house, he met Vincent Ogé, a free mulatto and goldsmith from the French colony of St. Domingue (today's Haiti), and five other mulattos. They had arrived just the day before, to demand seats in the new Assembly. But angry planters began insulting them in the Paris streets, and the Assembly, which included owners of St. Domingue slave plantations, wouldn't give them a hearing. The young Ogé, who first struck Clarkson as "*a very mild and placid man,*" turned furious as the weeks passed, and confided that the mulattos were ready to fight for their rights: "We can produce as good soldiers . . . as those in France." The planters, fearful of rebellion, sent word to all French ports asking ship captains to refuse passage to any mulatto delegates returning to St. Domingue.

Meanwhile, a crowd broke into the palace of Versailles and forced King Louis XVI and Queen Marie Antoinette to return under guard to Paris. (To the particular horror of conservatives in England, it was largely a crowd of *women.* The "furies of hell," Edmund Burke called them.) While French royalists and revolutionaries jockeyed for power, many of the wealthy fled abroad, the restive poor were short of food, and the public treasury was empty. Count Mirabeau, a leading figure in this phase of the revolution, gave Clarkson a draft of a speech on slavery he planned to make in the Assembly and asked for his comments. How heady this must have been—to be only four years out of university and consulted by one of the great orators of France! In serviceable schoolboy French, the delighted Clarkson answered Mirabeau's questions in installments that together ran to book length.

Months passed, and still Clarkson stayed on, hoping for a breakthrough. From London, the committee supplied him with more than a thousand copies of the slave ship diagram in French. "The Archbishop of Aix," wrote Clarkson, ". . . was so struck with horror, that he could scarcely speak." Louis XVI, now only precariously on his throne, noticed the clamor over slavery in the press and began asking questions. The French abolitionists sent him copies of Clarkson's writings and some African trading goods, but not the diagram, as the King's health was fragile and it was feared that the image would overwhelm him.

Across the Channel in England the abolitionists' enemies were growing more vocal and better organized. The two men who would be the proslavery lobby's most colorful public voices for years to come were just appearing on the scene.

The first of these was swept into office not by fervor for slavery but by outrage over ale. In Liverpool, one writer of the day noted, people "pique themselves greatly upon their ale, of which almost every house brews a sufficiency for its own use; and such is the unanimity prevailing among them, that if, by accident, one man's stock runs short, he sends his pitcher to his neighbour to be filled." In this ale-mad city, it had long been the custom for certain pubs to remain open extra hours at election time so that candidates could keep their supporters happily drunk until their votes were needed. In the parliamentary elections of 1790, however, the Liverpool city authorities supported an incumbent they thought was a shoo-in and, to save money, made the mistake of shutting off the usual free ale. Voters were outraged and swung their support to a popular challenger, Colonel Banastre Tarleton. A Tarleton backer "caused a cask of ale or porter to be rolled into the street, the head to be knocked out, and the contents to be distributed." The candidate's supporters sang:

> Come all ye noble Freemen,
> Who love an honest soul,
> Brave citizens and seamen,
> Come fill the flowing bowl;
> Let's drink our British Hero
> Of courage fam'd afar,
> Who fought for honor bravely,
> Amidst the smoke of war.

Along with ale, "the smoke of war" helped the dashing, boyishly handsome Tarleton into office, for he had been a British hero in the American Revolutionary War. He led a patrol that captured an American general, had his horse killed beneath him, his hat shot off his head, and still found time to be caught in bed with a superior officer's mistress. During a lull in the fighting, he acted in a series of plays in British-occupied Philadelphia. Known as "Bloody Tarleton" by the Americans, he had had two fingers shot off. "These gave I for King and country!" he would cry, waving his hand at campaign rallies. In parades his supporters wore green, the color of his dragoon's uniform. "Tarleton boasts," wrote the diarist Horace Walpole, "of having butchered more men and lain with more women than anybody else in the army."

Another boost to Tarleton's glamour came from his live-in romance with Mary Robinson, a novelist, poet, and actress. She had played Juliet, Ophelia, and Lady Macbeth, and was a discarded mistress of the Prince of Wales. Robinson loved the limelight, and caricaturists had a field day with her famous lovers and penchant for fancy carriages and liveried footmen. In poems to Tarleton that she published in the newspapers, fascinated readers could trace the ups and downs of her love and jealousy.* Clergymen were scandalized,

---

* One, written in a huff, begins:

> THOU art no more my bosom's FRIEND;
> Here must the sweet delusion end,
> That charm'd my senses many a year,
> Thro' smiling summers, winters drear . . .

and several marched in a parade for a rival candidate, which only won Tarleton more votes. Mary Robinson wrote his campaign songs and, once he was elected, his parliamentary speeches defending the slave trade. This did not stop her from simultaneously penning sentimental antislavery verse; frequently in need of money, she had a keen eye for what would sell.

Banastre Tarleton's father and various other Tarletons had been mayors of Liverpool. His family now lived in a castle, but the mansion they had graduated from was large enough to have been turned into a hotel—the King's Arms, where Clarkson had stayed on his visit to the city, braving slavers' taunts in the dining room. Tarleton's main interests were the army, women, and gambling, at which he ran up fashionably large debts; his family owned plantations in the West Indies and its shipping company was one of Britain's four top slave-trading firms. One vessel in its fleet was the 148-ton *Banastre.* Liverpool slave ship owners looked to Tarleton to defend them in the House of Commons, and he did. In the election some doggerel ran:

> If our slave trade had gone, there's an end to our lives,
> Beggars all we must be, our children and wives,
> No ships from our ports, their proud sails e'er would spread,
> And our streets grown with grass where the cows might be fed.

In his army days, Tarleton had become friends with the man who would be his counterpart in the House of Lords, the third son of King George III, soon given the title of Duke of Clarence. The two were part of a high-living set who bet heavily on horse races, prizefights, and once a ten-mile race between a flock of turkeys and a flock of geese (the geese won, costing the Prince of Wales £500).

As a thirteen-year-old, the future Clarence had been sent to sea in the vain hope of stopping him from taking after his dissolute older brothers. He made several Royal Navy voyages to the West Indies, where he gained a reputation for telling coarse jokes, ineptly designing midshipmen's uniforms that split when men climbed the rigging, ordering sailors flogged, and making his fellow officers drink themselves into a stupor by proposing endless, long-winded toasts—twenty-three in a row at one memorable dinner. "I never saw a man get so completely drunk," wrote one British officer of a visit Clarence made to the home of the chief justice of Nova Scotia. "He desired the General to order the whole garrison up to the Citadel Hill" to light a bonfire, although Clarence himself was too inebriated to attend. On another occasion, he and some boisterous companions did £700 worth of damage on a visit to a Barbados brothel. It was apparently in the navy that he picked up his lifelong habits of wiping his nose with the back of his fingers and spitting copiously in public. A distinctively oblong head, topped with red hair, won him the nickname of "Coconut." He reacted grumpily to the long letters of disapproval he received from his father: "My Christmas box or New Year's gift will be a family lecture for immorality, vice, dissipation and expense," he complained one year.

The surest way to Clarence's heart was through parades, banquets, and multi-gun salutes. When his navy ship stopped at Dominica, reported the *London Chronicle,* "a very elegant supper and ball, which surpassed any thing ever known in this part of the world, was given to his Royal Highness." The Barbados authorities presented him with a sword of honor and named a street after him, and he presented a Jamaican militia regiment, used for putting down slave rebellions, with a royal flag. Naval officers were always entertained lavishly by West Indian planters, and at countless dances and parties their daughters fluttered about the young member of the royal family. He returned their attention, rashly strewing marriage proposals and cases of venereal disease in all directions, and was always spirited away by his fellow officers—in one case by the young Horatio Nelson—in the nick of time. Not surprisingly, the future Duke of Clarence quickly absorbed the plantation owners' views about slavery.

It was rumored that he fathered both black and white progeny in the West Indies; cartoonists sometimes pictured Clarence's egg-shaped head beside that of a black mistress in a ship's cabin or hammock. On returning to England he began pursuing Dora Jordan, the finest comic actress of the day. She set gossips talking when she promptly performed in the role of a woman who turns away a royal seducer, but any spurning did not last long, and the two were soon living together. Mrs. Jordan was a kind and generous woman, a mentor to younger actors and dedicated to her craft, who deserved someone better than the oafish Clarence. There had, however, never been a

Mr. Jordan; she had adopted the name after an affair with a married theater manager who abandoned her when she became pregnant. That history and her unaristocratic origins meant that she and Clarence could never marry. This did not stop them from living together and happily having ten children, all of whom took the name FitzClarence.

The Duke, nonetheless, had no hesitation in fulfilling his royal duties by condemning adultery as "a most pernicious crime . . . destructive of the best interests of society" in a House of Lords debate on a measure called the Adultery Prevention Bill. "Jordan" was slang for chamber pot, and cartoonists had another round of sport showing the Duke in his naval uniform trying to fit inside one. Money flowed through the hands of Clarence and Mrs. Jordan like water, and she had to return to the stage regularly to make ends meet. At the urging of his disapproving father, the King, Clarence once proposed to cut the allowance he was paying her from £1,000 to £500 a year. Her answer was the torn-off bottom half of a playbill that bore the warning "No money returned after the rising of the curtain."

Clarence was not exactly a poster boy for the proslavery forces, but he was a member of the royal family and they were glad to have his voice. And have it they did, in debate after debate. In his maiden speech before the bewigged lords in their red and ermine robes, he called himself "an attentive observer of the state of the negroes" who found them well cared for and "in a state of humble happiness." Above all, he parroted the abiding national belief, elaborated with less boorishness and greater refinement by other proslavery legislators, that the health of the navy, the merchant fleet, and the Caribbean colonies all rested on the slave trade; remove that one vital link and the empire was gone. Whatever the personal oddities of Clarence and Tarleton, the West Indian interest was widely seen as the strongest lobby in late-eighteenth-century Britain. It would be a formidable obstacle in the abolitionists' path.

As the next round of conflict in Parliament loomed, Clarkson was summoned home from France. His visit to Paris had been thrilling, dangerous, inspiring, but not a success. Nearly six months of strenuous effort by him and his French friends had exposed a painful truth:

the nation now swept by the greatest revolution Europe had yet seen was not ready to end the slave trade. France's vaunted Rights of Man were still for white men only. The first move against the trade would have to come from Britain.

As the abolitionists focused their efforts on the House of Commons, the proslavery forces were worried; slave prices in the West Indies had soared because planters feared the supply might be cut off. Prime Minister Pitt jokingly referred to Clarkson and his comrades as Wilberforce's "white negroes"; they met often at the Parliament Coffee House or at Wilberforce's spacious home nearby, where once a week they had dinner. "I cannot invite you here," Wilberforce wrote a friend, "for, during the sitting of Parliament, my house is a mere hotel." So many petitioners of one sort or another came to see him that the books which began disappearing from the shelves of his anteroom had to be replaced with larger folio volumes that could not so easily fit into a visitor's pocket.

Clarkson once again rode the length and breadth of England in search of witnesses to testify at the endless hearings. He was on the road so much that his own mother wrote to him care of bookseller-printer James Phillips, "as I conclude you always know where he is to be found." On one expedition, he rode nearly two thousand miles meeting nothing but refusals, as people "fled [me] as they would a wild Beast." His hosts worried for his health. "I never in my Life saw a Man so devoted to any Cause as T Clarkson is to that which he has undertook," wrote one Quaker poet and farmer he stayed with. "He seems sensible his Constitution is wearing out fast, yet seems perfectly satisfied with being the slave of slaves."

For three entire weeks Clarkson searched for one key witness, a former shipmate of his brother John, who was reportedly willing to speak about British expeditions in heavily armed canoes that traveled up the Niger River delta kidnapping slaves. Such testimony would refute the slave ship captains who maintained that they acquired their cargo only from black dealers, buying people who were already slaves in Africa. Methodically boarding vessels in six ports across southern England, Clarkson worked his way through 317 ships—some three quarters of the Royal Navy. Finally, to his "inexpressible joy," he found his man and returned to London with him and five other witnesses in tow.

The parliamentary hearings, which had dragged on intermittently for nearly two years, ended in early 1791. The abolitionists then faced a curious problem. There were nearly 1,700 pages of House of Commons testimony, on top of the hefty 850-page volume from the Privy Council hearings of several years earlier, filled with eyewitness accounts, tables, and excerpts from slave laws of different colonies, some of them in French. No one could expect even the most sympathetic M.P. to master this mountain of material. And so, in the weeks before the next debate on the slave trade began, a group of abolitionists embarked on a feverish collective editing marathon—Wilberforce even working on Sundays, so urgent did he feel the task—to distill some three years of testimony into an account short enough to be given to each M.P. to read. The committee then sent it to all of them.

The abolitionists were optimistic about their chances, until news came that a slave revolt had broken out on the British island of Dominica. There had been many such uprisings on the Caribbean slave islands, of course, but now the planters could blame the abolitionists. The West India Committee declared the rebellion "to have been founded on no pretence of ill-treatment, as to food, clothing or other particulars, but to have occurred in pursuit of what [the slaves] term their 'rights.' . . . These doctrines, which are novel among the negroes, have originated from the new language and proceedings in this country respecting the Slave Trade." The abolitionists had done everything possible, said one angry proslavery writer, "to excite a rebellion, except that of furnishing the objects of their solicitude with fire arms and ammunition." And soon enough Clarkson would be accused of doing just that.

When the debate opened on April 18, 1791, Clarkson, watching from the House of Commons gallery, counted votes in advance and told friends their side would lose. On the House floor, Wilberforce insisted emphatically, as usual, that ending the trade would only help, not hurt, the plantation economy. Banastre Tarleton, who for effect often wore his green dragoon's uniform, immediately jumped up to respond, shaking his three-fingered fist in a long speech—presumably written by Mary Robinson—in which he declared that "the Africans themselves had no objection to the trade." Another proslavery speaker declared that the slaves loved ornaments, and he appealed "to the observation of every gentleman, whether it was the characteristic of miserable persons to show a fondness for finery." A still more bizarre argument came from Brook Watson, M.P., an alderman and later Lord Mayor of London, who had one leg (the other had been bitten off by a shark in Havana harbor when he was a young crewman on a smuggler's vessel). Abolition, he swore, would "destroy our Newfoundland fishery, which the slaves in the West Indies supported, by consuming that part of the fish which was fit for no other consumption." Even sympathizers found this argument unconvincing; one colonial landowner later said, "We never had but two things to say in favour of the slave trade, the first that it was a nursery for seamen, this has been completely disproved, it now rests upon the stinking fish of Brook Watson."

The debate, one M.P. commented, was between the giants and the pygmies of the House. Never had the abolitionist arguments been marshaled so brilliantly, until, as Horace Walpole put it, "commerce clinked its purse." After two days of debate the House voted, 163 to 88, against abolishing the slave trade. The church bells of Liverpool rang and Bristol celebrated with a cannon salute, a bonfire, fireworks, and a half-day holiday.

When the abolition committee met after the vote, the members were too discouraged for any small talk. "The looks of all bespoke the feelings of their hearts," wrote Clarkson.

His main consolation was his continued faith in the changes in France. Titles had now been abolished, and so it was to just plain Madame Lafayette that he wrote of his hope that "your Revolution will be established beyond the Possibility of being shaken by any human Power." Granville Sharp, also in his curmudgeonly way an instinctive radical, shared these hopes and wrote to French revolutionaries urging them to consider frankpledge. While English opinion on the upheaval in France was increasingly divided, to millions of Britons it seemed an unprecedented victory of liberty over privilege. The barrister and ardent abolitionist Samuel Romilly felt it to be "the most glorious event, and the happiest for mankind, that has ever taken place since human affairs have been recorded." On July 14, 1791, Clarkson was among the thousand people who attended a dinner at London's Crown and Anchor Tavern* to celebrate the second anniversary of the storming of the Bastille. The banqueters drank many toasts, including "May Revolution never cease until Despotism is extinct."

Not all agreed. Henry Dundas, the home secretary, wrote to Wilberforce, "What business had your friend Clarkson to attend the Crown and Anchor last Thursday?" When Clarkson saw him soon afterwards, "almost the first word Mr. Wilberforce said to me was this: 'O Clarkson, I wanted much to see you to tell you to keep clear from the subject of the French Revolution & I hope you will.' "

However, he could not have kept clear of the revolution's impact even if he had wanted to. One morning while he was having breakfast in his lodgings at 7 Frith Street, just off Soho Square, into the room unannounced walked the fiery Vincent Ogé from the French colony of St. Domingue, still intent on organizing the mulatto revolt he had told Clarkson about in Paris. Broke, he was trying to get back to St. Domingue. He asked to be introduced to Wilberforce, who adamantly, as Clarkson put it, "forbad me . . . to bring him to his house." It was clear to Clarkson that the longer his unexpected visitor stayed in London, "the greater chance there was that his acquaintance with me might become known." And this indeed happened: although traveling under a false name, Ogé was being shadowed by agents of the French planters. They leaked word of his doings, and proslavery writers lost no time in accusing Clarkson of giving him money to buy arms. All he gave Ogé, Clarkson later maintained, was £30 to pay for his passage across the Atlantic.

With the cause temporarily stymied in Parliament, Clarkson went on the road again. Through an admirer's diary we have one close-up glimpse of him hard at work on this trip. He was staying with a Shropshire clergyman named Plymley, who was supposed to leave

---

* A favorite venue for such events, the tavern's banquet hall was overlooked by a balcony. The Crown and Anchor's owner, Thomas Simkin, was famed for his corpulence, and as he leaned against the balcony railing one evening, it gave way. He fell, fatally, into the midst of the dinner preparations he had been supervising.

with him one morning at seven on a fund-raising mission. When Plymley's two sisters came downstairs to see them off, they found Clarkson waiting for their brother, who had just gone to get dressed. "If I had known Mr. Plymley wou'd not have been quite exact," he told them, "I cou'd have written some letters." Katherine Plymley offered to help, and "whilst he went for his papers, Ann & I with pleas'd alacrity ran for a table & desk. . . . He said, 'now we shall gain time if you will seal the letters.' I felt elated with the thought of doing any thing for him & answer'd that I will, & think myself honour'd by so doing."

Katherine Plymley was thrilled by Clarkson's visit, drinking in his news of the political scene in London, his hopes for France, and his faith that many M.P.s had voted against abolition only because they had been persuaded by West Indian friends "perhaps over a bottle" and had never read the evidence. He patiently answered the questions of her brother's children, although it meant keeping a carriage waiting. They had a wooden map puzzle, and after he left, her four-year-old niece kissed the piece showing Cambridgeshire because that was where he was from. Clarkson planned to enter Liverpool only by night, for, as Archdeacon Plymley told his sister, "Mr. C had had several letters to tell him his life would be in danger should he be seen there." Despite the threats, on this journey Clarkson took heart. Whatever the abolitionists' troubles in Parliament, they were clearly gaining support in the country at large. Most dramatic was the contagious spread of a new tactic the committee itself had never considered —and those putting it into action were women.

From the Plymley household in the west to the North Sea, from Josiah Wedgwood's home in the Midlands to the highlands of Scotland, hundreds of thousands of people had stopped using sugar. Ignited by several pamphlets,* one of which sold an estimated seventy

* One was in dialogue "between a Negro and an English Gentleman":

Mr. English. Why, Cushoo, what's the matter?

C. Ah! Massa, poor Negro worse usé den dog.

E. What have I to do with that, Cushoo? I am no planter.

C. But you drinké Rum and Sugar, Massa.

thousand copies in four months, the sugar boycott burst into life in response to Parliament's 1791 rejection of the abolition bill. For some the boycott meant self-denial; those with an incurable sweet tooth instead ate sugar from India. As with so much else, Quakers were in the vanguard: an eighteen-year-old named William Allen had already stopped eating sugar two years earlier.

Wilberforce, wary of anything that smacked of stirring up popular feeling, thought the time was not right for a boycott. Careful to avoid offending him, for several years the abolition committee took no stand. But Clarkson spurred on the boycotters, delighted to find a "remedy, which the people were . . . taking into their own hands. . . . There was no town, through which I passed, in which there was not some one individual who had left off the use of sugar. In the smaller towns there were from ten to fifty . . . and in the larger from two to five hundred. . . . They were of all ranks and parties. Rich and poor, churchmen and dissenters. . . . Even grocers had left off trading in the article. . . . By the best computation I was able to make from notes taken down in my journey, no fewer than three hundred thousand persons had abandoned the use of sugar."

Committee member William Dillwyn agreed with Clarkson's calculation; a Methodist minister named Samuel Bradburn set the number at 400,000. After an exhaustive study of provincial newspapers and other sources, Seymour Drescher, a careful modern scholar of British abolitionism, believes such estimates reasonable. Two Quakers in Cornwall, reported one newspaper, "have lately made a tour through that county on foot, and . . . have found, by actual enumeration, that not less than 12,000 persons . . . have left off sugar on principle." (If their "enumeration" was correct, and if the same percentage of the national population "left off sugar," then well over half a million Britons joined the boycott.) A woman wrote from Buckinghamshire, "There is more people I think that drinks tea without sugar than drinks with." In several parts of the country, grocers reported sugar sales dropping by a third to a half in a few months' time. Over a two-year period, the sale of sugar from India increased more than tenfold. One clergyman carried some with him at all times so that if parishioners gave him tea he would not have to use any slave-grown sugar. Advertisements resembled the "fair trade" food labeling of today: "BENJAMIN TRAVERS, Sugar-Refiner, acquaints the Publick that he has now an assortment of Loaves, Lumps, Powder Sugar, and Syrup, ready for sale . . . produced by the labour of FREEMEN."

Then, as now, the full workings of a globalized economy were invisible, and the boycott caught people's imagination because it brought these hidden ties to light, laying bare the dramatic, direct connection between British daily life and that of slaves. The poet Southey spoke of tea as "the blood-sweetened beverage," and one pamphleteer urged the tea drinker: "As he sweetens his tea, let him . . . say, as he truly may, this lump cost the poor slave a groan, and this a bloody stroke with the cartwhip."* William Cowper wrote:

I own I am shock'd at the purchase of slaves,
And fear those who buy them and sell them are knaves;
What I hear of their hardships, their tortures, and groans,
Is almost enough to draw pity from stones.

I pity them greatly, but I must be mum,
For how could we do without sugar and rum?
Especially sugar, so needful we see,
What? give up our desserts, our coffee and tea!"

Like many such actions today, the sugar boycott was partly symbolic. Systematically giving up all slave-grown products would have required Britons to also stop using tobacco, coffee, and cotton clothing (much of it woven in the mills of staunchly antislavery Manchester). Nonetheless, a boycott of sugar was potentially a powerful weapon because the country consumed so much of it. In the eighteenth century, sugar was Britain's largest import. Besides sweetening

---

* William Fox, author of the most widely read boycott pamphlet, went wildly overboard in a sequel. He claimed that sugar contained, literally not just figuratively, the sweat of slaves, as well as their lice, germs, and pus. And one barrel of Caribbean rum had been found to hold, he insisted, "the whole Body of a roasted Negro." The exploited cane cutters described or pictured in such pamphlets, incidentally, were almost always male. Even abolitionists seemed unaware that the majority of Caribbean field laborers were women.

the naturally bitter tea, coffee, and chocolate, sugar was used in pastries, puddings, biscuits, and candy, and in making many kinds of liquor. It was a preservative in candied fruit, jam, and marmalade, and a 1760 cookbook had recipes for sugar sculptures. One enthusiastic physician, Dr. Frederick Slare, urged the use of sugar for cleaning teeth.

Everyone could understand the logic of the sugar boycott, even children. Equiano was another visitor to the Plymley family, and gave a boycott pamphlet to six-year-old Panton Plymley—who soon stopped polishing his shoes because someone had told him that shoe polish contained sugar. An abolition organizer in Scotland recorded his amazement at "the vast circulation & great attention wh[ich] had been paid to a little tract ag[ains]t the use of sugar. . . . Dined w[ith] the Rev. Mr. Alice. . . . His grandson 10 yr. Old won't taste sug[a]r since he read Fox's tract."

A boycott was such a novel idea that the very word would not come into the language for nearly another century. This may not have been the world's first consumer boycott—arguably that title goes to the chain of events leading to the Boston Tea Party—but it was certainly the first to be so widespread. Slavery advocates were horrified. One rushed out a counter-pamphlet claiming on medical authority that "sugar is not a luxury; but . . . a necessary of life; and great injury have many persons done to their constitutions by totally abstaining from it."

Quietly but subversively, the boycott added a new dimension to British political life. At a time when only a small fraction of the population could vote, citizens took upon themselves the power to act when Parliament had not. "The legislature having refused to interpose, the people are now necessarily called on," wrote one boycotter. The boycott was radical in yet another way, made explicit in at least one pamphlet: it struck not just at the slave trade but at slavery itself. And, finally, the boycott was largely put into effect by those who bought and cooked the family food: women. Sometimes men were startled. One complained to a newspaper: "Happening lately to be sometime from home, the females in my family had in my absence perused a pamphlet. . . . On my return, I was surprised to find that they had entirely left off the use of Sugar, and banished it from the tea table." A young Quaker poet, Mary Birkett, wrote:

Yes, sisters, to us the task belongs,
'Tis we increase or mitigate their wrongs.
If we the produce of their toils refuse,
If we no more the blood-stained lux'ry choose. . . .
Say not that small's the sphere in which we move,
And our attempts would vain and fruitless prove;
Not so—we hold *a most important share,*
In all the evils—all the wrongs they bear. . . .

"Say not that small's the sphere . . ." Not surprisingly, the second year of the sugar boycott saw publication of the first great feminist manifesto in any language, Mary Wollstonecraft's *Vindication of the Rights of Women.* "Is one half of the human species," she asked, "like the poor African slaves, to be subjected to prejudices which brutalize them . . . ?"

Just as the movement helped to pioneer the consumer boycott, so it helped forge another great tool of modern civil society. From Yorkshire, now Wilberforce's constituency, a friend reported to him, "Who do you think we had in yesterday but T Clarkson who has been disseminating the Abstract through all the realm I trust with such effect that it will grow up & ripen to an abundant harvest." The Abstract was the *Abstract of the Evidence delivered before a select committee of the House of Commons in the years 1790 and 1791, on the part of the petitioners for the Abolition of the Slave Trade.* At the committee's request, Clarkson had taken its 648-page distillation of testimony before Commons and further boiled it down to a quarter of the size. He then took to the road to distribute these books throughout England and Wales, traveling more than six thousand miles "by moving upwards and downwards in parallel lines . . . of almost incessant journeyings night and day."

To everyone's surprise, this condensation of a condensation would become probably the most widely read piece of nonfiction antislavery literature of all time. The abolition committee in Newcastle upon

Tyne alone ordered two thousand copies. More editions quickly appeared in London and the provinces. The booklet would be reprinted often in future years, and was still being printed and used by abolitionists in the United States sixty years later, when slavery in the British Empire was long gone. The pocket-sized *Abstract of the Evidence* also reached some slaves, for the alarmed Governor's Council of Jamaica reported to London, "Perhaps nothing has contributed so much to the dissemination of these notions [of freedom] among our Negroes than the publication of the witnesses' examinations before the House of Commons, most industriously sent out by persons in England, and explained to our Slaves by free people of colour."

The *Abstract* reads more like a report by a modern human rights organization than the moralizing tracts against slavery that had preceded it. The book was a masterpiece of force and clarity, as well as one of the first pieces of antislavery literature printed in modern typography, without those *s*'s that look like *f*'s. It began with telling excerpts from West Indian colonial legislation, quoting, for instance, from a 1784 St. Kitts law "to prevent the cutting off or depriving any slaves in this island of any of their limbs or members, or otherwise disabling them," a law enacted, its preamble said, because "some persons have of late been guilty of *cutting off and depriving slaves of their ears.*" It excerpted runaway slave advertisements from a Jamaican newspaper, in which slaves were identified by brands, some on the face.

The bulk of the book distilled and reorganized hundreds of hours of testimony to bring the strongest evidence to bear on each aspect of the system. (Its italics, incidentally, should not be read as clumsy editorializing. To some extent, eighteenth-century writers used these as we would quotation marks today.) The summary can still produce a shiver of horror:

> When [slaves] are flogged on the wharves . . . they are described by H. Ross, Morley, Jeffreys, Town, and Captain Scott, to have their *arms* tied to the *hooks of the crane,* and *weights of fifty-six* pounds applied to *their feet.* In this situation the crane is wound up, so that it lifts them nearly from the ground and keeps them in a stretched posture, when the whip or cowskin is used. After this they are again whipped, but with *ebony bushes,*

(which are more prickly than the thorn bushes in this country,) in order to *let out the congealed blood.*

The book contained hundreds of such descriptions: of slaves being worked to death; of whipped women miscarrying their babies, of slaves tied up in painful positions and left in the broiling sun. But where Clarkson in his prize-winning *Essay* half a dozen years earlier had cited this or that unnamed "gentleman" familiar with the West Indies, and where John Newton had interwoven his memories of the slave trade with forecasts of God's punishment for sin, in the *Abstract* Clarkson simply cited, in a crisp and businesslike way, statistics, documents, and sworn testimony by military officers, planters, sea captains, physicians, and businessmen.

What also makes the *Abstract* feel surprisingly contemporary is what it does *not* contain. At a time in history when a large portion of all books and pamphlets were theological tracts or sermons, and in a book that quoted several clergymen as witnesses, the *Abstract* had no references to the Bible. Clarkson and his comrades somehow sensed that they could better evoke sympathy if they stood back and let the evidence speak for itself, supported by the damning quotations from West Indian laws and newspapers. The argumentative political pamphlet was very familiar to Britons, but this book was something different. In its carefully selected excerpts from documents and eyewitness accounts—illustrated, of course, with the famous slave ship diagram—the *Abstract of the Evidence* was, although the term did not then exist, one of the first great works of investigative journalism.

14

PROMISED LAND

THE STAGE ON WHICH the drama of British slavery and the fight against it was being played out was now a wide one, encompassing several continents. Increasingly, events in Britain in the struggle for abolition reverberated in far corners of the empire. One place where this impact was now felt was the province of Nova Scotia, where the three thousand blacks who had crossed to the British side in the American Revolutionary War had arrived from New York in 1783, hoping to build new lives in freedom.

Some half-dozen years later, they were having a hard time doing so. The wet, cold territory was crowded with white refugees from the war; food, farm tools, and relief supplies were short, and the blacks were always last in line. They had to pay taxes but couldn't vote, and living in the same province were more than a thousand other blacks—brought by pro-British masters fleeing the American South—who were still slaves. Canada was a British colony, after all, slavery was legal, and the newspapers carried runaway slave advertisements. Free blacks were not safe, for professional kidnappers roamed the region, hustling people onto ships bound for the Southern states or the West Indies, to sell them back into slavery.

Nova Scotia held other hardships too. "Great riot today," a surveyor recorded in his diary. "The disbanded soldiers have risen against the Free negroes to drive them out of the Town, because they labour cheaper." The white ex-soldiers destroyed some twenty black houses. One town passed an ordinance "forbidding negro dances and frolicks." After several years in Nova Scotia, said the carpenter Boston King, now a Methodist minister as well, "the country was visited with a dreadful famine. . . . Some killed and eat their dogs and cats." Finishing one carpentry job, he reported, "On my way home, being pinched with hunger and cold, I fell down several times, thro' weakness, and expected to die upon the spot." The British government had promised the blacks land, but unlike white refugees, few received any. At best, in the words of one former slave, they got "small allotments in a soil . . . over run with rocks and swamps." To stay alive, many ex-slaves had become indentured servants or sharecroppers for white farmers. They were learning a bitter truth that would become all too familiar to others in the decades ahead: the end of slavery may not mean a better material life.

It was a former slave working as a house servant who first heard the news of a possible way out. As Clarkson described it: "Some company at dinner happened to be conversing on the projected scheme of the Sierra Leone colony. . . . A sensible black, who waited at table, heard the accounts with eagerness, and took the first opportunity of spreading them among his countrymen. The hope of relief animated them, and they resolved to send over their agent, one Thomas Peters, a respectable, intelligent African, to . . . learn if they might expect encouragement to go to the new colony. . . . Never did [an] ambassador from a sovereign power prosecute with more zeal the object of his mission than did Thomas Peters the cause of his distressed countrymen."

A legend among Peters's descendants has it that he was of royal birth in Africa and had tried to escape three times from slavery in Louisiana. All we know for certain is that when the American Revolution began, he was the slave of a planter in Wilmington, North Carolina, from whom he fled to join the British forces in 1776. He was wounded twice and by the war's end was a sergeant.

Evacuated to Nova Scotia, the husky Peters worked as a mill mechanic, and he and a fellow ex-sergeant became the spokesmen for a group of landless black families. In a complaint to colonial authorities, they wrote, "When We first Inlisted & swore we was promised that we should have land & provitions the same as the . . . [white] Disbanded Soldiers, Which We have not Received." He was twice an eyewitness when kidnappers captured former slaves for sale in the West Indies—in one case seeing sixteen men and women abducted: "I follow them to water side where several of the slave holders followed me with Pistolls and Cutlasses—in order to murder me; but by the assistance of Providence got clare of them all."

Might his community be free from such dangers in Sierra Leone? In late 1790, Peters, in his early fifties, sailed to England in search of an answer. It was a risky journey, for a black man alone at sea could easily fall victim to an unscrupulous captain and be sold to a passing ship heading for the American slave states or the Caribbean. We do not know if Peters worked his way across the Atlantic as a sailor or whether the two hundred black families who had given him power of attorney were able to raise the £17 fare. In London, he looked up his old commanding officer, who introduced him to General Sir Henry Clinton, British commander in chief in the American war. Peters asked Clinton to give him a letter of introduction to the home secretary; Clinton did so, and before long, Peters was meeting with a group of M.P.s in the committee room of the House of Commons.

He also met Granville Sharp, and soon was moving in London's antislavery circles, where there was much talk of the news the abolitionist doctor Alexander Falconbridge was sending back from Sierra Leone. Whatever the tensions he was having with his wife, his reports to London were guardedly optimistic. Although the whole scheme, Falconbridge said, was still menaced by "that lump of deformity the *Slave Trade,*" the food situation was improving and the settlers were rebuilding their village. To both abolitionists and former slaves, the "Province of Freedom" remained a shining hope, a community whose success would be a more powerful argument against slavery than any sermon or pamphlet. With abolition stymied in Parliament—only temporarily, they hoped—they saw Sierra Leone as the place they could put their ideas about freedom into practice. Clarkson always talked up Sierra Leone on his travels and suggested that a coming boom in sugar grown by free blacks there would soon leave the West Indian slave economy far behind. Additional settlers could only strengthen the colony.

Peters petitioned the British government, saying that "at much Trouble and Risk" he had "made his way into this Country in the Hope that he should be able to procure for himself and his Fellow Sufferers some Establishment where they may . . . by their industrious exertions . . . become useful subjects to his Majesty." The government agreed to give the free blacks in Nova Scotia passage to Africa, and the Sierra Leone Company promised every male of "Honesty, Sobriety, and Industry" at least twenty acres of land.

Although the abolitionists' optimism about the colony remained unbounded, the need for new capital to keep the place going meant that Granville Sharp had essentially lost control to the larger circle of abolition-minded investors who had bought shares in the Sierra Leone Company. The black settlers continued to elect the headboroughs and hundreders he had planned for, but real power was now vested in a council of eight administrators the Company sent out from England —another attempt by white men in London to shape a new community on a continent they had never seen. Even as Sharp's influence waned, some amazingly idealistic touches stayed in force. At least half of every Sierra Leone jury had to be of the same race as the defendant, and the Company practiced what we would today call affirmative action. It ordered its officials "to employ in your service, so far as you are able, black and white men indiscriminately, and when you discern in any of the former, talents which might render them useful in any way, to endeavour to call these talents into action and afford them all possible means of cultivation and encouragement." There was no death penalty, and all children as well as many adults were in school, something not remotely the case in the United States or Britain. Although the administrators sent by London kept most power out of the hands of the electorate, the colony was the only place in the world where—if they were heads of households—women could vote. Compared to the harsh life the black refugees were living in Nova Scotia, Sierra Leone sounded like paradise.

"At a publick dinner at the Tontine Tavern" in Glasgow, a London newspaper reported, a gathering of abolitionists drank a toast to "Thomas Peters, the worthy Negro, the conductor of his countrymen from Nova Scotia to Sierra Leone." His mission in England accomplished, Peters triumphantly returned to Canada in the summer of 1791 to gather his fellow ex-slaves for the move to Africa. Jubilant that this would greatly increase the number of settlers in the colony, Clarkson wrote to Mme. Lafayette that Sierra Leone would be "one of the greatest Wounds that the Slave-Trade ever received."

The Sierra Leone Company, however, was not willing to consider a black man as the principal "conductor" of the epic migration. It had someone else in mind, a guarantee of future tensions. For this job, the Company wanted an Englishman, a firm abolitionist, and an experienced sailor—and, of course, anyone entrusted with spending the government's money paying for the voyage would have to be Anglican. And so they turned to Clarkson's younger brother, John, who soon followed Peters across the Atlantic to Nova Scotia.

John Clarkson was twenty-seven years old. He had entered the Royal Navy just before his thirteenth birthday, at the beginning of the American war. His time at sea was as filled with flying cannonballs and blood in the scuppers as a Patrick O'Brian novel; he saw battle on nine of the ten ships on which he served. Enemy guns killed and wounded men beside him and shot away topsails above him. He served under one captain who ordered sixty-two floggings in eight months (driving a sailor to hang himself), watched press gangs at work, crossed paths with slave ships at sea, and saw men from his ship capture a French frigate in hand-to-hand fighting.

Surprisingly, he emerged a kind and gentle man. When once challenged to a duel, he invited his would-be opponent to dinner instead. In peacetime England, with its surplus of naval officers, John became an active, much-liked volunteer for the abolition committee. Close as they were, the two brothers seemed from different families. Thomas was a big man, solemn, hard-driving, with little small talk; he bore the world's sorrows on his shoulders and developed ulcers. John, by contrast, was much shorter; in one portrait, his remarkably peaceful face looks almost dwarfed by the high collar of his naval uniform. Unlike his relatively humorless brother, he had a reputation for charm and social ease. John was a favorite of Wilberforce, who enjoyed his good cheer and sea stories and called him "My dear Admiral." The diarist Katherine Plymley caught something of his ready wit in a conversation he had with a proslavery bishop the brothers were lobbying:

"My Lord, what makes you so angry with these poor black people?" John asked the bishop one day.

"O, they are a disagreeable set of people," the bishop replied. "They have such ugly noses."

"Well, my Lord," retorted John, "you'll be pleased to recollect they did not make their own noses."

John Clarkson's fiancée, Susan Lee, agreed to wait for him while he gathered the Canadian blacks and took them to Sierra Leone. In this highly religious age there was something distinctly biblical about the planned exodus of a suffering people across a wide and stormy ocean to a fertile Promised Land on a far shore. That neither Clarkson nor his London employers had ever seen that Promised Land made it seem all the more alluring. Another biblical chord was struck by the name of the ship that took him to Canada, the *Ark*.

Like his brother, John Clarkson was a ferociously hard worker. In slightly more than three months in Nova Scotia, with just the help of Peters and one or two others, he chartered a fleet of ships, oversaw their provisioning, and toured the province by schooner and horseback answering questions in black churches and sharecroppers' huts. He found himself acting as the ex-slaves' representative in their struggles with provincial authorities. A black minister warned him not to walk around after dark: white farmers were "violent people," angry at the emigration plan that would deprive them of low-paid field hands.

Ever upbeat, Clarkson took to the families he met. "The majority of the men are better than any people in the labouring line of life in England," he wrote in his diary. In London, the Company had planned on 220 "Adventurers," as Clarkson called them, but thanks to him and Peters, 1,196 black men, women, and children streamed to the assembly point at Halifax. One determined group of four walked 340 miles through the snow to get there. It took fifteen ships (one of them, ironically, named after the Duke of Clarence) to hold them all. Among those boarding was a Baptist preacher, David George, who as a slave had been pastor of the first black church in North America, on the Silver Bluff plantation in Aiken County, South Carolina. Another emigrant was Henry Washington, an escaped slave whose former master was now President of the United States.

On two facing pages in his diary, Clarkson sketched each ship, sails rigged. He and Peters inspected the ships together, and Clarkson ordered holds scrubbed and berths and ventilation holes installed. Just before leaving, he had himself rowed from vessel to vessel, gathered on deck the families in each, and gave them all certificates entitling them to a tract of land in Sierra Leone. On January 15, 1792, the convoy bid goodbye to the tidy colonial harbor of Halifax, where rows of yellow and white houses climbed up a hillside to a fortress, and the first voyage of North American settlers to Africa was under way. As he headed out to sea, Clarkson dipped his main topgallant sail in salute to the curious crowd gathered at the harbor, a gesture, he wrote, that "was returned by the waving of hats and handkerchiefs."

Since roughly one third of the "Adventurers" had been born in Africa and sold into Atlantic slavery there, Clarkson did his utmost to make the voyage as unlike the middle passage as possible. He ensured that there was far more space in the ships; that meat or fish was provided once a day; and that pregnant women were given special quarters in one vessel. Another, his own flagship, he turned into a hospital ship for the sick and elderly.

As his small brig and its fourteen companions plunged bravely into the North Atlantic in mid-winter, gales carrying snow and hail scattered the fleet. "We met with a dreadful storm which continued sixteen days," wrote one black settler. "Some of the men who had been engaged in a sea-faring life for 30 or 40 years, declared, that they never saw such a storm before." Sixty-five settlers died on the way, including one who was washed overboard and one who died as his ship entered the Sierra Leone River. Clarkson himself fell ill with a high fever, lying below decks for a month. A huge wave smashed his cabin porthole cover and the captain "found me rolling from side to side, quite exhausted, covered with blood & water and very much bruised." At another point, after he had remained still for many hours, the ship's doctor pronounced him dead. Crewmen were preparing his body for burial at sea when he stirred.

As soon as he was well enough, he had a small boat take him to the handful of other vessels not blown out of range by the storms. "Upon my going alongside each ship, the Black passengers had collected themselves upon deck with their Muskets, and fired three volleys, and afterwards gave three cheers, as they had entirely given up all hopes of my recovery." Nearing the African coast, the convoy saw a Bristol ship on its way to pick up slaves, which must have struck a chill in the passengers' hearts. At last the shore was in sight, and through a spyglass Clarkson recognized the clasped black and white hands on the colony's flag.

As the battered fleet dribbled into the Sierra Leone estuary over a ten-day period, its sails ragged from the storms, each new shipload of immigrants noticed how the famous lion-shaped mountain relieved the long, flat coastline. "It was a great joy to see the land," wrote the minister David George. "The high mountain, at some distance . . . appeared like a cloud to us. I preached the first Lord's day, it was a blessed time, under a sail." The settlers offered prayers and hymns, made tents out of sails and spars, and began cutting down trees to build a new hillside settlement, Freetown.

All was not well, however, in this outpost of the abolitionist dream. Alexander Falconbridge and the other white administrators on shore, it turned out, had done nothing to prepare for the convoy's arrival. Then there was a growing rift between John Clarkson and Thomas Peters. Peters's mission to England had made the whole voyage possible, and he had personally recruited more than a third of the migrants. But waiting for the convoy in Sierra Leone were orders from London unexpectedly appointing Clarkson—who had intended to head directly back to England to be married—the colony's superintendent. Peters thus had to remain subordinate to a white Englishman half his age. Unfortunately the written record of this dispute is almost entirely Clarkson's, whose diary is full of entries like, "I was extremely mortified and distressed at the behaviour of Peters this evening . . . he still persisted in his obstinacy; he vexed me extremely." Eventually he decided that "this rascal had been working in the dark from the time he landed to get himself at the Head of the People"—a reasonable ambition, it would seem, and one clearly supported by many black settlers. But Clarkson preferred to think of himself as the paternal Moses of the venture. He took an obvious pleasure in donning his full-dress naval uniform to impress an African chief, who exclaimed that he "had never seen so young a king before." Clarkson wrote somewhat grandiosely to Lafayette that "the poor people I brought with me from America begin to feel the sweets of free government."

Peters's supporters wanted to elect him governor, and more than a hundred blacks signed a statement making him their spokesman. Clarkson, whose personal popularity with the settlers seemed to blind him to their burning desire for democracy, rang a bell to summon the community and, under a tree, the two men had a bitter public confrontation. The conflict soon ended, however, when Peters suddenly fell ill and died. His ghost was said to haunt the colony for years afterwards, as did the issue he raised, the right to self-rule.

Besides being undemocratic, the colony's government was also strangely organized, for Clarkson's only power as superintendent was to cast a tie-breaking vote on the council of eight white administrators. "Your government," John Clarkson wrote his brother, a Company director, "is of the most absurd kind and calculated to make [the settlers] miserable." A military man of action, he fired off a letter to the Company demanding more authority, which he received, but only after frustrating months of waiting as ships went to and fro.

His conflict with Peters was not the only one, for the hot-tempered, burly Falconbridge was similarly put out that *he* had not been appointed superintendent instead of this much younger, diminutive man who had never even been to Africa before. His increasingly estranged wife, however, took a great liking to Clarkson's "winning manners" and found him "an aimiable man, void of pomp or ostentation." From her Clarkson got an earful about the bungling of Sierra Leone's white officials to date, whose "absurd behaviour," she wrote, "make[s] them the laughing stocks of . . . such masters of slave ships as have witnessed their conduct, who must certainly be highly gratified with the anarchy and chagrin that prevails through the Colony."

Company directors in London, with little idea of this discord, bombarded John Clarkson with optimistic proposals for further settlements and trading posts. "The eyes of England are upon you & this Infant Colony," wrote his brother. ". . . To your lot it falls to be Governor of the Noblest Institution ever set on foot . . . an Attempt to civilize and christianize a great Continent . . . & to abolish the Trade in Men." On a shrewder note, Thomas suggested that being superintendent would help John's prospects in the navy: "You cannot after having been the Governor of a great Establishment, the Colonel of troops & c, be allowed to serve as a Lieutenant on board of a Man of War . . . you must have Rank."

The immigrants Clarkson accompanied to Sierra Leone from Canada included several who had been taken into slavery from this very river mouth. Thirty-year-old Frank Peters, a former slave in South Carolina, found the precise spot where he had been captured, to be sold to an American slave ship, fifteen years before. Then one day, in the words of a Company official, an elderly local woman showed "very peculiar emotions" when she saw Peters; "she ran up to him and embraced him: she proved to be his own mother." He resettled for a time in his old village. John Gordon, a lay Methodist leader in North America, had been sold from Bance Island when he was about fifteen. Four years after arriving back in Sierra Leone, he would meet the man who kidnapped him. He gave his captor a present and told him, "Your thoughts were evil, but God meant it for good—I now know God and Christ." Another black settler, Martha Webb, recognized her mother in a chain of slaves being led into captivity and, with a gift of wine, persuaded a local chief to let her go. We can only imagine the emotions in these encounters, about which surviving documents reveal little more; they are almost unique in the records of Atlantic slavery.

As the months went on, the new settlers' Promised Land seemed filled with trials. Temperatures could reach 114 degrees at midday. Tornadoes tore down buildings. The brush that needed to be cleared for houses was twelve feet high and interspersed with razor-edged grass. A terrified settler found a leopard in his hut, and one night, John Clarkson wrote in his diary, "a large baboon entered one of the tents, and seized upon a girl about twelve years of age, by the heel, and dragged her out of the tent. Her cries alarmed a man who was sleeping in the same place, who immediately caught hold of her arm. . . . A trial of strength now took place between them; the baboon endeavouring all in its power to carry off the girl, and the man equally determined to prevent him. Some assistance coming, the animal let go his hold, and ran off into the woods." Insects were legion and some local snakes measured up to eighteen feet long. If allowed to graze freely, farm animals ate the poisonous fruit of a local tree and died.

Only a month after the convoy's arrival an unusually severe seven-month rainy season began. From leaking tents came, Clarkson gloomily recorded, "stench from rotten Cheese, rancid Butter, bad provisions, damaged pickled Tripe." In the incessant rain, "nothing made of steel can be preserved from rust. Knives, scissors, keys, etc., look like old, rusty, iron. Our watches are spoiled by rust, and laid aside useless." Leather turned moldy and cloth rotted. Little help were the supplies that arrived from England intact, such as machinery for processing sugar and cotton—crops that grew only in the Company directors' imagination. People in London had no sense of what those in Sierra Leone might need. To Clarkson, Wilberforce sent a custom-made writing desk, the Company directors an engraved sword, and Granville Sharp a plan for the layout of townships.

The Nova Scotia settlers soon started to fall sick and some two hundred were dead by the year's end. "It is quite customary of a morning," wrote Anna Maria Falconbridge, "to ask 'how many died last night.'" Malaria, known as "putrid fever," was rampant. The settlement's doctors were of little use. One tended to wander off overnight, visiting African women and collecting natural history specimens; another Clarkson first ran into when the doctor was "so drunk, as not to know who I was." The man died the following day. In firing a salute at his funeral, a gunner managed to blow his own hand off, and soon perished as well.

Even had it had no internal problems, Sierra Leone would have been at risk as long as the slave trade continued. Because the abolitionist colony was so close to Bance Island and other slave depots, escaped slaves and badly treated British sailors sought help there, and angry captains came after them. What to do with the "renegade seamen," wrote Mrs. Falconbridge, ". . . considerably perplexes Mr. Clarkson, who, on the one hand is . . . threatened with lawsuits by the masters and owners of ships detained for want of their sailors, but is well convinced of the injury they sustain." She, however, took the side of the slavers, and was shocked to her imperial bones when a white sailor who had stolen a settler's duck was sentenced by "a *Jury of twelve blacks*" of a "*sham* Court" to a flogging administered by a black man: "one of the most atrocious infringements on the liberty of British subjects . . . that has yet occurred among us."

Uneasy as the relationship between the slave traders and abolitionists of Sierra Leone was, it remained more cordial than either side might have predicted. Although Clarkson usually turned them down, other white colony officials often accepted invitations to eat dinner and drink West Indian rum on ships sailing past Freetown on their way to or from picking up slaves. Frustratingly, the slavers often were the only means through which colony officials could get their mail from London, and were the only people with whom they could trade for food, medicine, and British newspapers. "These little civilities and attentions are necessary in a country where you stand in need of mutual assistance," wrote Clarkson regretfully.

Meanwhile, he was increasingly disturbed to see Falconbridge drinking himself into a stupor. Officials in London had given Falconbridge the title of Commercial Agent, with the near-impossible task of developing trade from the colony. When there was no sign of results, they fired him, which, his wife wrote,

> proved a mortal stab . . . after this, by way of meliorating his harrowed feelings, he kept himself constantly intoxicated; a poor forlorn remedy you will say, however it answered his wishes, which I am convinced was to operate as poison and thereby finish his existence; he spun out his life in anguish and misery till the 19th instant, when, without a groan he gasp'd his last.!!!
>
> I will not be guilty of such meanness as to tell a falsehood on this occasion, by saying I regret his death, no! . . . His conduct to me for more than two years past, was so unkind, (not to give it a harsher term) as, long since to wean every spark of affection or regard I ever had for him."

Despite the many problems, after some months things appeared to be improving, and there seemed reason to believe that the little colony could at last prove that freed slaves could become prosperous citizens of the British Empire. The rains had finally stopped. Clarkson was recovering his naval officer's ebullience; more buildings were up; the church was filled on Sunday; the settlers' poultry was doing well; and their small fishing boats were bringing home a good catch.

As the first distribution of farmland began, Clarkson simply ignored orders from London reserving all prime shorefront land for the Company itself. Even when he had recruited settlers in Nova Scotia, his enthusiasm had led him somewhat beyond the Company's instructions when he told blacks how easily they would receive free land, a big incentive for emigration. Meanwhile, in London, the Company had decided that all settlers granted land would have to pay a large tax, plus an additional tax on their produce. To Clarkson and the black settlers, this felt like betrayal.

After nearly a year in Sierra Leone, Clarkson, whose fiancée was still waiting in England (in her honor he had named Susan's Bay, a cove just south of the settlement), set sail for a Britain that, he fervently hoped, was soon to abolish the slave trade. Despite their lack of self-rule, the settlers mourned his departure, fearing that London would never send them so good a superintendent again. Counting on him to lobby the Company into reversing the hated decision about land taxes, forty-nine black settlers wrote the directors, "From the time he met with us in novascotia he ever did behave to us as a gentilmon in everey rescpt. . . . We pray that his Excelency John Clarkson might Be preserved safe over the sea to his frinds and return to us again." Poverty-stricken though they were, the settlers raised a contribution for Clarkson to take to the abolition committee.

Even Anna Maria Falconbridge, who seldom had a good word to say about anyone, wrote that Clarkson's departure "operated more powerfully and generally upon people's feelings, than all the deaths we have had in the Colony." The settlers gave him a tremendous sendoff, with gifts of chickens, pigs, eggs, and yams for the voyage. He wept at their generosity, and told them he hoped to return, perhaps with his new wife. Once he arrived in England, though, he was too vocal for his own good about the colony's death rate, the incompetent white staff, and the black settlers' hunger for land. He also made too clear to the directors his feeling that they were living in an Evangelical dream world; they denied a promotion to someone he had recommended, for example, on grounds that the man was known to swear. The Company told Clarkson his services were no longer needed. Crushed, he was never to return to Sierra Leone.

Remaining behind in Africa, but not for long, was Mrs. Falconbridge. Only three weeks after her husband had drunk himself to death, she married a white official of the colony, Isaac DuBois. It was not abolition but the need for a job that had brought DuBois to Sierra Leone. He was the scion of wealthy North Carolina cotton planters, loyal to the British in the American Revolution, who had then fled to England to spend many years seeking compensation for their lost property and slaves. And who else now appeared on the scene but Anna Maria's brother-in-law, Matthew Morley, captain of a Bristol ship, the 197-ton *Nassau,* which had been cruising the African coast collecting slaves before buying a final batch at Bance Island. Anna Maria and her new husband had had enough of what she thought a foolish abolitionist experiment. What better way to return to England than via the Caribbean, in the "excellent accomodations" of her brother-in-law's ship, as it carried its cargo of 190 slaves to Jamaica?

Twelve slaves on board died before the ship had left the African coast, but neither that nor the voyage changed her mind about slavery. "I always entertained most horrid notions of being exposed to indelicacies, too offensive for the eye of an English woman, on board these ships; however, I never was more agreeably disappointed in my life. . . . [The slaves] experienced the utmost kindness and care, and after a few days, when they had recovered from sea sickness, I never saw more signs of content and satisfaction, among any set of people." Thanks to "excellent" clean quarters and fresh air on deck, they arrived "in much higher health than when they embarked."

In the West Indies, Anna Maria found blacks even happier than on the middle passage. "All the slaves I had an opportunity of seeing in Jamaica, seemed vastly well satisfied, their conditions appeared to be far preferable to what I expected, and they discovered more cheerfulness than I ever observed the Blacks shew in Africa." The couple returned to England and, her book of adventures quickly published, settled in Anna Maria's hometown of Bristol, where, as with so many women of her time, no further trace of her remains.

15

THE SWEETS OF LIBERTY

IF WE PAUSE and step back to consider the British antislavery movement so far, what is most astonishing is how quickly it caught the public imagination. When the twelve-man abolition committee first gathered in May 1787, the handful of people in Britain who openly called for an end to slavery or the slave trade were regarded as oddballs, or at best as hopelessly idealistic. Yet in less than a year something unprecedented burst into being. Britons were challenging slavery in London debating societies, in provincial pubs, and across dinner tables throughout the country. Antislavery arguments filled bookshop shelves and newspaper columns. By a few years later, Equiano's autobiography had become a surprise bestseller, at least 300,000 people were refusing to eat slave-grown sugar, and Parliament was deluged with the most petitions it had ever received on any subject. Few countries in any age have seen a social movement of such scope erupt so suddenly.

Why did it do so? Some credit, of course, goes to brilliant planning. Thomas Clarkson was a magnificent organizer, and his Quaker allies were dedicated, resourceful people with the determination of those who knew firsthand something about being an oppressed minority. The close alliance between the fiery radical Clarkson and the cautious Evangelical Wilberforce—and the political tendencies each man represented—was central and long-lasting. But superb organization by itself cannot bring a popular crusade into being. Clarkson's five months of travel around England in 1787 was a crucial spark that helped ignite the movement. Yet the six equally hard-working months he spent two years later in France—moreover, in a revolutionary France that had just adopted the Declaration of the Rights of Man and Citizen—resulted in nothing. The first French mass antislavery petition would not come until 1844, and even then it garnered fewer signatures than the city of Manchester alone had sent to the House of Commons in 1788.

Manchester, of course, was a birthplace of the Industrial Revolution, and some have suggested a link: industrialism's rationality, perhaps, or, conversely, the way uprooted, exploited workers identified with uprooted, exploited slaves. However, none of the other half-dozen European nations with slave colonies spawned antislavery movements when they industrialized. What was different about Britain?

Begin with geography. At a time when travel was mainly by horse, coach, or on foot, Britain was a compact country with rapidly improving roads. In 1754, it took an exhausting 230 hours to get from London to Edinburgh by coach; in 1792, an abolitionist organizer made the trip in only 75 hours, including an overnight stay at an inn en route. Most of the increased speed was due to better roads and some to the addition of "flying machines"—coaches that ran through the night. (If you wanted to save money, outside seats were half price.) By contrast, normal travel time from north to south in the United States, France, or Spain was more likely to be measured in weeks. In 1779, the former slave merchant Henry Laurens took a full month to travel from Philadelphia to South Carolina.

At the heart of Britain's highway boom was a massive investment in well-kept toll roads, or turnpikes. As it happened, Britain's first turnpike was opened at Wades Mill, Hertfordshire, more than a century before Thomas Clarkson got off his horse there and sat down beside the road, when he was riding from Cambridge to London in 1785. Within Clarkson's lifetime, England and Wales would be dotted with 7,796 tollgates, where a toll collector emerged from his hut to swing open a barrier and let you onto the turnpike. In 1740, one coach a week ran from London to Birmingham; by 1783, there were thirty; by 1829, there would be more than two hundred.

Furthermore, when outlying cities sent petitions to Parliament or when the London committee dispatched the latest antislavery pamphlets to the far ends of the country, these were carried by the world's best postal service. By the mid-1780s, you could send a letter from London to many towns in southern England overnight, and all the way to Dublin in just three days. Like everything else that mattered, it seems, the head post office for the entire British Empire was within two blocks of James Phillips's printing shop. The *City Press* describes the scene at its Lombard Street entrance:

> If you sought to cross the road, you had to beware of the flying postman, or the letter-bag express. As six o'clock drew near, every court, alley, and blind thoroughfare in the neighborhood echoed to the incessant din of letter-bells. . . . Such armies of clerks! such sacks of letters. . . . A post-chaise, with the horses in a positive lather, tore into the street, just in time to forward some important despatch. Hark! the horn! the horn! . . . The clock will strike in less than five minutes; the clamour deepens, the hubbub seems increasing; but ere the last sixty seconds expire, a sharp winding of warning bugles begins. Coachee flourishes his whip—greys and chestnuts prepare for a run—the reins move, but very gently—there is a parting crack from the whipcord—and the brilliant cavalcade is gone.

The British Post Office had undergone a major reform in 1784. That year, four horses pulled the first swift all-weather mail coach, painted handsomely in red, black, and maroon, from the Swan with Two Necks pub in London to Bristol in a mere sixteen hours, a time considered so amazing that crowds cheered the coach for the last few miles of its journey. Along the way, through the night, such coaches picked up mailbags without stopping. New services, which carried passengers as well, soon started up on seventeen other routes from London, racing along at up to ten miles an hour. "This speed was thought to be highly dangerous to the head," one high official later recalled; ". . . stories were told of men and women who, having reached London with such celerity, died suddenly of an affection of the brain."

"Even the brother-in-law of a coachman in the Royal Post would regard himself as a person of importance," wrote the essayist William Hazlitt. Highwaymen were notorious for attacking postal couriers, so on top of a locked box of mail at the rear of each new coach sat a guard, resplendent in a scarlet coat with blue lapels and gold braid, a blue waistcoat with brass buttons, and a beaverskin hat with a gold band. Each guard was armed with a blunderbuss, a pistol, two cutlasses, and a bugle to summon help. In the face of such a daunting arsenal, the highwaymen melted away and the guards took to shooting at chickens and tooting their bugles at pretty young women.

Besides mail, the swift new coaches carried something else vitally important to civil society: newspapers. There were so many of these that the postal authorities opened a special branch office in London to handle them, and many British papers still have "Mail" or "Post" as part of their names. By the mid-1780s, a dozen newspapers were published in London, almost all dailies. Four of them were more than sixty years old; by contrast, the first French daily, *Le Journal de Paris,* only appeared in 1777. There were forty-nine newspapers elsewhere in Britain and dozens of magazines as well. These provincial papers mainly paraphrased the London press; this was not great journalism, but it guaranteed that any trend in the capital spread almost instantly to every corner of the country. Newspapers were crucial to the spread of antislavery feeling: they reprinted articles, published fund appeals, and their reports of abolitionist meetings and petitions in provincial cities stimulated similar actions elsewhere.

Closely interwoven with newspapers was another institution famously central to British civic life, the coffeehouse—a place that might be the scene of anything from the sale of stocks to an actor reciting a new literary work. The coffee itself was served like soup, in one-penny bowls. More than five hundred coffeehouses were scattered around London alone, most with copies of competing dailies on hand for their customers. At Moses Dimmock's library-coffeehouse in Winchester, visitors could read three London dailies, three weeklies, three provincial papers, and various monthlies. Although the Swiss visitor

César de Saussure found the coffeehouses "not over clean or well furnished, owing to the quantity of people who resort to these places and because of the smoke," he noted that "all Englishmen are great newsmongers. Workmen habitually begin the day by going to coffeerooms in order to read the latest news." Visiting from France, the Abbé Prévost admired these establishments "where you have the right to read all the papers for and against the government." He declared coffeehouses the "seats of English liberty." Ironically, of course, both the sugar and the coffee consumed in these seats of liberty were almost all harvested by West Indian slaves.

It was not only in coffeehouses that Britons read their newspapers. The French philosopher Montesquieu was surprised to see a roofer having his paper delivered to him atop the house where he was working. Nikolai Karamzin, a Russian writer, marveled in 1789 that "here newspapers and magazines are in everyone's hands, not only in town but in small villages as well." Newspapers had particular impact because more than half the people in England were literate. Many of them had parents or grandparents who were not, and so they treasured the printed word. For Dissenting, or non-Anglican, churches, whose members would play a disproportionate part in the antislavery movement, reading was at the heart of a devout life. John Wesley urged his preachers to spend at least five hours a day reading "the most useful books," and the Methodist Book Room in London distributed literature by the ton.

At the eighteenth century's end there were more than a hundred libraries in London. And if you wanted to avoid finding an earlier reader's wig powder or candle wax in a book, you could buy it new. The country had well over a thousand bookstores, plus sidewalk bookstalls by the dozen in every city; twenty printers and twelve booksellers did business in Newcastle upon Tyne alone. The London book dealer James Lackington's Temple of the Muses in Finsbury Square—"Cheapest Booksellers in the World"—was so big, it was claimed, that a coach and six horses could drive around inside. Lackington boasted of an annual turnover of 100,000 volumes. Just as today's primary temple of retail commerce, the supermarket, has magazines, flowers, and school supplies, so a sign of the importance of the British bookstore of this era was that it might also sell sealing wax or fishing tackle or, like one in Bridport, Dorset, "excellent Pills, Worm Cakes, Eye-Water and a remedy for Warts."

As striking as their abundance was the fact that British newspapers and books were completely uncensored. They were free to poke fun at the royal family, to mock cabinet ministers, to attack slavery. By contrast, at the end of its *ancien régime* France had 178 censors at work. For almost the entire eighteenth century no Briton needed government permission to own a printing press—a freedom that citizens of many countries don't have today. Equally unfettered, as we have seen, were the debating societies, which surged into prominence less than a decade before the birth of abolitionism. In 1778, London had only five of them; two years later there were thirty-five. From capital punishment to polygamy to eliminating the word "obey" in the marriage ceremony, nothing was forbidden territory. Class differences were forgotten. One critic bemoaned how debates "level all distinctions" of rank, leading to the promiscuous mixing of "wits, lawyers, politicians and mechanics."

Such unrestrained argument, in speech and in print, gave the English a reputation for cheek, something curiously at odds with the society's rigid stratification by wealth and caste. De Saussure described a holiday crowd as "particularly insolent and rowdy . . . for the great liberty it enjoys. At these times it is almost dangerous . . . for a foreigner, if at all well dressed, to walk in the streets. . . . He is sure of not only being jeered at and being bespattered with mud, but as likely as not dead dogs and cats will be thrown at him."

What foreigners saw as insolence, Britons knew as freedom. Here lay a contradiction so deep, given the overseas British slave empire, that the abolitionists were ultimately able to build a movement on it. With cheerful disregard for their role as the world's biggest slave-trading nation, ever since the 1740s the British had proudly sung:

> Rule, Britannia! Britannia rule the waves.
> Britons never, never, never shall be slaves.

Whites might think slavery normal for black people, but when imposed on themselves, it was something shocking—although, surprisingly often, Britons *did* become slaves. As the historian Linda Colley points out, because of Britain's imperial reach, its relatively small army was always spread thin, and British men and women were forever being taken prisoner by darker peoples elsewhere: at least three thousand by Native American raiders in the 1750s and 1760s; more than 20 percent of the British soldiers in India in fighting that began in the following decade; and some twenty thousand held for ransom, often for years, by North Africa's Barbary pirates between about 1600 and 1750. The pirates' prisoners got the most attention; at one point British captives in Algiers included the Earl of Inchquin, who, with no apparent sense of irony, later went on to become governor of Britain's biggest slave colony, Jamaica. In 1751, more than a thousand people packed Covent Garden Theatre to watch a candlelit pageant featuring a group of emaciated, sunburnt men who had recently returned from nearly five years' captivity in Morocco. For this strange occasion, they again wore rags, fetters, and chains, which they rattled against the stage. That so many people flocked to see them is testimony to how outrageous seemed the idea of enslaving white people. It would be decades more before Britons began to feel similar outrage over the idea of enslaving blacks. But the many tales of suffering written by returned prisoners helped establish captivity as a metaphor for injustice and misery.

Why was it thought so horrendous when Britons were turned into slaves? One answer was that at a time when the vast majority of people in the world were living in servitude of some sort, people in Britain felt proudly different. Increasing numbers of them were working in cities as wage laborers, and ever fewer as tenant farmers under the thumb of the landed gentry. They boisterously, sometimes violently, staged public protests on issues that inflamed them: taxes, quarrels with Catholics, labor rights. In 1766, workers in Honiton, angry over wheat prices, seized grain from farmers, sold it at market at what they considered a fair price, and returned the money and the empty sacks to the growers. In 1775, some two thousand slave ship sailors, of all people, demonstrated for higher wages and better working conditions by marching through Liverpool under a red flag. They carried cutlasses, slashed sails, wrecked rigging, looted and burned the homes of wealthy ship owners, and briefly bombarded the stock exchange with a stolen cannon.

Agitation sparked by the populist journalist and politician John Wilkes in the 1760s introduced many Britons to tools like the petition and the political pamphlet. Wars traditionally muffle all dissent, yet both press and Parliament carried on a remarkably vigorous debate over the right of the North American colonies to secede.

Most Britons, however, lacked the right to vote. The unelected House of Lords comprised several hundred noblemen and twenty-six Church of England bishops. And less than 5 percent of the population, all men, were eligible to vote for the House of Commons. An encrusted mixture of near-feudal practices made even this limited franchise still more unfair. Some members of Parliament fought campaigns over real issues, but most in effect bought their seats, as Wilberforce had, or were chosen by major landowners who might control half a dozen or more constituencies. In "potwalloper" boroughs, voters included all adult men not on poor relief—that is, who owned a fireplace in which they could boil pots. In other constituencies voters had to own a certain amount of property, while in many districts only a handful of people could vote (exactly thirteen each in Buckingham and in Malmesbury). Nonetheless, however odd and unrepresentative was Parliament, Britons knew that few other countries in Europe had legislatures at all, and none of those had more power than the king, as was the case in Britain. Furthermore, electoral campaigns, with their colorful torrents of speechmaking, marching bands, ballads, and leaflets full of anonymous denunciations and insulting cartoons, were a spectacle seen by everyone, voters and the disenfranchised alike. Millions of people could applaud or jeer candidates. A French traveler in the early 1780s was startled to see British sailors fighting in a pub over speeches given in Parliament. Even if most of them couldn't vote, Britons still lived in a culture of democracy.

Moreover, they knew they lived under the rule of law. There was no torture or arbitrary imprisonment. In theory, at least, a laborer could take a lord to court and win. With the help of Granville Sharp, a string of former slaves *did* take their would-be masters to court and won. A free black footman working for the painter Sir Joshua Reynolds successfully had a white man prosecuted at the Old Bailey for theft. (The thief got the death sentence, which was commuted on appeal.) The judicial system served the rich better than the poor, but there was trial by jury. Britons' confidence in their rights ran proud and deep. Without it, the abolitionists could never have persuaded them that slaves had rights as well.

A sense of rights can be contagious, something that worried Sir John Fielding, a London police magistrate and half-brother of the novelist. Before the Somerset decision's de facto elimination of slavery in England itself in 1772, Fielding was alarmed that slaves brought to the country by West Indian masters "no sooner come over, but the Sweets of Liberty and the Conversation with free Men and Christians, enlarge their Minds, and enable them too soon to form such Comparisons of different Situations."

It is hardly unexpected that a slave suddenly surrounded by free men and women would make such comparisons. A recurring complaint among planters who brought slaves to England was that they soon began asking for wages. Clearly, servants and other working-class whites were telling them they should be paid for their labor. Britons who had some rights were already empathizing with slaves who had none.

Equiano experienced this leap of empathy more than once. When he found himself sold to a new owner by the naval officer Pascal, fellow sailors "strove . . . to cheer me, and told me he could not sell me, and that they would stand by me." In the end, the threat of draconian naval discipline intimidated them, but several slipped on board the ship of Equiano's new master with oranges and other presents for him. Some months later, still a slave, he recorded another act of kindness by "a British seaman . . . whose heart had not been debauched by a West India climate," who saved him from being beaten by a white man.

Equiano was not the only slave treated in a friendly manner by lower-class British whites. When nine black sailors from a Brazilian vessel in port at Liverpool were thrown into jail at their captain's demand under the pretense of being debtors, they explained to their fellow prisoners that he feared their escape to freedom. The white prisoners got word to a local abolitionist, who obtained a court order setting the men free. In Scotland in 1770, when a slave owner in Fife attempted to return a black man named David Spens to the West

Indies against his will, local coal miners and salt pit workers raised money for Spens's legal defense.

The question remains: What made these leaps of empathy possible? Americans also lived with the same stark contradiction between civil liberties for whites and slavery for blacks, yet no widespread antislavery movement would take hold among them until nearly half a century after it had done so in Britain. Even then it would have less popular support. One crucial difference, of course, was that Britain's slaves were not in Britain. To push for ending slavery was to threaten planters and ship owners, but it did not, as in the United States, risk secession or civil war. And with the slaves on the other side of the ocean, for Britons to oppose slavery did not threaten their own way of life. Slaves were not cooking the meals or doing the laundry or working the fields of people in Britain itself.

Yet distance does not fully explain why the movement took life in Britain. The Atlantic Ocean separated six other European nations—France, Spain, Portugal, Sweden, Denmark, and Holland—from their slave colonies, but no antislavery crusade to speak of arose in any of them. The absence of a popular movement in the last three is particularly striking: all three were relatively enlightened societies with far higher literacy rates than Britain, and the last two shared the compact geography that had made it so easy for new ideas to spread there.

Was there, in addition to the strength of its civil society, anything else that set Britain apart?

There was. People are more likely to care about the suffering of others in a distant place if that misfortune evokes a fear of their own. And late-eighteenth-century Britons were in the midst of a widespread firsthand experience with a kind of kidnapping and enslavement that stood in dramatic contradiction to everything about citizens' rights enshrined in British law. It was arbitrary, violent, and sometimes fatal. Equiano, as a sailor, took part in it. John Newton was a victim of it. John Clarkson, as a naval officer, was intimately familiar with it. Granville Sharp denounced it as heatedly as he did slavery. It was the practice of naval impressment.

The Royal Navy could rule the waves only because it was far bigger than any other fleet, and it expanded with every conflict throughout this era of battling empires; during the Napoleonic Wars, it would reach a peak of nearly 1,000 ships and more than 140,000 men. In wartime, at least a third to a half of all naval seamen were "pressed" into service, and by some estimates the proportion was far higher. Since the 1600s, press gangs of armed sailors had patrolled Britain's ports, rounding up any sturdy-looking seafaring men they could find. Just offshore, naval ships did the same; London-bound merchantmen might be stopped as they sailed up the Thames. Such incoming merchant vessels—a prime target for the press gangs—sometimes dropped off their able-bodied crewmen at remote spots along the coast and limped into port manned only by elderly or crippled sailors. But that just sent the gangs roaming inland. A newspaper in 1770 noted hundreds of men on the roads streaming north from London to avoid the press. A man might be walking down the street or tending his garden and a few hours later find himself on a frigate, eating hard biscuit and salt pork, bound for the Caribbean or the Indian Ocean for several years of floggings, scurvy, and malaria. Not surprisingly, these unwilling seamen deserted at a high rate whenever they could, which led to brutal punishments for those caught and the impressment of more men to fill their places.

Like any power based on violence, impressment lent itself to corruption. A bribe to the right officer and the press gang would cart off an errant husband, a personal enemy, a rival in business or love. A verse from one ballad ran,

> Now when the father came to know
> His daughter lov'd the young man so,
> He caus'd him to be prest to sea,
> To keep him from her company.

Press victims were not only from the working class. The fact that his father was a ship's captain did not save the young John Newton from the press. Men from the privileged classes were given written "protections," but even this wasn't foolproof: What if you didn't have your papers with you and couldn't get word to anyone before being shut under iron gratings in the hold of a ship about to sail? And when the navy was desperate for men, the Admiralty would order a "hot press" in which protections were ignored.

Societies of all kinds have had military conscription, but the press was not an orderly draft that followed bureaucratic rules. It was kidnapping by armed men, and people in seaports—including London—lived in constant fear. Prints from the time show press gangs barging into homes, grabbing men in their beds, or hauling the groom out of a wedding procession while the bride screams in horror. In one cartoon, a press gang with tricornered hats and wooden staves hustles a man away while his wife, on her knees, implores, "For goodness sake dear your Honour, set him free, he maintains his Father, Mother & Wife." An officer replies, "Let them starve & be damned, the King wants Men, haul him on board."

Many sailors seized by press gangs fought back. Between 1740 and 1805 more than five hundred violent brawls between press gangs and their victims were serious enough to be reported, and doubtless many more never made it into court records or the newspapers. After several months' work in Bristol in 1759, every member of a press gang there had been wounded, and one killed. When a London press gang passed a whaling dock with three sailors in custody, reported the lieutenant in charge, "they were violently assaulted by some hundreds of Men . . . who not only rescued the Men the Gang had Procured, but almost killed three of the press gang by Cutts and Bruises in their Heads and some broken Ribbs."

In the American Revolutionary War, the press kidnapped more than eighty thousand men, provoking riots in at least twenty-two British seaports. An Admiralty official investigating the resistance found it "very remarkable That almost every Inhabitant in the town of Deal saw the Rioters and yet they all pretend they can't name or with any Degree of certainty describe [them]." Britain had a tradition of strong local government, and justices of the peace and even the Lord Mayor of London intermittently refused to cooperate with the navy. Sometimes women attacked press gangs with mops, trying to rescue their husbands. In Bristol, a navy man with a pressed citizen in tow was halted by a local merchant "who raised a Mob and took the man from him in the course of which he, the Petty Officer, was very much beat," said an Admiralty report. Angry families filed a flood of private lawsuits against navy officials, including Equiano's former owner Pascal. When in charge of the press gang in the port of King's Lynn, he had made the mistake of seizing a man in a local pub who turned out to be an apprentice to the town's mayor.

The debating societies argued over impressment. Letters to newspapers attacked it. Granville Sharp came to the aid of press victims, brought prosecutions, accumulated "some large drawers" full of documentary ammunition, and bent the ear of any influential person who would listen. "Called on Dr. Johnson," he recorded in his diary. "Had a long debate with him on the legality of pressing seamen." He was delighted to hear of some London sailors who "on being attacked by a Press Gang shut the Wharf Gates & gave them a hearty drubbing, till the Lieutenant & his men cryed out for mercy." Thomas Clarkson loathed impressment, as he did any form of injustice. During one war scare when press victims were many, he spent three days on the banks of the Thames talking with the wives of men who had been pressed. He was so moved by the plight of one weeping woman with a baby in her arms that he hired a small boat and took her to a navy battleship offshore, in an unsuccessful search for her husband.

Clarkson and Sharp keenly saw the resemblance between Britons seized by press gangs and the nearly half-million blacks in the British Caribbean, and they were far from alone. "Poor Sailors," Captain Thomas Pasley of the Royal Navy wrote in his diary in 1780. "You are the only class of beings in our famed Country of Liberty really *Slaves.*" As with the outrage at Britons taken prisoner overseas, more than a century of public anger at the press gangs strengthened the idea that violently capturing other human beings to put them to work was cruelly unjust—and could and should be fought against. Impressment proved hard to uproot, and did not end until well into the nineteenth century. Curiously ignored by scholars, the long public struggle against it psychologically set the national stage for the much larger battle over slavery.

16

HIGH NOON IN PARLIAMENT

DESPITE THEIR DEFEAT in the previous year's parliamentary session, as 1792 began, the abolitionists hoped that at last they were at the edge of victory. "Of the enthusiasm of the nation at this time," wrote Thomas Clarkson, who had just finished another exhausting horseback marathon around the country, "none can form an opinion but they who witnessed it. There never was perhaps a season when so much virtuous feeling pervaded all ranks. . . . The current ran with such strength and rapidity, that it was impossible to stem it." The sugar boycott was at its peak, and slavery supporters felt they had their backs to the wall. "Is the imaginary cruelty of the *West India Planters,*" wrote one, "to be the theme of every *drinking club* and *psalm singing meeting?*" Before the year was out, a young student at Cambridge named Samuel Taylor Coleridge would win a gold medal for his "Ode Against the Slave Trade," written in Greek. ("O Death," it begins, "welcome respite for a race yoked to misery, passport out of hell . . ."). His future friend William Wordsworth declared that the abolition fervor of 1792 was nothing less "than a whole Nation crying with one voice."

In early January, the abolition committee sent a young clergyman, William Dickson, "to enquire into the progress of our cause" in Scotland. The small leather-bound diary of this trip in Dickson's handwriting is the only written record, other than Clarkson's, we have from an eighteenth-century abolition organizer on the road. A rigid type, he methodically classified people he met as having one of two degrees of sympathy: "Dundee . . . Rev. Mr. Davidson—*zealous.* . . . Ebenezer Anderson Merch[an]t hearty." He also classified some people as "*almost* hearty." Zealous and hearty friends of the cause met him everywhere.

A far prissier traveler than Clarkson, Dickson complains of "a flood of rain," a "violent snowstorm," "abominable deep roads," "most excerable roads," and "shocking roads." But what is chilling to the reader of Dickson's diary is the way, even in remote corners of Scotland, he keeps meeting people with hair-raising tales to tell about slavery. "Mr. McNeill mentioned . . . a Scotchman in Jama[ica] . . . who when his slaves were worn out and judged by the Doctor of the estate to be capable of no more work, had them carried to what he called the '*launch*' which consisted of a few boards whose ends inclined over a great precipice and from thence he had them launched into eternity."

For political reasons, the official position of the committee in London, of course, was that they were working only for the abolition of the slave trade, not for the emancipation of all slaves. But the cautious Dickson, who had once worked as private secretary to the governor of Barbados, seems to have been one of the few abolitionists who genuinely felt this way himself. He believed that slaves should be emancipated only "by *slow* degrees . . . because *the privileges granted to slaves must keep pace with their improvement in Christianity,* and because *the property of their owners must not be injured.*" On the list of reminders Dickson wrote to himself at the back of the diary, the first item is: "Impossible to be too earnest in pressing the distinction between emancipation and abolition." He was continually rattled, however, by running up against people who felt that if slavery was so evil, why shouldn't the slaves be freed?

The committee had instructed him to prepare sympathizers to quickly gather signatures on petitions to Parliament when asked, but not to let this get "to the ears of the planters, Slave merch[an]ts & W India Merchts [who would] endeavor to counteract the object, by getting counter-petitions." Nonetheless, Dickson found, as organizers often do, that local activists had not bothered to wait for orders from headquarters: "This day taken up chiefly about a popular petition here of 2000 names *already*."

Impulsive supporters were bad enough, but Dickson was still more upset that "there is scarce any preventing . . . improper people from signing." And who were the improper people? "By a mistaken zeal . . . 3 women have been allowed to sign—do not know how to act—Mr. J. Ogilvy advises me to say nothing." This was not the only place that improper people were penning their names. A newspaper reported that, on a petition from Belford, Northumberland, "Some of the 433 [signatories] are ladies, who were anxiously desirous to shew their abhorrence of this abominable trade." Women were supposed to keep demurely silent about politics, but once again the movement was drawing them into public life.

Huge numbers of Scots signed the petitions, which Dickson sent by coach to London. One can feel their enthusiasm even through his anxious eyes. He describes a massive "publick meeting" in Edinburgh in March, "so orderly it was and so silent . . . not a whisper but when plaudits made the place resound—No less than 3685 signed on the spot . . . all with the most admirable decorum—the magistrates had ordered the castle troops of the town guard to be in readiness—and 2 troops of Horse were brought in from the country—this was their duty." The calling out of cavalry for an entirely peaceful abolition meeting was an ominous sign of a shadow just beginning to fall across Britain: the eighteenth-century equivalent of a red scare, triggered by the French Revolution.

Not just in Scotland but in every major town and city throughout the British Isles there were now local abolition committees, sending petitions and contributions to London, and receiving, in return, the latest books and pamphlets from James Phillips's press. Their leaders were mostly clergymen, shopkeepers, merchants, skilled workers, and professionals; a few rivaled Granville Sharp in eccentricity, and one surpassed him. The chairman of the Scottish Abolition Committee, Francis, Lord Gardenstone, a retired judge, philanthropist, and landowner, was best known for his inordinate fondness for pigs. This came to light when a neighboring farmer called on him early one morning. Shown into the darkened bedroom, the visitor stumbled over a large object that gave a plaintive grunt. From his bed, Gardenstone hastened to explain: "It's just a bit soo [small sow], puir beast, and I laid my breeks [breeches] ower't to keep it warm a'nicht!" Another of his pet pigs followed him about like a dog. When one of his pigs was small, Gardenstone shared his bed with it.

As he jounced along the bad roads of Scotland, William Dickson had a worse problem to fret over than Lord Gardenstone's porcinophilia. For something had happened that would soon cause immense trouble for the abolitionists, and would before long disastrously involve Britain itself on a scale no one yet imagined. "Dundee. . . . Rev. Dr. Blunshall hesitates about St. Domingo insurr[ection]," Dickson wrote in his diary, "but hearty otherwise." The insurrection was a huge slave revolt in the French West Indian colony of St. Domingue (St. Domingo to the British), begun some months earlier but only now catching the attention of the public in Britain.

Back in London, "People . . . are all panic-struck with the transactions in St. Domingo," wrote Wilberforce to a friend. "I am pressed on all hands . . . to defer my motion till next year." The St. Domingue rebellion also undercut the sugar boycott. With the colony's slaves fighting instead of harvesting, its exports dropped drastically and the price of sugar in Europe shot up, instead of falling as the boycotters had hoped.

As Parliament approached a battle over the slave trade that threatened to end it for good, the slave interests launched what today we would call a media campaign. The West India Committee budgeted £1,600 for articles to be published "in the Newspapers and otherwise." By March 1792, a subcommittee of the group was meeting from noon to three every day at Ibbotson's Hotel to scour the press and reply "to what may be therein inserted by the Favourers of the Abolition."

A man named Bell was paid £5 a week simply to monitor provincial papers, especially in abolitionist strongholds, "to find out which will, and which will not, insert paragraphs from this Committee"; the group then hired a writer for £100 a year to churn out such items. Sometimes it paid newspapers directly to print this material—£50 went to London's *Whitehall Evening Post,* for example; sometimes it bought copies in bulk—six hundred of the capital's *Argus* on one occasion—"to give encouragement . . . for a favourable Report to the Interests of the Sugar Colonies." Far outspending the abolitionists, the committee rushed proslavery tracts to libraries in resort towns, in hopes that they would be seen by M.P.s taking the waters. They bought copies of a proslavery book for distribution "in the Country, particularly at Cambridge" (college towns leaned left even then); printed eight thousand copies of a pamphlet describing how each happy slave family had "a snug little house and garden, and plenty of pigs and poultry"; and paid one Mr. Clutterbuck to write a pamphlet saying that sugar "is a mild, nutritious, vegetable substance; possessing a power of correcting the ill effects arising from a too free use of animal food."

More money than ever was now at stake for the proslavery forces. First, with the sugar price so high, so were the plantation profits flowing back to England. And with France beset by revolution at home and a major slave revolt abroad, the British slave trade was in the midst of its peak year of traffic to date, with an average of three to four ships leaving English ports each week. British Caribbean planters were rushing new land into cultivation, and their demand for new slaves was higher than ever. "Everything in the shape of a ship . . . is fitting out for Africa," wrote one trader, and ". . . the money made by the voyages just now concluded exceeds anything ever known." Would Britons really turn their backs on such profits? Under the elegant chandeliers of his London club, Brooks's, Banastre Tarleton bet an officer friend 10 guineas that the slave trade would not be abolished.

Despite the pressure on him to do so, Wilberforce did not postpone his motion for abolition. Clarkson, Sharp, and several other committee members lobbied M.P.s intensively. As the debate drew closer, abolition petitions flooded Parliament as never before. When unrolled, the one Dickson had seen being signed in Edinburgh stretched the whole length of the House of Commons floor. Thirteen thousand people signed in Glasgow; twenty thousand in Manchester, nearly one third of the city's population. The petitions from some small towns bore the signatures of almost every literate inhabitant. Altogether, in a few weeks, 519 abolition petitions came from all over England, Scotland, and Wales bearing at least 390,000 names. (By contrast, only some 250,000 people had signed petitions on *any* subject whatever between 1765 and 1784, a politically stormy time that included the American Revolution.) They arrived at such a rate that one newspaper declared they "almost obstructed the proceedings of the House by their perpetual introduction"—this because petitions traditionally were read aloud before debates. More people had signed the petitions than were eligible to vote for Parliament.

Four petitions arrived in favor of the slave trade.

The debate, the climax of five years of antislavery organizing, ran through the night. And so we must imagine the House of Commons chamber, designed by Sir Christopher Wren, dimly lit by a chandelier and candles in sconces; the snuffboxes at the doors; the black-cloaked clerks; the Speaker in wig and gown in his pulpit-like chair, members bowing to him as they leave the floor; the candlelight faintly glinting off the heavy silver and gold ceremonial mace lying on a central table, an ancient symbol of the House in session; and, rising into the gloom, the tiers of benches where members sat, many wearing boots, spurs, and swords. When the debate began on April 2, 1792, the narrow visitors' galleries were filled to capacity. Equiano was there, but Clarkson, who slipped a doorkeeper a handsome 10 guineas to let in thirty abolitionists, was not. Either too exhausted or too anxious about the outcome, he would not hear Wilberforce praise him as a "Gentleman whose services in the whole of this great cause can never be over rated." Wilberforce, summing up all the evils of the trade, exclaimed: "Africa, Africa! Your sufferings have been the theme that has arrested and engages my heart—your sufferings no tongue can express; no language impart."

In reply, Banastre Tarleton leapt to the defense of the slave trade, calling the abolition campaign a sham: "The form and language of the Petitions bear too strong a resemblance to each other. . . . In some villages and towns, mendicant physicians, and itinerant clergymen [i.e., Clarkson], have exercised almost unexampled zeal and industry to extort names from the sick, the indigent, and the traveller: in others . . . boys have been indulged with the gladsome tidings of a holiday, provided they would sign." He scoffed at the "fabrications" about the horrors of the middle passage, saying that as the representative of the "great and flourishing commercial town" of Liverpool, he could assure his fellow M.P.s that the death rate on slave ships was a negligible 4½ percent.

When Henry Dundas, the powerful home secretary, rose to speak, no one knew where he stood. The abolitionists were hopeful, because some years earlier he had sided with a black Jamaican in Scotland who had resisted being returned to the Caribbean. A forceful debater, Dundas was in effect the Scottish political boss, controlling the votes of thirty-four M.P.s.

Dundas began by declaring himself in favor of abolition, at which the spectators looking down from the gallery must have felt their spirits rise. He then went boldly further and declared himself in favor of emancipation—but far in the future, he added quickly, and after much groundwork and education. Dundas's speech signaled a moment that comes in every political crusade when the other side is forced to adopt the crusaders' rhetoric: the factory farm keeps harvesting, but labels its produce "natural"; the oil company declares itself pro-environment, but keeps drilling. Dundas had called himself an abolitionist, but he asked that abolition be postponed. To the abolitionists' dismay, he introduced an amendment that inserted the word "gradually" into Wilberforce's motion to end the slave trade.

Replying to Dundas, the tall, slender Prime Minister, William Pitt, in office nearly a decade and still not yet thirty-three years old, spoke last. It was 4 A.M. when he began, and he said he was "too much exhausted to enter so fully into the subject . . . as I could wish." To read his speech, however, is to feel shame at the sound-bite political rhetoric of our own time. Even in an imperfect transcription ("Nothing was ever so absurd . . . so ludicrous, as what the short-hand men have furnished," Wilberforce fumed afterwards) we can feel the impact Pitt had, both on his fellow M.P.s and in the visitors' galleries, packed with abolition stalwarts including, almost certainly, some other ex-slaves besides Equiano.

Pitt spoke for over an hour, extemporaneously, it seems, for there is no evidence he knew in advance of his own home secretary's proposal, and abolition was not a measure introduced by his government. (The cabinet was divided on the issue, and at least one member owned property in Jamaica.) He began by taking the "gradualists" at their word, that they favored abolition, and then one by one showed how each of their points was a better argument for ending the trade immediately. He mocked the idea that if British ships stopped carrying slaves, other countries would take over: Where would they get the ships? Where would they get the capital? And how could anyone expect France to increase its slave trading while desperately trying to put down the St. Domingue rebellion? And as for the trade itself, "How, Sir! Is this enormous evil ever to be eradicated, if every nation is thus prudentially to wait till the concurrence of all the world shall have been obtained? . . . There is no nation in Europe that has, on the one hand, plunged so deeply into this guilt as Great Britain, or that is so likely, on the other, to be looked up to as an example."

Finally, Pitt made a grand historical comparison steeped in imperial arrogance, but which cleverly made use of just that sense of national superiority. Britain, he declared, and British laws, British commerce, British achievements, were the acme of human civilization. But was it fair for proslavery speakers to call Africa irredeemably barbarous and uncivilized, or to insist that the slave traders were doing no harm by removing people from that continent? In Britain, too, when the Romans invaded nearly two millennia earlier, they would have found slavery and human sacrifice. "Why might not some Roman Senator, reasoning on the principles of some Honorable Gentlemen, and pointing to *British Barbarians,* have predicted with equal boldness, '*There* is a people that will never rise to civilization.'" He finished by quoting some lines in Latin from Virgil, about darkness being dispelled by the light of dawn. At that moment, legend has it, the first rays of the rising sun burst through the large window behind the Speaker's chair.

Despite this alleged assist from nature, Pitt's eloquence was not enough. Dundas's "gradually" provided exactly what the timid majority of Commons needed: a way to end a divisive national controversy, to look enlightened and responsive to popular will—and to make no immediate changes. The gradualist proposal passed, and after more debate the House set 1796, four long years hence, as the date when the slave trade was supposed to end. In a sense, this was a historic achievement: the first law against the slave trade passed by a national legislature anywhere in the world. Nonetheless, Wilberforce, Clarkson, and their allies felt the gradualist plan to be a stab in the back, the latest in a long chain of delaying tactics.

An even stronger obstacle than Dundas's bill, however, was the House of Lords, which, like Commons, had to pass on any measure before it became law. The upper house wanted no abolition at all, gradual or otherwise. When the measure came before it, the Lords insisted on beginning their own lengthy hearings on the subject, and the slave interests monopolized these until Parliament adjourned for the year. The movement was stopped in its tracks.

The flow of contributions and letters to the abolition committee slowed to a trickle. Wilberforce received a death threat, and when he next returned to his Yorkshire constituency, an armed friend traveled with him as a bodyguard. In the autumn of 1792, Clarkson set out again on the always difficult job of looking for new abolition witnesses. Crossing the Bristol Channel, he badly bruised his face when his small boat was caught in a storm. Then he parted ways with a traveling companion, who reported that the only place Clarkson could find for the next leg of the journey was an outside seat on a coach. His coat was soaked from a night's rain, and he gratefully accepted a fellow passenger's cloak and wrapped it around himself as the coach moved out of sight. The movement faced a long, cold winter.

As the prospect of freedom for British slaves receded, the dream of expanding rights for whites swept across Europe. Thomas Paine, a key figure in the American Revolution who had now returned to his native England, commanded a huge audience. His egalitarian polemic *Rights of Man,* a London merchant warned Home Secretary Dundas, was "a dangerous book for any person who does not share in the spoil to be left alone with." Many Britons did indeed feel they were not getting a fair share of the spoils, at a time when French men and women seemed to be taking theirs. Radical societies sprang up in some twenty towns in England and Scotland. When the new French revolutionary army crushed the Austrians and Prussians in battle, London dissidents celebrated by burning in effigy the losing commander, who happened to be George III's brother-in-law. More than five thousand radicals marched in the streets of Sheffield. Labor unrest spread through

Britain and broadsheets circulated everywhere. "Lord Buckingham who died the other day had thirty thousand pounds yearly for setting his arse in the House of Lords and doing nothing," said one. "Liberty calls aloud, ye who will hear her voice, may you be free and happy." Messages of solidarity flowed across the water to France: "Frenchmen, you are already free, and Britons are preparing to become so." Few in England had yet noticed the rise through the French Army's ranks of someone who would eventually take his country in a different direction, the young Corsican artillery officer Napoleon Bonaparte.

Still prizing his memento stone from the Bastille, Clarkson tried to raise money to support the French National Assembly. Some months after the bitter failure in Parliament, he quietly took a boat across the English Channel, on his own, to spend a few weeks in France once again. As with Westerners who remained Soviet loyalists after Stalin's lethal purges began, Clarkson's hopes had by now perhaps outpaced his judgment. The guillotine was already in use, and, in a foretaste of much more bloodshed to come, some two thousand French royalists, clergy, and aristocrats were killed in September 1792. Nonetheless, wrote a friend in his diary two months later, Clarkson had "little doubt . . . that an excellent Republic will be established on the Ruins of despotism & arbitrary Power."

The British establishment, however, was horrified by the executions. "The streets of Paris," thundered the *Times,* "[are] strewed with the carcases of the mangled victims . . . Read this ye ENGLISHMEN, with attention, and ardently pray that your happy Constitution may never be outraged by the despotic tyranny of Equalization." After these massacres of its enemies, the revolution would soon begin devouring its own, including members of the small band of French abolitionists.

Ironically, moving in different circles than Clarkson, Banastre Tarleton also visited France in the summer of 1792. One day he was at dinner with the Duke of Orléans and other aristocrats when they heard a great uproar in the street and rushed to the window to look. A crowd had lofted a severed head on a pike, hair streaming behind it. The Duke observed: "*Ah! C'est la Lamballe; je la connais à ses cheveux.*" The red-haired Princess Lamballe had just fallen victim to an antiroyalist mob, now parading her head through the city to the window of her friend Queen Marie Antoinette. Tarleton, who quickly returned to England, was the only one of the twelve diners that day who did not end up being guillotined.

That same summer, Louis XVI was taken prisoner, which sent a chill through the ranks of British abolitionists, aware of how attached Britons were to their own monarchy. To Wilberforce's horror, the French government conferred honorary citizenship on him, Clarkson, and Thomas Paine. To make clear his disdain for the revolutionary cause, Wilberforce attended a public meeting to raise funds for the relief of refugee French clergymen.

On January 21, 1793, the French King, who had already lost his throne, lost his head as well. "Every bosom burns with indignation in this kingdom," raged the *Times* after the guillotine's blade fell, "against the ferocious savages of Paris." The British government expelled the French ambassador. With the monarchies of Europe desperate to stamp out the threat to their own thrones, and France eager to export revolution, a clash was inevitable. A few weeks before the King's execution, the "Betting Book" at Brooks's Club had recorded, "Col. Tarleton bets Mr. Clopton one hundred and five guineas to five gns. that Great Britain is at war with France within Six Months from the above date." Tarleton won easily: on February 1, France declared war.

With this, the prospects for abolition disappeared, for war fever is always the enemy of social reform. Wilberforce's motion against the slave trade in Parliament's 1793 session—which, with clumsy timing, he introduced only two weeks after the declaration of war—was promptly defeated. In a long-winded speech in the House of Lords, the Duke of Clarence called him a fanatic and a hypocrite. When Wilberforce tried introducing a much-watered-down bill the following year, Banastre Tarleton called it "a violent aggression upon property." In the Caribbean, the war reinforced slavery more than ever. A distraught black sailor came to tell Granville Sharp that when the Royal Navy captured French ships with free blacks and mulattos in their crews, it did not treat these men as prisoners of war, but sold them for profit.

Exhausted from years of unremitting work, Clarkson was beginning to experience what a later age would call a nervous breakdown. In the previous seven years, he wrote, "I had a correspondence to maintain with four hundred persons with my own hand. I had some book or other annually to write in behalf of the cause. In this time I had travelled more than thirty-five thousand miles in search of evidence, and a great part of these journeys in the night." He had gone through much of his modest inheritance, sending "whole Coaches full of Seamen" to London to testify at hearings, often paying their expenses out of his own pocket (although wealthier abolitionists eventually took up a collection to repay him). "My mind has been literally bent like a Bow to one gloomy subject. . . . I am often suddenly seized with Giddiness & Cramps. I feel an unpleasant ringing in my Ears, my Hands frequently tremble. Cold sweats suddenly come upon Me. . . . I find myself weak, easily fatigued, & out of Breath. My recollection is also on the Decline."

Although he kept the reasons to himself, around this time Clarkson made what was for his day a most unusual decision—Sharp, for instance, strongly disapproved—namely, never to enter the Anglican ministry for which he had been educated. He ceased wearing black clerical clothes and asked people not to address letters to him as "Reverend." He doggedly continued his search for new abolition witnesses, but doctors limited his travel to ten miles a day and prescribed rest and cold baths.

Little wonder his faith in organized religion, and possibly in himself, faltered. If the war went well for Britain, its overseas slave economy would become even stronger. European wars in this long era of clashing empires were fought globally, with countries raking in each other's colonies like so many chips in an endless poker game. (Britain and France were the usual players, but sometimes Holland, Spain, or Portugal joined in.) The island of Tobago, for example, changed hands twenty-two times over the centuries. If Britain succeeded in seizing lucrative French Caribbean colonies like St. Domingue, the number of slaves under British rule could more than double.

The conflict between monarchy and republic gave the traditional Anglo-French rivalry a far more deadly cast; what French revolutionaries called the "war of all peoples against all kings" was clearly not going to end with any quick, gentlemanly truce. Britain was swept by a wave of patriotic fervor. "No Jacobins Admitted Here" signs appeared on taverns. In Manchester, abolitionist stalwart Thomas

Walker, now president of the Manchester Constitutional Society, gathered friends with guns to defend his house against a mob, and for this was charged with attempting to overthrow the government. Clarkson visited, but warily: "I don't wish it to be known that I am at Manchester," he wrote, "and should therefore like to ride up to your House, and spend the day with you, and be off the next morning." Although Walker was acquitted, legal costs nearly bankrupted him. Soon more such "treason trials" were under way.

With both his friends and his cause in trouble, Clarkson's nerves grew worse. "On going to bed the very stairs seemed to dance up and down under me, so that, misplacing my foot, I sometimes fell." Everywhere, antislavery activists sensed that the times had turned against them. From the countryside, a Quaker father wrote his son, apprenticed to an abolitionist merchant in Liverpool, "I cannot but consider thy situation in the present times of disturbance rather a dangerous one. . . . My advice to thee is to be on thy guard, always watchful and careful to offend no party. Keep cool and say little."

IV

WAR AND REVOLUTION

17

BLEAK DECADE

IN THIS TIME of mounting paranoia about revolutionary ideas, the War Department in London quietly sent its deputy adjutant general, one Colonel De Lancey, on a tour of Great Britain. "There is a Spirit abroad very full of mischief, & which should be checked before it has made any greater progress," he reported. "The measures . . . to put a Stop to it must in my opinion depend very much on the Gentlemen of property in the Country . . . it is only [by] their uniting themselves that the evil can be remedied."

"Gentlemen of property" were indeed worried, about both homegrown British radicalism and the prospect of French subversion. France did send aid to Irish rebels during this decade, but its feared secret agents in England itself, we know now, were far less of a threat than the British imagined. Many sent their reports home written in invisible ink that was supposed to become legible when heated over a flame. When this was done, the frustrated foreign minister of France complained, the charred letters were "almost unreadable," and modern scholars have found the same.

Britain's treasured civil liberties steadily eroded. The police sent an undercover agent, for example, to sit in on a meeting of the Society for Free Debate, whose topic for the night was the "Alliance of Kings Against the Liberties of France." In his report, the agent recorded that the audience "enjoyed to a great degree the very liberal Abuse of Government." When several hundred people showed up for the next debate, they found constables blocking the entrance. Nearly fifty years old, the Society for Free Debate was shut down. A procession to plant a "tree of liberty" on London's Kennington Common, well known for its public gallows, was halted by troops. Government informers snooped on what radical groups remained, sowing suspicion and sending intelligence to competing spymasters. Signed with code names, their fascinatingly unreliable reports are still filed in the Public Record Office today.

Meanwhile, the authorities were encouraging another type of organization. Men gathered at the Crown and Anchor Tavern to form the Association for Preserving Liberty and Property Against Republicans and Levellers. The association resolved to fight "such nefarious designs as are meditated by the wicked and senseless reformers of the present time." About 1,500 other such "associations" sprouted elsewhere, sometimes sporting paramilitary trappings. Members of one group in London drilled several nights a week, in uniforms of blue and scarlet.

Some of these associations circulated patriotic declarations house to house in order "to discover the disaffected." In Halesworth, Suffolk, only seven people refused to sign; in Kettering, Northamptonshire, only three. An intimidated bookseller in Frome turned his entire stock over to the local association, and in Exeter a bonfire devoured the works of Thomas Paine and other radicals. Dissenting cartoonists drew John Bull's lips fastened shut with a padlock.

The associations published pamphlets, mostly aimed at the "lower orders," full of warnings against Paine-like figures: Judas MacSerpent, for example, who yearned to subvert those good Britons David Trusty, Sir John Blunt, and Justice Worthy. In such stories, decent, apple-cheeked, beef-eating Englishmen resisted the blandishments of conniving Frenchmen made thin by a diet of soup and frogs. Employers distributed the tracts to their workers, clergymen to their flocks, and officers to soldiers and sailors. One was a ballad in the voice of the doomed Marie Antoinette:

> Remember do, the injur'd Queen, that means this doleful ditty;
> Who many months of Sorrow's seen, and much deserves your pity.

Paine, in exile in France, was convicted in absentia of seditious libel. Booksellers and printers of his work could now be prosecuted. Within a few months, more than two hundred effigies of him had been burned in Britain, although how much popular feeling was involved is open to question. One pamphlet reported that men in Devon who had just set an effigy aflame asked the person who had hired them "if there was any other *gemman* among his friends who he wished to have burned, as they were ready to do it for the same quantity of beer."

"A general panic has seized the kingdom," wrote one abolitionist. None of the major antislavery figures were prosecuted, but their enemies condemned them more ferociously than ever. The most sophisticated literary voice of the West India lobby, Bryan Edwards, a planter and writer who owned 1,500 Jamaican slaves, indirectly blamed the ongoing revolt in St. Domingue on the London abolition committee, which he referred to disdainfully by its former street address. The slave rebels "were driven into those excesses—reluctantly driven—by the vile machinations of . . . imitators in France, of the Old Jewry associates in London." In 1794, the Earl of Abingdon declared in Parliament that "this proposition for the abolition of the slave trade, is . . . grounded in and founded upon French principles . . . namely, those of insubordination, anarchy, confusion, murder, havock, devastation and ruin." And, of course, in a broad sense, none of the critics were wrong. Despite the cautious paternalism of backers like Wilberforce, the cause of antislavery was deeply part of this age of revolutions.

In reply to attacks that sometimes targeted him personally, Clarkson rushed into print a pamphlet pointing out that slaves had been rebelling ever since the days of ancient Greece and Rome, and needed no incitement from French or British sympathizers. Although in later years he would take a much more cautious tone on the issue, at this time he was one of the few abolitionists to defend the Caribbean slave rebels, saying that they had "been fraudulently and forcibly deprived of the Rights of Men."

The gloomy Wilberforce complained about "madheaded professors of liberty and equality." At times it seemed to him that *only* the revolutionaries he so abhorred were now willing to support abolition. The Norwich Revolution Society sent the abolition committee a contribution of £10, 10 shillings, and an unhappy friend informed him,

"I do not imagine that we could meet with twenty persons in Hull at present who would sign a petition, that are not republicans. People connect democratical principles with the Abolition of the Slave Trade."

No one gave voice to the connection more forcefully than Thomas Hardy, a Piccadilly shoemaker. Not related to the nineteenth-century novelist, Hardy was both a strong abolitionist and the moving spirit of the London Corresponding Society, the city's first real working-class organization, which advocated universal male suffrage and other reforms. The French Revolution and the social upheavals of the beginning of the industrial age had reinvigorated the indigenous radicalism that had flourished at the time of the English Civil War a century and a half earlier.* Hardy, one of its leaders, was close to Equiano. "My friend Gustavus Vassa, the African," he wrote, ". . . is now writing memoirs of his life in my house." Equiano, to be more precise, was revising his memoirs for yet another edition. He was one of the first of the London Corresponding Society's several thousand members (dues were a penny a week), and on his travels promoting his book, he kept an eye out for potential recruits. Apparently it was he who steered to Hardy the society's first contact outside London, for to this activist in Sheffield Hardy wrote, "Hearing from . . . Gustavus Vassa . . . that you are a zealous friend to the abolition of that cursed traffic, the Slave Trade, I infer, from that circumstance, *that you are a zealous friend to freedom on the broad basis of the* RIGHTS OF MAN." Equiano, too, found this connection self-evident. In such oppressive times, it was brave and risky for him to openly identify himself with the society, several of whose members were soon convicted of sedition and sentenced to fourteen years in the new penal colony in Australia.

In 1794, the year after the war with France began, mobs sacked radicals' houses and, a comrade reported urgently, "Citizen Hardy was

* When, interestingly, the metaphor used for injustice was slavery. The epochal Putney Debates of 1647 among members of Oliver Cromwell's army laid bare the conflict between human rights and property rights that would run through British political life for several hundred years to come. "I would fain know what the soldier hath fought for all this while?" asked one Leveller, Colonel Thomas Rainborough, the most eloquent of the radicals. "He hath fought to enslave himself, to give power to men of riches, men of estates, to make him a perpetual slave."

taken away. . . . They seized everything they could lay hands on." Among Hardy's confiscated papers, which agents carried off wrapped in four large silk handkerchiefs, police discovered a letter from Equiano. If Hardy and his colleagues were convicted, Clarkson vowed, he would immigrate to the United States, "for if it was look'd upon to be treason to belong to such popular societies . . . no one was safe."

Guarded by soldiers with fixed bayonets and charged with high treason, Hardy was held in the Tower of London. Several weeks after his arrest, a stone-throwing mob celebrated a British naval victory over France by setting his house on fire. His wife, pregnant with their sixth child, was hurt escaping through a back window; she died in childbirth soon afterwards. When Hardy later came to trial, crowds gathered in the streets and troops were called out. Despite the witch-hunt atmosphere, Britain's courts showed some independence, and a brilliant legal defense won him acquittal. A group of supporters unhitched the horses from his lawyer's carriage and jubilantly pulled Hardy through the streets, but paused for a few minutes in silence outside his empty shop and damaged house. The London Corresponding Society was eventually outlawed.

Another person arrested was the fiery orator Henry Redhead Yorke, chair of a huge public meeting in Sheffield called to consider both "a reform in the representation of the people" and "the total and unqualified abolition of negro slavery." In a striking show of solidarity across racial lines, thousands of metalworkers attending the meeting unanimously endorsed freedom for the slaves, to "avenge peacefully ages of wrongs done to our Negro Brethren." Yorke seemed to approve of armed rebellion both in England and among slaves, writing, "Let the African, the Asiatic, the European, burst asunder their chains, and raise a pious war against tyranny. Should tyrants . . . refuse to expiate their crimes . . . let the PEOPLE roll on them in a tempest of fury, and compel them to expire in agonies!" A jury found him guilty of conspiracy, and he spent two years in prison.*

---

* When released, Yorke discovered something well known to survivors of modern red scares: a repentant radical can live the good life. Swiftly repudiating his earlier beliefs, he helped recruit a militia regiment, was set up as the editor of a well-financed right-wing newspaper, and coauthored a patriotic encyclopedia, *Lives of the British Admirals.* He married his jailer's daughter.

As heads rolled from French guillotines by the thousands in the Reign of Terror, Britain too, it seemed, could be facing revolution. The war was already straining the economy when 1794 brought the first of several bad harvests. That winter was one of the coldest in memory; in farmers' cow barns, milk froze in pails, and parts of the country suffered near famine. Death rates rose, food riots broke out, undernourished miners collapsed on the job, and children rummaged for scraps in garbage dumps. At increasingly rare radical meetings, large groups of policemen shouted "God save great George our King!" when anybody tried to speak. In 1795, a crowd jeered and stoned the King on his way to Parliament, and his coach window was shattered. "My Lords," he said as he entered the upper chamber, "I have been shot at." Two years later, in two major anchorages, great mutinies shook the bedrock of the empire, the Royal Navy. The rebel sailors' brief-lived "Floating Republic" shocked admirals; its suppression left the bodies of several dozen seamen hanging from ships' yardarms. Even guards at the Tower of London attempted mutiny.

Meanwhile, the government had pushed through the Seditious Meetings Act and the Treasonable and Seditious Practices Act. Any political meeting of more than fifty people now needed a magistrate's approval. Anyone who spoke or wrote in a way "to excite or stir up the people to hatred or contempt of the . . . constitution of this realm" was liable to immediate arrest. Could that include hatred of slavery? The law was vague. Although the Two Acts, as they were called, were not strictly applied, on paper they were draconian: a magistrate could proclaim a meeting illegal; if, an hour later, there were still twelve or more people present, they could be sentenced to death.

Wilberforce gave a speech in favor of the Two Acts. "Went to Pitt's, to look over the Sedition Bill—altered it much for the better by enlarging," he wrote in his diary. ". . . I greatly fear some civil war or embroilment." Before long, musket fire was sounding in Ireland as British troops suppressed a rebellion; the bitter fighting cost some thirty thousand lives. More than three thousand war poems appeared in the British press during the 1790s, as the government posted rewards for catching deserters. Radical newspapers were forced to close. It would not be until another devastating global war, from 1914 to 1918, that Britain would see such a crackdown on dissent again.

By the late 1790s Napoleon was gaining power in France, and his Army of England was camped on the other side of the Channel, threatening invasion. Rumors periodically swept the country that the French had already landed. Trains of wagons lined the streets of coastal towns, ready to take women and children away. Troops trained in village commons, although Wilberforce opposed drilling on Sundays.

With progressive politics almost entirely shut down by the war, Clarkson dropped out of public life and bought a piece of land in the Lake District. On it, he helped local workmen build a small stone house, his first home after nearly a decade of rented rooms, inns, and spare beds in the homes of sympathizers. Still, he could not help himself: there were "at least ten poor families to whose comforts he administers," reported a Quaker friend. ". . . He has been begging round the neighbourhood for a poor man who had lost his cows."

Apparently for the first time in his life, Clarkson was in love. He had met Catherine Buck several years earlier. The niece of a supporter he sometimes stayed with, she had seen his shackles and thumbscrews and his African cloth and spices in her uncle's parlor. She had helped him with some of the endless copying that was required in the days before carbon paper, but was no mere secretary. A family friend, the writer Henry Crabb Robinson, said that, except for Madame de Staël, Catherine "was the most eloquent woman I have ever known. . . . She . . . made her own whatever she learned." A vivacious woman who devoured the news of the day and read widely, she, too, was attracted by the great promise of the French Revolution, and in the circle of young people in which she grew up it had been the fashion to address one another as *citoyen* and *citoyenne.* She and Clarkson were married in early 1796, and she gave birth to a son ten months later.

Clarkson threw himself into farming, raising sheep and bullocks and growing wheat, oats, barley, and other crops, and into writing a massive three-volume history of the Quakers, the first major work on the sect by a nonmember. Most of the people he was closest to were Quakers, ranging from his publisher James Phillips to William Allen, a businessman and scientist and an early boycotter of sugar. Of the Quakers, Clarkson once said he felt "nine parts in ten of their way of thinking." Many in the sect suspected the final tenth of his soul belonged to them as well.

The Clarksons soon became fond of some new neighbors: William Wordsworth, Samuel Taylor Coleridge, and their families. Coleridge, in fact, seems to have been the only one of Clarkson's friends who called him "Tom." His bond with the two poets was an improbable one, for there was little poetic in Clarkson's temperament. Catherine wrote that when her husband "had a . . . tribute once forwarded to him in the form of an ode, the poet was forced *to promise him a prose translation.*" She herself may have been the spark that lit these friendships, for much of what we know about Wordsworth and Coleridge in these years comes from letters that Dorothy Wordsworth, the poet's sister, wrote to Catherine. Wordsworth and his wife named a daughter after her and kept silhouettes of both Clarksons over their mantel. Coleridge wrote, "I once asked Tom Clarkson whether he ever thought of his probable fate in the next world, to which he replied, 'How can I? I think only of the slaves in Barbadoes!'" (As for Wilberforce, Coleridge was convinced he didn't "care a farthing for the slaves," if only "*his soul were saved.*")

Clarkson remained close to his brother John, who shared his hopes for the revolution in France. Some months after the war began John was offered what naval officers usually dream of, the command of a ship. But, in an almost unheard-of gesture, he refused it, "giving, as his reason, that he did not approve the war," according to the diarist Katherine Plymley, who always seemed to know everything. Wilberforce, though fond of John, now said that he "fear'd to have him at his house, his conversation was so very unguarded in politics, even to a degree of imprudence," Catherine Clarkson wrote. Political divisions were reflected even in appearance—sympathizers of the French Revolution wore short hair instead of powdered wigs—and these turbulent times strained many friendships.

The war between Britain and France seemed to foil the abolitionists' plans on every continent. As if the Sierra Leone colony didn't already have enough troubles, in September 1794 a squadron of French warships sailed into the river estuary and raked Freetown with cannon fire for an hour and a half. Sailors then came ashore, looted the town, killed the settlers' pigs, smashed a new printing press, and burned all the Company's boats and buildings.

(Paradoxically, the attack temporarily revived some of Sierra Leone's early egalitarianism. Fearing more raids, the colony organized all its adult males into a militia, and each company elected its own officers. Most of the whites had never fired a gun, while many of the blacks had spent years in the British Army during the American war. Thus at times black officers commanded white troops—something virtually never seen on the continent again until the newly democratic South Africa reorganized its military in the 1990s.)

Sierra Leone was bombarded not just with French cannonballs but, like everyone else, with advice from Granville Sharp. To the colony's governor he wrote, "I send you two dozen copies of the Extract from Dampier, concerning fruit-trees, and one dozen copies of the tract on Maple Sugar." Despite the mood of the day, Sharp's connections in high places and his Anglican piety protected him from being considered a dangerous subversive. How could anyone fear this thin, sprightly, gray-haired man, who always walked fast and erect along London streets, on his way, perhaps, to the Crown and Anchor Tavern for a rehearsal of the Madrigal Society, or to St. Paul's for morning and evening prayers? Yet his instinctive sense of social justice was as strong as ever. He backed a minimum wage law and drew up plans for new towns to be settled on the American frontier, but stressed that on no account was land to be taken from the Indians. And when the United States passed its first Fugitive Slave Act, requiring even the nonslave states to capture and return runaways, he wrote to American friends and urged them to break the law.

Sharp was the only person in the abolitionist leadership, so far as we know, who stayed in touch with Equiano during these grim years. Another edition of the ex-slave's autobiography appeared in 1794, the last in his lifetime. Two years later, Equiano's wife, Susanna, died at the age of thirty-four, leaving him their two young daughters to care for. Her death may have weakened his will to live, for he died in London thirteen months later, in 1797, probably in his early fifties. We know almost nothing else of the final few years of his life except that Sharp, more than a decade older, was one of his last visitors: "He was a sober, honest man," Sharp wrote, "and I went to see him when he lay upon his deathbed, and had lost his voice so that he could only whisper."

Equiano had earned his way out of bondage. He had written more movingly and effectively about what it was like to experience slavery than would anyone else for decades to come. While he cultivated relationships with influential men, he also had the courage to openly befriend the radical democrats of his day. And he had done what most writers can only imagine, which was to earn a good living from his pen. His estate, when inherited by his surviving daughter on her twenty-first birthday—her sister had died as a child—totaled £950, more than $100,000 in today's money. If neither daughter survived him, Equiano's will stated, half his money was to be used for sending missionaries abroad, and half given to the school at Sierra Leone.

Wilberforce, during this time, was living in the village of Clapham. Today it is a stop on the London Underground, but in an era when open fields were half an hour's walk from the houses of Parliament and a large pig farm was next to the British Museum, Clapham was three miles from the city's outskirts. This was a welcome distance from the constant pall of smoke from London's tens of thousands of coal fires and the black grime it left on hair, clothes, and park benches. The trip cost 18 pence by coach. It was in Clapham that Wilberforce, his first cousin Henry Thornton, who headed the faltering Sierra Leone Company, and a circle of like-minded people lived, members of what was later called the Clapham Sect, or, more derisively, "the Saints." Another member of the circle was the lawyer James Stephen. After surviving a bout of yellow fever, he had returned from the West Indies to England in 1794, bringing with him a turtle, a local delicacy, as a present for Wilberforce.

Rich and pious Evangelical Anglicans all, the Saints worshiped at a church on Clapham Common. They were a group, as Thackeray later put it mockingly in his novel *The Newcomes,* whose aims were "to attend to the interests of the enslaved negro; to awaken the benighted Hottentot to a sense of the truth; to convert Jews, Turks, Infidels, and Papists; to arouse the indifferent and often blasphemous mariner; to guide the washerwoman in the right way; to . . . hear preachers daily bawling for hours." The families intermarried a great deal and were continually in and out of each other's lavish houses, four of which opened onto a garden that was considered common property. They were a wealthy, eighteenth-century version of what modern Americans would call a cohousing community. For some years, Wilberforce and Thornton shared a Queen Anne–style mansion, which grew to encompass a total of thirty-four bedrooms. The Clapham circle often gathered in its lofty oval library, designed by Prime Minister Pitt, whose high glass doors looked out on a magnificent view of farmland.

For several years, some of the rooms in this house were occupied by two dozen African children, brought to England from Sierra Leone to be educated at a school run by the rector of the Clapham church. The first time the children were taken on a walk across the common, a number of them failed to return. Curious residents, it turned out, had sent their servants to bring back an African child, to be examined as an exotic object. Sadly, most of the boys and girls did not survive the unfamiliar climate and bacteria of England.

Two members of the Clapham Sect, Thomas Bowdler and his sister Henrietta, added their name to the language when they edited the works of Shakespeare "to exclude . . . whatever is unfit to be read aloud by a gentleman to a company of ladies." When he was finished with Shakespeare, Thomas went to work on bowdlerizing the Old Testament. Critics had fun with the group's prudery: one cartoon shows Wilberforce using his top hat to block out the fig leaf on the statue of Achilles in Hyde Park.

Until now, "Wilber," as his friends sometimes called him, had not shown the slightest interest in women. It took another member of the Clapham circle, it seems, to choose one for him. "Babington has strongly recommended Miss Spooner for wife for me," he wrote in his diary. Barbara Spooner had been vetted as sufficiently highborn and Evangelical, and two days later he was introduced to her. Then the diary references come thick and fast: "After sad night haunted with Miss Spooner rose to prayer." "I could not sleep for thinking of her." "Sadly too sensual about Barbara. . . . Oh Lord God do thou forgive me for I have yielded too hastily to the Forces of affection or the impulse of appetite." Eight days after meeting her, he proposed. Friends tried to slow him down, but in less than two months they were wed. He was thirty-eight, and the bride twenty. Judging from her letters, Barbara Spooner was an odd duck, without the least interest in her husband's political activities and much obsessed by the dangers of illness, storms, and the fiery deaths awaiting sinners. But she and

Wilberforce were apparently happy together, and had six children.

He continued to support all the era's repressive measures, arguing in favor of a law that provided three-month jail terms for anything remotely resembling labor organizing, which he thought "a general disease in our society." And when Paine's attack on traditional Christianity, *The Age of Reason,* was published by a small bookseller named Thomas Williams, Wilberforce's Society for Carrying into Effect His Majesty's Proclamation Against Vice and Immorality got Williams jailed. To his credit, however, Wilberforce never wavered on abolition, and neither, as far as we can tell, did the British public. Before the Two Acts shut down such forums, audiences at London debating societies in 1794 and 1795 voted unanimously in favor of banning the slave trade. Year after year, Wilberforce introduced an abolition bill, but he remained as poor a strategist as ever. He would propose the bill either too late in the legislative session or when M.P.s were distracted by some other issue, and he was too disorganized to muster his supporters. Year after year, the bills went down to defeat. In 1796, the margin was painfully close: only four votes. The bill would have carried if a group of sympathetic M.P.s had not gone to see a new comic opera, *The Two Hunchbacks.* Clarkson was newly married and away. "Had he been in Town . . . he would have ferretted out the members & seen that they were in their places," felt James Phillips.

Of course, even that victory would have been only a moral one, since any abolition bill passed by Commons would, as in 1792, have died in the House of Lords. Furthermore, as the war with France dragged on, it became clear that Pitt was not going to risk his political capital by continuing to oppose the slave trade against the will of the majority of his cabinet. His support became more and more perfunctory. Wilberforce kept introducing abolition bills throughout the 1790s, until at the decade's end, despairing, he stopped.

The Clapham group was a close one, and its pet projects stayed within the family. When troubled Sierra Leone needed a new governor in the mid-1790s, Thomas Babington, the man who found Wilberforce his wife, steered the job to his brother-in-law, a priggish, somber young man named Zachary Macaulay, who had turned against slavery while working as an assistant manager on a Jamaica sugar plantation. Macaulay had enough dour Evangelical piety to make Wilberforce look like a libertine; even the bust of him in Westminster Abbey seems to wear a slight, thin-lipped grimace of disapproval. He was known for his boundless appetite for work. "State papers were child's play to him, however dull or voluminous," one colleague remembered. "He would attend half-a-dozen charitable committees . . . during the day, and refresh himself after dinner with a parliamentary folio that would have choked an alderman by the sight of it alone." In humid, sweltering Sierra Leone, he read the New Testament in Greek before dawn and after dinner. Unpopular with the black settlers, he was opposed to self-government, quick to order corporal punishment, and fixated on blasphemy and sin.

"What struck me as . . . most lamentable," he wrote to his fiancée about visiting a dying English settler, ". . . was that though he was continually reiterating his cries for mercy, and declaring himself a wretched sinner, when I came to ask what were the sins which lay heaviest on his conscience, he said he could not fix on any particular sins. I was at no loss, however, to remind him of numberless particular sins of the commission of which I myself had been a witness. I set them before him with all their aggravations."

Paradoxically, this humorless and unlikable man performed the boldest feat of abolitionist investigation since Clarkson had prowled the docks of Bristol and Liverpool. In 1795, Macaulay fell ill and went back to England to recover. Wilberforce had written asking for any "damning proof" he could find about the slave trade, and so he decided to return home via the West Indies, on the *Ann Phillipa* of Liverpool, which had been collecting slaves along the Sierra Leone coast. One of the vessel's owners was the brother of the city's blustery spokesman in Parliament, Banastre Tarleton. Either at his own request or because the captain wanted to make things unpleasant for his abolitionist passenger, at night Macaulay's hammock hung in the slaves' quarters, where they slept just below him. He kept a diary, writing in Greek letters to disguise it from the ship's crew.

> May 5. Captain Y—— told us we should see that a slave-ship was a very different thing from what it had been reported. We should find the slaves rejoicing in their happy state. . . . He ac-

cordingly said a few words to the women, to which they replied with three cheers and a laugh. He went forward on the main deck and spoke the same words to the men, who made the same reply. "Now," says he, "are you not convinced that Mr. Wilberforce has conceived very improperly of slave-ships?" . . .

[May] 7th. I observed one woman handcuffed, and inquired the cause. I found she had lately attempted to drown herself, and had been caught by the leg just as she had thrown herself over the side. . . .

[May] 8th.The men-slaves were brought on deck for the first time since our sailing. . . . While the ship was on the coast they had made an unsuccessful attempt to get possession of her. . . . The two ringleaders are now chained to each other by the neck; besides having on the same fetters which are worn by the others. . . .

[May] 23rd. I observed to-day, as on former occasions, several of the slaves rejecting their food. The officer on duty began to threaten and shake his *cat* at such as refused to eat. . . . The slaves then made a shew of eating by putting a little rice into their mouths; but whenever the officer's back was turned, they threw it into the sea. . . .

[May] 29th. About ten o'clock in the forenoon, to my great joy, the island [of Barbados] appeared in sight. The slaves set up a great shout; but in a few seconds their countenances fell. Possibly they thought that some great change was now about to take place in their condition, and their ignorance of what it might be filled them with painful forebodings. . . .

From the above account you will conceive that my situation could not have been a pleasant one. During the night I hung over a crowd of slaves huddled together on the floor, whose stench at times was almost beyond endurance. . . . Their cup is full of pure, unmingled sorrow. . . . Eight died during the three weeks I was on board.

Macaulay's journey was an unhappy reminder that the British slave trade was more entrenched than ever. By the end of the 1790s it was enjoying a major surge, with an average of more than 150 slave ships leaving Liverpool, Bristol, and London each year. The slave-based economy of the British West Indies was increasing its proportion of the empire's trade and, with French merchant ships largely swept from the seas by the Royal Navy, its share of world coffee and sugar production. Parliament authorized the building of the great new West India Docks in London. War fever seemed to wrap slavery tightly in the British flag, as the country's most popular military hero, Lord Nelson, declared that he would battle any threat to "our West Indian possessions . . . while I have an arm to fight in their defence, or a tongue to launch my voice against the damnable doctrine of Wilberforce and his hypocritical allies."

By contrast, political repression had paralyzed local abolition organizing. The group in Manchester, once the most vigorous outside the capital, had not met since 1792. In London, the abolition committee itself gave up its office space in 1794, and met only half a dozen times in the following three years. Then, for the next seven years, it did not meet at all. Stephen Fuller, London lobbyist for the Jamaica planters, wrote to his employers rejoicing in "the defeat of the absurd attempt of abolishing the Slave Trade, which I think we shall hear no more of."

Across the Atlantic, however, the slaves were not quiet.

18

AT THE FOOT OF VESUVIUS

THE 1790S WERE a time of upheaval around the Western world. In France, revolutionaries removed not just the heads of their opponents, but every visible vestige of the old regime, including its calendar: they started over again with Year I, ten-day weeks called *décades,* and a cycle of twelve freshly named months that began on the autumn equinox. In Venezuela, a slave revolt erupted, and white patriots issued a declaration of independence from Spain; both attempts failed, but anticolonial zeal spread through Latin America. But nowhere was the social order overturned so dramatically as by the rebellion that shook the French colony of St. Domingue. It was the largest and bloodiest slave revolt the world has ever seen.

Count Mirabeau, whom Clarkson had met in Paris, once said that the whites of St. Domingue slept "at the foot of Vesuvius." In the summer of 1791 the colony was swept by slave escapes. A series of secret slave gatherings took place on St. Domingue's rich northern plain, the heartland of its agricultural wealth. (Caribbean planters, who had spoken condescendingly for years about the slaves' peculiar willingness to travel long distances for funerals and dances, did not understand black communication networks.) Finally, a large group of slaves representing many plantations met under the night sky in a remote spot called Alligator Woods, slaughtered a pig, ceremonially drank its blood, and swore an oath to rise up at an appointed time.

"Throw away the image of the god of the whites who thirsts for our tears," a leader reportedly told the group, "and listen to the voice of liberty which speaks in the hearts of all of us."

At 10 P.M. on August 22, the volcano erupted. Drumbeats gave the signal. Slaves attacked plantation buildings with pruning hooks, machetes, and torches. For miles around, they set fire to everything connected with the hated work of sugar cultivation: cane fields, mills, boiling houses, and warehouses. Machinery that would not burn they smashed with sledgehammers. They murdered white men in their beds and raped the women atop their husband's corpses. They nailed one member of the slave-catching militia alive to the gate of his plantation and chopped off his arms and legs. They tied a carpenter between two planks and sawed him in half. Two sons of a white planter and a slave woman stabbed their father to death. Planters had been meting out similar violence to their slaves for generations, but news of these atrocities sent waves of horror through Europe because for the first time white people were being killed by the hundreds, a toll that would soon mount into the thousands. The world was turned upside down.

Terrified white refugees, some in nightclothes, filled the road to elegant Cap François, the major city in the north. "Imagine all the space that the eye can see," wrote one, ". . . from which continually arose thick coils of smoke whose hugeness and blackness could only be likened to frightful clouds laden with thunderstorms. They parted only to give way to equally huge flames, alive and flashing to the very sky. . . . For three weeks we couldn't tell day from night. . . . The most striking thing about this terrible spectacle was a rain of fire composed of burning bits of cane-straw which whirled like thick snow and which the wind carried, now toward the harbor and ships, now over the houses of the town."

"Desolation and fear were painted on all faces," another refugee recalled. ". . . Guns could be heard from afar and the bells of the plantations were sounding the alarm. . . . Young children transfixed upon the points of bayonets were the bleeding flags which followed the troop of cannibals."

While flames signaled the spread of the revolt, some blacks protected their masters, at least temporarily. At the Bréda plantation, near

Cap François, a slight, wiry, taciturn black man in his late forties named Toussaint held the privileged position of livestock steward and coachman, a job that had taken him throughout the colony's north. Known for his skill as a veterinarian and herbalist, he was said to be the son of a West African chief, although almost everything about his origins is a matter of rumor. We do know that, born a slave, he had been freed some years earlier. He was now literate and a slave owner himself—both were common for the colony's many mulattos, but extremely unusual for a man, like him, of pure African blood. He managed to deflect the rebels for some days until Bayon de Libertat, the plantation manager who had freed him, could safely leave with his family. Then Toussaint, too, joined the revolt.

French soldiers were confident they could put down the uprising, as they had suppressed various small revolts in the past. One group of officers calmly continued their dinner even when an alarm warned that the rebels were approaching. "We were eating heartily until the moment a cannon ball passed through the window and carried away, right under our beards, the table and all the plates. The general, infuriated by this mishap, mounted his horse with food still in his mouth, and left camp with six hundred men and four pieces of artillery. Two hours later one could not find a living Negro within a circle of two and a half miles, and the roads were strewn with their bloody remains."

St. Domingue had the largest slave population in the Caribbean, and slavery there was as harsh as anywhere. Some owners put tin masks on slaves to keep them from chewing sugar cane in the fields. A wealthy French planter named Jean-Baptiste de Caradeux used to entertain his visitors by placing an orange on a slave's head; male guests would then compete with each other to see who could knock it off with a pistol shot at thirty paces. Another plantation owner wrote instructions for his managers on how to inflict pain to maximum effect: "Slow punishments make a greater impression than quick . . . ones. Twenty-five lashes of the whip administered in a quarter of an hour, interrupted at intervals to hear the cause which the unfortunates always plead in their defense, and resumed again, continuing in this fashion two or three times, are far more likely to make an impression than fifty lashes administered in five minutes."

Like all revolts, the one in St. Domingue was blamed on outside agitators. And indeed, copies of Josiah Wedgwood's medallion, with the inscription "*Ne suis-je pas ton frère?,*" had appeared in St. Domingue, along with news of the British parliamentary debates and of the formation of the Société des Amis des Noirs in Paris. But the final goad to the slaves' long-simmering anger was the French Revolution, more news of which came with each successive ship. When word of the Bastille's fall first arrived, the colony's superintendent wrote, "the blacks are all in agreement . . . that the white slaves have killed their masters . . . and have come into possession of all the goods of the earth."

All over the West Indies, such news from Europe spread with lightning speed because at white dinner tables, as one resident put it, "every Person has his own waiting man behind him." "To discuss the *Rights of Man* before such people," wrote a shocked European visitor to St. Domingue. "What is it but to teach them that power dwells with strength and strength with numbers!" As slaves at the wharves wrestled barrels of sugar and indigo or sacks of coconuts and coffee beans onto ships bound for France, they heard more from French sailors, who wore the tricolor cockade. Freedom is never far from the minds of slaves anywhere, and for those in St. Domingue, it was not far from their experience: the majority had been born in Africa.

The rebellion threw into embarrassing relief the contradiction between slavery and the stated goals of the French Revolution. When a general inspected a battalion from the Loire region as it was about to be rushed across the Atlantic to fight the slave rebels, he was horrified to find the unit's banner emblazoned "Live Free or Die," and to discover that the soldiers were planning to plant a "tree of liberty" on their arrival. He saw to it that a new motto was sewn onto the banner, "The Nation, the Law, the King," and that the battalion would plant a "tree of Peace."

When French soldiers captured one black rebel in St. Domingue, "we found in one of his pockets pamphlets printed in France." But it was the slaves of St. Domingue themselves who unexpectedly, and undirected by any of the revolution's architects in Paris, made universal and immediate its promise of freedom. Everyone knew full well, when the slaves rose up, that this was the long-feared nightmare of every West Indian white: revenge. On an island where harvesting crops was all, this was truly the reaping of the whirlwind.

On both sides, it was a war of unsurpassed brutality. The bodies of black rebels swung from tree branches where they had been hanged, while fortifications they built were lined with French skulls. An Englishman was witness to the execution of two slave leaders: "They were broken on two pieces of timber placed crosswise. One of them expired on receiving the third stroke on his stomach, each of his legs and arms having been first broken in two places. . . . The other had a harder fate. When the executioner, after breaking his legs and arms, lifted up the instrument to give the finishing stroke on the breast . . . the [white] mob, with the ferociousness of cannibals, called out '*arretez*' (stop) and compelled him to leave his work unfinished. In that condition the miserable wretch, with his broken limbs doubled up . . . seemed perfectly sensible, but uttered not a groan. At the end of some forty minutes, some English seamen, who were spectators of the tragedy, strangled him in mercy."

Returning to his family's plantation, a young Frenchman found everything destroyed: "The sugar refinery, the vats, the furnaces, the vast warehouses, the convenient hospital, the water-mill which was so expensive, all is no more than a specter of walls blackened and crumbled, surrounded by enormous heaps of coals and broken tiles." Within a mere two months' time, the rebels had looted and burned more than a thousand plantations and controlled a large swath of the northern part of the colony. The more news like this that reached England, the harder it made things for the beleaguered abolitionists. "If all the shocking enormities committed at St. Domingo . . . be true," a correspondent wrote to *Gentleman's Magazine,* "it is to be hoped, for heaven's sake, we shall hear no more of abolishing the slave trade. . . . The Negro race . . . are but a set of wild beasts let loose."

The rebellion sent shock waves throughout the world, not just because of its size and ferocity, but because St. Domingue was no ordinary colony. Although hard to imagine when we see the desperately poor Haiti of today, St. Domingue was the undisputed crown jewel of all European colonies anywhere. Such was its mystique that slave merchants in France sent their shirts across the Atlantic to be washed in its mountain brooks, which were said to whiten linen better than European rivers. St. Domingue was more than twice the size of the largest British Caribbean island, Jamaica; its soil was so rich and so well irrigated that its plantations yielded half again as much sugar per acre as the best land in Jamaica. It produced more than 30 percent of the world's sugar and more than half its coffee, not to speak of cotton and other crops. Thousands of slaves were at work clearing mountainside forests for new coffee estates, but the massive erosion this caused would not take its toll until the next century. The colony's eight thousand plantations accounted for more than one third of France's foreign trade, and its own foreign trade equaled that of the newly born United States. St. Domingue's annual production of sugar and other crops was roughly double that of all the British West Indian islands put together. No colony anywhere made so large a profit for its mother country.

William Pitt called St. Domingue "the Eden of the Western world"; the French, guarding their treasure with troops and a large naval base, referred to it as *la perle des Antilles.* It was, of course, neither Eden nor pearl for the slaves. Some half million of them far outnumbered the nearly forty thousand whites and slightly fewer "free people of color"—most of them mulatto. Fifteen hundred oceangoing ships called each year at the territory's thirteen international ports, and a few more smuggled goods ashore elsewhere to avoid customs duties. Much of what the ships landed, both legally and on remote beaches by lantern light at night, was human cargo: St. Domingue was the largest single market for the Atlantic slave trade, importing many of them on British ships from Bance Island and other depots.

Most of the wealth flowed back to France. But enough of it stayed in St. Domingue to allow well-to-do whites to live in luxury unmatched in the Caribbean. Planters and merchants in their splendid imported carriages could visit two resident orchestras, gambling houses, military parades, horse shows, and a traveling wax museum with figures of Louis XVI, Marie Antoinette, and George Washington. In March 1784, St. Domingue was the scene of the first lighter-than-air balloon flight in the Americas. Ten days later, the governor and other officials gathered by a sugar cane field to watch a larger balloon, also unmanned but thirty feet tall, take off and ascend to 1800 feet, its cloth envelope decorated with painted garlands and the coats of arms of colonial dignitaries.

In the capital city of Port-au-Prince there were street magicians and jugglers, a botanical garden, a bathhouse, and several bookstores. Six towns had repertory theaters, and in 1791, the year the great upheaval began, the colony staged more than 150 performances. The theater in Cap François held 1,500 spectators and had a special box for the governor-general guarded by a sentry. It was a favorite rendezvous for white men and their black or mulatto mistresses; there were separate sections for these women in the upper balcony. The star of the resident company, named Chevalier, died on stage. "Close the curtain," he said. "The farce is played out."

"The practice of dueling," wrote one white resident, ". . . was . . . an everyday sport among the young and dissipated." There was also much sport in the bedroom—too much, in the opinion of a prostitute just off the boat from France, who wrote to a St. Domingue newspaper in 1786 to complain angrily about all the competition she faced, both amateur and professional. The life of a colonial Frenchwoman, a visiting American reported, "was divided between the bath, the table, the toilette and the lover. . . . The *faux pas* of a married lady is so much a matter of course, that she who has only one lover, and retains him long in her chains, is considered as a model of constancy and discretion." Sometimes discretion did not prevail: "One lady, who had a beautiful negro girl continually about her person, thought she saw some symptoms of *tendresse* in the eyes of her husband. . . . She ordered one of her slaves to cut off the head of the unfortunate victim, which was instantly done. At dinner her husband said he felt no disposition to eat, to which his wife, with the air of a demon, replied, perhaps I can give you something that will excite your appetite; it has at least had that effect before. She rose and drew from a closet the head of Coomba. The husband . . . left the house and sailed immediately for France."

Besides such preoccupations, the whites of Cap François, who fancied themselves the colony's most cultured, could boast a museum, public fountains, several newspapers, a Royal Society of Arts and Sciences, and separate gallows for blacks and whites. The city was as large as Boston, and many of its streets were paved (something not the case in much of provincial France), and most had brick or stone sidewalks. Its whitewashed homes were built of stone brought from Europe as ships' ballast; their wrought-iron balconies and garden trellises bore vines of muscat grapes. For the wealthier settlers, local fruits and vegetables were supplemented by Médoc wine, Périgord truffles, and fowl imported from the United States. Despite the veneer of elegance, however, there was something of the frontier town about the place, reflected in names like Devil's Fart Street.

Absconding to St. Domingue was a way to escape gambling debts, the Paris police, or a pregnant girlfriend demanding marriage. *Passer aux îles* meant to flee a tight spot. Although those on the run might first have to wait for the trouble to blow over, most French people in the colony wanted to make their money and then head home. As one observer put it: "All wish to be gone. Everyone is in a hurry; these people have the air of merchants at a fair."

When word of the St. Domingue revolt first reached London, stock prices fell. Further news of the upheaval spread panic among slaveholders everywhere. In Virginia, the state legislature tightened restrictions on slave gatherings and passed an "Act against divulgers of false news." Fears were still higher in the Caribbean, where British planters had long known that they, too, were at the foot of a volcano. In Jamaica, whites were proportionally even more outnumbered than in St. Domingue. Authorities on the island declared martial law, begged London for soldiers, and called up the militia. Rumors flew that French revolutionaries and St. Domingue mulattos had sent secret agents to stir up slaves on Jamaica's north coast, only a day's sail away. Runaway slaves often fled from one Caribbean island to another in small boats or as stowaways, and so the revolt was treated like a communicable disease. British warships cruised the channel between the two islands. Then a new path for the virus suddenly opened: slave servants brought to Jamaica by French planters fleeing the rebellion. Magistrates were ordered to be on the alert for any sign of contact between these slaves and Jamaican ones. White fears were further inflamed when a runaway French slave was found in Jamaica with the brand marks of several different masters on his breast (a sign of a troublemaker who had been repeatedly sold), and gave his name as "John Paine." "I am convinced that the Ideas of Liberty have sunk so deep in the minds of *all* Negroes," an alarmed slave owner on the island wrote, "that whenever the greatest precautions are not taken they will rise."

Where should the greatest precautions be taken? The St. Domingue upheaval forced government officials in London to assess risks in their own slave colonies. A wellborn Royal Navy officer, Captain George Cranfield Berkeley, wrote a shrewd, confidential report to the foreign secretary about which British islands were most in danger from rebellion and why. Barbados he thought secure: a high proportion of whites, most slaves "Born and Bred up in the Island and habituated," and "No Woods, nor Places where they could hide or assemble in." But Grenada was in danger: "Impassable Woods" in the interior, plus the slaves were mostly new arrivals. Antigua was safe: a fort "commanding the Whole Island, and the King's Dock Yard . . . where in general some of our men of War are constantly stationed," plus missionaries to the slaves "whose Preachers constantly recommend in the strongest terms the Necessity and Duty of Subordination and passive Obedience to their Masters."

There was no way British planters could contain news of the uprising. Within a month, Jamaican slaves were singing songs about it, and rumors spread that slave blacksmiths were secretly forging cutlasses. The slaves seemed to think freedom was imminent: one who was whipped said to her tormentor, "Slapp me again if you please, 'tis your time now, but we shall drink wine before Christmas." A letter from the island reported the rumor among slaves that "the King of England wished Slaves in Jamaica to be on the same footing [as whites] but that their owners were against it."

The myth of a benevolent king betrayed by others recurs throughout history, and it is not surprising that it should repeatedly do so in the Caribbean. After all, hundreds of thousands of slaves had grown up in African chiefdoms or monarchies. Rarely did they demand freedom as an inherent right; more often, in both the French and British colonies, they were convinced that the king had already freed them. Although many of their leaders were stirred by the promise of the

French Revolution, most rebel slaves in St. Domingue did not generally wear the tricolor cockade. To them it symbolized the emancipation of the whites only; instead they wore the white cockade, signifying loyalty to King Louis XVI.

Sometimes the imagined benevolent king took a different form. In December 1791, a worried Jamaican white man reported that "a body of Negroes . . . had assembled drinking King Wilberforce's health out of a Cat's Skull by way of a cup, and swearing Secrecy to each other." Wilberforce would no doubt have been appalled. Nor was this the only slave celebration of the best-known abolitionist: the same year, before being dispersed, some three thousand Jamaican blacks gathered peacefully to mark his birthday.

Besides its vast scale, the upheaval in St. Domingue differed from previous slave risings in other ways. For one thing, the colony's mulattos —almost all of them descended from liaisons between Frenchmen and slave women—were also in rebellion. Although traditionally free, they had long been treated as second-class citizens; the very word "mulatto" comes from the Spanish term for a young mule. Those in St. Domingue had no political rights and faced a humiliating set of prohibitions: against riding in carriages, wearing fine clothing, or mixing with whites in churches or restaurants. Nonetheless, they owned one third of the colony's plantations and one quarter of its slaves; many sent their children to France to be educated.

A first wave of rebellion by mulattos had been suppressed just months before the slave revolt broke out, and many of the rebels were hanged. For the two top leaders, hanging was considered too mild: they were sentenced to kneel and apologize while holding a burning torch, then to be broken alive on a scaffold and finally beheaded. One man refused to kneel; the other, whose last-minute tearful repentance brought him no reprieve, was Vincent Ogé. Clarkson must have been shocked when he got the news. Ogé had apparently used some of the £30 Clarkson had given him in London to buy arms in South Carolina on his way home.

What also made the turmoil in St. Domingue unprecedented was that the island's whites were deeply and sometimes violently divided.

Many workers, shopkeepers, seamen, and soldiers of fortune identified with the French Revolution, wore the tricolor cockade, and started a plethora of political societies. Although they considered themselves far superior to blacks and mulattos, they were hostile to the wealthy white planters. Whites in St. Domingue were thus bitterly at odds over who should control the colonial government. One regiment of French troops in the colony mutinied; they and revolution-minded local whites beat their royalist colonel to death, cut off his genitals, and paraded the corpse around town. Before long there were white, slave, and mulatto armies in the field, and at times several of each. Woe to the newcomer to St. Domingue history who tries to keep straight the bewildering array of ever-changing alliances, fissures, and betrayals among rival armies and warlords that unfolded throughout the 1790s. Underlying them all, however, was the struggle between blacks in rebellion and whites who wanted them to remain slaves.

France, convulsed by revolution, had for several years sent its prize colony a stream of contradictory messages. In 1789, the National Assembly passed the Declaration of the Rights of Man and Citizen, but as the frustrated Clarkson saw when he was in Paris, "Man" did not include slaves. In 1791, the Assembly decreed that free mulattos born to free parents—a tiny minority of a minority—would have the right to vote. When the slave revolt erupted, Paris reversed its decree, enraging the mulattos and setting off a new rebellion by them in the colony's south.

Meanwhile, slaves in the north continued their fight. Fast emerging as their leader was Toussaint, the former coachman of the Bréda plantation. He soon would also be using the name L'Ouverture—the opening. This may have come from the way his troops forced a breach when they attacked, or from his desire for opportunity open to all, or from the gap in his mouth where a spent cannonball had knocked out some teeth. Perhaps Toussaint L'Ouverture intended all of these echoes in his chosen name.

In 1792 the French government reversed itself once again and granted full political rights to all mulattos and free blacks. The colony's governor was called home and guillotined, while the feud between royalist and republican whites in St. Domingue broke into open civil war, the republicans promising freedom to all slaves who joined them.

Planter families in the colony's north continued to flee the burning countryside for Cap François, which was hit, as if symbolically, by a large earthquake. Republican whites and rebel slaves captured the city, killing thousands in bitter fighting and forcing ten thousand white refugees and royalist troops onto ships bound for the United States. From the rails of these vessels, those leaving watched the black troops load long mule trains with the contents of their shops and houses, then head off into the country. A visitor to Cap François soon afterwards described "the great squares where the bodies of the dead had been burned. The bones were lying in long rows. . . . Warehouses that were so lately loaded with merchandise from all parts of the world lay smouldering."

Léger-Félicité Sonthonax, a portly lawyer and journalist who became the senior French official in the colony, was a militant revolutionary opposed to slavery, but he was riding a tiger. Nominally in charge politically, he saw that his only hope for keeping St. Domingue for the French republic lay in an alliance with rebel slaves. Exceeding the authority given him, on August 29, 1793, he proclaimed the end of slavery in St. Domingue. The government of revolutionary France then had little choice but to make official what was already a fait accompli. On February 4, 1794, by formal decree in Paris, France became the first European country to free all the slaves in its empire, arguably the most radical, and most overlooked, act of the French Revolution. Thousands of Parisians came to a grand ceremony in the Cathedral of Notre-Dame, now rechristened the Temple of Reason. In towns all over France, people celebrated with street theater pageants, where whites in blackface had their chains undone. It was the slaves of St. Domingue, however, who had freed themselves.

What was Britain to do? Caribbean history was filled with revolts, almost always quickly suppressed, but the rebellion that raged across the plains and mountains of St. Domingue was clearly of a different order of magnitude. In the face of it, the traditional rivalry between French and British planters vanished. From St. Domingue came pleas for help, and British arms and ammunition were shipped to the colony's beleaguered whites.* Then, when war between Britain and France broke out in early 1793, Britain did much more. Conquering the colony, the British reasoned, would both gain Britain an immense treasure house of sugar and coffee plantations and stop the virus of rebellion from spreading. Henry Dundas, author of the 1792 "gradual" amendment and now secretary for war, later admitted, "Had not St. Domingo been attacked, Jamaica would not have been worth one year's purchase [i.e., rent]." Then as now, however, stated war aims had to be lofty. The conquest of St. Domingue, Dundas said—sounding like many an American President since then—was "not a war for riches or local aggrandisement, but a war for security."

In the field, military men were more blunt. Their main mission, the commanding British general and admiral in the Caribbean said in a joint message to their officers, was "to prevent a circulation in the British Colonies of the wild and pernicious Doctrines of Liberty and Equality." Filled with optimism, British forces sailed for France's Caribbean colonies. One lieutenant later recalled the day of departure: "The morning was brilliant beyond conception, the sight grand above description. The bands of music, the sounds of trumpets, drums and fifes, the high panting ardour, zeal and discipline of the soldiers and sailors, the confidence in the warmth, bravery and experience of the Commanders-in-Chief, and, in short, the cause we were employed in, created . . . a true loyal joy."

In September 1793, the first British forces came ashore in St. Domingue. At Jérémie, in the south, they were met by welcoming cheers and a banquet. A British commander found his troops "received by the inhabitants with every demonstration of joy and fidelity." These were the white inhabitants, of course; the reception from others would be a different story.

A mulatto army put up the first resistance, preventing the surprised British from capturing the fortified port of Tiburon. But soon town after town was falling into their hands as, from two sides, British

---

* A thousand muskets, other military supplies, and eventually some $400,000 also came from the United States, whose President and secretary of state, George Washington and Thomas Jefferson, were both slave owners. Jefferson was so appalled by the revolt that he declared, "Never was so deep a tragedy presented to the feelings of man."

troops closed in on Port-au-Prince. When news reached London that they had captured the city in time to celebrate the birthday of George III, church bells pealed all morning. With the capital in their hands, the British acted as if they had almost won the war. A French settler wryly noted, "It would be easy to live amicably with our Britannic comrades. All that is needed is to drink strictly hard liquor with them each day, and not to contradict when they repeat to satiety that the English Nation is the greatest in all the world, in war, commerce, agriculture, manufacture, customs, sciences, arts, manly strength, womanly charm, social accomplishments, etcetera—and there are countless etceteras."

The British assumed that taking control of the remainder of the colony would now be easy. But unknown to them, Toussaint L'Ouverture was rapidly turning illiterate rebel slaves into a formidable force. Roughly forty-seven years old when the fighting began, he was described as "small, frail, very ugly." Nonetheless, like his similarly short contemporary Napoleon, he had a powerfully commanding presence. He lived frugally and ate little. Everyone noticed his ever-moving eyes that missed nothing. Perhaps only in Leon Trotsky in the Russian Civil War has history seen another person with no military training or experience so quickly become a leader who could hold great armies at bay.

On the same day the French representative Sonthonax officially freed the slaves, Toussaint had issued a proclamation of his own:

> Brothers and Friends,
>
> I am Toussaint L'Ouverture. My name is perhaps known to you. I have undertaken to avenge you. I want liberty and equality to reign throughout St. Domingue. I am working towards that end. Come and join me, brothers, and combat by our side for the same cause.

The British invasion galvanized thousands of ex-slaves. If they wanted to keep their new freedom, it was clear that the French republic's formal emancipation was not enough. They would have to fight for it. A masterly maker and breaker of alliances, Toussaint first formed a temporary coalition with Spain, which had a colony (today's

Dominican Republic) on the eastern half of the same island and was eager to gain French territory. The Spanish naturally expected to dominate this army of former slaves, but Toussaint no more wanted Spanish masters than French ones. After he had received the Spanish arms and money he needed, he suddenly broke off the alliance.

Some of the greatest tributes to Toussaint come from the European generals who fought against him. One, Pamphile de Lacroix, later wrote: "He slept only two hours a night. . . . You never knew what he was doing, if he was leaving, if he was staying, where he was going, where he was coming from. Often it was announced that he was at Cap François, and he was at Port-au-Prince. When you thought he was at Port-au-Prince, he was at Cayes, at Môle, or at Saint-Marc. . . . Toussaint Louverture had the best and fastest horses . . . it was his only luxury. . . . While racing across the colony on horseback at lightning speed, while seeing everything for himself, he prepared his plans and thought things out while he galloped."

Toussaint hired French deserters to train his troops, and he chose his officers shrewdly. "Never was a European army subjected to more severe discipline than that observed by Toussaint Louverture's troops," wrote de Lacroix. "Each officer ruled with pistol in hand, and had the power of life or death over his subordinates." Toussaint rapidly grasped how to use the ambushes and booby traps that are the essence of guerrilla warfare. As one exasperated French soldier wrote, "Each tree, each hole, each piece of rock hid from our unseeing eyes a cowardly assassin." As they stormed one British stronghold, 1,500 men found their assault ladders too short and stood on each other's shoulders while the dead dropped beside them. The British drove back four of these attacks, leaving 500 black dead. When their ammunition ran out, Toussaint's soldiers fought with stones or fashioned bows and arrows. His men often went into battle, in his words, "naked as earthworms."

Whites in St. Domingue were repeatedly stunned by the skill and determination of these troops, especially since many of their commanders were illiterate: surviving orders and reports from some show their signatures first written by someone else in pencil, then shakily traced over in ink. The historian John Thornton suggests one reason why the soldiers were such good fighters: many had fought before.

Massive slave imports in the 1780s to feed St. Domingue's booming sugar plantations meant that the great majority of Toussaint's troops were African-born. In Africa, many had fallen into local slave merchants' hands by becoming prisoners of war. Among the wars they were veterans of were those on the Angola-Congo coast, where about half of St. Domingue's slaves came from. Thornton has traced specific tactics used by Toussaint's commanders—both guerrilla raids and sophisticated attacks by masses of troops—to well-documented battles in that coastal region between local Africans and the Portuguese.

With his soldiers, Toussaint was a natural teacher. As his opponent General de Lacroix described it: "He spoke to them in parables. . . . Into a glass vase filled with black corn, he mixed a few kernels of white corn, and said to those who surrounded him: 'You are the black corn; the whites who want to enslave you are the white corn.' He shook the vase, and held it before their fascinated eyes, shouting, as if inspired, 'See the white ones only here and there.' That is to say: See what the whites are in proportion to you."

Toussaint was equally shrewd in speaking to his enemies. When a captured British officer was found to be carrying the written order "Take no prisoners!" Toussaint sent a letter to the commanding British general: "You have demeaned yourself. . . . Were I to be guilty of so infamous an act, I should feel I had sullied the honor of my country."

British officers were starting to realize that even if they were able to conquer St. Domingue, the victory would be a hollow one, for the colony's blacks were determined never to be slaves again. They were also dismayed by the terrain. It is said that a British officer, in answer to a question from King George III about the look of the countryside, took a piece of paper off the table, crumpled it up, and said, "Your Majesty, it looks like that." Still worse were the tropical diseases. Doctors, of course, did not know that malaria and yellow fever were carried by mosquitoes, which breed in stagnant water. The main British hospital in Port-au-Prince was next door to a swamp.

About other matters the British should have known better; after all, they had had soldiers in the Caribbean for well over a century. Nonetheless, pomp triumphed over common sense, and successive shiploads of fresh troops disembarked in tight-fitting red uniforms of heavy wool, made for fighting on the snowy plains of northern Europe. The army refused to abandon the famous red coat, or the regulation flannel underwear. In the intense, humid heat, the layers of flannel and wool became drenched in sweat, creating a covering as thick and clammy as a modern surfer's wetsuit and bringing on heat stroke.

Tsar Nicholas I once said that Russia's best generals were January and February; similarly, Toussaint made shrewd use of his best generals, malaria and yellow fever. Using the other months to train troops and regroup, he saved his most brilliant surprise attacks for the malarial rainy season, when British troops were sometimes up to their knees in mud that sucked their boots off.

When a Hospital Corps was established to help overwhelmed military doctors, British infantry officers used it to get rid of all their misfits. "Such a collection of incorrigible and incapable villains I believe never was brought together," wrote one surgeon, "and it was a true relief to the army when their drunkenness and the yellow-fever killed them off." This left the hospitals with few staff, but many dying men. Of one of these, an officer wrote, "Having seen the dead bodies merely sewed up in blankets before they were thrown into the graves, and feeling great horror at the idea of being buried without a coffin, he took care to buy one, and kept it at his bedside, until he . . . fancied that he was recovering, and sold the coffin to the patient on the stretcher next to his; but, relapsing soon after, he died, and was buried without one."

The effects of the yellow fever virus, which multiplies in the body to attack various internal organs, were especially horrendous: incontinence, delirium, pus oozing from the gums, bleeding from the nose and eyes, and then the dreaded "black vomit" of digested blood that often preceded death. Equally appalling was the medical treatment the ill soldiers received: doses of mercury, of diluted vinegar, of tartar to induce vomiting; and, above all, pre-scientific medicine's favorite treatment for everything, bleeding—typically the draining of twenty to thirty ounces of blood at a time. In search of something strong to attack the disease, one medical officer gave his patients balls of dough wrapped around cayenne pepper, which only made things worse, for yellow fever weakens the stomach lining. Small wonder that a French official set free a British military surgeon he had captured, telling his surprised prisoner that "wherever he went he would do much more harm than good with his medicines and flannel shirts."

Alcohol was thought to protect against fever, and the meat preserved in salt that the troops ate increased everyone's thirst. Doctors believed Madeira had particularly medicinal qualities, and so the Royal Navy sent a hospital ship to fetch supplies of it at the Portuguese island of that name. The officers' drink was claret, and some consumed up to twenty bottles a week. Sick or well, enlisted men were issued rum daily, and they liberally supplemented it by filling their canteens with more from the bars and cafés of the ports. In addition to leaving the troops in a stupor, much of the rum was badly distilled moonshine with a high ethanol and lead content, which added lead poisoning to the army's woes.

A vivid microcosm of the British military experience in St. Domingue can be found in a detailed journal kept by Thomas Phipps Howard of the York Hussars. He was a bluff career cavalry officer, filled with thoroughly conventional ideas about the splendor of his regiment, the rightness of slavery, the generosity of masters, and the character of slaves ("extremely sulky," "obstrepolous" [*sic*], and full of "Obstinacy"). Even after seeing his own regiment mauled by the greatest of all slave armies, his beliefs never changed, nor did he consider it the least bit odd that two brother officers, in the midst of the deadly campaign, took time out to fight, over "some trifling dispute," a duel.

The magnificent uniforms of the York Hussars made them a favorite of military painters: scarlet jackets with green cuffs and high collars, red breeches, long leather boots, high cylindrical black helmets with white cord and plume. After Howard and his men disembarked, the officers unwisely waited until well into the morning before marching the troops off to an attack.

> The Sun being so extremely hot & not a drop of Water to be meet with on the Road[,] none but those who have been obliged to March in this Country can have an Idea of the extremities to which the Army was reduced. [S]o great was it that before they halted, which was about 3 oClock in the Afternoon, no less than between 50 & 60 Men had absolutely perished with thirst & were lying dead along the Road. . . . At

> every three or four hundred yds you met Men lying on their backs, their tongues lolling out of their Mouths & in the agonies of Death for want of Water. Many were absolutely by way of moistening their Mouths obliged to drink their own Urine. . . . We were . . . infinitely Obliged to the Humanity of Dr. Baillie, our Surgeon, who tho' ill himself & suffering every Deprivation with the rest of the Army, exerted himself in the relief of the Unfortunate Men by bleeding.

Soon came malaria and yellow fever. "The Dead Carts were constantly employed, & scarcely was one empty, tho' they held from 8 to 12 each, but another was full. Men were taken ill at dinner, who had been in their most apparent Health during the Morn:, & were carried to their long Homes at Night. . . . Hundreds, almost, were absolutely drowned in their own Blood, bursting from them at every Pore. [S]ome died raving Mad, others forming Plans for attacking, the others desponding."

Although the horrors that loomed largest for Lieutenant Howard were those of heat and disease, between the lines of his journal we catch repeated glimpses of Toussaint's ragtag, unexpectedly disciplined ex-slaves. Howard never dignifies them with any name other than "Brigands," and talks contemptuously of how "they for the most part go naked except perhaps a peice of Cloth tied round their mid[d]les," but it is clear that they ran circles around the gloriously plumed and redcoated York Hussars. All Howard's training in sword-waving cavalry charges was for naught. "Their Method of making War consists chiefly in Ambuscades, for which the face of the Country is particularly calculated, & surprises. [A]s to meeting you openly on the Plains or having any regular System of Tacticts, they are totally unaccquainted with it, & seldom or ever have been able to be brought up in a regular manner against our Troops. . . . Five hundred European Cavalrie would destroy five thousand of them in [the] Plain, but the Case is much altered when they fight in their own woods & Mountains." In Howard's voice is the same bewilderment that conventionally trained army officers have felt over the centuries when faced with guerrillas. As another British observer described it, the British advances were "like a vessel traversing the ocean;—the waves yielded indeed for the moment, but united again as the vessel passed."

Howard could not get over the fact that the barely clothed "Brigands" attacked again and again, often against great odds. Their ranks bloodied and diminished by these assaults, Howard's own men began melting away. "On the 21st: eight Men deserted to the Enemy. [O]n the 22th we lost two more; & on the 23th another which made eleven in three Days, out of which four were Corporals." Did these eleven soldiers end up fighting in Toussaint's army of ex-slaves? Unfortunately, at this point they vanish from our sight.

Besides suffering a heavy toll in St. Domingue, the British were battling French republicans or rebel slaves elsewhere in the Caribbean, including several British islands on which the long-feared slave uprisings had finally begun. On Grenada in 1795, for example, rebel blacks and mulattos captured the governor, massacred whites, destroyed most of the plantations, and held the bulk of the island for months. When the rebels used up their cannonballs, they loaded their artillery with blocks of sugar wrapped in cloth, and fired these at the British.

The army was running out of soldiers and something had to be done. British officers had long experience in India of getting colonial subjects to do their fighting for them, and after watching successive waves of British soldiers die, they began to raise regiments of blacks, who were already acclimated to tropical weather and diseases. The army bought slaves quietly, in small groups, to conceal what it was doing and to avoid making Prime Minister Pitt, who still gave lip service to abolition, look like a hypocrite. Nonetheless, the news leaked out and Wilberforce wrote a mild, very belated letter of protest to Pitt. Over time, the British Army purchased some 13,400 slaves, which probably made it the largest single buyer of slaves in the Caribbean. This program, of course, gave the government itself a huge vested interest in preventing abolition, and helps explain why Pitt, who had once denounced the slave trade with memorable eloquence, now did so no longer.

Paying £60 to £70 apiece, depending on a man's strength and fitness, the army bought many of these slaves directly off ships from Africa. At the wharf, a slave would be poked, prodded, measured, found fit to bear arms, and given a name, which might be anything from Hannibal to Othello. Then, in the words of Roger Buckley, historian of these black regiments, "He was tagged around the neck with a white card bearing his new name, to which the now-recruited African was abruptly introduced by the repeated shouts of a splendidly uniformed black noncommissioned officer. Still silent, and, perhaps, still ignorant of his new vocation, he was marched off . . . to a West India regimental depot where he would be adorned with a dazzling scarlet tunic and begin immediately to earn the King's shilling. All this for his troubles in coming across the ocean!" To better motivate them, some slaves were promised freedom after five years of service, but, as the British commander in St. Domingue dryly noted, "At the expiration of that period, probably very few of these individuals will be alive to partake of the terms now offered."

St. Domingue remained embattled and divided. On one side were British troops, white and black, and the white slave owners and French royalists who had welcomed them so enthusiastically. On the other were Toussaint and his slave rebels, plus a small number of French troops. Toussaint was nominally in the service of the French republic, which had also sent thirty thousand muskets, supplies, and money. But the money ran out, and disease felled many French soldiers. It was really Toussaint's war. He had to scrounge for supplies, trading coffee and rum to American smugglers for barrels of gunpowder. French republican officials in the colony, despite their speeches about the rights of man and Toussaint's protestations of loyalty to France, were increasingly uneasy with a black man as the de facto leader of much of the territory. They suspected that he had independence on his mind.

After suffering additional defeats at the hands of a mulatto army in the southern reaches of St. Domingue, the British decided to reinforce their battered forces there and on the other islands with a vast fleet of troopships in late 1795. As they waited to board, soldiers filled thousands of white tents lined up in farmers' fields on the south coast of England and seized final moments of comfort in dingy local boarding houses offering, as a cartoon had it, "Lodgings for Single Men and Their Wives."

The expedition was the largest that had ever left Britain. Sometimes, however, it seemed to be sailing directly out of a comic opera. British forces in the Caribbean in this era included a Colonel Quarrell, a Colonel Riddle, and a Captain Muddle. The names seemed to describe the expedition's departure, delayed by internecine rivalries, a creaky military bureaucracy, and naval manpower shortages that had press gangs roaming the streets of British cities. The military repeated all its earlier mistakes on a huge scale. Service in the West Indies had never held the same glamour as that in Europe or India, and officers assigned to the region were traditionally those who failed to win other posts. "Blockheads at the heads of Regiments. . . . The most indolent, ignorant and negligent men," one frustrated general called them. Nor were the enlisted men any better: "The very scum of the Earth," a West Indian governor exclaimed. "The Streets of London must have been swept of their refuse, the Gaols emptied. . . . I should say the very Gibbets had been robbed to furnish such Recruits."

Two regiments in Ireland briefly mutinied when word came that they were being sent to the Caribbean. Several units of German mercenaries resisted the assignment with gunfire. When the expedition finally set sail, a storm promptly wrecked five of the ships, strewing some six hundred redcoated corpses along the beach and the bottom of the English Channel. Reorganized for a second attempt, the armada grew still larger: 218 ships carrying 19,284 soldiers. Some officers, as was the custom of the day, brought their wives and children.

In this and earlier convoys, an estimated one thousand soldiers died before they even arrived, for the small, packed troop transports that tossed and dipped their seasick passengers across the Atlantic were no cruise liners, especially once they reached tropical waters. An army doctor wrote, "You will readily imagine . . . such a body of men, sick, and ill, and crowded in every quarter of the ship. . . . They lie down in their clothes at night, where they have been standing or sitting the whole of the day, and from making the deck at once their sitting bench, their dinner board, and their bed, all about them soon grows filthy and offensive: pieces of broken food—sloppings of broth, or grog, bits of meat, old bones, crumbs of biscuit, and various other kinds of filth collect under them, and about their clothing; and, from the great heat of climate, and still more unpleasant heat of the crowd, this dirty commixture soon becomes sour and fetid."

After weeks in conditions like these, the troops were not exactly in top fighting form. Those who straggled off their ships in St. Domingue found that the British were steadily losing territory and thousands of men—to disease, to roving black guerrilla bands known as *congos*, to Toussaint's troops, and to those of his rival in the south, the skillful mulatto general André Rigaud.

Before long, War Secretary Dundas seemed to realize the cause was hopeless. He toyed with several face-saving schemes that would have turned the British-controlled portion of St. Domingue over to someone else. At one point he considered giving it to a coalition of French royalist planters—the very people who had not been able to maintain control in the first place; at another, to Britain's ally, Russia. By 1798, it was clear that the redcoats could not keep their foothold much longer, and Parliament and the press were filled with contentious debate about the costs of the campaign in money and lives. In Edmund Burke's memorable phrase, it was like fighting to conquer a cemetery.

Toussaint had been wounded in combat many times, but never seriously, and the legends around him grew. From a local black corps fighting for the British, three hundred men deserted en masse to Toussaint's side. The crackle of musketry grew ever closer to the major British stronghold of Port-au-Prince. The few hundred followers Toussaint had started with some five years earlier were now an experienced army of fourteen thousand. "Do not disappoint me," he said in a proclamation to his soldiers. ". . . Do not permit the desire for booty to turn you aside. . . . It will be time enough to think of material things when we have driven the enemy from our shores. We are fighting that liberty—the most precious of all earthly possessions—may not perish." Before long, he captured Morne l'Hôpital, a hill overlooking Port-au-Prince, and British soldiers below could hear the ex-slaves singing a martial song to the tune of "La Marseillaise."

The British had had enough, and agreed to withdraw. A strange episode during the evacuation of the capital shows how hard it was for British troops to acknowledge that blacks had gotten the better of them. Two sentries of the 69th Foot Regiment, standing guard at the city's Government House, were forgotten in the confusion of withdrawal. Toussaint's men found them at dawn, still on duty. They refused to believe that their fellow troops had all left, and refused to leave their posts unless relieved. Finally they were sent off under guard to catch up with the last of their departing compatriots.

Britain agreed to leave Toussaint alone, and to have a trading relationship. In return, Toussaint promised not to invade Jamaica or to spread "dangerous principles," as a later, more formal treaty put it, to Jamaican slaves. Although still nominally under the French republic, Toussaint acted like a head of state in negotiating the peace agreement. He knew he would need friendly relations with Britain to declare independence from France.

"Thank God I have at length got Great Britain rid of the whole of the incumbrance in this Island," wrote Thomas Maitland, the British commander. Of the more than twenty thousand British soldiers sent to St. Domingue during five years of fighting, over 60 percent lay buried there. In October 1798, the Union Jack was lowered and Toussaint rode as liberator into Port-au-Prince and Cap François—on whose streets he had once driven as a liveried coachman.

British newspapers now spoke of him with a new note of respect. "According to all accounts," said the *London Gazette,* "he is a negro born to vindicate the claims of this species and to show that the character of men is independent of exterior color." The *Times* acknowledged his skill and bravery as a commander but assured its readers, erroneously, that he had been educated in France.

British mythmaking has long turned military withdrawals or defeats into moments of heroism—consider, in later times, the charge of the Light Brigade or Dunkirk—but with the five-year campaign in St. Domingue this never happened. The colony's name has never appeared on a single British regimental banner. Although the evacuation was negotiated and orderly, with salutes and drumrolls and honor guards and a dinner given for Toussaint by General Maitland, and although departing redcoats smartly marched towards their ships in ranks four abreast, and although disease took a greater toll than combat, there was no disguising one central fact: the soldiers of the world's greatest slave-trading nation had given way before an army of ex-slaves.

19

REDCOATS' GRAVEYARD

CURIOUSLY, it was during these years when the abolitionist movement in England was brought to a dead halt by the war, with Clarkson living in the country and Wilberforce deep in Evangelical projects at Clapham, that war brought far more Britons than ever before face to face with slavery. It was not only in St. Domingue that British soldiers were battling slave rebels; total casualties, chiefly to disease, were even higher in fighting on the smaller islands of the eastern Caribbean. Early in the war with France, for example, British forces had swiftly taken Guadeloupe, but the French had a weapon they could not match: the revolutionary decree emancipating the slaves. Blacks flocked to join them. Suddenly the British, appalled at the new twist France had given the rules of warfare, found themselves fighting a sizable number of determined ex-slaves.* Since the black soldiers fought barefoot, British troops in one fort threw broken glass into a surrounding ditch. Still the siege continued, and the British lost the island. In London, the abolitionist lawyer James Stephen, though now high in his country's establishment, wrote to Wilberforce

* The British therefore assumed that all blacks on Guadeloupe were now the enemy. A British grenadier officer named Burnet, whose face had been completely blackened by a gunpowder explosion, was mistaken for a rebel slave by his own men and bayoneted three times before they realized their error. He survived.

that he welcomed the victories of the French and their ex-slave allies as proof of God's plan to end the "horrid system" of slavery.

Even some victories felt like defeats. The British took St. Lucia, lost it, then took it again. The final recapture required more than twelve thousand troops who faced, in the end, only two thousand on the other side, almost all of whom were black. "The negroes in the island are to a man attached to the French cause," General John Moore, a rising star in the British Army, confided to his diary. "Neither hanging, threats, or money would obtain for me any intelligence from them." Death and illness badly depleted Moore's own troops. "The army you left in this country is almost entirely melted away," he wrote to his commanding general.

Moore tried to tempt blacks to lay down their arms by promising a new, better version of slavery with "kind treatment and good feeling," but the former slaves would have none of it. When the last guerrillas surrendered after more than a year of fighting, they did so only on condition that they never again be slaves.

Britain sent more soldiers to the West Indian campaign than it did to suppress the North American rebels two decades earlier, and the war cost far more lives. Long rows of officers' names filled the obituary columns—enlisted men usually did not merit such mention—and it was said on the floor of Parliament that every member had lost someone he knew in the Caribbean. Of the nearly 89,000 white officers and enlisted men who served in the British Army in the West Indies from 1793 to 1801, over 45,000 died in battle or of wounds or disease. Another 14,000 were discharged, mainly because of wounds or illness, and more than 3,000 deserted. In addition, among sailors on British naval or transport ships, deaths are estimated as at least 19,000. Proportionally, this would be as if the United States today lost more than 1.4 million soldiers and sailors in a distant war. The impact of the toll only grew as shiploads of ragged survivors returned, bringing news of the senseless waste of lives. Some men also brought with them other stories: about the nature of slavery—and about the blacks fighting to free themselves from it.

One officer with such a story to tell returned from Jamaica. In 1795, the British faced a rebellion on that island from a community of free blacks known as Maroons. (The name comes from the Spanish *cimarrón,* or savage, derived from the Symarons, an Indian tribe in Panama who had rebelled against Spain.) The Jamaican Maroons were descendants of fugitive slaves who had long before taken refuge in the "cockpit country," the extremely rugged interior, which European troops had always found almost impenetrable. Much of Jamaica is white limestone, and in the mountains of the island's western end heavy tropical rains over the millennia have carved the soluble limestone into caverns, sinkholes, and ridges that have a strange honeycombed appearance when seen from the air, like the bottom of an egg carton or an endless, densely moguled ski slope. The cockpits are narrow ravines walled by steep, bush-covered cliffs, ready-made for ambushes.

By treaties of some sixty years earlier, the Maroons had been guaranteed freedom and some cultivatable land. In return they accepted British authority, and agreed to hunt down and return any runaway slaves. But Jamaican whites, with St. Domingue on their minds, feared these independent black communities on their island, and tensions between them and the Maroons rose. The Maroons were outraged when soldiers seized and handcuffed six of their leaders, on the way to present some grievances to government officials. In response, they staged an ambush that killed three dozen British cavalrymen.

Plantations went up in flames, and yet another war was on. Some locally based British military units had just been dispatched to St. Domingue, but the Earl of Balcarres, Jamaica's acting governor, sent a fast boat to overtake the troopships at sea and order them back to Jamaica. The Maroons, fighting as guerrillas from the natural fortifications of the cockpits, were such good marksmen that they killed five times as many British as they wounded, including two colonels. Eerily for the British, for some weeks there were no signs of any Maroon casualties. Balcarres, himself the owner of several hundred slaves, was horrified by reports that more than 150 slaves had run away to join the Maroons.

The British posted rewards for the capture, dead or alive, of several Maroon leaders, including Leonard Parkinson, one of the few black rebels from this time of whom we have an image. An engraving shows a sinewy young man, bare-chested and barefoot; he is equipped with a musket, a pouch for powder and shot, and a cutlass. His features are in profile only; in the eyes of the white artist, he is almost faceless, all muscle and weapon. A white plantation overseer witnessed one of Parkinson's raids, escaping death himself by hiding up to his chin in a muddy pond. He testified that the raiding party, including seven women and girls, killed one of the plantation's white managers, set the house and stable on fire, and took arms and food. "What they could not carry away they distributed amongst the Negroes belonging to the Plantation. *Parkinson told them not to be afraid,* they only intend to kill Backras [whites]. He tried to get the Men to enlist with them, and finding them averse to it, he said that 'he did not mean to force them, but he was fighting to make all the Negroes free.'"

Roughly five hundred Maroon men, women, and children were in rebellion, with a mere 150 muskets; some five thousand British troops and Jamaican militia went into action against them. The Maroons knew their territory. They camouflaged themselves with leaves and built traps of pits concealed by branches. They used drums and animal sounds to signal each other, and were said to make fires of woods that emitted little visible smoke. They sometimes took shelter in "back-o-water" caves, whose mouths were hidden by waterfalls. Plantation slaves gave them information on British troop movements.

Commanding the forces sent against them, including nearly one hundred bloodhounds and their handlers imported from Cuba,* was Major General George Walpole, whose great-uncle had been a British Prime Minister. Walpole trained his men carefully, found concealed firing positions, and worked out a system of signal rockets for communicating with far-flung units. At one point his men marched for five days with no water except that which collected in certain trees and plants, particularly the spout-shaped leaves of the wild pine, a survival trick he copied from the Maroons. Like commanders in

---

* To the British, putting down black rebellions was business as usual, but some felt that using bloodhounds to do so, particularly *Spanish* bloodhounds, was improper. The eccentric George III was so outraged that he at once ordered the secretary of state for the colonies to write to Balcarres to express his "Abhorrence of the mode of warfare" and to demand that he "remove forthwith, and to extirpate from the Island, the whole Race of those tremendous animals, of whose ungovernable ferocity you have already seen a very shocking effect." By the time the order had crossed the Atlantic, however, the hounds had ended their British military careers.

twentieth-century antiguerrilla conflicts, he cleared brush and seized his enemy's cropland. But, as would also happen among his counterparts in future wars, Walpole came to admire the Maroons as an enemy who "had manifested great Fortitude, great Generalship and has preserved a secrecy in their manoeuvres unparralled among European Soldiers. . . . The Velocity of their Movements and the knowledge of the Grounds was so superior to ours as to make them be considered as almost unconquerable."

Walpole also realized that the very fighting was turning the Maroons into symbols of freedom in the eyes of slaves, "a rallying point for more runaways to resort to, and thus the wars be perpetuated by years." (In a more cynical moment, he suggested that the only way to subdue the Maroons would be to resettle them near one of the large towns selling liquor: "The access to spirits will soon decrease their numbers.")

After more than half a year of fighting, high British casualties, and a cost of £500,000, the revolt was at last defeated. As a sign of good faith, Walpole went into the woods unarmed to negotiate with the remaining Maroons. They agreed to surrender, kneel, and ask the King's pardon, return any recent runaway slaves who had joined them, and be relocated elsewhere on the island. But they would not, Walpole promised, be transported away from Jamaica, where they had lived in independence so long. Alarmed at the apparent trust that had developed between Walpole and the enemy, Balcarres wrote him, "We are staggered here at the engagement you have entered into."

On December 28, 1795, Balcarres, as governor, reluctantly ratified the agreement, but insisted all Maroons surrender within the next four days, knowing there was no way word could reach many of the backwoods Maroons in time. Walpole and Balcarres angrily disagreed over whether the Maroons had handed over enough recently escaped slaves to keep that part of the bargain. Then Balcarres and the planter-controlled Jamaican Assembly simply refused to honor Walpole's treaty. Whites took over much of the Maroon land. Some rebel Maroons, including Parkinson, were whipped and jailed—a particular humiliation for people living proudly free for several generations. Finally, 568 Maroons, some in irons, were deported to cold and distant Nova Scotia.

Walpole was furious. He wrote to Balcarres that "the Maroons were Induced to Surrender from a Reliance which they had in my word; from a Conviction impressed upon them by me that the white people would never break their faith. All these things strongly call upon me . . . to declare the facts to the world." He refused a gift from the Jamaican Assembly of a 500-guinea sword, returned to England, and left the army to begin a public campaign to force the British government to honor the promises he had made.

Other British officers were also forced to think long and hard about the system of slavery they found themselves defending. George Pinckard, for example, was an army physician. On arriving at Barbados in 1796, Pinckard wrote home after visiting a newly arrived American slave ship in the harbor. "We were pleased to observe that an air of cheerfulness and contentment prevailed." The ship's slaves were well fed, clean, and well exercised, Pinckard said; they danced, and "they all seemed to regard the master of the vessel more in affection than fear." On shore, where Barbados landowners wined and dined Pinckard and other officers, he visited the Church of England's Codrington plantation, and there, too, found the slaves happy.

But gradually, as he traveled on, the tone of his letters changed. At a slave market, "I saw numbers of our fellow beings regularly bartered for gold, and transferred, like cattle, or any common merchandise, from one possessor to another." Buyers made the slaves jump, stamp their feet, and open their mouths, and marked the slaves they wanted by tying bits of colored string or cloth around their arms or necks. "In one part of the building was seen a wife clinging to her husband, and beseeching, in the strongest eloquence of nature, not to be left behind him. Here was a sister hanging upon the neck of her brother, and, with tears, entreating to be led to the same home of captivity."

On another occasion, a slave couple ran away from a notorious plantation. After they were captured, the husband was whipped to death; his wife nearly so. "I found the wretched and almost murdered woman lying stark-naked on her belly, upon the dirty boards, without any covering to the horrid wounds which had been cut by the whips, and with the still warm and bloody corpse of the man extended at her side." Some days later, Pinckard was startled to find several slaves carrying her outside in the rain. "You will scarcely hold it credible, when I tell you that they were employed a full half-hour *picking maggots out of her sores.*"

Pinckard's fellow soldiers shared his horror. Once he met a slave wearing a common instrument of punishment: "a heavy iron collar about his neck, with three long iron spikes projecting from it, terminating in sharp points at the distance of nearly a foot and a half from his person, and with his body flogged into deep ulcers from his loins to his hams. . . . The poor man followed me to the fort; the soldiers grew indignant . . . his neck was quickly freed from its load, and the massive yoke and its spikes were speedily converted into pot-hooks for the use of the mess."

Unlike British civilians in the West Indies, military men like Pinckard had not gone there in hopes of getting rich off the slave economy, and their memoirs, letters, and even cartoons often exhibit disgust at slavery. Jonathan Leach was on a hunting expedition a few days after arriving in Antigua when he was shocked to see "a huge slave-driver flogging most unmercifully an old decrepit female negro, who appeared bowed down with misery and hard labour." Impulsively, he and another officer peppered the man's legs with pellets from their shotguns. A best-selling memoir by an English officer who had fought slave rebellions in the Dutch South American colony of Suriname gained impact from a powerful set of illustrations by the artist and poet William Blake. Blake's engraving of a slave bound and suspended from a meat hook through his ribs became one of the most widely reproduced pieces of all antislavery art.

Besides Walpole, one other senior commander came to question what he was fighting for. Writing to his brother from the midst of the fighting in St. Domingue, Thomas Maitland, who would negotiate the British withdrawal with Toussaint, declared it was useless to try to subdue the rebel slaves fighting for a "Negroe free Government arising out the ruins of European Despotism. . . . We have no business on that Island." And in the House of Commons, an M.P. named Benjamin Hobhouse had pointed to the "surprising feats of valour" in St. Domingue performed by the determined ex-slaves set free by France, and went on to argue: "To be a match for France in the West Indies, we must meet her with her own weapons; we must adopt, towards our negroes, the same line of conduct she has observed towards hers: we must follow her example."

The long campaign in the Caribbean had sent tens of thousands of British soldiers to their graves, but, abolitionists wondered, was there any way in which the endless war with France might also bring their movement back to life? It would take many more deaths before that question would have an answer.

20

"THESE GILDED AFRICANS"

IN ENGLAND the movement was still frozen, but for the first time in a Caribbean colony, slavery was ended. In 1799, an awed Captain Marcus Rainsford of the now withdrawn British Army visited St. Domingue and several times met Toussaint L'Ouverture. "Though Europe waste her armies, and exhaust her navies in the endeavour, the blacks of St. Domingo will be unsubdued," he later wrote. ". . . No power on earth will be able to reduce them." France, as it would turn out, had yet to learn this lesson.

St. Domingue was a land in ruins. Fields were burned, plantation buildings destroyed, and several hundred thousand people of all colors had died. Many of those still alive had little to eat. White and mulatto skilled workers, teachers, doctors, and other professionals who had not been killed had fled. In the cities, people were living in makeshift shelters in the rubble of what had once been the Caribbean's grandest buildings. The well-armed mulatto general Rigaud still controlled the southern portion of the territory. The son of a black woman and a French official, Rigaud opposed slavery but wanted mulattos to be the dominant caste. A goldsmith in civilian life, he had learned war in Georgia and South Carolina, as a sixteen-year-old in a regiment of St. Domingue mulatto volunteers on the rebel side in the American Revolution. There was no love lost between his supporters, many of whom had been slave owners, and Toussaint's.

Indeed, the conflict between desperately poor blacks and the more middle-class mulattos would run like a bloody thread through the territory's politics for the next two centuries.

In the two years after the British withdrawal, Toussaint and Rigaud fought a civil war, known as the War of Knives, as brutal and bereft of mercy as all that had gone before. Captured mulatto leaders were blown from the mouths of cannons; at Port-au-Prince some six hundred Rigaud sympathizers were tied back to back, towed out to sea on barges, bayoneted, and tossed to the sharks. Blood stained the beaches red. Rallying his troops and urging on his generals, Toussaint sometimes rode sixty-five or seventy miles a day. The defeated Rigaud fled to exile in France.

By then a worse threat loomed. In Paris, Napoleon, dreaming of expanding France's empire, seized full political power in 1799. And he was no abolitionist, nor was his wife, Josephine, who had grown up on her father's slave plantation in Martinique. In 1801, after eight years of war, Napoleon signed a peace treaty with the British, in order to free up troops to regain France's most lucrative colony and make further conquests in the Americas.

The hopes of slaves everywhere were embodied in this one territory where they had won freedom. But St. Domingue was vulnerable. The former slaves, now mostly scraping out a hand-to-mouth living on small plots of land carved from the old plantations, were producing little that could be traded for arms and ammunition. In a shattered country desperately arming to protect itself, democracy would have been difficult even if its iron-willed strongman, Toussaint, had been any sort of democrat, which he definitely was not. Forcibly returning land to sugar and coffee production, he confiscated the old plantations, leasing them out to his generals, other trusted officials, and the few white planters he could persuade to return. The government took a share of the profits. Black farmworkers were offered slightly better living conditions, at least in theory. But they were attached to particular plantations like serfs, under strict military discipline. The whip and fifty-five-man gendarme companies in each parish made the system run, and people were conscripted as forced labor to build roads. To those living under it, the new regime seemed not so different from slavery.

Not surprisingly, revolts broke out, which Toussaint met with guns. Firing squads or cannons loaded with grapeshot executed some two thousand people suspected of disloyalty, including Toussaint's own adoptive nephew, who bore scars of slave whippings on his back. But however authoritarian Toussaint was, blacks, whites, and mulattos all held high positions in his regime and army. "Whatever their color," he wrote, "only one distinction must exist between men, that of good and evil. When blacks, men of color, and whites are under the same laws, they must be equally protected and they must be equally repressed when they deviate from them." Toussaint did far more repressing than protecting, but no other leader anywhere would even give lip service to such an ideal for many decades to come.

He issued a constitution abolishing slavery, granting himself power for life and establishing, in effect, a military dictatorship—a striking parallel to what Napoleon was doing in France. Sleeping only a few hours a night, he rose at dawn, attended Mass, dictated scores of letters and orders, then headed into the countryside on his favorite horse, Bel-Argent. Although he was only five feet one inch tall, Toussaint dressed like an emperor, which was what he clearly wanted to be, and is perhaps what his subjects, so many with memories of African monarchies, expected of him. "His uniform," Rainsford wrote, "was a kind of blue jacket, with a large red cape falling over his shoulders; red cuffs, with eight rows of lace on the arms, and a pair of large gold epaulettes thrown back; scarlet waistcoat and pantaloons, with half boots; round hat, with a red feather, and a national cockade; these, with an extreme[ly] large sword, formed his equipment." His bodyguards were adorned in equal brilliance; at ceremonial functions two trumpeters with red-plumed silver helmets preceded him. He used Creole dialect when addressing local crowds, but insisted officials speak to him in French. In his letters, he never used the informal French *tu.* He drank no alcohol and ordered that women's dresses show no cleavage. He was said to never forget a face.

Fearful of assassins, he accepted food only from trusted aides or, when in the field, on a banana leaf he had cut himself. He never appeared at a window. "He never pardoned," said a Frenchman who had been his secretary. "His unknown, resolute, terrible will was the supreme law without appeal. His spies . . . were everywhere, around his generals, on the estates, in the huts of the blacks. . . . He succeeded, so to speak, in making himself invisible wherever he was and visible where he wasn't; he seemed to have stolen the spontaneity of his movements from a tiger. . . . Frequently he arrived alone at night to surprise the troops and people. . . . Speedy horses were placed along all his routes. . . . Thus there was neither thought of betrayal nor time for treason. Impenetrable in his designs . . . he confided to no one."

All the while, Toussaint's wary eyes were on Napoleon, to whom, legend has it, he sent a letter addressed "From the first of the blacks to the first of the whites." Napoleon's reply was an invasion force, the largest that had ever set sail from France and designed, in his words, "to annihilate the government of the blacks in St. Domingue." In command was his twenty-nine-year-old brother-in-law, Victor-Emmanuel Leclerc, who cheerfully boasted that the sight of French bayonets would put the blacks to rout. "Rid us of these gilded Africans," Napoleon wrote Leclerc, "and we shall have nothing more to wish."

Still fearing the virus of slave rebellions, London confidentially told Napoleon that it would not regard his invading St. Domingue as a hostile act. "Toussaint's Black empire is one, amongst many evils, that has grown out of the War," a British cabinet minister wrote privately to the governor of Jamaica, "and it is by no means our Interest to prevent its Annihilation." The British representative in St. Domingue was withdrawn and all trade cut off. Almost alone in England, James Stephen spoke out against this "bare-faced annulling" of the British peace and trade agreement with Toussaint.

"We are lost," Toussaint said after the sails of the great invasion flotilla of French ships appeared over the horizon in early 1802. "All France has come to St. Domingue." The French had sent thirty-five thousand men, over half again as many as were in Toussaint's experienced but ill-equipped ranks. But, as Leclerc ominously reported to France, "Toussaint and his generals appear to me to have decided to burn down the colony and entomb themselves under the ruins before surrendering." Toussaint sent a message to one of his officers: "The only resources we have are destruction and fire. Annihilate everything and burn everything. Block the roads, pollute the wells with corpses and dead horses."

Toussaint's desperate troops rolled rocks down mountainsides into the path of the invaders. French commanders, like the British before them, were nonplused by guerrilla tactics. "The enemy held no territory, yet never ceased to be master of the country," wrote Alexandre Moreau de Jonnès, a French lieutenant. "Victors everywhere, we possessed nothing beyond the range of our rifles. . . . War was no better than hunters shooting at hares hiding in the thickets."

Nonetheless, French firepower took its toll, and after some months of fighting, several of Toussaint's generals went over to the French side, lured by promises that they could maintain their ranks. Finally, in May 1802, Toussaint began negotiating. Afraid of turning him into a martyr, the French promised him the position of lieutenant general if he would agree to retire to one of the plantations he now owned. Slavery, Leclerc promised, would never be restored. When Leclerc offered him dinner, Toussaint took nothing except water from a carafe whose contents had already been tasted, and a chunk cut from the middle of a piece of cheese.

A month later, under Leclerc's orders, another French general asked Toussaint to meet with him. In a rare lapse of judgment, Toussaint fell into the trap. Seized and bound on the spot, he was rushed to the coast and on board a ship for France. To the captain, Toussaint said, "They've only cut the trunk of the tree of black liberty. It will spring up again by the roots, for they are deep and plentiful." Attempting to cut the roots as well, the French transported across the Atlantic as prisoners more than eight hundred of Toussaint's officers and personal guard.

It seemed as if the French had won. General Leclerc's wife, Napoleon's beautiful and pleasure-loving sister Pauline, settled in great comfort in a mountainside villa, sleeping in a canopied bed with carved cupids and white satin curtains trimmed with gold. When an American visitor found her at home, "She reclined . . . on the sofa and amused general Boyer, who sat at her feet, by letting her slipper fall continually, which he respectfully put on as often as it fell. . . . She has a voluptuous mouth, and . . . an air of languor which spreads itself over her whole frame. . . . Madame Le Clerc is very kind to general Boyer, and . . . her husband is not content." While Pauline dallied with her husband's subordinate, the French, like the British, steadily succumbed to yellow fever and malaria, burying their dead in mass graves at night so no one would see their losses. Meanwhile, a series of decrees from Napoleon, held secret for the time being, stripped mulattos of equal rights and restored slavery and the slave trade.

However, when a ship called at Cap François, filled with captured black rebels from the French island of Guadeloupe, some of the prisoners jumped overboard and escaped to tell people that slavery had been reinstated there. The French could keep the secret no longer, and announced that slavery was to be restored in St. Domingue. The blacks rose again. From all the years of fighting, many muskets remained in their hands, but they fought even when they had no weapons: one group of unarmed farm laborers tricked a French general into thinking he was being attacked by calling out military commands at night.

Leclerc, who was growing desperate, wrote the minister of the navy, "50 prisoners have been hung; these men die with an incredible fanaticism; they laugh at death; it is the same with the women. . . . It appears to me from the orders that you send me that you have not got a clear idea of my position here. . . . It is not enough to have taken away Toussaint." To Napoleon, he added, "Here is my opinion. You will have to exterminate all the blacks in the mountains, women as well as men. Except for children under twelve. Wipe out half the population of the lowlands, and do not leave in the colony a single black who has worn an epaulet. . . . Send 12,000 replacements immediately, and 10 million francs in cash, or St. Domingue is lost forever." It was Leclerc's last letter. Three weeks later, he was dead of yellow fever. Pauline, more devoted in death than in life, cut off her long hair and put it in his coffin.

The rebels fought on and the French were ruthless: the general who took over from Leclerc ordered one rebel leader's epaulets nailed to his shoulders in front of his wife and children, who were then drowned before his eyes; he staked naked prisoners to the ground in front of dogs who had been deliberately deprived of food. By packing black and mulatto prisoners into a ship's hold and burning sulfur through the night, he created what may have been history's first gas chamber. In the morning, the bodies were dumped overboard to make room for more. By these and other atrocities, the French succeeded in uniting St. Domingue's blacks and mulattos against them.

Then Napoleon went to war with England again, supplies from France were cut off, and British warships arrived to bombard French positions.

Meanwhile, Toussaint was being held incommunicado in the massive ninth-century Fort de Joux in the Jura Mountains near the Swiss border. He refused to speak to an emissary sent by Napoleon, who then ordered his food and fuel allowance cut back.

Although virtually no Britons had praised Toussaint while Britain was fighting his slave rebels, many rushed to do so now that he was prisoner of the hated Napoleon. The image of a brave victim locked in a cold cell far from his native land was much more appealing than that of a black general leading an insurgent army. Laudatory articles poured forth in the press, and the *Annual Register*, hardly a revolutionary publication, chose him as its man of the year. The abolitionists, for the most part never comfortable with the idea of slaves fighting to free themselves, joined in the chorus. Coleridge declared Toussaint had more "true dignity of character" than his captor, Napoleon. Wordsworth wrote him a sonnet. After suffering through a northern European winter for the first time in his life, "in some deep dungeon's earless den," in Wordsworth's phrase, Toussaint died on April 7, 1803, ten months after his capture.

Ironically, the remnants of Napoleon's army were just then going down to defeat in St. Domingue. Demoralized, half-starving French soldiers, desperate for fruit and vegetables, sold bags of gunpowder to black women in the market, who smuggled these beneath their dresses to rebel forces. By the year's end, the last French troops had been forced from the island's soil. In its twenty-two-month attempt to retake the colony, France had lost more than fifty thousand soldiers, including eighteen generals. Napoleon suffered more casualties in St. Domingue than he would at Waterloo.* The territory, however, was

* The defeat of the French had vast consequences for the United States. Planning to use a reconquered St. Domingue as a base for further empire-building on the mainland, Napoleon had earlier acquired from Spain a huge tract of land. If he had not lost an army and depleted his treasury in the vain effort to subdue St. Domingue's ex-slaves, he would never have hastily sold this territory to the United States for a much-needed $15 million, in the transaction known as the Louisiana Purchase.

devastated. In more than a dozen years of scorched-earth warfare, near famine, and race-based mass murders (in one final spasm, Toussaint's successors ordered the three thousand French people remaining in St. Domingue slaughtered), it had lost more than half its population. The legacy of violence has crippled the land to this day. But the invaders—the two greatest European military powers—were defeated.

On January 1, 1804, St. Domingue's leaders proclaimed it the Republic of Haiti—the name for the island in the language of its earliest inhabitants, the now vanished Arawak Indians. Haiti's new constitution forbade land ownership by whites, and an amendment offered citizenship to any black or American Indian settler. It was the second independent nation in the Western Hemisphere. In the two hundred years to come, the country's path would not be an easy one: a nearby United States that imposed its own kind of domination, a France that successfully extracted restitution for the confiscated plantations, dire poverty, a string of corrupt dictators. Nonetheless, Haiti's independence was a historical turning point: three centuries of slavery on its soil were over.

Today we usually refer to these tumultuous years of fighting as the Haitian Revolution. It led to a spate of insurrection scares all over the American South, and inspired slave rebellions in Virginia and Louisiana that left more than one hundred dead. So afraid of revolutionary currents from the Caribbean were South Carolina's lawmakers that they passed the Negro Seaman Act, which permitted the jailing of any free black sailor as long as his ship was in the port of Charleston.

If there were always justice in history, the suffering and deaths of hundreds of thousands of ex-slaves in defeating first the British and then the French, and the transformation of colonial St. Domingue into independent Haiti, should have immediately brought freedom throughout the Caribbean, especially to the nearby British islands. But a strong British military presence prevented this, and both British slavery and—for the moment, anyway—the British slave trade seemed intact. Yet the events in St. Domingue forever changed the way people in Britain thought about their own West Indian colonies. Their image as a glorious, dependable source of imperial wealth, writes the historian David Brion Davis, "already tarnished by years of antislavery literature and iconography, never recovered from Britain's defeat."

In the minds of both slaves and their owners, the Haitian Revolution altered the idea of what was possible, and it thereby raised the stakes in all the struggles that followed. For the first time, whites saw a slave revolt so massive they could not suppress it, and for the first time blacks saw that it was possible to fight for their freedom and win. Two months after Haiti was born, Lady Nugent, the ever-observant wife of the Jamaican governor, wrote in her journal that whenever her dinner guests discussed the new nation, "the blackies in attendance seem so much interested, that they hardly change a plate, or do anything but listen. How very imprudent, and what *must* it all lead to!"

V

BURY THE CHAINS

21

A SIDE WIND

ONE AFTERNOON not long after the last British troops withdrew from St. Domingue, two small groups of men, keeping an aloof distance from each other, walked onto Putney Heath. This was a wild area outside London where criminals were hanged; the corpse of a well-known highwayman was still swinging in the breeze. One group surprised a pair of furtive lovers in the bushes. They were heading for a dell lined with gorse and silver birches, with neither a hanging nor an assignation in mind. Spurred by an obscure insult on the floor of the House of Commons, Prime Minister William Pitt and an M.P. named George Tierney were preparing to face off with pistols in hand at twelve paces. Tierney was plump and Pitt cadaverously thin; a joke was making the rounds that, to even the contest, an outline of Pitt should be marked on Tierney and only shots inside it should count. "Never did two men meet more ignorant of the use of their weapons," wrote one dignitary. Two exchanges of bullets missed, and it was quickly agreed that the affair had been settled with honor to all.

The duel, however, seriously damaged Pitt's relationship with Wilberforce, who was aghast not only that Pitt had fought a duel, a practice the Clapham Evangelicals abhorred, but also that he had done so *on a Sunday.* "I am more shocked than almost ever," he wrote in his diary. The friendship between the two men was already strained by Pitt's loss of interest in abolition; after the duel it became cooler still.

Tierney's second at Putney Heath was someone we have met before, former general George Walpole. As the war with France continued, Walpole's strenuous efforts to force the British government to honor his promises to the Jamaican Maroons had gone nowhere. To further his campaign, he got himself elected to Parliament, where he met Tierney, a longtime abolitionist who backed his efforts wholeheartedly. At last they achieved a partial victory, persuading the government to order the Maroons sent from Nova Scotia to Sierra Leone. In the area of Freetown where they settled, the Maroons named a street in Walpole's honor. Some thirty years later, still remembering his promises, a group of Maroons wrote him that "we all lie begging" and asked his help in returning to Jamaica. Only a handful were ever able to do so.

Despite the addition to the antislavery ranks of a few returned veterans of the Caribbean fighting, like Walpole, the dawn of the nineteenth century found British abolitionists deeply discouraged. Repressive legislation had brought almost all reform-minded political activity to a stop. Pitt subordinated everything to the long war with France. The slave economy appeared more firmly rooted than ever: the West Indian colonies accounted for more than 30 percent of British imports, and British slave traffic was near record levels, averaging more than forty thousand Africans carried to the New World each year. For the first time, a former slave ship captain sat in the House of Commons, John Anderson. He and his brother had inherited from their uncle, Richard Oswald, part of the Atlantic trading empire that included Bance Island.

In an England bled and impoverished by war, its sons and husbands being killed by the hundreds of thousands on foreign seas and battlefields, no one knew if people still felt the abhorrence of slavery they had once shown. One development, however, did offer the abolition forces some hope. In contrast to the revolutionary France that had formally liberated its colonial slaves in 1794, the France that Britain was fighting at the beginning of the 1800s was, of course, trying to *restore* slavery. Paradoxically, the archenemy Napoleon had thereby opened up some political space for British antislavery forces: they could associate abolition with British moral superiority. Was there any additional way the ongoing war could be made to work against slavery? The very question seemed, to one man who asked it, "half mad, and wholly presumptuous." But, as it turned out, he had an answer.

In Clarkson, the movement had an inspired organizer; in the Quakers, a network of dedicated activists; in Wilberforce, a parliamentary spokesperson of great respectability; in Granville Sharp, a venerable father figure, even if he made people's eyes roll when he rattled on about frankpledge. Until now, though, what the abolitionists had lacked was a first-rate thinker who could figure out how, within the confines of Britain's tradition-bound, half-democratic political system, they could transform into law the great reservoir of public opinion that—they hoped—was still on their side. This sorely needed strategist was now on the scene.

James Stephen had put behind him the multiple romantic infatuations of his youth to become a prominent lawyer, a writer on the affairs of the day, and a behind-the-scenes adviser to M.P.s and cabinet members. A portrait of him catches an intense, penetrating gaze beneath prominent eyebrows. Like Wilberforce, he was a conservative on most issues other than slavery, and was firmly convinced of the superiority of British culture. But unlike Wilberforce, his hatred of slavery, visceral and born of a decade of living in the West Indies, was the central, driving passion of his life. His conventional opinions on other subjects were, one senses, just part of the normal intellectual furniture of his class and time. He once said that while his fellow members of the Clapham Sect had come to abolition through Evangelical Christianity, he had come to Christianity through his horror at seeing slavery firsthand.

The best intellect among the abolitionists, Stephen was one of the empire's leading maritime lawyers—and it was this grounding in the world of international commerce that would give him a crucial tool in the fight for abolition. In the years he was searching for that tool, we can trace his restless mind at work in his writing. In 1802, in *The Crisis of the Sugar Colonies,* he used the St. Domingue revolution as an argument against slavery. Recalling the costly British military disaster, he correctly predicted the same for Napoleon's armies. Britain's islands in the Caribbean, filled with slaves ready to rebel and with climate and terrain difficult for European troops to fight in, would, he assured his readers, prove a huge drain on national resources. Addressing a war-weary country, he presented himself as a clear-thinking realist, speaking "not to the *conscience* of a British Statesman, but to his *prudence* alone." His arguments were practical and impeccably patriotic; his loathing of slavery was carefully kept under wraps.

In 1805, Stephen wrote an influential, widely read book, *War in Disguise, or, The Frauds of Neutral Flags.* The Royal Navy, he argued, had effectively cleared the Atlantic of the ships of France and its allies, Holland and Spain. Yet their New World colonies were thriving, because they carried on trade with the mother country through neutral ports and neutral ships, mostly flying the American flag. An American-flagged ship, for instance, would pick up a cargo of sugar at a French Caribbean island like Martinique and take it to South Carolina, where another American ship—or perhaps the same one, with a change of name and papers—would carry it to France. Why, Stephen argued, advancing a very twentieth-century notion of economic warfare, should Britain not seize such vessels? Wise in the ways of the sea, Stephen knew he was covertly appealing to a powerful lobby. Under the wartime "prize" system of the day, navy officers and sailors plus the crews of privateers—privately owned armed vessels—were entitled to a share of the value of the enemy ships and cargoes they captured. This was how officers dreamed of getting rich, and deckhands of supplementing their miserable pay. If neutral-flagged ships became fair game, they would be a huge new source of prize money. Artfully, Stephen scarcely even referred to the nature of the cargo many of these ships would be carrying: slaves.

One day in early 1806, as Wilberforce was about to leave his house in Old Palace Yard for Parliament, planning doggedly to introduce another doomed abolition bill, Stephen called on him to suggest and help draft something different. It was a bill that banned British subjects, shipyards, outfitters, and insurers from participating in the slave trade to the colonies of France and its allies. In the short debate over this proposal, abolitionists barely mentioned the evils of slavery, and Wilberforce himself did not speak.

The bill was hard to argue against, for how could anyone object to impeding trade with the country Britain had been fighting for more than a decade? But this piece of legislation was more far-reaching than it appeared. A well-concealed secret was that many, possibly the majority, of the supposedly neutral "American" slave ships were in fact owned by Britons, manned by British crews, and outfitted in Liverpool. The only thing American on them was the flag. The new bill, the so-called Foreign Slave Trade Act, in the name of the war effort, would in effect cut off approximately two thirds of the *British* slave trade. Stephen himself, with his intimate knowledge of the maritime world, was one of the few people who understood the potential impact of the act.

One other person, representing some of these ship owners, knew full well. Banastre Tarleton, now in his fifties and with his boyish good looks somewhat aged, fumed helplessly in the House of Commons that the abolitionists "were now coming by a sidewind on the planters." Tarleton was seriously handicapped, however, for he no longer had the skilled pen of his mistress, Mary Robinson, to write his speeches.* Stephen's "sidewind" was particularly ingenious because it split the parliamentary slave lobby, dividing slave ship–owning families like Tarleton's from British West Indian plantation owners, who did not mind seeing competing French and Spanish planters deprived of new slaves. With few members bothering to attend the debate, the Foreign Slave Trade Act sailed through the House of Commons with surprising ease. But by the time it got to the House of Lords, slave trade backers had begun to realize that this sidewind might ultimately blow them aground.

---

* Tarleton had left her to marry the twenty-two-year-old daughter of a rich duke. Robinson promptly returned the insult by making him the easily recognizable central character of her novel *The False Friend*—conniving, untrustworthy, and lecherous, "too witty to be learned; too youthful to be serious: and too handsome to be discreet." While eloping with another man's wife, he is shipwrecked and drowned. Robinson, it turned out, could take revenge only in fiction; in real life Tarleton long outlived her.

The revived abolition committee needed to put pressure on the Lords, but was the public still with them? The great river of antislavery books, pamphlets, and newspaper articles had all but dried up. Under the wartime sedition laws there had been no abolition mass meetings and almost no petitioning of Parliament on any subject whatever for more than a decade. Clarkson, now back in harness, had made a months-long journey around England and Scotland, reactivating the network that had lain dormant so long. The diarist Katherine Plymley found him as upbeat as ever, but noticed that he now tired easily. His face was developing furrows, and his hair was turning white.

In the Lords, the Duke of Clarence, with his red-haired, coconut-shaped head, still was known for swearing as colorfully as he had in his navy days. He protested that the bill would yield the bulk of the British trade in slaves to foreigners "who would not use them with such tenderness and care." Five of his royal brothers denounced the bill as well. And in Manchester, where owners of cloth mills felt threatened by anything that might curtail the supply of slave-grown cotton from the Americas, 439 people signed a petition to the Lords against the measure. Clarkson swiftly contacted his own Manchester friends and asked them to circulate a counter-petition. Within a few hours, they had one on a coach to London with 2,354 names. And, they wrote Clarkson, they could have gathered twice as many signatures if they had had just one more day. Although only one city, this was an early sign that the widespread public feeling against the slave trade had not changed. The bill passed.

In the wake of this startling success, the exuberant, reenergized abolitionists now felt sudden optimism that they might be able to wipe out the portion of the slave trade that remained. Several recent events further raised their hopes. For one thing, the volatile price of sugar had fallen to an unprecedented low point, leaving planters with little money to purchase new slaves from Africa and less incentive to fight for their right to do so. Another change was that, in 1806, his health broken by the strain of the Napoleonic Wars, Pitt had died. Not only was his successor as Prime Minister, Lord Grenville, much more committed to abolition, but as a member of the House of Lords he was in a better position to influence the chamber where the idea had always met its chief roadblock. No one knew, however, if such developments were enough to bring victory.

The West India Committee ran a two-week campaign of newspaper advertisements opposing any new legislation and allotted £500 to produce new pro–slave trade pamphlets, but the revived abolition campaign seemed ever stronger. In parliamentary elections in late 1806, the slave trade for the first time became a major election issue in some constituencies. Several candidates switched to the abolitionist side. In Bristol, of all places, a newspaper observed that "during the course of the election in various parts of the kingdom the popular sentiment has been very strongly expressed against the continuance of that traffick in human flesh." In Yorkshire, Wilberforce won his seat with a campaign song against the slave trade. Perhaps the best tribute to the strength of public feeling came from a proslavery Liverpool M.P. who complained bitterly of the "popular clamour . . . resorted to on this occasion. The church, the theater, and the press . . . laboured to create a prejudice against the Slave Trade."

As the long-awaited parliamentary debate began in 1807, John Anderson and his brother vigorously protested that the entire value of their investment at Bance Island would be wiped out. Knowing that only continual imports of new slaves had kept the West Indian slave population from dropping, almost everyone on both sides still saw ending the trade as leading inevitably, in a few generations, to the end of slavery itself. Believing this, Wilberforce did not want to risk going too far by suggesting anything that smacked of emancipation. When a young member of Parliament proposed that all infants born to slaves henceforth be free, he strenuously opposed the idea.

In both houses of Parliament, this was the first full-scale debate on the issue in a decade. The abolitionists left nothing to chance, renting a house on Downing Street as temporary headquarters for their lobbying. "How popular Abolition is, just now!" an amazed Wilberforce wrote in his diary. "God can turn the hearts of men." The hearts of men had not been turned enough in the past, but as the debate unfolded, it was clear that much had changed since the early 1790s. One clear difference was that British soldiers had now seen what unexpectedly determined fighters rebellious blacks could be. George Walpole, now in Commons, was a strong supporter, of a sort the abolitionists had never before been able to call on, and it may have been through his influence that another military man in the House, Lieutenant General Richard Vyse, declared he "supported the bill most strenuously," and backed all efforts to stop "so infamous a trade." The abolitionists reprinted long passages from army doctor George Pinckard's descriptions of the atrocities he had seen.

A decade and a half earlier, small groups of M.P.s had heard firsthand accounts of slavery from the eyewitnesses Clarkson had laboriously rounded up for hearings. Now the full House of Commons could hear such stories, in mid-debate, from one of their own colleagues. The newly elected Sir John Doyle, another former officer who had served in the Americas, described how he and his troops were once out on patrol and heard terrible groans. They broke open the door of a hut and found a slave in irons "stretched upon the ground, where for four days he had remained without being able to change his position. . . . The rats had actually eaten off the greater part of both his ears." Another time, "a neighboring Planter came into the camp, and . . . said, how spiteful his neighbors were. 'Only think, they have killed two of my Negroes, and I should not have thought so much about it, if they had not been two of my very best Negroes.' . . . This planter told us . . . that he would take an opportunity to shoot a Negro or two belonging to the person who had killed his."

When a Liverpool M.P. made the familiar argument that other nations would profit from slave trade business lost to Britain, and that city's investment in ships and docks would go to waste, Doyle replied, acidly, that this was like a highwayman saying, "If I had not committed the robbery, Will Bagshot, who was further on the road, would. . . . Besides, I have gone to a great expence . . . and have bought four or five horses which are good for nothing but to stop gentlemen on the road."

Although it went virtually unmentioned in the debate, every M.P. was well aware of one immense change: independent Haiti had now replaced French St. Domingue, which had once produced the most sugar of any slave colony in the Caribbean. No more, therefore, could anyone claim that if Britain ended its slave trade, its perennial rival, France, might dominate the world sugar market once the war was over. Toussaint's victorious slave rebellion had destroyed that long-time argument against British abolition for good.

The abolitionists, it turned out, now had more members of Parliament with them than they had previously dared dream of. As it became apparent which way the wind was blowing, many pro–slave trade M.P.s, preferring to appear enlightened, jumped to the winning side. There were attempts at delays and amendments, but the momentum was unstoppable. In early 1807, a bill abolishing the entire British slave trade passed both houses of Parliament, the climax of twenty years of effort. Clarkson spent the day writing joyful letters to friends throughout the country. The abolitionists could still barely believe it when, a few weeks later, on March 25 as the clock struck noon, King George III signed the bill into law. The traffic that had taken more than three million captive Africans onto British ships for the middle passage was now officially reaching its end.

This was not a case where the government provided leadership, commented the *Edinburgh Review,* but one where "the sense of the nation has pressed abolition upon our rulers." With the country bogged down in a war straining the social fabric, the British elite had good reason to yield to "the sense of the nation" in granting a demand that threatened them far less than reforming gross inequalities at home. Nonetheless, the impact of the abolition bill, which stopped all slave ships from leaving the world's major slave-trading nation after May 1, 1807, gave hope to millions of people around the Atlantic.

To take part in the trade was later defined as a felony, and, eventually, as piracy. In Liverpool, slave ship sailors rioted, and Banastre Tarleton paid two young blacks to carry a placard through the streets announcing his promise to get the trade restored, but all was in vain. The West Indian planters felt furious and betrayed. In revenge, some members of the legislature in Jamaica threatened to cut off supplies to the three thousand British troops on the island. But since these were the main force standing between the planters and a slave uprising, that, too, came to nothing.

The abolitionists savored their triumph. When word came that the bill had passed, Granville Sharp reportedly fell to his knees. At Clapham, Wilberforce asked his cousin Henry Thornton, "Well Henry, what shall we abolish next?" Thornton, a solemn Evangelical, replied, "The Lottery, I think." British self-congratulation knew no bounds. A commemorative medallion showed a queenly Britannia sitting on a dais inscribed "I have heard their cry." Wilberforce wept during one tribute paid to him in Parliament. In another, an M.P. praised him for "his unwearied industry, his indefatigable zeal, and his impressive eloquence, in thus bringing to a happy conclusion, a measure . . . which washes out this foul stain from the pure ermine of our national character." The Duke of Norfolk declared that abolition was "the most humane and merciful Act which was ever passed by any Legislature in the world."

But to the more than half-million blacks in the British Caribbean at work in baking-hot fields, sugar mills, and boiling houses, their situation did not seem humane nor the British character pure ermine. They were, after all, still slaves.

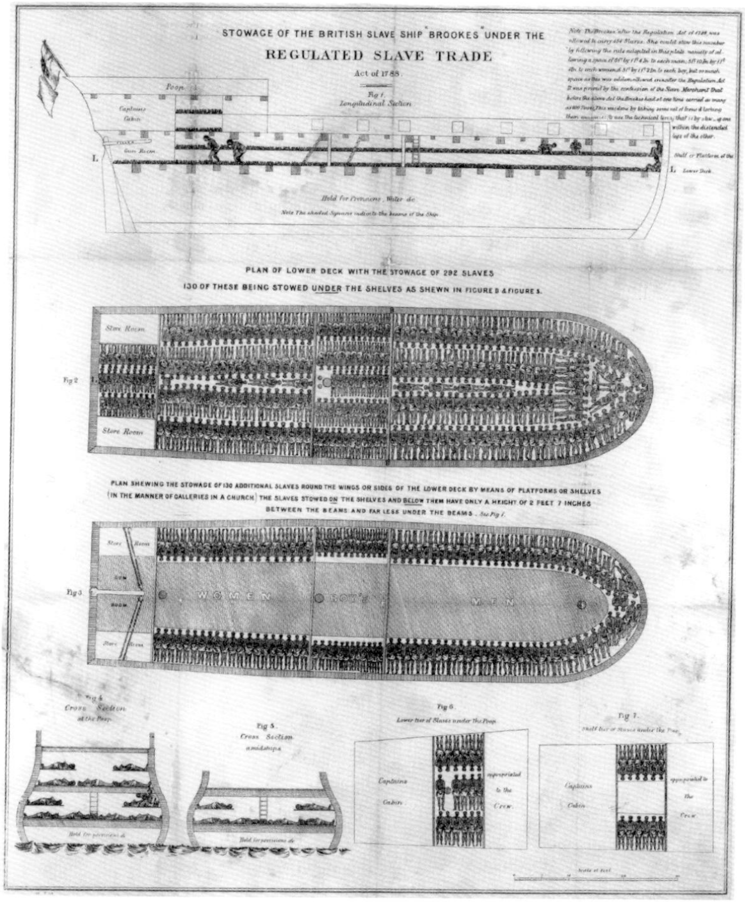
STOWAGE OF THE BRITISH SLAVE SHIP "BROOKES" UNDER THE
REGULATED SLAVE TRADE
Act of 1788
Poop
Fig 1.
Longitudinal Section
PLAN OF LOWER DECK WITH THE STOWAGE OF 292 SLAVES
Store Room
Fig 2
Store Room
PLAN SHEWING THE STOWAGE OF 130 ADDITIONAL SLAVES ROUND THE WINGS OR SIDES OF THE LOWER DECK BY MEANS OF PLATFORMS OR SHELVES
(IN THE MANNER OF GALLERIES IN A CHURCH) THE SLAVES STOWED ON THE SHELVES AND BELOW THEM HAVE ONLY A HEIGHT OF 2 FEET 7 INCHES
BETWEEN THE BEAMS AND FAR LESS UNDER THE BEAMS.
Fig 3
WOMEN
BOYS
MEN
Fig 5
Cross Section
amidships
Fig 6
Fig 7

The famous diagram of the slave ship *Brookes.* In an age before photography, this was one of the first widely reproduced political posters and one of the abolitionists' most powerful tools.

The model of the *Brookes* that Wilberforce showed to his fellow members of Parliament.

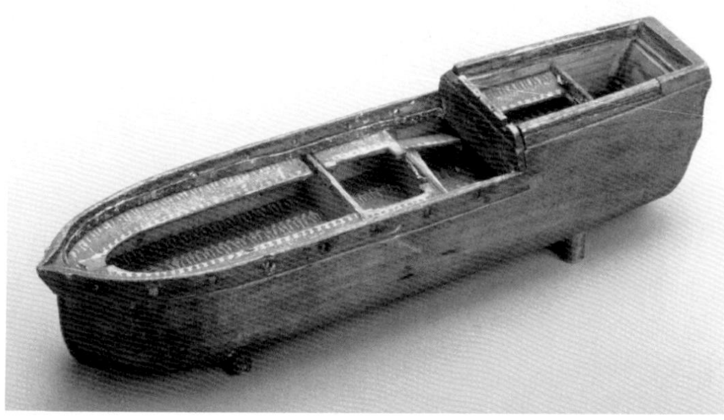

THE PROPOSED FORM OF

An INDENTURE for FREE, or PUBLIC, LABOUR:

Whereby *private* Individuals, by engaging a part of their *own Labour* to the *public* Exchequer, may obtain, in return, the infinite advantages of *accumulated Labour* to cultivate their own *private* Lots of Land: for inſtance, inſtead of the tedious and ſolitary labour of *one ſingle Man for* 100 *Days, day* after *day*, the Man may obtain the ſpeedy, ſpirited and much more effectual, Labour *of* 100 *Men in one Day*, with all proper Engines, Screws, Ploughs, and Inſtruments, belonging to the public, and with the advice of experienced Men, for clearing his Lands; whereby the proportion of *time* ſaved for *vegetation* will be no leſs than 99 Days out of every 100 Days to enable him to pay an adequate compenſation to the *public revenue* in return for the *public* Labour out of his own property of *produce from the Land*, even *long before* his *own Debt of Labour* for that advantage is demanded, if he pays a ſmall Intereſt to the *public* for *poſtponing* it.

The adopted MOTTO of our Free Community is the *Inſignia* of CHRIST's Kingdom, the STANDARD which GOD has ſet up to diſtinguiſh HIS *Government* among Men, viz.

"Glory in the Higheſt to GOD,
"And on Earth PEACE,
"Towards Men GOODWILL." (Luke ii. 14.)
—— "and all Nations ſhall flow unto it." (Iſaiah ii. 2.)

To the Exchequer of the Province of Freedom.

Dated from the Hundred, in the Thouſand, the day of

An Indenture to LABOUR, for the Benefit of the Community, in public Works, or cultivating either public *or* private *Lots of Land. under the direction of the Public Adviſers in Labour, when duly ſummoned thereto by the Truſtees of the Public Exchequer, for*
Day, ſigned by
of the Tithing of this Hundred.
Witneſs Hundreder.

Entered, in the Public Books of this Hundred.
Town-Clerk.

—"Render unto God the things that are God's."—

"Thou, O GOD, haſt prepared of thy goodneſs for the poor." (Pſal. lxviii. 10.) "Thou viſiteſt the Earth, and bleſſeſt it: Thou makeſt it "very plenteous." (Pſa. lxv. 9.) "THY WILL be done in earth as in heaven." (Matt. vi. 10.) viz.—RIGHTEOUSNESS—PEACE—BENEVOLENCE— (Luke ii. 14.) And, "if any will not WORK neither ſhould he EAT." (2 Theſſ. iii. 10.)

To the Public Exchequer of the Province of FREEDOM, in } Africa, { From the Hundred, } the day
in the Thouſand, } of

THIS Indenture witneſſeth, *that, by the favour and generous Indulgence of the* Britiſh Government, *a FREE COMMUNITY hath been formed, conſiſting of People from various Nations, and of various complexions*, from the four Quarters of the World, *who, diſdaining national prejudices, and partial* "reſpect of perſons." *have agreed to unite in BROTHERLY LOVE, and to promote and maintain the* juſt Rights *of* Humanity, *to which, as MEN, ALL are equally entitled: And, whereas the ſaid FREE COMMUNITY propoſe (with all due ſubmiſſion to the providence of GOD and with humble confidence in HIS DIVINE PROTECTION) to procure, by fair treaty, an* Eſtabliſhment for FREEDOM in Africa *founded on the principles of* Righteouſneſs, *without which no government can be conſiſtent with the revealed purpoſe of Chriſtianity:* Glory to GOD in the higheſt, and in earth PEACE,—GOOD WILL toward Men, *the indiſpenſible Rule of a true Chriſtian Community, and the adopted* Motto *of this:*] I, a *Member of this FREE COMMUNITY, duly pledged in the* Tithing of this Hundred, *do hereby promiſe obedience to the LAWS (not inconſiſtent with the LAWS of GOD) which have been or ſhall be duly enacted by the Majority of the Common Council of the ſaid* Free Community; *and having alſo engaged, with the* Bank of this Hundred, *to LABOUR, in the free Service of the Public Exchequer, (during the uſual time of work,) for DAY under the direction of ſuch perſons as ſhall have been appointed by* common council *to adviſe the beſt mode of proceeding in any public work, or in cultivating any* public, *or even* private, *Lot of Land, (if the owner hath duly contracted with the Truſtees of the Exchequer for the value of the public labour to be beſtowed upon it,) which is, in either caſe, for the common profit of the whole Community: I do therefore promiſe my beſt endeavours punctually to attend the Summons of the Public Exchequer (after receiving due previous notice) to fulfil this my contract for Public LABOUR, and faithfully to obey all lawful commands of the appointed Adviſers for the public benefit therein. As witneſs my hand.*
Witneſs Hundreder. *So help me GOD.*

"Shew me the Tribute-Money. * * * Whoſe is this Image and Superſcription? * * * Render therefore * * * * " * * * * * * * * * * unto GOD the things that are GOD's."—(Matt. xxii. 19—21.)

Granville Sharp's Utopian currency for Sierra Leone, redeemable for human labor instead of gold.

The House of Commons in the early 1800s.

With abolition catching the British imagination, the caricaturist James Gillray drew this antislavery cartoon in 1791.

Later, turned reactionary by the wartime jingoism that brought the movement to a halt, he mocked Wilberforce and a sympathizer (a bishop, at right) in 1796.

Take-no-prisoners fighting between French and slave rebel armies in St. Domingue.

Toussaint L'Ouverture, the leader of history's greatest slave revolt, defeated both British and French armies.

The Jamaican Maroon leader Leonard Parkinson, 1796, in the only known portrait of a British slave rebel or Maroon drawn from life.

Wayne Rowe of Accompong Town, Jamaica, with the sword said to have been captured by his ancestors from a British officer in the Maroon War of 1795.

A treadmill for punishing slaves, Jamaica.

A trap placed in high grass to capture runaway slaves, Jamaica.

***Head-Quarters, Montego-Bay, St. James's, Jan.* 2, 1832.**

TO

THE REBELLIOUS SLAVES.

NEGROES,

YOU have taken up arms against your Masters, and have burnt and plundered their Houses and Buildings. Some wicked persons have told you that the King has made you free, and that your Masters withhold your freedom from you. In the name of the King, I come amongst you, to tell you that you are misled. I bring with me numerous Forces to punish the guilty, and all who are found with the Rebels will be put to death, without Mercy. You cannot resist the King's Troops. Surrender yourselves, and beg that your crime may be pardoned. All who yield themselves up at any Military Post ***immediately***, provided they are not principals and chiefs in the burnings that have been committed, will receive His Majesty's gracious pardon. All who hold out, will meet with certain death.

WILLOUGHBY COTTON,
***Maj. General Command*^g.**

GOD SAVE THE KING.

The 1831–32 revolt by more than twenty thousand slaves in western Jamaica shocked the British government and hastened the coming of emancipation.

The author at a 1797 slave hospital at Orange Valley plantation, Jamaica.

An 1838 portrayal of emancipation as a gift from Britannia to grateful slaves.

22

AM I NOT A WOMAN AND A SISTER?

IF THIS BOOK were a novel, it might now read: "Twenty years passed . . ." Not because nothing happened in these decades, but because in history, as in our own lives, there are moments of sudden transformation and times when change that has been passionately yearned for does not come. And so it was with slavery in the wake of the 1807 victory in Parliament. The long-imagined goal, the liberation of all British slaves, the great hope of abolitionists from the time that Thomas Clarkson set off on horseback on the first of his many journeys, and the dream of all slaves through generations of early death in the sugar cane fields, still hovered in the distance. Yet nothing seemed to bring it closer.

Almost simultaneously with Parliament's action, the United States also banned the slave trade. However, this had not been the result of so prolonged and tumultuous a battle as had taken place in Britain. Southern planters were resentful, but with the South's large slave population long and rapidly increasing on its own, they did not feel as threatened as their Caribbean counterparts by the cutting off of slave imports. Since there was as yet no widespread American antislavery movement, the U.S. government felt little pressure to enforce the ban at sea. The British activists now pushed forcefully to get the Royal Navy to do just that.

There was Britain's self-interest involved as well: if planters in its colonies could no longer buy fresh shiploads of slaves, they wanted them denied to their competitors too. Ironically, then, having fought the abolitionists bitterly for two decades, the West India interests now also lobbied hard for enforcement of the ban. A lucrative market for imported slaves continued, particularly in Latin America, even after countries there also officially banned the trade. British warships eventually began stopping vessels all over the Atlantic, and troops of armed sailors boarded them to search for cargoes of slaves. In time, as many as one third of Royal Navy vessels would be engaged in such patrols. With surprising swiftness Britain had gone, it has been said, from chief poacher to chief gamekeeper.

There were plenty of poachers from all nations out there, for banning anything, as with illegal drugs today, always raises the price. When the Royal Navy did manage to intercept ships full of slaves on the high seas, and rewarded its captains with prize money for their pains, what was to be done with the cargo? Many slaves were promptly put into soldiers' red coats or the navy's blue jackets. Bance Island in Sierra Leone, now closed as a slave depot, found a new lease on life serving the British military as the home of the euphemistically named African Recruiting Establishment. As with slavery, the blacks had no choice; they found themselves "recruited" for terms of up to fourteen years, with no pension rights. Later, once the wartime need for soldiers and sailors was over, Britain simply left slaves captured at sea in Sierra Leone—more than fifty thousand of them over the decades, speaking more than two hundred languages.

The abolitionist dreams of Sierra Leone as a cornucopia of agricultural products had never been fulfilled. The early black settlers' long-festering grievances over land and taxes had flared into an armed revolt in 1800 that was quickly suppressed. Among its leaders was the ex-slave Henry Washington, who was, one historian remarks, "less successful in rebellion than his former owner." Sierra Leone had always been one part bold, multiracial Utopian experiment, one part the planting of a British imperial foot in West Africa. Under the impact of continuing economic losses, the remnants of the first gave way to the second, and in 1808 Sierra Leone became a colony of the British crown. For slaves taken from the captured ships, being set at liberty there meant having to build new lives as colonial subjects hundreds or thousands of miles from home and family, but perhaps that was better than life on the sugar plantations.

The winding down of the transatlantic slave trade left African slave owners and dealers looking for local customers. With the European or American ships now sailing the coast to buy products like nuts, palm oil—to make soap and lubricants—and gold, African rulers quickly bought new slaves and put them to work gathering these commodities. Ever since Clarkson had exhibited his box of African woods, cloth, and spices on his tours of Britain, abolitionists had wished to see a bustling trade between Britain and Africa in something other than slaves. But, ironically, the very growth of commerce in the decades after the slave trade ban greatly increased the number of indigenous slaves in West Africa.

Not long after the victory in Parliament, two actors from early scenes in the drama left the stage. Since testifying before the Privy Council and parliamentary hearings nearly twenty years before, John Newton had made only a few passing references to slavery in his voluminous writings and sermons. Widowed and increasingly shaky in moving his rotund figure about, he rebuffed friends' suggestions that he retire. "What!" he told one. "Shall the old African blasphemer stop while he can speak?" Conducting a church service one day, he forgot the subject at hand until someone climbed to the pulpit to remind him. He did not preach again. He told a friend, "I am packed and sealed and waiting for the post," and died at eighty-two, at the end of 1807. His most painful memory, it is clear, was not of captaining shiploads of chained human beings, but of the brief period when he himself had been held captive on the Sierra Leone coast by a slave trader's black concubine. He once referred to himself at this time as "the most abandoned of slaves," and on the epitaph he wrote for his own tombstone is the line "once an infidel and libertine, a servant of slaves in Africa."

Granville Sharp, possessed of a far stronger moral compass, survived until a few years later. He continued firing off tracts and letters on everything from frankpledge as a means of combating the Hindu caste system to the popular election of judges, bishops, and even some military commanders. His many brothers and sisters all died before him, and the family's open-air orchestra, once so grandly borne by barge along the rivers and canals of England, was now but a memory. One day in the summer of 1813, when he was seventy-seven, Sharp took a stagecoach to bring a donation of books to a library, but he got lost wandering the London streets until a worried coachman found him and brought him home. He died a few weeks later.

Among proslavery figures, the Duke of Clarence remained as vocal as ever; the only change was in his personal life. Various princes and bishops convinced him it was high time he got married, for George III was very short of legitimate grandchildren. Furthermore, Parliament would grant a far larger allowance to a married son of the King than an unmarried one. And so, despite two happy decades of life together, he ditched the talented actress Dora Jordan. Soon after, playing a role on stage that called for her to laugh, she burst into tears instead. A poet urged Clarence to return to

> Your faithful friend for twenty years;
> One who gave up her youthful charms,
> The fond companion of your arms!
>
> Brought you ten smiling girls and boys,
> Sweet pledges of connubial joys;
> As much your wife in honor's eye,
> As if fast bound in wedlock's tie.

But Mrs. Jordan died, alone and brokenhearted, a few years later. Clarence found a German princess judged suitably royal for him to marry, and she turned out to be a good stepmother to the ten FitzClarence children.

Portraits of Thomas Clarkson from this period show his red hair whitening and receding a bit on the sides, and his ruddy face framed by sideburns. With the trade now banned, Clarkson sat down to write a stirring, autobiographical two-volume history of the abolitionist movement. He worked mostly in a room above the kitchen at the house of his close friend William Allen, the Quaker businessman and scientist, a block away from the Phillips printing shop. James Phillips had died, leaving the business to his son. Clarkson was extremely nearsighted, a child who grew up in the Allen house remembered years later: "I used to fancy that he went about . . . with his eyes shut, for I have often had to get out of his way, so as not to be stumbled over. . . . He never used spectacles, and when he read or wrote his nose almost touched the paper." He came to life when the subject was slavery: "His countenance . . . would be lighted up, and that noble enthusiasm . . . become visible in every feature."

Although Clarkson went out of his way to give credit to almost everyone, his history managed to offend some people who thought he trumpeted his own role too much. They kept quiet at the time, but years later their hurt feelings would return to haunt him. The book, particularly its 150 pages on his first horseback trip to Bristol and Liverpool, remains perhaps the greatest memoir of a political organizer ever written. His friend Samuel Taylor Coleridge exclaimed, "Nothing can surpass the moral beauty of the manner in which he . . . relates his own [part] in that Immortal War—compared with which how mean all the conquests of Napoleon and Alexander!" The poet ordered twenty-five copies for friends.

As the years passed, Clarkson also wrote a history of Sierra Leone, a biography of the Quaker leader William Penn, and more tracts and pamphlets about slavery. He threw himself into a variety of projects: a nonsectarian school open to all, which he hoped could improve on the strict, brutal elite schools that tended to "harden the heart"; a campaign to reform criminal law and reduce the huge number of crimes carrying the death penalty; and, as Europe's two decades of war came to an end, the Society for the Promotion of Permanent and Universal Peace. He carried on a voluminous correspondence with Henri Christophe, one of Toussaint's former commanders, who, in the divisive, bloody aftermath of Haitian independence, crowned himself King of the northern part of the country in 1811. Clarkson helped him recruit British schoolteachers and college professors and acted as the King's unofficial ambassador in Europe. When the King shot himself (with a golden bullet, according to legend) after being deposed in a military coup, his wife and two daughters fled to England. They stayed a month with the Clarksons. "A more delightful family never entered a person's house," he wrote.

Wilberforce continued to fret about sin, protesting, for example, the "indecency" that would occur if public bathing was allowed in the Thames. Even when writing to the ill-fated Henri Christophe—who, surrounded by plotters and abject poverty, surely had more pressing matters on his mind—Wilberforce boasted that in Britain "our women are much more generally faithful to their husbands than the ladies of any other country in Europe; Switzerland and Holland perhaps excepted." He urged the Haitian monarch to set up "voluntary associations in the different classes of your society, [to] which . . . those females only were to be admitted who were of unstained reputation." In contrast with Clarkson's welcome of the black king's widow and children, when Wilberforce in 1816 chaired a public dinner at Freemasons' Tavern for something called the African and Asiatic Society, the handful of Africans and Asians present ate at one end of the room, behind a screen. Once the slaves were finally free, he believed, they should still know their place in the social order. "Taught by Christianity, they will sustain with patience the sufferings of their actual lot . . . [and] will soon be regarded as a grateful peasantry." In the meantime, he remained as wary as ever about any proposals for reform of the system. Completely banning the use of the whip, for instance, he felt was going too far. Instead slave whippings should be done only "at night after the day's work."

Although the two men remained friends and collaborators, Clarkson's pacifism was attacked as subversive in the *Christian Observer,* the unofficial organ of Wilberforce's Clapham circle. And while Clarkson passionately backed legislation to improve working conditions in England, Wilberforce wrote that "the progressive rise of Wages" was "an evil . . . sufficient to accomplish the ruin . . . of the whole commercial greatness of our country." The poor should know, he declared, "that their more lowly path has been allotted to them by the hand of God; that it is their part . . . contentedly to bear its inconveniences." His suggestions for how government could best help the indigent included the idea of "having comfortable causeway walks for them along the public roads."

Critics then and now have attacked Wilberforce for showing more pity for slaves than for suffering Britons. He was entirely faithful to his own view of the world—one divided into generous rich and grateful poor, into those wise enough to vote and those too unpropertied for the privilege, into Christians who knew God's truth and heathens who did not. Nonetheless, to his credit, it was a world in which slavery ultimately had no place. Furthermore, although he supported harsh legislation against sin, to sinners he met personally he was the soul of kindness. He gave generously to charity; in one year of food shortages, he contributed far more than his own income. When he bought a piece of land with tenant farmers on it, he lowered the rents and never complained if people fell years behind in their payments. He frequently paid the bills of debtors he took a liking to, so they could get out of jail. He was so honest that he would not permit his servants to tell a visitor he wasn't home if he was, and as a result his hospitality was always larger than his table. A friend wrote: "His old butler . . . would sometimes suggest to a favoured guest the advisableness of keeping near the door [to the dining room] when waiting dinner, as there were several more guests than there was room for."

People constantly besieged him with requests of all kinds: for help in obtaining military promotions, professorships, clergymen's "livings"; for money; for his influence in getting a death sentence reprieved; for support in establishing chapels for coal miners or mission stations in India; for advice on whether it was proper for a young woman to sing. He continued to powder his hair in the fashion of the previous century. Unfailingly conscientious, he tried to answer every letter, and often did so at rambling length. A founder of the Society for the Prevention of Cruelty to Animals, he once rushed up to a cart driver in Bath to stop him from beating and kicking his fallen horse. The man was about to turn on him as well when a fellow carter stepped up and whispered "Wilberforce" in the driver's ear.

The most vivid pictures we have of Wilberforce in this period come from Marianne Thornton, daughter of Henry Thornton of the Sierra Leone Company. Decades later, she recalled how he could never bear to fire any employee. She makes him sound like a character out of Dickens. His house, for instance, was continually "thronged with servants who are all lame or impotent or blind, or kept from charity; an ex-secretary kept because he is grateful, and [the ex-secretary's] wife because she nursed poor Barbara [Mrs. Wilberforce], and an old butler who they wish would not stay but then he is so attached, and his wife who was a cook but now she is so infirm. . . . [One would] sit in despair of getting one's plate changed at dinner and hear a chorus of Bells all day which nobody answers." The number of superfluous elderly servants only grew; one guest found thirteen of them shuffling about the dining room while the two Wilberforces and three visitors ate dinner.

As he aged, the diminutive Wilberforce grew visibly smaller, for his head was always bent forward onto his chest. His oddities multiplied. He filled his diaries with lists of his sins and faults, few of them worse than "late rising." He read while walking, and friends were astonished at the quantity of books and papers stuffed into his extra-large pockets —one of which burst open under the load as he was kneeling with his family at prayer one day. Another pocket carried an inkstand, and his rumpled suit was black so that spills wouldn't show; others within range, dressed in lighter colors, were not always safe.

James Stephen, who had now become a member of Parliament, remained a part of Wilberforce's circle, and his hatred of slavery was unchanged. "I would as soon affiance myself in the bonds of friendship with a man who had strangled my infant child," he said in Commons, "as lend my . . . support to an administration disposed to violate the sacred duty of adhering to and enforcing the Abolition of the Slave Trade." After his wife, Nancy, died he married Wilberforce's sister, a clergyman's widow. "She was," wrote Stephen's grandson, "a rather eccentric but very vigorous woman. She spent all her income, some £300 or £400 a year, on charity, reserving £10 for her clothes. She was often to be seen parading Clapham in rags and tatters. Thomas Gisborne, a light of the sect, once tore her skirt from top to bottom at his house . . . saying, 'Now, Mrs. Stephen, you *must* buy a new dress.' She calmly stitched it together and appeared in it next day."

When Britain and its allies defeated Napoleon in 1814, sending him into exile on Elba, the victorious kingdoms and empires gathered in Paris to sign a peace treaty. In response to pleas from French planters and ship owners, France was allowed to resume the slave trade to its Caribbean colonies for the next five years. The British antislavery forces, horrified, called a mass meeting at Freemasons' Hall, and from it sent an appeal to all parts of the country for petitions denouncing this article of the treaty. Even Wilberforce was willing to see the dangerous beast of public opinion mobilized. The old network swiftly pulled itself together, and Clarkson ran the campaign from temporary headquarters at the New London Tavern in Cheapside. He asked his wife to bring their small son to the city so that "Tom can give us a little assistance by sitting for an Hour or two at my Elbow & see our Work going on."

At first it was far from certain how successful the work would be, for the nation was distracted by victory celebrations. But in a matter of weeks, the committee gathered petitions containing more than three quarters of a million names, an amazing number, for the total population was only some twelve million. Clarkson, feeling his oats, wrote to a member of the Foreign Office staff that unless the "obnoxious article" of the peace treaty was changed, "both houses of Parliament, as well as the newspapers will be let loose against you."

Meanwhile, George III had gone mad again, spending his days playing the harpsichord and talking to people who weren't there; the Prince of Wales was ruling in his place as Prince Regent. Although the Prince was proslavery, Wilberforce persuaded him to talk, royalty to royalty, to Louis XVIII of France about dropping the offending treaty article. Antislavery activists were able to lobby more monarchs when Tsar Alexander I of Russia and King Frederick William III of Prussia came to confer with their British allies. Most bizarrely for an autocrat guarded, even in London, by a troop of fierce-looking Cossacks, the pious young Tsar was intensely interested in Quakerism. He found time to visit a Quaker family and attend a Quaker meeting. He granted audiences to Wilberforce and to Clarkson's friend William Allen, who, true to Quaker custom, did not remove his hat before a mere earthly monarch. Clarkson had copies of the *Abstract of the Evidence* specially bound and presented to both rulers. Leaving Britain, Tsar Alexander became ill on crossing the English Channel. When an aide consoled him, the Tsar pointed to the famous slave ship diagram and said, "It is that book . . . which has made me more sick than the sea."

Clarkson proposed a trip to Vienna, where the European powers were scheduled to meet again, so he could keep up the pressure. Wilberforce, dismayed at the prospect of the hotheaded Clarkson let loose among kings and emperors, refused to allow it. But by 1815, spurred by continued lobbying from antislavery activists, the British government successfully pushed the French King to abolish the slave trade. (The law was not enforced, and French slaving continued.)

Several months after the defeat of the resurgent Napoleon at Waterloo that year, Clarkson, on a tight rein, was dispatched to Paris to see Tsar Alexander. An ardent democrat can still have a soft spot for the trappings of monarchy, and Clarkson was awed when he was ushered into the English-speaking Tsar's presence. "He said, continuing [to hold] my hand in his own, that . . . he had always been an enemy to the slave trade. . . . He considered [it] an outrage against Human Nature . . . but when . . . he had read my book, which furnished him with particulars on the subject, and when he had seen the print of the slave ship, he felt he should be unworthy of the high situation in which Providence had placed him, had he not done his utmost . . . to wipe away such a pestilence from the face of the earth." At one point, the Tsar asked Clarkson if he was a Quaker: "I replied, that I was not so in name, but I hoped in spirit. . . . They had been Fellow Labourers with me in our Great Cause, the more I had known them, the more I had loved them. The Emperor said (putting his hand on to his breast) 'I embrace them more than any other People; *I consider myself as one of them.*'" It apparently did not occur to either the Tsar or the dazed Clarkson that a form of slavery was the lot of Russia's many millions of serfs.

The Tsar's sympathy, of course, made no difference to the slaves of the Caribbean. Their lives remained ruled by the whip and the sun that beat down through the long tropical day, its start marked by the 5 A.M. signal gun fired from each of the many British forts that dotted the islands and helped keep slavery in place. Nowhere did it seem more firmly established than on Barbados, so long under British rule and with no slave rebellions or conspiracies for well over a hundred years. But on the evening of Easter Sunday, 1816, white colonists were shocked to see flames rising into the night sky. Unknown to them, slaves from different plantations had been secretly using a string of social gatherings, ending in a dance to celebrate Good Friday, to plot rebellion. Within a few hours, the fires spread across a third of the island. Slaves on seventy plantations were in revolt, and they seized an armory full of weapons before the militia could assemble. Panicky whites, remembering the slaughtered French families of St. Domingue, fled for the capital, Bridgetown. The colonel commanding British troops on the island claimed that "among the Flags used by these Insurgents, a rude drawing served to inflame the Passions, by representing the union of a Black Man with a White Female."

As so often before, slaves' hopes had been provoked by word of the latest round of agitation in England, news that was often magnified and embellished as it was passed on. One slave later testified he had heard that "Mr. Wilberforce had sent out to have them all freed." Unusually, one of the leaders of the Barbados revolt was a woman, Nanny Grigg, a literate domestic servant. "She said she had read . . . in the Newspapers" that the slaves were to be freed, a slave witness testified, "and that her Master was very uneasy at it . . . she was always talking about it to the negroes, and told them that they were all damned fools to work, for that she would not, as freedom they were sure to get. . . . And the only way to get it was to fight for it, otherwise they would not get it; and the way they were to do, was to set fire, as that was the way they did in St Domingo." As both slave and woman, Nanny Grigg is doubly written out of history, and we know nothing else about her except that she was carried on the inventory of the Simmons plantation at the exceptionally high value of £130.

By the time soldiers crushed the revolt, a quarter of the island's sugar cane crop had gone up in smoke. White troops burned slave houses to flush out rebels in hiding. At least fifty slaves died fighting, well over two hundred were executed, and more than a hundred transported to penal servitude in British Honduras—whose officials didn't want them and sent them on, ironically, to Sierra Leone.

The effects of the rebellion reverberated through the British Caribbean. The governor of one colony addressed a message to its slaves: "Should the contagion of this mad insurrection spread . . . I will be among you like an arrow from the bow to execute an instant and terrible justice on the guilty." In Jamaica the same year several slaves were brought to trial, accused of singing:

Oh me good friend, Mr. Wilberforce, make we free!
God Almighty thank ye! God Almighty thank ye!
  God Almighty, make we free!
Buckra [the white man] in this country no make we free:
What Negro for to do? What Negro for to do?
  Take force by force! Take force by force!

"The Insurrection has been quelled, but the spirit is not subdued," wrote the Speaker of the Barbados Assembly, "nor will it ever be subdued whilst these dangerous doctrines which have been spread abroad continue to be propagated among the Slaves."

Dangerous doctrines were in the air, not only of the slave colonies, but of England itself. The immense dislocations of the Industrial Revolution led to high unemployment and a rise in the price of bread that squeezed poor families. Although labor unions were harshly repressed, there was an upsurge in radical agitation. In 1819, eleven people were killed and more than four hundred wounded in the notorious "Peterloo massacre," when militia and cavalry, swords slashing, broke up a meeting at St. Peter's Field, Manchester, of sixty thousand workers demanding universal male suffrage.

One figure among the London radicals of this time was a Jamaican-born mulatto, Robert Wedderburn. His mother was a slave; his father, whom he hated, the Scottish owner of eight sugar plantations. Wedderburn had been free from birth, but as a child he had seen his mother whipped while pregnant. "My heart glows with revenge," he wrote four decades later, "and cannot forgive." Wedderburn moved to Britain as a teenager and joined the burgeoning workers' movement. A pamphleteer and agitator, he was several times in jail, where Wilberforce, who liked to visit prisoners and admonish them to repent of their ways, once went to see him. If only we could have overheard their conversation . . .

According to a report by one of the ubiquitous police spies, Wedderburn told a London meeting that he planned to "*write home and tell the Slaves to murder their Masters as soon as they please.*" He managed to send copies of the radical journal he published to Jamaica, apparently with black sailors. In one issue, he warned the planters, "Prepare for flight . . . for the fate of St. Domingo awaits you. Get ready your blood hounds, the allies you employed against the Maroons."

The planters so feared such propaganda reaching the slaves that one member of Jamaica's Assembly suggested an extraordinary reward for anyone who turned in a copy of one of Wedderburn's incendiary tracts: a slave would receive freedom—and a free person the gift of a slave.

In 1820, urged on at every step by a police agent provocateur, a group of London radicals plotted to murder the entire cabinet at a moment when, according to a newspaper article, they were due to be having dinner at a mansion in Grosvenor Square. This attack was to be the first blow of a general insurrection: sympathizers would then, the radicals hoped, seize arms, set fire to barracks, and proclaim a provisional government. The authorities were on to the whole plan from the beginning, and even the announcement of the cabinet dinner had been a ruse. The members of the Cato Street Conspiracy, as they were called, after the stable loft where they kept their weapons, were arrested as they were about to leave for Grosvenor Square. In the ensuing fight, they killed a constable but were overwhelmed by a force of police and soldiers under the command of Lieutenant Frederick Fitz-Clarence, one of the ten illegitimate children of the Duke of Clarence and Mrs. Jordan. The five key conspirators were sentenced to be hanged, beheaded, and quartered. In one of the more meaningless pardons on record, the last part of the sentence—but only the last part—was remitted by the King.

Thousands of angry sympathizers flocked to the execution, on a special platform erected in front of Newgate Prison. Cavalry, foot soldiers, and artillerymen with six cannons stood by to prevent any last-minute attempts at rescue. One of the condemned men, William Davidson, bowed to the crowd and called out calmly, "God bless you all! Goodbye." Like Wedderburn, he was a Jamaican mulatto; his father had been the colony's white attorney general. "Black Davidson," as he was called, was a large, strong man who had spent part of his restless life in Jamaica, part at sea, and part in England, where he became secretary of the shoemakers' union. He seemed to have anticipated an end like that of many slaves: "Death's countenance is familiar to me," he wrote his wife just before his execution. After the conspirators' bodies dangled for half an hour, they were cut down and a man with a black mask and a knife swiftly decapitated them. As Davidson's severed head was provocatively brandished before the furious crowd, hissing and booing the executioner, it was as if the violence of British slavery had finally come home to haunt the motherland.

The dangerous doctrine of freedom was in the air elsewhere as well: thousands of British volunteers, for instance, were fighting with Simón Bolívar to win the independence of Latin American countries from Spain. Others, including the poet Lord Byron, had gone to help the Greeks fight for liberation from the Ottoman Turks. But on the most dangerous doctrine of all, immediate freedom for slaves, the leading antislavery figures remained conspicuously silent. West Indian slavery was bound to disappear, they continued to believe, if the trade was completely stopped by all countries. (With long experience in the slave colonies, James Stephen, always more of a realist than his comrades, did not share this comforting illusion.)

What accounted for such wishful thinking? For one thing, class ties meant that upper-crust abolitionists had always had an easier time attacking the slave trade than attacking slavery itself. Those who carried on the trade were rough, uncouth men from a different social world, sea captains and sailors. Absentee owners of slave plantations, on the other hand, included friends, fellow M.P.s, members of the same London clubs. Wilberforce on occasion visited the elegant estate of his good friend Henry Lascelles, who also represented Yorkshire in Parliament, even though Lascelles's family owned more than 1,200 slaves in Barbados. "I sincerely believe many of the owners of West-Indian estates to be men of more than common kindness," Wilberforce wrote, ". . . utterly unacquainted with the true nature and practical character of the system with which they have the misfortune to be connected."

Even Clarkson, who should have known better, believed that "Emancipation, like a beautiful plant, may, in its due season, rise out of the ashes of the abolition of the Slave-trade." But as the years went by, it became painfully clear that nothing was rising from the ashes except more slave-grown crops. Without newly imported slaves, owners knew, in the words of Thomas Roughley, author of an 1823 manual for planters, that they had to "encourage healthy propagation." And so they began offering their slaves better diets and treating them somewhat less harshly; they also installed improved sugar mill machinery, including a relatively simple safety screen that made it less likely that slaves' hands would get caught between the rollers. As a result of such changes, slave birth rates were increasing.

The Church of England's Codrington plantation, for example, had improved food, housing, clothing, and working conditions, and built a small hospital for sick and pregnant slaves. The treatments dispensed there by slave nurses—gin, port, brandy, and bleeding with leeches—were surely not much help, but respite from twelve-hour days cutting cane undoubtedly was. Thanks to measures like these, Codrington's slave population grew from 303 in 1807 to 355 in 1823; its managers boasted of having the most successful "breeding" program on Barbados. Plainly, opponents of slavery began to see, enforcing the slave trade ban was hardly enough.

In 1823, the core of the old abolition committee, some of its membership lost to death but filled out by a second generation, met at the King's Head Tavern and formed a new group whose very name reflected timidity: the London Society for Mitigating and Gradually Abolishing the State of Slavery Throughout the British Dominions. Gradual or not, it was unthinkable that a new antislavery organization be set up without Thomas Clarkson. His friend William Allen wrote him that "we have . . . put thy name on the Committee in the midst of those, with whom thou has always delighted to work."

Now sixty-three and more nearsighted than ever, Clarkson set out to mobilize the public one more time. Some of the rough dirt roads he had first ridden over thirty-six years earlier were now paved. He traveled ten thousand miles in two installments lasting more than twelve months. In his diary he noted the miles covered each day, and in the left-hand margin kept a cumulative total. He pulled together meetings of a dozen people here, twenty people there, and sent a stream of upbeat messages back to his colleagues. The Clarkson who treasured his keepsake stone from the Bastille, whose fiery radicalism worried more sober heads in London, had always been in tension with the Clarkson respectful of the peers and bishops and M.P.s whose support the abolitionists so cultivated. On this journey, Clarkson dutifully echoed the paternalistic rhetoric of the new society, whose wishes for the slaves, he said, were "to civilise them, to Christianise them . . . to make them better servants to their masters, and to make them more useful members of the community."

Better servants to their masters? Clarkson and his comrades were making clear that they opposed only slavery, not the plantation system itself. Even so, the West India interests knew their prime enemy was on the road once more, and immediately allocated £1,000 to pay for an onslaught of proslavery newspaper articles and pamphlets. But nothing they did could stop him. By the time the new society held its first big public meeting in 1824, there were 230 branches around the country, almost all of them founded by Clarkson in his marathon travels, and 777 petitions had been ceremoniously placed on the table in Parliament.

The society's "gradual" nature, however, bogged it down. It had been willing to send the venerable Clarkson on one last tour, but a proposal to put more organizers in the field to set up mass meetings was defeated, on grounds that these were dangerous in times of labor unrest. Not feeling under much pressure, Parliament merely passed some vague resolutions about such matters as encouraging marriage and religious instruction for slaves and ending the whipping of women. Responsibility for turning these suggestions into law was left in the hands of Caribbean island legislatures, which of course did nothing. The West India Committee promptly drafted its own lofty-sounding code of similar recommendations—an early instance of something familiar today, when an industry tries to fend off government regulation by proclaiming that it can regulate itself. Planters ignored these guidelines as well.

Although too loyal to openly criticize his colleagues, Clarkson saw full well that the public was impatient. "Everywhere People are asking me about *immediate abolition,* and whether that would not be the best," he wrote in his diary while on the road, "and whether they should not leave off West India sugar." The strongest such voices were those of women, and foremost among them was Elizabeth Heyrick, a former schoolteacher and convert to Quakerism. In 1824 she published a widely read pamphlet called *Immediate, not Gradual Abolition.* A blast of fresh air, Heyrick, unlike virtually every other writer on the subject, roundly criticized the mainstream antislavery figures for their "slow, cautious, accommodating measures." She mocked their decorum in Parliament: "The West Indian planters, have occupied much too prominent a place in the discussion of this great question. The abolitionists have shown a great deal too much politeness and accommodation towards these gentlemen. . . . Truth and justice, make their best way in the world, when they appear in bold and simple majesty."

A woman, Heyrick wrote, was "especially qualif[ied] . . . to plead for the oppressed." It was as if she had given women permission to speak, for more than seventy women's antislavery societies now sprang into being. Also, Heyrick was openly sympathetic to the black insurrections in the West Indies: "Was it not in the cause of self-defence from the most degrading, intolerable oppression?" Why were these revolts, she asked, any less "heroic and meritorious" than the Greek battle for independence from the Turks?

On issues closer to home, Heyrick did more than just write. She stopped a bull-baiting contest by buying the bull and hiding it in the parlor of a nearby cottage until the angry crowd went away. To experience the life of Irish migrant workers, she lived in a shepherd's cottage eating only potatoes. She visited prisons and paid fines to get poachers released. Her feelings about slavery were of a piece with those about all injustice. The poor in England suffered because the rich treated them with "the spirit of the slave trade"; a man could be hanged for petty theft, while society did nothing to punish "robberies en masse which impoverish . . . millions." She called for laws reforming prisons and limiting the workday; she supported a strike by weavers in her hometown of Leicester, even though her own brother was an employer in the industry. At nineteen, she had been married to an apparently overpossessive and volatile army officer who died eight years later. A friend wrote: "How they lived together I know not, it was always either my plague or my darling."

Heyrick began campaigning among the people of Leicester to promote a new sugar boycott, visiting all of the city's grocers to urge them to stock no slave-grown goods. Her message was clear and bracing: "The West Indian planter and the people of this country, stand in the same moral relation to each other, as the thief and the receiver of stolen goods. . . . Why petition Parliament *at all,* to do that for us, which . . . we can do more speedily and more effectually for ourselves?" As in the 1790s, the boycott was an inherently radicalizing tactic, because its effectiveness depended on everyone's participating: men and women, rich and poor. Heyrick hoped that the poor, in particular, would rally to the cause, because they "have themselves tasted of the cup of adversity." Inspired by her, women's societies put out boycott pamphlets and began compiling a national list of everyone who pledged to abstain from West Indian sugar.

Although virtually all the prominent male opponents of slavery were still talking about varieties of gradualism—emancipating the slaves in thirty years or raising money to buy women out of slavery—Heyrick would have none of it. In parliamentary elections in 1826 she called for people to vote only for candidates who supported freeing the slaves *now.* Other women agreed, and that year the women's society in Sheffield, ignoring the gradualist men's committee in the same town, became the first antislavery group in Britain to demand immediate emancipation. A few years later, it repeated its call for freedom "without reserve, without limitation, without delay." "Men may propose only *gradually* to abolish the worst of crimes," a woman in Wiltshire wrote, "and only mitigate the most cruel bondage, but why should *we* countenance such enormities? . . . We must not talk of *gradually* abolishing murder, licentiousness, cruelty, tyranny . . . *I trust no Ladies' Association will ever be found with such words attached to it.*"

Women's groups canvassed communities house to house, over four years visiting more than 80 percent of the homes in Birmingham, for instance. One woman, Sophia Sturge, personally called on three thousand households. The women reworked Josiah Wedgwood's famous image; now the legend read "Am I Not a Woman and a Sister?" The woman slave in chains was still kneeling and imploring, however. In celebrating the slave rebels who were not on their knees, Elizabeth Heyrick was virtually alone.

Another woman activist, Lucy Townsend, was an Evangelical Anglican from Birmingham who had been inspired as a girl by Clarkson; she wrote to him for advice on forming a women's antislavery society. In reply, Clarkson cautiously suggested that Townsend call her new group the "Female Society for ameliorating the condition of Female Slaves in the British Colonies, but with a view ultimately to their final emancipation there." But he embraced the revived sugar boycott and was unrestrained in his enthusiasm for the women's societies. "I am, & long have been of opinion, that such Committees *would, in time finish the great work.*" Unusually for a man of his day, he believed women deserved a full education and role in public life and admired the way his beloved Quakers allowed women to speak in their meetings. He objected to the fact that "women are still weighed in a different scale from men. . . . If homage be paid to their beauty, very little is paid to their opinions." He wrote to Townsend as one organizer to another, with advice about printers and congratulations on the opening of new branches.

The women's societies were almost always bolder than those of the men. Women in Worcester not only stopped buying slave-grown sugar; they refused to patronize bakers who used it and shopkeepers who sold it. This was the first time on record that the sugar boycott had been used this way, making it a sharper political tool and less a matter of virtuous personal sacrifice. The Birmingham women declared that they would give their annual £50 donation to the national antislavery society only "when they are willing to give up the word 'gradual' in their title." In vain did Wilberforce—now frail and recently retired from his forty-five years in Parliament—protest that "for ladies to meet, to publish, to go from house to house stirring up petitions—these appear to me proceedings unsuited to the female character as delineated in Scripture."

Wiser men, however, recognized that it was the women who were keeping the movement alive at a difficult time. "Ladies Associations . . . did everything," a prominent male activist later acknowledged. "They circulated publications: they procured the money to publish; they dunned & talked & coaxed & lectured: they got up public meetings & filled our halls & platforms when the day arrived; they carried round petitions & enforced the duty of signing them. . . . In a word they formed the cement of the whole Antislavery building—without their aid we never should have kept standing."

Whether for personal reasons we do not know or out of hopelessness at the failure to end slavery, Elizabeth Heyrick was depressed in her last years. "Nothing human can dispel that despairing torpor into which I have been plunging deeper and deeper for many months past," she wrote to Lucy Townsend. She died far too soon, at the age of sixty-one, in 1831; her diaries and most of her letters have been lost. Except for the fierce moral clarity of her pamphlets, we know little about her life and can only wonder what gave her such a burning passion for justice and to what else she would have applied it if she had lived longer. Not one portrait of her survives.

As the decades passed, an ever-higher proportion of Caribbean land passed into the hands of absentee owners in England. One of the wealthiest of these, with more than a thousand slaves to his name, was Sir John Gladstone of Liverpool, father of the future Prime Minister. Among his holdings were several plantations in steamy, tropical Demerara, part of what is today Guyana. Sugar prices were in decline in the 1820s, and so British owners pushed their overseers to increase productivity. One witness to the results in Demerara was John Smith, a young Protestant missionary to the slaves. "A most immoderate quantity of work has . . . been expected of them, not excepting women far advanced in pregnancy," he wrote. And again: "The first thing as usual which I heard was the whip. From ½ past 6 until ½ past 9 my ears were pained by the whip. Surely these things will awaken the vengeance of a merciful God." Smith was no less dismayed to find that "the planters will not allow their negroes to be taught to read."

The deacon of Smith's chapel was an African-born slave carpenter, Quamina, from one of the Gladstone plantations. "The Planters often talk of the many little comforts enjoyed by the Slaves," Smith wrote angrily. "Let the following serve as a specimen. Peggy and Quamina, a very superior and loving couple, had lived together as man and wife for nearly 20 years. One would have expected that while Peggy was so ill as to be thought near her end, Quamina would have been permitted to remain, at least a part of his time, with his dying wife." But like all slaves, Quamina was forced to work from sunup to sundown, and one evening he returned to find that his wife had died an hour before.

Planters usually loathed missionaries as meddlesome do-gooders. If, as the preachers wanted, slaves went to church on Sundays, they would soon be demanding other time off for cultivating their small vegetable gardens, and where would that slippery slope end? The planters also feared that missionary chapels would prove handy meeting places for plotting rebellion. On that score, they were entirely correct. Smith apparently didn't notice that the parishioners who gathered at his church well before each Sunday service were not talking about religion. The London Missionary Society had instructed him that "not a word must escape you in public or private which might render the slaves displeased with their masters or dissatisfied with their station." But he and other missionaries invariably found that the most popular of all Bible stories was that of Moses leading the children of Israel to the Promised Land.

More than four out of ten slaves in the colony were African-born, and Smith was unexpectedly touched when a slave seemed to empathize with the missionary's own disorientation. "This morning one of the negroes . . . so precisely described the circumstances of my leaving my friends, the tender anxiety of my mother, my own feelings . . . in a strange land that this . . . affected my mind more deeply than anything had done since I have been in this country." Without telling the planters, he began teaching some slave children to read.

The colony's capital, Georgetown, was a bustling port full of coffee and sugar warehouses and palm-shaded white mansions with red tile roofs, their courtyards planted with orange, lemon, and banana trees. In the summer of 1823, word reached the city about the formation of the new antislavery society in London, and Parliament's vague declaration about the need for reforms. As so often before, rumors flew among the slaves that the King of England, the "Big Massa," had freed them. Some believed Wilberforce next in line for the throne. Without his knowledge, members of John Smith's church began planning a rebellion. When they were victorious, it was agreed, deacon Quamina would be king of their liberated territory. Before church one morning, Quamina and his son, Jack Gladstone, a tall, handsome man who had taken the last name of the plantation's owner, met with many others and swore an oath on the church Bible. Unaware, Smith arrived to conduct a communion service, and his solemn words about the body and blood of Jesus Christ were taken as further sanctifying the oath.

Flames from burning plantations licked the sky. The colony's governor, heading from Georgetown in the direction of the fires, encountered a mass of armed slaves on the road. He asked what they wanted, and was answered, "Our rights." After racing back to the capital, he declared martial law. Soldiers arrested Quamina and Jack Gladstone, but a group of supporters with cutlasses managed to set them free. At least nine thousand slaves were now in revolt, but armed mainly with knives and pikes. The crucial battle took place at a plantation whose name echoed the image that had drawn so many young Englishmen to the Caribbean: Bachelor's Adventure. A one-sided slaughter left its cotton fields littered with dead and wounded slaves. Quamina and several others fled to the colony's interior. More than three weeks later, an expedition finally found them and shot Quamina dead. In the fighting and by execution afterwards, some 250 slaves were killed. Quamina's body slowly decomposed as it hung in chains in front of one of the Gladstone plantations. One witness wrote that a "colony of wasps had actually built a nest in the cavity of the stomach, and were flying in and out of the jaws which hung frightfully open."

The planters, needing an outside villain, blamed everything on John Smith. He was arrested and put on trial. Captured slaves were pressured to name Smith as the revolt's instigator; Jack Gladstone gave in, saving his own life by doing so. From jail, Smith, gravely ill with tuberculosis, smuggled out a message: "2 Corinthians, IV, 8, 9." His Bible-reading supporters knew these verses well: "We are troubled on every side, yet not distressed; we are perplexed, but not in despair; persecuted, but not forsaken; cast down, but not destroyed." The court sentenced him to be hanged, but made a recommendation to the King for mercy. George IV, who had at last succeeded his mad father, agreed and signed the pardon, but by the time the messages traveled by ship to England and back, the imprisoned Smith was dead of TB. To avoid any occasion that might prove a rallying point for slaves, he was buried in an unmarked grave by lantern light, at 4 A.M. For good measure, some white colonists also hanged him in effigy.

The missionary's martyr-like death provoked great outrage in Britain. Newspapers throughout the country published editorials praising him. Two hundred petitions arrived at Parliament, and M.P.s thundered out denunciations of the colonial authorities on the House of Commons floor. "This single case of a persecuted individual," one antislavery activist later noted, ". . . produced an impression far more general and more deep than all that had ever been written or declaimed against the system of West Indian slavery." The movement had stretched Britons' empathy, but the death of one white man moved them more than those of 250 slaves.

This latest rebellion, the furor over John Smith, and the determined women's antislavery societies were still not enough to move a grossly unrepresentative Parliament to end slavery. In the face of this unyielding obstacle, by the end of the 1820s, the movement lost steam. James Stephen, who now backed immediate emancipation, published a brilliant, learned, two-volume work on slavery in the West Indies, reflecting his lifetime of gathering evidence against it. In the book, he said "I shall not live to see" the end of slavery. He was right: he died soon after, at the age of seventy-four. The prospect that Parliament would ever vote to free the slaves seemed to recede further than ever. The *Anti-Slavery Reporter* spoke despairingly of the "torpor" that had come over the movement. At four meetings of the gradualist national society, the group could not even muster a quorum.

Disturbingly, the next person in line for the British throne was the Duke of Clarence. These days, he seemed filled less by enthusiasm for slavery than remorse for having abandoned the love of his life, the late Dora Jordan. Portraits of the actress adorned the house Clarence shared with his wife, and, in tears, he later commissioned a sculpture of her for Westminster Abbey. At one point, he consoled himself from these sorrows by taking a group of warships from the Channel fleet out to sea for ten days without orders. The Admiralty was outraged, for no one knew where the ships had gone.

A steadily growing, well-organized bloc of more than fifty M.P.s had West Indian landholdings or commercial ties. And no longer were they blusterers like Banastre Tarleton. Their spokesmen were smooth and articulate types who professed themselves deeply concerned about the slaves' welfare. So did the government bureaucracy, which had even established in various colonies a new position of His Majesty's Protector of Slaves. These officials actually did more tabulating than protecting. Extrapolating from figures supplied by one of them, a parliamentary opponent of slavery estimated that the backs of British West Indian slaves were now receiving more than two million whip lashes a year. These were the recorded punishments only, and did not include routine use of the whip in the fields to prod the slaves as one might teams of horses. Flaunting their power, slave owners introduced a method of punishment new to the West Indies, the treadmill, and drawings of it quickly reached England. Tied and suspended by their arms, slaves had to keep climbing a large, rapidly turning cylinder or else its wooden steps would bang painfully against their shins as they dangled.

In 1828, John Clarkson, then sixty-three, was listening to a member of his family read aloud to him about conditions in the West Indies. "It is dreadful to think," he said, "after my brother and his friends have been labouring for forty years, that such things should still be." These were his last words; a few minutes later he was dead of a heart attack. Thomas Clarkson had lost his best friend and most loyal supporter. Two years later, one of Clarkson's worst enemies, the Duke of Clarence, took the throne as King William IV, his boorish manners and habit of making coarse and garrulous speeches untamed by the passage of time. His famously oblong head requiring padded hats, he raced about in an open carriage accepting women's kisses and grinning with undisguised glee over becoming King at last.

23

"COME, SHOUT O'ER THE GRAVE"

As the 1830s began, the tiny percentage of British citizens who could vote had barely changed for more than 150 years. The House of Commons was a bizarre anachronism, perhaps best symbolized by a famous episode in which one member, leaving in full court dress to attend the opera, unintentionally speared a seated colleague's wig on the tip of his sword and strode out of the chamber unawares. Booming Manchester, the second-largest city in the country, had no representatives at all, while the virtually uninhabited hill of Old Sarum, like Cambridge and Oxford Universities, sent two. (Oxford candidates were not allowed to campaign, and had to be at least ten miles from the university at election time.) The county of Cornwall elected almost as many members as all of Scotland—and several Scottish constituencies were allowed to send representatives only in alternate elections. Not only were there varying property qualifications for voters, but parliamentary candidates came from an even more limited group: they could only be men with incomes of at least £300 a year or, for certain constituencies, £600. This antiquated crazy quilt, weighted in favor of wealthy landowners, left the West India bloc in Commons much stronger than when the slave trade had ended a quarter century earlier—although, in the interim, the importance of the West Indies to the British economy had somewhat declined.

Millions of Britons were exasperated by the undemocratic way in which Parliament was chosen. A variety of ideas for electoral reform—or Reform, as it came to be known—were in the air, and all who cared about freeing the slaves knew that the fates of the two movements were linked. In France, where restricted suffrage was also a sore point, a revolution in 1830 brought barricades to the Paris streets, forced the King to abdicate, and was a warning signal to Britain's elite: Why not stave off such upheaval by giving the rising middle classes more of a stake in government? Reform agitation, like every progressive movement for a generation, was modeled on the drive for abolition: a media campaign, cheap pamphlets, mass meetings, petitions to Parliament. The bolder petitions demanded universal male suffrage, but even far more modest Reform looked like an uphill battle, for no politicians anywhere like to reform themselves out of office.

The growing pressure for Reform reignited the antislavery movement. Many younger members of the London Society for Mitigating and Gradually Abolishing the State of Slavery Throughout the British Dominions had had enough of mitigation and gradualism. Hoping that Reform might yield a more responsive Parliament, they pushed for another great mobilization of public opinion against slavery. Although none of them would openly acknowledge a woman's influence, Elizabeth Heyrick's example had been powerful. Like her, they wanted slavery ended *now.*

This feeling burst dramatically into the open at a May 15, 1830, public meeting of the society at Freemasons' Hall, on Great Queen Street. A high ceiling, chandeliers, clerestory windows, and pilastered walls lined with larger-than-life portraits made this one of the city's most majestic meeting places. Some two thousand people jammed into the hall, and hundreds more had to be turned away. Both now in their seventies, Clarkson and Wilberforce were on the platform—together for the very last time, it would turn out. Clarkson, his sight impaired by cataracts, moved that "the great leader in our cause" should chair the meeting. Stooped, and with his once powerful speaker's voice barely audible, Wilberforce did so.

With them was Thomas Fowell Buxton, antislavery leader in Parliament since Wilberforce's retirement. Although as large and athletic as Wilberforce was small and frail, he matched his mentor in caution, believing that adult slaves were not ready for emancipation, though their children might be. The meeting, however, belonged not to Buxton and Wilberforce but to a later generation, including one of James Stephen's sons, George, a lawyer. "The very demon of procrastination seemed to have possessed our leaders," he later wrote.

> A string of resolutions was proposed by Buxton; admirably worded; admirably indignant, but—admirably prudent! They wound up with "an unalterable determination to leave no proper and practicable means unattempted for effecting, at the earliest period. . . ." But it was too much for the patience of young Antislavery England. Mr. Pownall . . . in defiance of frowns and remonstrance, and cries of "Order!" . . . moved an amendment in a few pithy words . . . "That from and after the 1st of January, 1830, every slave born within the King's dominions shall be free." It was a spark to the mine! the shouts, the tumult of applause were such as I never heard before, and never shall hear again. Cheers innumerable thundered from every bench, hats and handkerchiefs were waved in every hand. Buxton deprecated, Brougham interposed, Wilberforce waved his hand for silence, but all was pantomime and dumb show. I did my best in a little knot of some half-dozen young men to resist all attempts at suppression. We would allow no silence and no appeals. At the first subsidence of the tempest we began again. . . . nor did we rest, or allow others to rest, till Wilberforce rose to put the amendment, which was carried with a burst of exulting triumph that would have made the Falls of Niagara inaudible at equal distance.

The following year, even more impatient, George Stephen and his friends formed a subcommittee of the society and hired a full-time staff of half a dozen lecturers, each paid £200 a year to travel a particular part of the country rousing the public. They were given materials about slavery to study and detailed instructions on how to handle questions and interruptions. Although Stephen's memoirs make it sound as if he were the first to plan such a campaign, this was not so.

The women had already done it. Beginning in 1829, the Birmingham Ladies' Society for the Relief of Negro Slaves had put several paid lecturers in the field, and the first two lecturers for the new national group had already been doing the same for the Birmingham women.

One lecturer, Captain Charles Stuart, who dressed in Scotch plaid and a long cape, carried a slave whip with him. He found a friendly reception everywhere; a hotel manager "treated me like a brother, and would receive no compensation." Huge numbers of people flocked to hear the speeches: six thousand reportedly filled a hall in Leeds; second lectures were scheduled when crowds overflowed the first. In Baldock, reported one sympathizer, "the Friends' Meeting House . . . was thronged; persons stood on benches to hear through the open windows, and I have been assured that about 200 could not get in." With local dignitaries also wanting to have their say on the subject, these occasions sometimes lasted four to seven hours, resembling, as one scholar puts it, "more what would today be called 'teach-ins,' rather than the stately proceedings which the old Society conducted . . . proposing lofty but useless resolutions." The West India lobby mobilized groups of hecklers to try to break up the meetings—and quietly instructed its own paid lecturers to attend and see what techniques they could learn.

Before long the new committee separated from its more hesitant parent body and named itself the Agency Antislavery Committee. There were many hurt feelings when the younger activists accused the elderly veterans of timidity. Anne Knight, who would become a pioneer feminist, later spoke of the gradualists as sleeping "the slumber of the daddies." Together with the women's committees already at work in the provinces, the young Agency Committee enthusiasts breathed new life into the national movement. In parliamentary campaigning in 1831, activists displayed blacks (or, where they could find none willing, chimney sweeps with sooty faces) in chains. The number of local antislavery groups around the country soared to more than 1,200. Quakers were still crucial, but they were joined by Britain's fast-growing ranks of Methodists—a denomination far more democratic and egalitarian than the Church of England.

A more equitably chosen Parliament would likely reflect the country's revived antislavery feeling, and so the fate of slavery ultimately depended on whether Parliament would pass the Reform bill, introduced in March 1831. Knowing that they were at a critical moment in history, M.P.s debated furiously for months. At last, in September, a watered-down bill passed the House of Commons—only to be defeated in the House of Lords, which looked on Reform with horror. Commons then passed a still tamer bill, which the Lords sat on, debated, and finally passed after gutting its few meaningful clauses. To no one's surprise, a proposal to emancipate the slaves also failed to pass.

Even conservatives began to worry that no Reform would mean growing public unrest. At Nottingham, rioters set the castle of an anti-Reform duke on fire. The bishops who voted against Reform in the Lords were burned in effigy. Angry workers cut gas pipes, set coal pits on fire, sabotaged factories. What could be done? The reluctant King, who would doubtless have preferred to be adventuring at sea with his beloved navy, came under mounting pressure to appoint enough new pro-Reform peers to get a meaningful Reform bill through the Lords. Crowds rampaged in Bristol, horrifying Wilberforce, who was taking the waters at nearby Bath. "Not a single gaol," he wrote to one of his sons, ". . . is left undestroyed. The Bishop's Palace (and Deanery too I am told), burnt to the ground. The Custom House ditto, Mansion House ditto. . . . The redness of the sky from the conflagration was quite a dreadful sight." If there were any further "grumblings of the volcano," he planned to flee Bath for his son's country parsonage "before the lava bursts forth."

As word of the revived antislavery movement reached the Caribbean, planters feared another eruption of their own volcano. The system was already fraying at the edges: there had been several abortive Jamaican slave conspiracies during the 1820s, and authorities there were reporting more than 2,500 escaped slaves a year. Most were recaptured, although several thousand were believed to be living in the rugged backcountry. In the summer of 1831, Jamaican whites began holding meetings to strategize about how to keep the slaves under control. There was even talk of seceding from the British Empire and joining up, in some undetermined way, with the American South. In November, the Assembly defiantly refused, almost unanimously, to ban the flogging of slave women. In an earlier debate on the subject, when it had considered only whether female slaves were to be flogged "decently" or "indecently" (i.e., naked), indecently won.

As was so often true in the British colonies, the harshness of Jamaica's social order coexisted with a surprisingly free press. Almost all the island's newspapers echoed the viewpoint of the white planters, but from 1829 on, one, the *Watchman,* was co-owned and edited by Edward Jordon, a free mulatto. He was the best known of a brave but tiny handful of mulatto and white West Indian journalists who called for slavery's end, and he both wrote his own exposés and reprinted many antislavery articles from Britain. Further enraging the planters, dozens of Baptist, Presbyterian, Moravian, and Methodist missionaries were now working among the slaves. Police had several times found excuses to briefly throw some of them in jail, and one missionary's house was shot at.

Like John Smith in Demerara, the missionaries had come to Jamaica as preachers, not antislavery crusaders. Almost any church, however, was bound to be far more revolutionary in this world of oppression than the London missionary societies could have imagined. As a Jamaican slave, you were not a citizen, had no rights, and faced a life of unremitting hardship and humiliation. But in a mission chapel you could learn to read and write and could gain the status of a member, a deacon, a respected elder. Moreover, you were part of an international fellowship; Baptist and Methodist membership cards were printed in England. And despite the care the missionaries took to avoid challenging slavery directly, you could hear them preach that all men and women, black and white, slave and free, were equal in the sight of God. "It was easy most unintentionally to err," wrote Reverend Hope Waddell, a young Presbyterian who arrived in Jamaica in 1829, ". . . and to say things in a slave congregation fit only for a free one."

The Christian message had power, and so did the ritual, which sometimes echoed elements of African religion. The hymns, the prayers, the call-and-response cadence of the church service, the vision of the Promised Land, all spoke of a human dignity starkly different from the world of slave labor. To join the Baptist Church, for instance, was to take an initiative fraught with great spiritual meaning, in a life otherwise without choices. In the mission chapel, the new converts would spend a long night of solemn meditation, towards the end of which, writes historian Mary Turner, "In the very early hours of the morning the missionary joined them for prayer; then, before sunrise, the company moved to the nearest river or seashore. The candidates, all robed in white, were assembled by their class leaders while the missionary waded waist-deep into the water and the ceremony began. Each one was led by his class leader to the missionary, who, emphasizing once more that baptism must mark a change of heart, immersed him. On the bank the waiting crowd sang hymns while some made fires and boiled coffee. . . . The orderly crowds, the white-robed candidates, the sacrificial fires, and the holy music under the luminous blue dome of the sky before sunrise created a memorable occasion." The missionaries themselves had never experienced such fervor in their congregations back home, and were sometimes moved to tears.

As agitation in England continued, "the negroes had begun to look for the arrival of the mail packet," wrote Waddell, "and inquire the home news." Wild rumors swirled. A popular Baptist missionary named Thomas Burchell left his chapel in Montego Bay in mid-1831 for home leave, to return at Christmas. He was the one, the slaves now said, who would bring the "freepaper" from the King, or perhaps even arms. And, people swore, the King's own soldiers would fight on the slaves' side if the planter militia denied them freedom. Adding to the tension, a severe drought ravaged the slaves' vegetable plots.

Although Christmas Day, 1831, fell on a Sunday, the Jamaican authorities announced that the slaves would not get an extra day's holiday. The governor released a Colonial Office proclamation saying specifically that the King had *not* freed the slaves. The militia was put on alert. Just after Christmas the storm broke. Waddell, staying in the "great house" of a plantation, was awakened at night by the cry of a rebel messenger running through the slave quarters: "No watchman now! No watchman now! Nigger man, nigger man, burn the house—burn buckra house! Brimstone come! Brimstone come! Bring fire and burn massa house!" Houses did burn, and with them warehouses full of crushed, dried sugar cane, the fuel for the hated boiling houses. More than two hundred plantations in northwest Jamaica suffered over £1.1 million worth of damage. And that did not count the thousands of slave huts and gardens that whites destroyed in revenge, to which the government naturally assigned no value.

Just as one of the first heroes of the long fight against British slavery was named Sharp, so (although he spelled the name differently) was one of the last. Thirty-one-year-old Samuel Sharpe, known variously as "Daddy" or "Schoolmaster," was the leader of the rebels. Literate, widely respected, and a mesmerizing speaker, he was chief deacon temporarily in charge of the absent Thomas Burchell's Baptist missionary chapel in Montego Bay, the largest town in this part of the island. A nephew who worked for a printer brought Sharpe extra copies of the local newspaper, so he must have known that no emancipation bill had yet passed. Nonetheless, many slaves later testified, he told them the King had decreed their freedom. An earnest Bible reader, Sharpe was certainly convinced that God, at least, had made such a promise.

As deacon, for months he had been preaching on various plantations; he would begin with a prayer meeting, then invite a select few slaves to stay on. One told a missionary later how Sharpe spoke "in a low, soft tone, that his voice might not be heard beyond the walls of the building. He . . . kept all his hearers fascinated and spell-bound. . . . He concluded by observing, that because the king had made them free, or resolved upon doing it, the [planters] were holding secret meetings with the doors shut close . . . and had determined . . . to kill all the black men, and save all the women and children and keep them in slavery; and if the black men did not stand up for themselves, and take their freedom, the whites would put them at the muzzles of their guns and shoot them like pigeons." Sharpe made the slaves at this meeting swear an oath not to work after Christmas unless the planters freed them and met their demand—a surprisingly moderate one—for half the going wage rate.

Although he appointed "colonels" and "captains" and himself was referred to as "General," Sharpe seems to have originally planned something like a sit-down strike. Only if the slaves were attacked would they take up arms and destroy plantation property—and even then, only the great houses, not the sugar fields or mills or boiling works that would be the basis of their future paid labor. But in a society ruled by the whip and the gun, the slaves could not build the organizational network necessary for an effective, coordinated strike.

Instead the rebellion took on a momentum of its own and swiftly became the greatest slave uprising the British Caribbean had ever seen. Planters had long liked to build their great houses on ridges and hilltops, and as these were set alight, the flames acted as signal beacons that spread the revolt. As the militia was closing in on one plantation, a woman put down her washing and ran to set fire to the sugar works, shouting, before she was shot, "I know I shall die for it, but my children shall be free!" The rebels forced into retreat a militia detachment under a particularly brutal and hated plantation manager, who declared, "I am now convinced the contest must be decided in the streets of Montego Bay." White women and children were evacuated to ships in the harbor.

More than twenty thousand rebels seized control of a wide swath of territory, while regular-army redcoats were rushed around the island by ship to join the militia in the attempt to contain them. Remarkably, some rebels were in uniform, the British general in command reported: "It appears beyond doubt that the burnings [of plantations] are conducted by regular parties; they are dressed many in blue jackets and black cross belts; some thus accoutred (four or five) were distinctly seen yesterday by Captain Burnett." A few days later, other soldiers saw a rebel chief dressed in red, with black sleeves and blue pantaloons. The origin of these uniforms is unknown; did women slaves sew them in advance?

It required almost all of January 1832 for troops to subdue the outgunned rebels and take Sharpe into custody. Some 200 slaves and 14 whites died in the fighting, and the gallows or firing squad claimed at least another 340 rebels—and possibly many more, for court records from two key regions are missing. "The powerful influence which Sharpe exercised over the people around him," wrote the Methodist missionary Henry Bleby, "will appear from the fact, that he succeeded in enlisting several free men in the struggle." Fourteen of them were convicted of aiding the rebels, and several of these were executed. Most were apparently mulattos, but one was a white sailor, and a white plantation official had shown the rebels how to make bullets.

Bleby described the executions in Montego Bay: "Generally four, seldom less than three, were hung at once. The bodies remained stiffening in the breeze. . . . Other victims would then be brought out and suspended in their place, and cut down in their turn to make room for more; the whole heap of bodies remaining just as they fell, until the workhouse negroes came in the evening with carts, and took them away, to cast them into a pit dug for the purpose, a little distance out of the town."

Limiting the deaths was the fact that to hang a slave was to destroy a planter's property, for which the colonial government had to pay compensation. And so the executions were selective. Women were usually spared, and if all the slaves on a plantation had rebelled, one or two were swiftly dubbed "ringleaders" and hanged or shot, while the others were whipped or let go. Seldom, then, did any owner lose more than a handful of slaves.

In the perennial search for outside agitators, white colonists targeted the missionaries. One island newspaper called for them to be hanged. A hissing, spitting white mob surrounded Thomas Burchell, Samuel Sharpe's pastor, when he returned from England, and he had to flee back on board his ship. His colleague Bleby was beaten and covered with tar; only the arrival of black supporters rescued him from being set on fire. Several other missionaries were jailed, and white mobs or the militia burned down some twenty Baptist and Methodist chapels. "I shall return to England," Reverend William Knibb wrote to his mother, "as I am not safe from assassination in this part of the world."

Some missionaries played a curious role in the uprising's aftermath. Anxious to extract information about just how the revolt was planned, officials asked them to talk to the imprisoned rebels. The missionaries agreed, hoping to obtain pardons for the men by proving that they had been coerced or manipulated into participating. In a few cases they succeeded. Whatever the moral ambiguities involved, it is only through the missionaries that we have any record of the last days of the doomed slaves. Bleby, for instance, visited Samuel Sharpe several times in his death cell.

> I had much conversation with him whilst he was in confinement; and found him certainly the most intelligent and re-

> markable slave I had ever met with. He was of the middle size; his fine sinewy frame was handsomely moulded, and his skin as perfect a jet as can be imagined. . . . He had teeth whose regularity and pearly whiteness a court-beauty might have envied, and an eye whose brilliancy was almost dazzling. . . . I heard him two or three times deliver a brief extemporaneous address to his fellow-prisoners . . . in the same cell, and I was amazed both at the power and freedom with which he spoke, and at the effect which was produced upon his auditory. He appeared to have the feelings and passions of his hearers completely at his command. . . .
>
> His execution excited a good deal of interest; and a considerable number of spectators assembled to witness it. He marched to the spot . . . with a firm and even dignified step, clothed in a suit of new white clothes, made for him by some female members of the family of his owner, with all of whom he was a favourite, and who deeply regretted his untimely end. He seemed to be entirely unmoved by the near approach of death [and] addressed the assembled multitude at some length in a clear unfaltering voice.

Bleby wept at the scene. One sentence Sharpe said to him in jail has echoed over the decades and made Sharpe a national hero in Jamaica today: "I would rather die upon yonder gallows than live in slavery."

Sharpe's owners were paid £16, 10 shillings, in compensation for their loss of property.

As Sharpe mounted the scaffold, the Baptist missionary William Knibb was on his way home. When his ship approached port in Liverpool in June 1832 and the pilot climbed on board, Knibb eagerly asked for the latest news: had the Reform bill passed Parliament? When the pilot answered yes, Knibb exclaimed, "Thank God. Now, I'll have slavery down."

Under the threat of more unrest and the force of overwhelming public opinion, the House of Lords had finally, reluctantly given in. The King signed the bill, Parliament was dissolved, and it was clear that in the upcoming elections Reform would slash the bloc of M.P.s with economic ties to the West Indies almost in half.

Reform and the revived antislavery movement were two of the events that would help doom British slavery. A third was the insurrection in the crown jewel of Britain's Caribbean colonies. From the moment the first dispatches from Jamaica had been rushed from an arriving ship to a cabinet meeting, the country's ruling establishment grasped that the price for maintaining slavery might be too high. No one needed to be reminded of the revolt that forty years earlier had cost France the riches of St. Domingue.

Freeing the slaves was the only alternative to a widespread war that might be beyond the government's military capacity, Lord Howick, parliamentary undersecretary of the Colonial Office and the son of Earl Grey, the Prime Minister, warned a House of Commons committee in the summer of 1832. He was even more frank in writing to the new governor taking office in Jamaica that year: "The present state of things cannot go on much longer . . . every hour that it does so, is full of the most appalling danger. . . . Emancipation alone will effectually avert the danger . . . in the meantime it is but too possible that the simultaneous murder of the whites upon every estate in the island . . . may take place." To his own journal Howick confided, "I would not be surprised any time to hear that Jamaica is in the possession of the negroes." Fearing renewed rebellion, the government dispatched five hundred additional British soldiers to reinforce the Jamaica garrison.

An especially forceful witness before the parliamentary committee was the British naval commander for the West Indies, Vice Admiral Charles Fleming, who said, in the wake of the rebellion, "The only reason why [the slaves] are tranquil now is, that they . . . hope to be emancipated." If they were not freed, he declared, "insurrection will soon take place." William Taylor, a former Jamaican plantation manager and police magistrate, testified that the revolts "will break out again, and if they do you will not be able to control them. . . . I cannot understand how you can expect [slaves] to be quiet, who are reading English newspapers."

The revolt strengthened the antislavery movement, for it made the British public demand an end to slavery more loudly than ever. They identified, however, less with the slave rebels who fought and died than with the white missionaries. Knibb and others traveled the country on speaking tours and testified at length before the parliamentary hearings. The burning of churches by white mobs shocked the public. Knibb spoke of how he had been prodded in the chest with a bayonet, and, to the gasps of his audience, exhibited the neckerchief of his colleague Bleby, still coated with tar. The missionaries were especially effective in reaching their fellow Baptists and Methodists in the lower middle and working classes, which now had the highest proportion of emancipation supporters. At least one canvasser, forwarding signatures on a petition to Parliament, apologized for the scrawls of signers who were barely literate.

Although they edged out the hundreds of dead slaves for the role of martyrs, the missionaries had great impact. To loud boos and hisses, Knibb brandished a spiked punishment collar on the lecture platform and called for freedom. Crowds packed the halls—the Quakers, as always, not removing their black hats—singing antislavery hymns and weeping with emotion. "My fellow Christians," Knibb said in one speech, "I appear as the feeble and unworthy advocate of 20,000 Baptists in Jamaica, who have no places of worship, no Sabbath, no houses of prayer . . . the greater part of those 20,000 will be flogged every time they are caught praying. . . . I call upon children, by the cries of the infant slave whom I saw flogged on Macclesfield estate. . . . I call upon parents, by the blood-streaming back of Catherine Williams, who, with a heroism England has seldom known, preferred a dungeon to the surrender of her honour. I call upon Christians, by the lacerated back of William Black, of King's Valley, whose back, a month after a flogging, was not healed." If Samuel Sharpe had been a nobleman fighting to free the Poles from Russian rule, Knibb declared, Britons would have built a monument to him.

It was a changing Britain that now waited to see what would be the fate of slavery. Top hats had replaced the three-cornered hats of the previous century; where horses once towed the Sharp family's musical barge along the Thames, steamboats now ran; steam power was driving cloth mills and Britain was the industrial powerhouse of Europe. How much change would be reflected in the new, reformed Parliament an expanded electorate would choose in December 1832, no one knew. In the months before and after the election, antislavery campaigning reached its peak, as the movement concentrated first on getting an emancipation-minded Parliament into office, and then on pressing it to act. It was the culmination of a half century's work.

Where once Clarkson alone had traveled the country, the Agency Antislavery Committee's staff of lecturers, paid and volunteer, now fanned out; and where he had gone by horseback from Liverpool to Manchester, they could take the world's first steam-powered passenger railway. (Like many British landmarks of the Industrial Revolution, it was partly financed by slave profits; the Gladstones and other planters were shareholders.) Where once William Dickson had jotted down the names of "hearty" or "zealous" Scottish recruits in his notebook, now candidates for Parliament were categorized by the Agency Committee, which published its lists in the newspapers and on posters, showing every man's position on emancipation: "Anti," "Doubtful," or "Recommended with perfect confidence."

To more traditional M.P.s this very listing seemed a shocking invasion of privacy, a portent of mob rule. But other candidates sent a flood of letters to the committee's headquarters mentioning any fact—such as once having had dinner with Wilberforce—that might establish their bona fides. At an unprecedented mass meeting at Exeter Hall, on the Strand, sixty-six members of Parliament pledged to vote to free the slaves. Yet it remained uncertain how the new Parliament would act. Some of the outlandish inequities of the old had been removed, but even after Reform, four out of five adult males in England could not vote, and the proportion was higher in Scotland and Ireland. Of the new M.P.s, George Stephen worried, "I do believe that they will give Emancipation to a distant day . . . and thus quiet the country. The practical effect of this will be to work the slaves to death before abolition occurs."

After the new Parliament began meeting in 1833, antislavery forces increased the pressure, organizing a rare street demonstration in which a large, orderly crowd marched to the Prime Minister's office on Downing Street. Even the elderly Wilberforce, no fan of inflaming public opinion, was persuaded to publicly initiate a petition to Parliament. He told a friend he felt "like a clock which is almost run down." Writing to Clarkson, he addressed him warmly as "My dear Old friend" and sent "every good Wish for you & yours, in time & for Eternity." He died quietly later in the year.

As the final battle over emancipation raged in Parliament, it was clear that what happened in Britain would be also felt in the United States. John Quincy Adams thought that emancipation in the British Empire might "prove an earthquake on this continent." Hoping for just such an earthquake, the fiery young American abolitionist William Lloyd Garrison, making his first visit to England, closely studied the British movement's tactics and eagerly joined the antislavery activists each morning for breakfast at the Guildhall Coffee House as they plotted strategy inside and outside Parliament. American newspapers printed long excerpts of House of Commons speeches.

The debate lasted more than three months, making this session of Parliament one of the longest in memory. As emancipation began to seem ever more likely, the West India lobby shrewdly switched its target, mounting an aggressive fight to be paid for the human property that, it appeared, might be taken from them. To the absentee plantation owners particularly, money mattered far more than the continuation of slavery. Elizabeth Heyrick had presciently warned nearly a decade before, "let compensation be first made to the *slave*." But this was not—and would never be—on any government's agenda.

The triumph came at last when the emancipation bill passed both houses of Parliament in the summer of 1833. It felt less glorious than expected, however, to many of those who had worked for it so long. For them it was tarnished by the price attached, for Parliament voted the plantation owners £20 million in government bonds, an amount equal to roughly 40 percent of the national budget then, and to about $2.2 billion today. Compensation satisfied financial interests in Britain as well as in the West Indies, for many plantations were mortgaged, and it was their London creditors who ultimately pocketed much of the money. For Britain's landed gentry who, even after Reform, controlled the country's politics, compensation was the perfect compromise, bowing both to public opinion and to the sacredness of private property.

When the compensation money was finally passed out, the Church of England's Codrington plantation was rewarded with £8,823, 8 shillings, 9 pence, or some $950,000 in today's money, for its 411 slaves.

To further soften the blow to planters, Parliament decreed that emancipation was to happen in two stages. The slaves would become "apprentices" in 1834, obligated to work full time for their former owners, in most cases for six years, without pay. Only after that would they be fully liberated. Buxton said that he hoped that the slaves would "by every motive of duty, gratitude and self interest . . . do their part towards the peaceful termination of their bondage." Gratitude? Whatever the legalities, in practice apprenticeship was little different from slavery. Activists waged a vigorous campaign against it that climaxed in a huge petition from more than half a million women. In the Caribbean, angry apprentices themselves staged stormy, widespread strikes, marches, and demonstrations that forced troops to be called out. As a result of pressure on both sides of the ocean, the term of six years was shortened to four.

The real victory, then, came on August 1, 1838, when nearly 800,000 black men, women, and children throughout the British Empire officially became free. The Quaker William Allen, who had sworn off eating sugar as an eighteen-year-old in 1789, was now able to put a spoonful in a cup of tea. In the British Caribbean there were parades and flags and banners, some, ironically, with the slogan "Am I Not a Man and a Brother?" But those now gaining freedom had little resemblance to the pleading, kneeling figures of the white imagination of only fifty years earlier.

William Knibb had returned to Jamaica, and on the sweltering night of July 31, he presided over a thanksgiving service in his church there. Its walls were hung with branches, flowers, and portraits of Clarkson and Wilberforce. In a coffin inscribed "Colonial Slavery, died July 31st, 1838, aged 276 years," church members placed an iron punishment collar, a whip, and chains.

As midnight drew near, the congregation sang:

> The death-blow is struck—see the monster is dying,
> He cannot survive till the dawn streaks the sky;
> *In one single hour,* he will prostrate be lying,
> Come, shout o'er the grave where so soon he will lie.

"The hour is at hand!" Knibb called from his pulpit, pointing at a clock on the wall. "The monster is dying!" When midnight struck, he called out, "The monster is dead!" The congregation burst into cheers and embraces. "Never, never did I hear such a sound," Knibb wrote to a friend. "The winds of freedom appeared to have been let loose. The very building shook at the strange yet sacred joy."* An open grave lay waiting in the yard of the church school. Still singing, the parishioners lowered the coffin into it. At the graveside they planted a coconut tree, as a "tree of liberty"—a symbol from the American and French revolutions now adopted by former slaves.

Slavery was still in place in the southern United States, in the Caribbean colonies of other European countries, in most of South America, and, in different forms, in Russia, most of Africa, and the Islamic world. But in the largest empire on earth, it was ended. Of the twelve men who had walked through the door of James Phillips's bookstore and printing shop fifty-one years earlier to begin planning their campaign, only Thomas Clarkson was still alive.

As with any crusade, there was soon a struggle over just how the antislavery movement in Britain was to be remembered. This sprang from the tension always at the heart of a campaign both revolutionary and conservative in nature. Although radical in confronting a practice so interwoven with the economy of the empire and accepted throughout the world, the movement generally argued against slavery not in the name of a new social order, but of Christianity and British law.

Clarkson and many like him were deeply affected by the new political currents of the day—revolution, the rights of man, pacifism. Granville Sharp, coming to the defense of child laborers in the Scottish salt pits and coal mines, said they were "involved in an *unjust Slavery* almost equally wretched" as that of blacks in the West Indies. In the glaring wrongs of slavery Clarkson, Sharp, Elizabeth Heyrick, and many others saw parallels to injustices at home.

Wilberforce and the "Saints" of Clapham, on the other hand, often contrasted slavery with the happy lot of British workers and craftsmen, who—except when led astray by Frenchmen or outside ag-

---

* Like James Stephen and other visitors to the West Indies before him, Knibb was profoundly changed by what he saw of slavery. After emancipation, he outraged Jamaican planters and startled many of his fellow Baptists by advocating that ex-slaves should have full citizenship rights, including the vote. His daughter married a mulatto.

itators—were patriotically content with their place in the social hierarchy. For the M.P.s who were almost entirely from the upper classes, voting for abolition of the trade and then for emancipation might stem from heartfelt conviction, but it was not a vote to redistribute political and economic power in England—or in the West Indies. Naturally, the movement had different meanings for its two wings.

How, then, was it to be celebrated? As a historic, pioneering mobilization of public opinion, via boycotts, petitions, and great popular campaigns, all powerfully reinforced by the armed slave revolts? Or as a great gift to poor slaves by a group of pious, benevolent men? In this battle of memory, the heirs of Wilberforce won out for well over a century. After his death Wilberforce was the object of a massive and successful feat of image-making: a laudatory five-volume biography by two of his sons. Both were influential, extremely conservative churchmen; one was a bishop and chaplain to the House of Lords, with the ceremonial post of Lord High Almoner to Queen Victoria. They both deeply resented Clarkson, feeling that he had hogged too much credit in his history of the movement's early days, published some thirty years before. Egging them on was a brother of George Stephen, angry that the quiet but crucial role of their father, James, in banning the slave trade in 1807 Clarkson had failed to mention.

The two Wilberforces termed Clarkson merely the paid "agent" of a movement led by their father, not even referring to him as a member of the abolition committee. They altered wording in their father's letters and completely ignored the numerous warm and friendly references to Clarkson in them. They never used a word from the many letters of Wilberforce to Clarkson that Clarkson had graciously sent them. They lost or destroyed these and other Wilberforce correspondence loaned to them, thus further ensuring that their picture of their father would prevail. They claimed that while still a boy, Wilberforce had written a prescient letter to a Yorkshire newspaper opposing slavery—a letter no researcher has ever been able to find. Some twenty more biographies of Wilberforce have followed, most of them reinforcing the view that slavery in the British Empire came to an end almost entirely because of the dogged, idealistic persistence of this saintly man and his saintly friends. Reflecting a similar outlook, a children's board game of the 1830s ended in a square where the King grants freedom to a kneeling slave. A century later, when Wilberforce's hometown of Hull marked the one hundredth anniversary of his death and of the passage of emancipation, the Lord Mayor led a procession of dignitaries past his home and statue, the Archbishop of York gave his blessing, and the flags of fifty nations were unfurled before an audience of twenty thousand. In 1935, Sir Reginald Coupland, an Oxford professor and advisor to the Colonial Office, imagined a posthumous interview with Wilberforce in which he asked the great man to explain the overthrow of slavery. Wilberforce's "reply": "It was God's work. It signifies the triumph of His will over human selfishness. It teaches that no obstacle of interest or prejudice is irremovable by faith and prayer."

Not only were Clarkson, radicals like Elizabeth Heyrick, and popular protests like the sugar boycott long slighted in British memory, so were the huge slave revolts, especially the final great rising in Jamaica that so clearly hastened the day of freedom. The deliberate forgetting of these began early. When sympathizers in Birmingham celebrated emancipation in 1838 at a public breakfast, a speaker referred to the slaves' "relying on their own peaceful and persevering efforts for the removal of every vestige of oppression," ignoring the fact that these efforts had the most impact when they were anything but peaceful.

For many Britons, the idea that emancipation had sprung from the benevolence of a wise elite was deeply comforting. Such confidence in British good intentions was gradually transformed into justification for more than a century of conquests and colonialism in Africa and a dramatic and often bloody expansion of British imperial holdings in India and the Far East. Indeed, one of the iron paddle-wheel steamers sent up the Niger River in 1841, to explore what would become the British colony of Nigeria, was proudly named the *Wilberforce.*

Clarkson, deeply hurt by the Wilberforce sons' biography and grown somewhat long-winded and querulous in his old age, wrote a whole book in reply. Many reviewers and former colleagues sided with him. Letters and statements of support came flooding in, and the Common Council of London unanimously voted him the ancient honor of the "Freedom of the City." The two Wilberforces eventually made a private, halfhearted apology, but the damage had been done, and their five volumes largely blotted Clarkson out of history for well over a century. Not until 1989 did he get the full scholarly biography he deserved, from Ellen Gibson Wilson, an American-born writer living in England. And he was not granted a memorial stone on the floor of Westminster Abbey—beneath the larger-than-life statue of Wilberforce that had been there more than 150 years—until 1996. But Wilberforce, to give him the credit he deserves, fully belongs there, and Clarkson would be the first to agree. The one spent forty years pushing Parliament to act in accord with the outpouring of antislavery feeling that the other was mobilizing in the country at large. They were one of history's great partnerships, and both men knew it.

In its final phase, the British antislavery movement drew considerable criticism from the left. A ballad about a child worked to death in a factory ran:

> Their tender hearts were sighing as negro wrongs were told,
> But the white slave lay there dying who earned their father's gold.

Leaders of Britain's working-class movements were usually against slavery, but they distrusted the politics of aristocratic benevolence, and modern critics have occasionally echoed them. Freeing the slaves, they have charged, was a much easier pill for the country's ruling elite to swallow than permitting trade unions, banning child labor, recognizing the rights of the Irish, and allowing all Britons to vote. And all this fuss about the slaves in the West Indies helped distract the public from the oppression of labor at home. The first point is certainly true. But the second is not, for, once awakened, a sense of justice is something not easily contained. It often crosses the boundaries of race, class, and gender. The movement's impact spread far more widely than the pious Evangelicals among its early backers ever wished for. If slaves should have rights, why not women? If the brutal working conditions of slavery should be outlawed, why not those in British factories? The sailors and ships' doctors Clarkson rounded up to testify on the slave trade paved the way for parliamentary hearings on child labor forty years later, a landmark on the path to modern social legislation.

Again and again, agitators for domestic reform of all sorts drew on the antislavery movement as a tactical model and on slavery itself as a powerful metaphor. The great nationwide petition campaign for abolition sparked later petitions from clothing-mill laborers demanding better working conditions and minimum-wage laws, and from pacifists fed up with Britain's endless wars with France. When the movement revived in 1823 with emancipation as its goal, the new round of agitation led to a torrent of petitions to Parliament on other issues. One from Manchester declared that to be deprived of the vote was as much a mark of degradation "as the visible brand on the person of a bought and sold negro." Women in Wiltshire asked for poor relief, saying that if the lot of slaves was on Parliament's agenda, then it was no longer "improper even for females to petition the House." A procession to a mass Reform rally in Manchester was led by a flag showing a maimed factory worker, with the words "Am I Not a Man and a Brother?" Among the campaign banners in the 1832 elections was one in Yorkshire calling for "the immediate abolition of slavery both at home and abroad."

Reverberations from the antislavery movement also spread down through the generations. Some descendants of its leading figures ended up questioning the status quo in ways no less far-reaching than had their forebears, as if the spirit of this first international human rights crusade had somehow been in their blood. The one-legged pottery entrepreneur Josiah Wedgwood had a grandson who turned the world upside down, Charles Darwin. William Smith, for many years Wilberforce's closest ally in Parliament, was the grandfather of Barbara Bodichon, who founded a pioneer feminist journal, the first women's college at Cambridge, and the first Women's Suffrage Committee. Samuel Blackwell was an antislavery leader in Bristol; his daughter Elizabeth, against great opposition, became the first female physician in either Europe or the United States. Robert Goulden was an active supporter of the movement at the time of emancipation; three quarters of a century later, his daughter, Emmeline Pankhurst, repeatedly went to jail in her battles for women's suffrage. James Stephen, whose life was forever changed in a Barbados courtroom when he saw the trial that ended with slaves sentenced to be burned alive, had a great-granddaughter who left her mark on the twentieth century and beyond. Her name was Virginia Woolf.

• • •

In Thomas Clarkson's final years, he watched comrades from the long struggle die one by one. Among the few survivors was William Allen. Clarkson wept when Allen left after a last visit, and Allen, in turn, wrote in his diary, "We have been dear to each other for nearly half a century, and it is doubtful whether we shall ever meet again." Despite his age and ill health, the lines of Clarkson's handwriting slanted optimistically upwards across the page as he continued to turn out letters and memoranda to antislavery activists, an exposé on the dreadful working conditions of British seamen—something he had first encountered nearly sixty years before—and several pamphlets on American slavery. In 1846, when he was eighty-six years old, he was almost alone among the antislavery veterans in believing Britain should cease buying all slave-grown produce, whether Cuban or Brazilian sugar, the American cotton that was the foundation of the British textile industry, or anything else. His last political act was to send the House of Lords a petition urging that tariffs on sugar imports be set not according to whether the sugar was grown in a British colony, but whether it was grown by free labor or slaves.

Ever since the abolition committee had dispatched bundles of its pamphlets to Benjamin Franklin nearly six decades earlier, the movement in England had been a model and inspiration for American antislavery leaders. Two of them, William Lloyd Garrison and Frederick Douglass, called on Clarkson that summer for what they knew was a final visit. As Clarkson talked with the two much younger men, all three understood that the Americans still had a difficult struggle ahead of them to end slavery, although they could have scarcely imagined that it would require a long and bloody civil war. "We found the venerable object of our visit seated at a table, where he had been busily writing a letter to America against slavery," the former slave Douglass wrote. Clarkson told them he had spent sixty years in the struggle, "and if I had sixty years more they should all be given to the same cause." He died some five weeks later.

In both the funeral procession and the overflowing church where the service was held, the mourners included many Quakers, and the men among them made an almost unprecedented departure from long-sacred custom.

They removed their hats.

EPILOGUE

"TO FEEL A JUST INDIGNATION"

ALTHOUGH THE great majority of British slaves were in the West Indies, emancipation's impact sent ripples around the globe, freeing slaves in territories as far flung as the Cape Colony, at the southern tip of Africa, and the Indian Ocean island of Mauritius. And their liberation raised hopes beyond the British Empire, for so much of the rest of the world's population was still in slavery, forced labor, or serfdom. When emancipation came in 1838, there were, for example, more than 1.5 million slaves working in mines and on plantations in Brazil, roughly 400,000 slaves in Cuba, and more than 2 million in the United States.

Brazilian and Cuban slaves would have to wait another fifty years for freedom. Nonetheless, the fact that the unrivaled superpower of the era had freed its slaves made clear that slavery's days were numbered. Nowhere was that felt more than in the United States, where bondage would last another quarter century. For American slaves, the British West Indies, once a dreaded place to which troublemakers might be banished, to be worked to an early death in the sugar fields, were now an oasis of hope and refuge. In 1841, 135 slaves on board the American brig *Creole,* who were being shipped from Richmond, Virginia, to New Orleans, rose up and seized control of the vessel. They forced a mate to sail it to the nearest port in British territory—Nassau, in the Bahamas—where, despite furious protests from their owners and the American consul, they gained their freedom.

During the two and a half decades before the American Civil War, free blacks in the Northern states celebrated not July 4, when they were at risk of attack by drunken whites, but August 1, Emancipation Day in the West Indies, a date Frederick Douglass called "illustrious among all the days of the year." In 1838, blacks in Cincinnati held an overnight church vigil, remaining silent for the last fifteen minutes before midnight, then bursting into cheers, hymns, and prayers when the hour struck. Black churches in Philadelphia remained open all day, and a mass meeting was held in New York. The commemorations on August 1, which often included sympathetic whites, grew as the years passed. In black communities throughout the North there were outdoor meetings and parades with banners that showed a slave with fetters broken. Seven thousand people attended an August 1 celebration in New Bedford, Massachusetts, in 1855. When blacks from throughout the state gathered in the same city three years later, one of the speakers they heard was the veteran missionary to Jamaica Henry Bleby, who told the crowd, "I saw the monster die."

In the British Caribbean, what had replaced the monster was less than glorious. Most of Britain's slaves left bondage just as their ancestors had entered it, with little but the clothes on their backs. It was, after all, the plantation owners or their creditors and not the slaves who received the £20 million compensation; more important, they still owned the plantations. White planters, merchants, and bankers kept a tight grip on local government, the tax structure, and the franchise. In an 1863 election in Jamaica, out of a population of more than 440,000, only 1,457 people voted. On Barbados fewer than one in twenty adults qualified to vote until after the Second World War. For decades, blacks continued to cut sugar cane in conditions not much better than slavery. And now, for the same modest huts and gardens they had long had, they had to pay rent to landlords and taxes to the government. Plantation owners manipulated the system in various ways. On Barbados, many ex-slaves were allowed to remain in their homes rent free—if they worked the landlord's fields five days a week. On St. Lucia, an observer noted in 1844, "on the abolition of slavery almost every planter was induced to establish a shop upon his estate" to recapture the ex-slaves' wages as profits, and often force them into lifelong debt. Pay, abysmal to begin with, was undercut further by competition from hundreds of thousands of penniless indentured laborers imported from India, in effect a subsidy to planters. Taxes paid by ex-slaves helped finance the immigration of their competition.

Antislavery M.P.s in Britain for the most part paid little attention to these hardships. "The Negro race," declared parliamentary antislavery leader Thomas Fowell Buxton, "are blessed with a peculiar aptitude for the reception of moral and religious instruction, and it does seem to me that there never was a stronger call on any nation than there is now . . . to send missionaries, to institute schools, and to send out Bibles. It is the only compensation in our power. It is an abundant one! We may in this manner recompense all the sorrows and sufferings."

The Bibles proved small recompense. As mills and plantations mechanized, blacks often found themselves unemployed, especially when it was not harvest season or when the sugar price dropped. In most of the colonies there was little land they could farm—the best having been long taken for sugar—and so they ran afoul of laws against squatting and vagrancy. Harsh labor legislation took the place of slavery in guaranteeing a compliant and inexpensive work force. In British Honduras, "insolence and disobedience" to an employer, or being absent without leave from work, commonly drew a sentence of three months at hard labor. Throughout the British Caribbean, the budget for prisons and courts soared; in Barbados between 1835 and 1840, the first doubled and the second tripled. Numbers were even higher elsewhere.

Discontent simmered, then exploded in revolts. The most notable broke out in precisely those British colonies that had seen the strongest slave uprisings: Jamaica, Barbados, and Demerara—then part of British Guiana. An 1856 revolt in the latter, led by an apocalyptic preacher who gathered his followers with trumpet blasts, ended with more than one hundred "ringleaders" being sentenced to hard labor, with fines or floggings as well. A massive 1865 black uprising in Jamaica took six weeks to suppress and left almost as many dead as the slave revolt of 1831–32. On Barbados in 1876, nearly forty years after emancipation, workers paid as little as twopence a week started protests that led to 8 blacks being killed and 450 being taken prisoner.

Although he had other struggles in mind, the British socialist William Morris could have been speaking of the decades after emancipation when he wrote, "Men fight and lose the battle, and the thing that they fought for comes about in spite of their defeat, and when it comes turns out not to be what they meant, and other men have to fight for what they meant under another name." And yet men—and women—have fought those later battles in the former slave colonies, and have won many of them: for the rights of labor, for the vote, for independence from Britain, and for much more. Could any of these battles have been fought at all if the first and greatest, against slavery, had not been won?

The end of slavery did not mean the end of injustice, but one measure of human progress, surely, is that today enslaving others is a "crime against humanity" under international law. Those charged with all crimes against humanity, genocide, and war crimes are, at least in theory, subject to trial. Although that justice has been applied only sporadically and inconsistently, and far more to the weak than to the strong, the very idea of such a criminal proceeding would have astonished someone from the era of slavery. Could they have seen forward across the centuries into our own time, the slave rebels and abolitionists might have been pleased that when the long trial of former Yugoslav strongman Slobodan Milosevic began in 2002, one of the three judges he faced each day, a respected expert on human rights law, was a descendant of British slaves: Patrick Robinson of Jamaica.

Traces of the world of British slavery remain on all of the continents it touched, and on the floor of the ocean that connects them. In 1972, divers discovered the wreck of the *Henrietta Marie,* sunk by a hurricane near Key West in 1700 after delivering 190 slaves to Jamaica and loading up with sugar, indigo, cotton, and dyewood for the voyage back to its home port of London. Similar in size to the ships John Newton captained, the *Henrietta Marie* carried slaves whom scholars believe were Igbo, Equiano's countrymen and -women. Among the cargo in the wreck was leftover slave-buying currency: English pewter mugs now white with encrusted coral, small mirrors, thousands of yellow and green beads, and flat iron bars a foot or so long. (In Africa at the time, the going rate was thirteen bars for a man and ten for a woman.) African slave dealers sometimes melted down the bars to make chains and shackles for transporting slaves to the coast. The wreck also yielded weapons kept on shipboard for putting down slave revolts: a blunderbuss with a thick bronze barrel and a cutlass, its blade now ragged from rust. Divers found seventy-five pairs of corroded shackles, some sized to fit the legs of children. Wrecks like that of the *Henrietta Marie* are the only remnant of the vast armada that carried slaves across the Atlantic for more than three and a half centuries; afloat or ashore, not a single slave ship plank remains.

All three corners of the deadly Atlantic triangle, however, hold other reminders of the trade. Along the coast of West Africa, some thirty old slave-trading forts still survive, in various states of repair: the largest are massive, imposing structures with thick walls, chapels, graceful archways and colonnades, and rows of black iron cannon standing out against whitewashed ramparts. In several you can see the narrow "door of no return" through which captives were herded, single file, to begin their journey across the ocean. After the slave trade ended, some of these forts got a new lease on life in wars of colonial conquest. When the Asante people of what is now Ghana fought British invaders in 1873, the British bombarded them from Elmina Castle. In putting down a later Asante revolt, British officers (including future Boy Scouts founder Robert Baden-Powell) deployed West Indian troops, quartering them in the same forts through which some of their ancestors must have passed on the way to slavery a hundred years or more earlier. Today Christiansborg Castle is the official residence of the President of Ghana—symbolizing, in the minds of some critical Africans, a continuity between the indigenous slave dealers who supplied captains like Newton and the unhappy continent's current oligarchy.

Several former slave castles have been refurbished by countries eager for euros and dollars, and are visited by tourists each year, many of them black Americans. There have been bitter disputes, akin to arguments about Auschwitz, over whether restaurants, shops, and concerts should be allowed on the premises. One favorite spot for travelers is the Île de Gorée, just off the coast of Senegal, which played a minor role in the slave trade. The little surf-rimmed island is mesmerizingly beautiful: a visual symphony of narrow streets lined with houses in Mediterranean pastels with terra-cotta roofs and wrought-iron balconies, their walls covered with brilliant red bougainvillea. Goats graze; palm and baobab trees sway in the ocean breeze; the Rue des Gourmets runs parallel to the Rue des Donjons. Ironically, a building christened the "House of Slaves"—the destination over the years of hundreds of thousands of pilgrims, including Nelson Mandela, Pope John Paul II, and two American presidents—was a merchant's home and not a depot from which slaves were shipped overseas.

On the rocky bluff of an island off Sierra Leone, a recent visitor found the roofless enclosure, with a single opening in one wall, where the youthful John Newton once kept slaves when he worked for a shore-based trader. "The pen is a square of stone walls, ten metres along each side and over two metres high, mortared and plastered: stout solid walls, with sharp fragments of eighteenth-century bottle-glass still firmly embedded along the top." But in this war-torn country, there is no money to rebuild the fort on Bance Island to lure visitors, and it lies as it long has, in crumbling ruins.

In Jamaica, in the Caribbean corner of the triangle, not a single slave dwelling is left standing. These were almost always built of cheap boards or wattle and daub, and none have survived hurricanes and the passage of time. What was built to last, however, were the various plantation work buildings made of stone. If you drive an hour or two off the tourist track, into the interior and onto the dirt roads that cross the land of some of the old estates—Windsor, Orange Valley, Retreat, Hampstead—you can find the shell and chimney of an old sugar mill, a stone wall with an archway that once surrounded a military garrison, and, the roof long gone, four walls of a 1797 slave hospital with a tablet over the door inscribed in Latin, "Not unmindful of the sick and wretched."

Those treated in slave hospitals, however, were not necessarily there out of planters' mindful benevolence. A physician who worked in the West Indies before emancipation observed that the effect of a severe whipping often "confines the delinquent to the sick-house for five or six weeks." Thomas Roughley's instruction manual for planters advised them to be vigilant about admitting slaves to such facilities, otherwise "the whole population of an estate . . . would present themselves . . . and enjoy their supine, idle, propensities."

A few miles away a sugar boiler red with rust lies on the ground, along with a jumble of stones from the building that once held it. The experience of visiting such spots is not like that of seeing Nazi concentration camps, where the tours are organized, the visitors numerous, and the crematoria and other evidence of deliberate murder so painfully visible. Rather, it is like seeing the remnants of the old gulag camps strewn across Arctic Siberia: few pilgrims, nothing preserved, only ghostly scatterings of rusted iron and blocks of stone, with nature taking over—there snow and ice, here fast-growing tropical foliage. It is the visitor, and not a tour guide, who must ask the questions that hang in the air, unanswerable. How many slaves were worked to death feeding this boiler? How many had their arms crushed in the rollers of the mill that must have been next to it?

Much better preserved and restored are some of Jamaica's plantation great houses. A few of these are occupied by wealthy families; others have been converted into small hotels or charge admission for tours given by women in period costumes of white blouses and long flowing skirts. As in the American South, the old days have been commercially burnished into a time of gracious comfort, with the assumption that the tourist will identify with the slaveholder, not the slave. At the great house of the Barnett estate, on the outskirts of Montego Bay, you can find life-size mannequins of a slave maid serving tea to her seated white mistress. There are, of course, no mannequins of women field laborers.

A dozen miles east of town stands the majestic Greenwood great house, which once belonged to the family of Elizabeth Barrett Browning. Its original library of books and its handsome, darkly gleaming rosewood and mahogany furniture are still intact, as is a fearsome "man-trap" with saw-toothed iron jaws, like a trap used for catching bears, which could be hidden in the tall grass on a route that might be taken by an escaping slave. On the wall is a framed list of some of the plantation's slaves, one named "Bob Trouble." Greenwood sits on a high ridge a mile or two back from the sea, and the very grandeur of the commanding view makes it easy to feel how the slave owners who once enjoyed it could imagine that their way of life would go on forever. Looking at the 180-degree expanse of turquoise ocean, you can actually see the slight curvature of the earth. Perhaps forty miles of coastline are in sight: first the long fringe of beach and surf, where slaves once loaded barrels of sugar onto coasting vessels from now vanished plantation wharves; then a green ribbon of fields, some still bearing stands of sugar cane; then back of the fields the rising slopes that once held many more great houses on their heights.

At the beginning of the 1831–32 uprising led by Samuel Sharpe, the missionary Hope Waddell stood almost at this very spot. "Scarcely had night closed in," he wrote, "when the sky towards the interior was illumined by unwonted glares. . . . As the fires rose here and there in rapid succession, reflected from the glowing heavens, we could guess from their direction, and the character of masters and slaves, what estates were being consumed. Soon the reflections were in clusters, then the sky became a sheet of flame, as if the whole country had become a vast furnace. . . . That was a terrible vengeance which the patient drudges had at length taken on those sugar estates, the causes and scenes of their life-long toils and degradation, tears and blood."

Today Jamaica and the other former British sugar islands are not without their problems, some shared with other countries of the world's South. But their citizens have much that those who fought and died in the great revolt could never have dreamed of, from public health systems to almost universal schooling. The ships that visit Jamaica's harbors unload cruise passengers, not slaves. Far from the beach hotels, plaques throughout the western end of the island mark sites associated with the uprising. Many of Jamaica's schoolteachers are graduates of Sam Sharpe Teachers' College. On two sugar plantations just north of Kingston, Papine and Mona, slaves once lived and worked under the same regime as throughout the West Indies: draconian whippings, spiked iron punishment collars, scanty food, early death. Now, on this land, their descendants can attend the flagship campus—including law school, medical school, and its teaching hospital—of the University of the West Indies.

The final point of the triangle trade was, of course, Britain. What was once a dirt road from Cambridge to London has become a busy highway, and as it descends a hillside in Hertfordshire few drivers notice a small weathered stone obelisk on one side. It was erected by admirers long ago to mark the spot where, in 1785, Thomas Clarkson got off his horse, sat down beside the road, and decided that "someone should see these calamities to their end." One recent autumn day, a puzzled telephone repairman descended from the top of a nearby pole to see why an American couple were studying this marker he had not examined before. But when he heard the name Clarkson he recognized it as having something to do with ending slavery.

The slave ports of Bristol and Liverpool, where Clarkson traveled two years later, are now changed beyond recognition. But there are still Clarence and Tarleton streets in Liverpool, and both cities have elegant homes built with the trade's profits, among them several of the neoclassical red brick mansions that surround Bristol's Queen Square. Nearby, the Seven Stars pub, whose owner took Clarkson out at night to show him how drunken, indebted sailors were dragooned onto slave ships, is still in business.

In London, no signs mark where either the abolitionists or the slave traders had their offices, even though in that part of the financial district, if you don't lift your eyes above ground-floor level, a few of the narrow alleys look somewhat as they might have in the eighteenth century. The Jamaica Coffee House, where slave captains once collected their mail, is now the Jamaica Wine House. But another building in the city reflects the abolitionist heritage in a way that matters more than plaques or monuments. After emancipation passed, the British activists reorganized to agitate for the freedom of those enslaved elsewhere, especially in the United States. The linear descendant of one of these organizations is the human rights group Anti-Slavery International, which works today for the freedom of the millions of people who still live in some form of bondage: to cross-border traffickers in women, to employers of child labor, to rural landlords in Asia, and more. Its London headquarters is named Thomas Clarkson House.

To the British abolitionists, the challenge of ending slavery in a world that considered it fully normal was as daunting as it seems today when we consider challenging the entrenched wrongs of our own age: the vast gap between rich and poor nations, the relentless spread of nuclear weapons, the multiple assaults on the earth, air, and water that must support future generations, the habit of war. None of these problems will be solved overnight, or perhaps even in the fifty years it took to end British slavery. But they will not be solved at all unless people see them as both outrageous and solvable, just as slavery was felt to be by the twelve men who gathered in James Phillips's printing shop in George Yard on May 22, 1787.

All of the twelve were deeply religious, and the twenty-seven-year-old Clarkson wore black clerical garb. But they also shared a newer kind of faith. They believed that because human beings had a capacity to care about the suffering of others, exposing the truth would move people to action. "We are clearly of opinion," Granville Sharp wrote to a friend later that year, "that the nature of the slave-trade needs only to be known to be detested." Clarkson, writing of this "enormous evil," said that he "was sure that it was only necessary for the inhabitants of this favoured island to know it, to feel a just indignation against it." It was this faith that led him to buy handcuffs, shackles, and thumbscrews to display to the people he met on his travels. And that led him to mount his horse again and again to scour the country for witnesses who could tell Parliament what life was like on the slave ships and the plantations. The riveting parade of firsthand testimony he and his colleagues put together in the *Abstract of the Evidence* and countless other documents is one of the first great flowerings of a very modern belief: that the way to stir men and women to action is not by biblical argument, but through the vivid, unforgettable description of acts of great injustice done to their fellow human beings. The abolitionists placed their hope not in sacred texts, but in human empathy.

We live with that hope still.

APPENDIX
SOURCE NOTES
BIBLIOGRAPHY
ACKNOWLEDGMENTS
INDEX

APPENDIX:
WHERE WAS EQUIANO BORN?

OLAUDAH EQUIANO'S AUTOBIOGRAPHY, a bestseller in its time, was later out of print for more than a century. Ever since it was rediscovered in the 1960s, scholars have valued it as the most extensive account of an eighteenth-century slave's life. Equiano's description of the middle-passage crossing appears in many anthologies.

Nigerians, eager to celebrate him as a native son, have searched for the birthplace he described in the book, the "charming, fruitful vale, named Essaka." One researcher maintains, unconvincingly, that she found it in a town named Isseke, where she interviewed a ninety-five-year-old man who claimed to remember ancestral lore about Equiano's capture. But nearly two and a half centuries after the fact, any such evidence is totally in the eye of the beholder. Curiously, no one seems to have followed up another reference of Equiano's, in a newspaper article, to "my estate in Elese, in Africa," which might, or might not, refer to today's Nigerian town of Alese.

Recently, however, a leading scholar has asked: Was Equiano born in Africa at all? The question comes from Vincent Carretta, professor of English at the University of Maryland and the editor of the definitive Penguin edition of Equiano's memoir and letters, first published in 1995. Although noting that the London parish record of Equiano's baptism described him as "a Black born in Carolina" and that the muster roll for the Royal Navy ship on which he sailed to the Arctic listed him as born in South Carolina, Carretta did not, in his introduction and notes to that volume, question

Equiano's account of his African birth and childhood. But in a 1999 article, subsequent writings, and a 2003 edition of Equiano's book, he does.

What threw Equiano's story of his early life into question for Carretta was newly found evidence suggesting that Equiano first arrived in England more than two years sooner than the date he names in his autobiography. Furthermore, in all the years he was free, Equiano went by his slave name of Gustavus Vassa, and never claimed an African name until he was about to publish his book. Was his name, as well as his childhood in Africa, invented?

Although Carretta finds Equiano's account of his Royal Navy voyages as the young slave of Lieutenant Pascal "almost all verifiable and impressively accurate," there are, of course, no records in Africa that could verify his description of his birth, childhood, or chiefly lineage. Equiano's picture of an idyllic, pastoral Africa and of the terrible voyage across the Atlantic could easily have been drawn from abolitionist and African travel books of the time, and indeed he openly acknowledges several of them. Presenting himself as born in Africa and a veteran of the middle passage was certainly a significant help in selling his book and promoting the antislavery cause. That he had gone on from a heathen childhood in Africa to become a literate British Christian was the most dramatic possible proof, to his Anglocentric readers, of the equal potential of all human beings. In addition, agitation against the Atlantic slave trade was at its peak, and he wanted to speak with authority as a survivor of its horrors.

In Equiano's own time, an anonymous proslavery writer who wanted to undermine his credibility did so by charging he was not African-born. There were two such brief attacks in London newspapers, one apparently repeating the other, in 1792. Both claimed, with no evidence cited, that he had been born on the West Indian island now known as St. Croix. In the later editions of his book, Equiano published a vigorous denial and several supporting letters from others, as well as a list of six British witnesses who knew him when he first arrived in England and could testify that he "could speak no language but that of Africa" (although this in itself was not necessarily proof of African birth). The accusation about not being African-born, Equiano complained to his friend Thomas Hardy, "has hurted the sale of my Books."

At this point in his life, with the movement under way, Equiano had strong motives to present himself as African-born. If this claim was true, what, then, might have been his motives much earlier in life for presenting himself as born in North America?

There is one possible answer, which may also be the reason why several additional free blacks in London, like Quobna Ottobah Cugoano, are not on record as using their African names until after the antislavery movement began. Throughout the world of North Atlantic slavery, whites feared African-born slaves to be far more prone to rebellion. They had good reason to think so, particularly during the decades when Equiano claimed North American birth. The 1760 revolt in Jamaica, which spread through much of the island and left more than four hundred slaves and some sixty whites dead (see page 37), was accompanied by African drum signals and war cries and spearheaded by Coromantee slaves, from what is today Ghana. A committee of the Jamaican legislature was so alarmed that it recommended banning the import of slaves from that part of Africa. The rebels aimed, according to a white Jamaican writer of the time, at "the entire extirpation of the white inhabitants . . . and the partition of the island into small principalities in the African mode." More Jamaican Coromantees rose up in 1765 and 1766. In a 1776 rebellion on the island, Coromantee and other African-born rebels were joined by people of Equiano's own ethnic group, the Igbo; among the posts the chief slave conspirators planned to name themselves to was "King of the Eboes." African-born slaves led other uprisings in the British Caribbean, from Bermuda to the Bahamas to British Honduras to a later Igbo conspiracy in Jamaica.

British military authorities were even more skittish than the planters about slaves born in Africa; when they began raising slave regiments, they tried hard (though unsuccessfully) to recruit only "old English negroes"—that is, those born in the West Indies. Equiano, canny observer of white people, would have known full well the reputation of African-born slaves. The first time he named a birthplace in the Americas, he was still a slave. On the second occasion, he was free, but was signing on for a berth in the Royal Navy. He knew that the reputation of Africans as troublemakers was as notorious at sea as on shore, for navy ships patrolled West Indian waters and two of them had been used as floating prisons for the rebels of the 1760 Jamaica revolt. In his early life, therefore, Equiano could have had good reason not to name a birthplace in Africa. (However, skeptical of this argument, Carretta points out that two other black sailors on the Arctic expedition did not hesitate to list African birthplaces.)

Barring the appearance of new evidence, Carretta and many other scholars believe we will never know for certain where Equiano was born, and any responsible historian must agree. But there is one additional factor outside the immediate evidence that may strengthen his claim of an African birthplace. It seems somewhat improbable that he invented the first part of his life story when the rest of it, to use Carretta's words, is "remarkably accurate whenever his information can be tested by external evidence." There is a long and fascinating history of autobiographies that distort or exaggerate the truth, by writers as varied as Sir Henry Morton Stanley, Frank Harris (*My Life and Loves*), the Guatemalan Nobel Peace Prize winner Rigoberta Menchú, and "Binjamin Wilkomirski," the Swiss author of a prize-winning bestseller about the Holocaust childhood he never had. But in each of these cases, the lies and inventions pervade the entire book. Seldom is one crucial portion of a memoir totally fabricated and the remainder scrupulously accurate; among autobiographers, as with other writers, both dissemblers and truth-tellers tend to be consistent. In any event, whatever the mystery of his origins, the bulk of Equiano's book, from his teenage years on, is undeniably authentic, and remains one of the great survivor's tales of his or any other time.

SOURCE NOTES

IN QUOTING FROM secondary sources, when the original source is a personal letter or else a book, periodical, or newspaper that is accessible in many libraries, I have used the form "Clarkson to Wilberforce, 5 April 1793, quoted in Smith, p. 67," or "*Morning Chronicle*, 5 April 1793, quoted in Smith, p. 67." But when a secondary source fails to cite the original source precisely or the latter is neither a dated letter nor a book, periodical, or newspaper, I have usually omitted the original citation and simply used "quoted in Smith, p. 67."

INTRODUCTION

1 *"anything more extraordinary": Le Siècle,* 22 October 1843, quoted in *Tocqueville and Beaumont on Social Reform,* ed. Seymour Drescher (New York: Harper & Row, 1968), p. 138.

2 *"the peculiar institution":* Drescher 1, p. x.

3 *three times as many Africans:* Richardson 2, p. 462.

5 *"the Petitioners themselves":* quoted in Davis 2, pp. 410–411.

"as their own": Humble Petition of Several of the Freemen of the Corporation of Cutlers, in Hallamshire in the County of York, 24 April 1789, in *Diary,* 11 July 1789, quoted in Drescher 1, p. 266 n. 2.

cost the British people: Drescher 8, p. 232 ff. See also Kaufmann and Pape, p. 637.

1. MANY GOLDEN DREAMS

11 *"All* that *sugar!":* Quoted in Ragatz 2, p. 50.

12 *"my future fortune":* Newton 1, p. 17.

"from my waking thoughts": Newton 1, p. 19.

"no Relish without you": Quoted in Martin, pp. 39–40.

13 *"who all perished":* [James Mitchell], "Voyage of H.M.S. Harwich to India in 1745–1749," *Bengal Past and Present* 45, part 2, April–June 1933, p. 80.
"sodomy with a sheep": George Ratcliffe diary, quoted in Steve Turner, p. 22.
"going to leave us": Newton 1, p. 38.
"tall and strong men": Richard Hakluyt, *The Principal Navigations, Voiages, Traffiques and Discoveries of the English Nation* (Glasgow, 1904), vol. 6, p. 176, quoted in Walvin 3, p. 1.

14 *"this globe moves":* James Houston, *Some New and Accurate Observations of the Coast of Guinea* (London, 1725), p. 43, quoted in Gratus, p. 34.
"industry and riches": An African Merchant, *A Treatise upon the Trade from Great Britain to Africa, humbly recommended to the Attention of Government* (London, 1772), p. 7, quoted in Anstey, p. 37.
William Davenport: Richardson 1, pp. 64, 69, 76, 77, 80, 82–83.

15 *"orphans my children":* William Barrett, *The History and Antiquities of the City of Bristol* (Bristol, 1789), p. 655, quoted in Kenneth Morgan, p. 4.

16 *"brutish lusts":* quoted in Phipps, p. 29.
"sinned with a high hand": Newton 1, p. 40.

17 *"utterly in vain":* Newton 2, p. 105.
"improving my fortune": Newton 1, pp. 40–41.
"their own slender pittance": Newton 1, pp. 46–47.

18 *"Business flourished":* Newton 1, p. 54.
"invented new ones": Newton 1, p. 60.

19 *"Lord have mercy on us":* Newton 1, pp. 65, 67.
"the habit of swearing": Newton 1, pp. 77, 79.
"more wild Inhabitants": Newton 1, p. 88.
"happy in my life": Newton to Jack Catlett, quoted in Martin, p. 90, and Phipps, p. 31.
"the fleshly appetites": quoted in Phipps, p. 47.

20 *"when business would permit":* Newton 1, p. 93.
"get a word out": Newton to Mary Newton, 8 January 1751, in Newton 3, vol. 5, p. 343.

22 *"take her on shoar again":* Newton 2, pp. 14, 16, 32.
"first came on board": Newton 2, pp. 29, 48, 56.
"ever seen 3 days": Newton 2, p. 31.
a higher death rate: Newton 2, p. 95.

23 *"down to the deck":* Newton 2, pp. 33, 75, 18.
"take the ship from me": Newton 1, p. 104.
"Divine Providence": Newton 2, p. 69.
"in neck yokes": Newton 2, pp. 22, 71, 77.

24 *"they have passed":* quoted in Martin, pp. 110, 118.
"a man born blind": Newton to Mary Newton, 26 January 1753, in Newton 3, vol. 5, pp. 404–405, 407.
Bance Island: Also sometimes known as Bence, Bense, Bunce, or George's Island.

24 *active trading posts:* see Ball, pp. 419–431. *Golf:* see Hancock, pp. 1–2, and Henry Smeathman's journal, 5 May 1773, whose brief passage on the subject is reprinted in Fyfe 3, pp. 70–71.

25 *"of being overheard":* Newton to Mary Newton, 19 April 1753, in Newton 3, vol. 5, p. 413.

"drink away their senses": James Low to Captain Archibald Grant, 10 May 1762, quoted in Hancock, p. 195 n.

"admitted at a time": House of Commons, *Parliamentary Papers,* 1821, vol. 23, "Second Annual Report of Sir G[eorge] R. Collier, Bt.," in "Further Papers Relating to the Suppression of the Slave Trade," p. 55.

half the island's . . . population: Hancock, p. 197 n.

26 *"trafic in human flesh":* Afzelius, p. 135.

"misfortunate *flycatcher":* Smeathman to Drury, 10 May 1773, UUB D26, Manuscripts and Music Department, Uppsala University Library, Uppsala, Sweden.

"make them swallow": Smeathman journal, 10 July 1773, in Fyfe 3, pp. 76–77.

27 *of some £500,000:* Hancock, p. 385.

"and Ready Conversation": Alexander Carlyle, quoted in Hancock, p. 69.

28 *"quarter of the world":* Newton to Mary Newton, 10 April 1753, in Newton 3, p. 412.

"our white people": Newton 2, p. 80.

"and Florence [olive] Oil": quoted in Martin, p. 132.

"myself too long was": Newton 2, pp. 64–65.

29 *"of the Lord to me":* Newton 1, pp. 102–103.

2. ATLANTIC WANDERER

31 *"we kept as slaves":* Equiano, pp. 32–41.

"young people in it": Equiano, pp. 46–47.

"ran off with us": Equiano, p. 47.

nearly half . . . died on the way: Thomas, p. 386.

the Ogden: Carretta 1, p. 100.

32 *9.6 million survived:* Eltis, Tables I and III. His estimates are 11,062,000 departures and 9,599,000 arrivals. This is for the transatlantic slave trade only. European or American ships also took slaves from Africa to other destinations, such as Mauritius, Réunion, and the various islands off Africa's Atlantic coast. These numbers are close to estimates made by other scholars in recent decades, but the compilation of all available Atlantic slave trade shipping records in the Eltis et al. CD-ROM database has made such calculations far easier and more accurate. Over a longer period of time, a roughly equal number of people were transported as slaves from the east coast of Africa to the Islamic world.

"horror almost inconceivable": Equiano, p. 58.

"done a brute": Equiano, pp. 59, 57.

33 *"what to think":* Equiano, p. 60.
"all in motion": Ross-Lewin, p. 16.
biggest British slave population: Philip D. Morgan, p. 466.
34 *"parcel they like best":* Equiano, pp. 60–61.
"rice and fat pork": Equiano, p. 62.
35 *"to gratify my curiosity":* Equiano, p. 59.
36 *"good tempered Black Boy": Gazetteer and New Daily Advertiser,* 18 April 1769, quoted in Shyllon 1, p. 6.
"to the heart": Equiano, p. 98.
"a pot boil over": Equiano, p. 107.
37 *"nine-pence a pound":* Equiano, pp. 104, 110.
38 *"executed the day after":* George Scott to John Allen, 21 July 1776, quoted in Craton 1, p. 175.
"I have had . . .": Equiano, pp. 117, 137.
"till I had left them": Equiano, p. 122.
39 *"used me very ill":* Equiano, pp. 171, 167–168, 165.
"squeezed to pieces": Equiano, pp. 174–175.
"motives of curiosity": Equiano, p. 223.
40 *"swore he would sell me":* Equiano, pp. 210–212.

3. INTOXICATED WITH LIBERTY

41 *aquatic concert:* Lascelles, pp. 119–126; Hoare, pp. 143–147.
"3 or 4 different songs": Eliza Sharp Prowse, quoted in Lascelles, p. 123.
42 *"to be impracticable":* William Shield to Prince Hoare, 1816 n.d., in Hoare, Appendix VI, p. xiii.
"best voice in England": "Conversations with George III," Sharp Papers, quoted in Woods 2, p. 281.
43 *"A glass. Horsegear.":* Lascelles, pp. 121–122.
"separated from the Stock": Granville Sharp, *Letter Book, 1768–1773,* p. 195 and p. 93, quoted in Walvin 3, p. 117.
"where I was going": Hoare, p. 33 n.
"ready to die": Quoted in Shyllon 1, p. 19.
"becoming totally blind": Granville Sharp, *Letter Book, 1768–1773,* p. 195 and p. 93, quoted in Walvin 3, p. 117.
"sold as a Slave": quoted in Shyllon 1, p. 20.
44 *"these are my witnesses":* Clarkson 1, vol. 1, p. 70.
"to touch him": quoted in Shyllon 1, p. 21.
"law could give him": quoted in Hoare, p. 36.
45 *"in an unjust War": Remarks on the opinions of some of the most celebrated writers on Crown Law, respecting the due distinction between manslaughter and murder* (London, 1773), pp. 67–70, quoted in Staughton Lynd, *Intellectual Origins of American Radicalism* (New York: Pantheon, 1968), pp. 112–113.
46 *"in their action":* quoted in Shyllon 1, p. 30.

simply were no statutes: Drescher 9, p. 87.

"no man but the Black": *Times,* 11 and 12 February 1794.

47 *"begin to expect Wages":* Sir John Fielding, *Extracts from Such of the Penal Laws, as Particularly Relate to the Peace and Good Order of this Metropolis* (London, 1768), pp. 143–145, quoted in Equiano, p. 268, n. 281.

"her needle tolerably": *Public Advertiser,* 28 November 1769, quoted in Hoare, p. 49.

the American Revolution: Christopher L. Brown's forthcoming study of British abolitionism speculates how the movement against the slave trade and slavery might have unfolded if the American Revolution had never occurred and the Southern and West Indian slave societies had remained part of the same empire.

"my fellow-subjects": quoted in Lascelles, p. 40.

48 *"worth the expense":* James Sharp to Granville Sharp, 5 October 1775, quoted in Hoare, pp. 126–127.

The man whose flight: The most thorough treatment of the Somerset case is in Shyllon 1, pp. 77–176. See also Cotter, Paley, and Davis 2, p. 472 ff.

"Mr. Charles Stewart": quoted in Hoare, p. 70.

49 *"thank God!":* quoted in Hoare, p. 77 n.

50 *"obey my commands":* quoted in Fryer, p. 123.

"thro' the crowd": Philip C. Yorke, ed., *The Diary of John Baker: Barrister of the Middle Temple, Soliciter-General of the Leeward Islands* (London: Hutchinson, 1931), p. 234 (14 May 1772).

"contest with Lord Mansfield": Quoted in Hoare, p. 91.

"a foreign country": Peter Hutchinson, *The Diary and Letters of His Excellency Thomas Hutchinson Esq.* (Boston, 1886), vol. 2, p. 277.

51 *"a single negro":* J. Bigelow, ed., *The Works of Benjamin Franklin* (New York, 1887), vol. 4, p. 507, quoted in Walvin 5, p. 41.

"arm within the other": Peter Hutchinson, *The Diary and Letters of His Excellency Thomas Hutchinson Esq.* (Boston, 1886), vol. 2, p. 276.

"and the whole family": a Jamaican planter, quoted in Peter Hutchinson, *The Diary and Letters of His Excellency Thomas Hutchinson Esq.* (Boston, 1886), vol. 2, p. 276.

"Dido Elizabeth her freedom": quoted in Shyllon 1, p. 169.

"for Blacks or Dogs": Matthew Dyer in the *London Advertiser,* 1756, quoted in Shyllon 1, p. 9.

"men's sable countenances": *London Chronicle,* 22 June 1772, quoted in Shyllon 1, p. 110.

"they will be free": *Virginia Gazette,* 30 September 1773, quoted in Scott, p. 118.

52 *"parted by consent":* Equiano, p. 179.

"might not know me": Equiano, p. 180.

"unhappy man his liberty": Equiano, pp. 180–181.

"hands of his tyrants": Equiano, p. 181.

53 *"return to England":* Equiano, p. 181.

4. KING SUGAR

54 *"stirs the Universe":* G.-T. Raynal, *Histoire philosophique et politique des établissements et du commerce des Européens dans les deux Indes* (new edition, Paris, 1820), vol. 7, p. 453, quoted in Duffy, p. 6.

"Port in the West Indies": quoted in Dava Sobel and William Andrewes, *The Illustrated Longitude* (New York: Walker, 1998), p. 67.

importing 100,000 hogsheads: Walvin 1, p. 23.

value of British imports: Thomas, p. 481.

55 *imports from tiny Grenada:* Williams 1, p. 114.

60 percent of all slaves: Finkelman and Miller, vol. 2, p. 723. It was less than 50 percent, however, over the entire span of the Atlantic slave trade.

"sweet jellies": Nugent, p. 57 (6 February 1802).

56 *"tobacco was lighted":* Anon., *A Short Journey in the West Indies* (London, 1790), vol. 2, pp. 26–34, quoted in Brathwaite, pp. 117–118.

57 *"in a high degree":* Stephen 1, pp. 116–117.

58 *"I ever saw":* Stephen 1, p. 273.

"loved them, in return": Stephen 1, p. 305.

"discovery of the truth": Stephen 1, pp. 317, 321–322.

59 *"England no more":* Stephen 1, pp. 328, 330.

"attachment towards me?": Stephen 1, pp. 389–390, 393.

"given to the other": Stephen 1, p. 409.

60 *"appeared . . . pretty strong":* Stephen 2, vol. 2, pp. xix, xviii.

felt the same way: see, for instance, Dickson, p. 20.

61 *"depicted in her countenance":* Stephen 2, vol. 2, pp. xx, xxii.

"giving false evidence": Barbados Mercury, 20 December 1783.

"roasted to death": Stephen 2, vol. 2, pp. xxvi–xxvii.

62 *276 men, women, and children:* Bennett, p. 11.

63 *"hang'd himself":* Bennett, p. 49.

one third of Africans died: Craton 2, p. 94.

"in the night time": James Grainger, *An Essay on the More Common West Indian Diseases, and the Remedies which that Country Itself Produces. To which are added some hints on the management, &c. of Negroes.* In Bewell, p. 288.

64 *"poor sufferer's life!":* Nugent, pp. 62–63 (24 February 1802).

footnote: Senhouse Papers. Joseph Senhouse Memoirs (Cumberland County Record Office), vol. 3, f. 60, quoted in Sheridan, p. 189.

"puerile work field": Roughley, p. 104.

"improper to mention": quoted in Bennett, p. 22.

"return of runaway slaves": quoted in Bennett, p. 4.

65 *"over their shoulders":* Stephen 2, vol. 1, pp. 48–49.

"Any Wicked Designe": quoted in Bennett, p. 29.

"White people there to the Sword": General Report, Assembly Minutes, 3 January 1737, quoted in Gaspar, p. 4.

"the Distill house": quoted in Bennett, pp. 56–57.

66 *three inches shorter:* Finkelman and Miller, vol. 2, p. 613.
majority . . . were women: Philip D. Morgan, p. 472; Ward, p. 431; Craton 2, pp. 208–209.
67 *half . . . never bore a child:* Philip D. Morgan, p. 469.
3 percent a year: Ward, p. 431.
"fill up their places": Newton 2, p. 112.
68 *"as they are at present":* Secker to Drummond, 3 March 1760, quoted in Bennett, p. 89.

5. A TALE OF TWO SHIPS

70 *"a little world":* Equiano, p. 72.
71 *"creditable way of life":* Newton 2, p. xii.
"usually very profitable": Newton 1, p. 114.
"than that of breathing": Newton 1, p. 115.
73 *"pursuing a fox":* Arthur Young, *Enquiry into the State of the Public Mind Amongst the Lower Classes* (London, 1798), pp. 22–23, quoted in Ford Brown, p. 33.
"even of transcribing them": A Biographical Dictionary of the Living Authors of Great Britain and Ireland (London, 1816), p. 253, quoted in Ford Brown, pp. 32–33.
the raucous country: Roy Porter, p. 171.
74 *"this world of ours":* quoted in Roy Porter, p. 171.
"a purge or a vomit?": quoted in Andrew, p. 46.
"strangers in the Gallery": Morning Post, 12 June 1779, quoted in "The Reporting and Publishing of the House of Commons' Debates, 1771–1834" by A. Aspinall, in Richard Pares and A.J.P. Taylor, eds., *Essays Presented to Sir Lewis Namier* (London: Macmillan, 1956), p. 233.
"and to smell too": Henry Fielding, *An Inquiry into the Causes of the Late Increase of Robbers* (London, 1751), in Briggs, p. 307.
"they proceed to drink on": [Thomas Wilson], *Distilled Spiritous Liquors the Bane of the Nation* (London, 1736), in Briggs, p. 307.
75 *sometimes showed up drunk:* Furneaux, p. 56.
"to invade private life": Lord David Cecil, *Lord Melbourne* (London: Constable, 1954), p. 168, quoted in Furneaux, p. 42.
"visits till towards daybreak": Newton 1, p. 113.
"officiating myself": Newton 1, p. 98.
76 *In December 1772:* Earlier writers have not tried to date its composition, but Steve Turner, p. 79, has effectively done so.
1,100 recordings: Steve Turner, p. 177.
had the courage: In a passing reference to Newton in an earlier book, I myself was guilty of this oversimplification.
reported the Associated Press: Lawrence Knutson, "Washington Yesterday: Poetry Charts the Course of Slavery Across 150 Years," 2 December 2002.

77 *"set his human cargo free":* Kathleen Norris, *Amazing Grace: A Vocabulary of Faith* (New York: Penguin Putnam, 1998), p. 97, quoted in Phipps, p. 206.
"Our *national sin":* Newton 4, vol. 9, p. 141.
committee of six: There was also a larger, more formal, less activist twenty-three-person Quaker committee to consider the issue of slavery.
79 *"on board an English slave ship":* quoted in Hoare, p. 236.
80 *"Perils . . . of the Seas":* in Donnan, vol. 2, p. 624.
"the embrace of death": Hoare, p. 238.
"and was saved": Sharp to the Lords Commissioners of the Admiralty, 2 July 1783, in Hoare, p. 243.
81 *"had been cast overboard":* Sharp to the Lords Commissioners of the Admiralty, 2 July 1783, in Hoare, p. 244.
"the Blacks were property": quoted in Hoare, p. 240.
"as if horses were killed": Court minutes, 21 May 1783, quoted in Hoare, p. 237 n.
"to have been no necessity": quoted in Shyllon 1, p. 191.

6. A MORAL STEAM ENGINE

85 *"a very good thing":* Thomas Grosvenor in the House of Commons, 18 April 1791, *PH,* vol. 29, col. 281.
"chains, bolts, and shackles": Newton 1, p. 114.
86 *"their cruel tyrants":* J. Philmore [pseud.], *Two Dialogues on the Man-Trade* (London, 1760), p. 54, quoted in Davis 6, p. 594. Also see Davis 6, p. 585 ff., on Wallace.
"anonymous tract writer": [Maurice Morgann], *A Plan for the Abolition of Slavery in the West Indies* (London, 1772). Morgann and a number of other overlooked antislavery figures of this era are described at length in Christopher L. Brown.
"negroes in the West-Indies": Boswell's Life of Johnson (Oxford: Clarendon Press, 1934–64), vol. 3, p. 200, quoted in Fryer, p. 69.
"Bricks without Straw": John Pinney, *Letter Book,* 1764, quoted in Fryer, p. 14.
"the masters and the slaves": Politics, Book I, quoted in Thomas, p. 28.
87 *"make it perpetuall":* Adam Smith, *Lectures on Jurisprudence,* ed. R. L. Meek, D. D. Raphael, and P. G. Stein (Oxford: Clarendon Press, 1978), p. 187.
name a vessel after him: Thomas, p. 465.
"cultivated without Negroes": quoted in Alan Gallay, "The Great Sellout: George Whitefield on Slavery," p. 25, in *Looking South: Chapters in the Story of an American Region,* ed. Winfred B. Moore, Jr., and Joseph F. Tripp (New York: Greenwood Press, 1989).
directly or indirectly: Correspondence between Peckard and Sharp survives from later years, but not, so far as I have been able to find, from the 1780s.
"most barbarous and cruel traffick": quoted in Clarkson 2, p. 154.

88 *"deprived him of his life":* Catherine Clarkson to Shewell, 31 March 1836, quoted in Wilson 1, p. 6.

"so great a cause": Clarkson 1, vol. 1, pp. 208–209, 214–215.

89 *"calamities to their end":* Clarkson 1, vol. 1, p. 210.

90 *"Friend, Exemplar, Saint":* Coleridge to Stuart, 18 February 1809, quoted in Wilson 1, p. 140.

"ever I was with Clarkson": Austen to Cassandra Austen, 24 January 1813. R. W. Chapman, ed., *Jane Austen's Letters to Her Sister Cassandra and Others* (London: Oxford University Press, 1969), p. 292.

"stout and earnest persons": "Self-Reliance," in Brooks Atkinson, ed., *The Complete Essays and Other Writings of Ralph Waldo Emerson* (New York: Random House, 1940), p. 154.

"person should interfere": Clarkson 1, vol. 1, pp. 210–211.

"think and act with me": Clarkson 1, vol. 1, p. 212.

91 *"hitherto known nothing!":* Clarkson 1, vol. 1, p. 215.

"meet with in London": Clarkson 2, p. 127 n.

92 *"in the medical line":* Clarkson 2, pp. 70 n., 72 n., 125 n.

"their different plantations": Capt. Edward Thompson, *A Seaman's Letters* (London, 1756), vol. 2, p. 24, quoted in Kemp, p. 144.

"no man here is without one": Nugent, p. 29 (1 October 1801).

Thistlewood: see Hall.

93 *"sentiment for liberty": On the Treatment and Conversion of African Slaves* (London: James Phillips, 1784), pp. 176–177, in Craton, Walvin, and Wright, p. 245.

"almost overpowered with joy": Clarkson 1, vol. 1, p. 223.

showered him with curses: Shyllon 2, pp. 3–13.

"kindling within me": Clarkson 1, vol. 1, p. 238.

94 *"distribution of my books":* Clarkson 1, vol. 1, pp. 239–241.

"seemed to be fast asleep": Clarkson 1, vol. 1, pp. 242, 247.

Scholarly studies today: see, for instance, Behrendt 1, p. 55, who finds Liverpool crew mortality above 20 percent in every year from 1784 through 1787.

"though many go in": quoted in Furneaux, p. 62.

95 *"wish of making of them":* Clarkson 1, vol. 1, p. 245.

"Trade now instituted": William Dillwyn, 19 May 1787, quoted in Anstey, p. 231. Either Dillwyn had other business for several days or committee members gathered informally before their first recorded meeting.

96 *"impolitick and unjust":* Minutes, 22 May 1787.

7. THE FIRST EMANCIPATION

99 *"emancipating our slaves":* quoted in Quarles 1, p. 20.

"cannot be hit upon": Washington to R. H. Lee, 26 December 1775, quoted in Quarles 1, p. 20 n.

99 *"the use of a Horse":* Lowndes to James Simpson, 20 May 1780, quoted in Quarles 1, p. 119.
"dinner for her": St. George Tucker to Fanny Tucker, 11 July 1781, quoted in Quarles 1, p. 119.
100 *"an agreeable sale":* Laurens to Richard Oswald & Co., 29 June 1756, in Donnan, vol. 4, pp. 354–355.
"advice and assistance": Laurens to Oswald, 24 May 1768, in Donnan, vol. 4, pp. 422–423.
101 *"pleased to accept":* Laurens to Livingston, n.d., quoted in Wilson 3, p. 49.
"dine with Dr. Franklin": John Adams, *The Works of John Adams, Second President of the United States,* ed. Charles Francis Adams (Boston: Little, Brown, 1850–1856), vol. 3, p. 335, quoted in Wilson 3, p. 48.
"your securing them": Washington to Parker, 28 April 1783, in Washington, vol. 26, p. 364.
102 *"before the Door":* Smith typescript, p. 585.
"kept with all Colours": Smith typescript, p. 586.
103 *"Repast under a Tent":* Smith typescript, p. 587.
"people of any complection": Carleton to Washington, 12 May 1783, quoted in Wilson 3, p. 54.
"restored to them": Washington to Harrison, 6 May 1783, in Washington, vol. 26, p. 401.
104 *"got safe over":* King, pp. 355–356.
"departed from our eyes": King, p. 356.
"loyal subjects suffer": Thomas Jones, *History of New York During the Revolutionary War and of the Leading Events in the Other Colonies at That Period,* ed. Edward Floyd De Lancey (New York: Arno Press, 1968, reprint), vol. 2, pp. 84–85, quoted in Wilson 3, p. 65.
105 *"left him 4 years ago": Inspection Roll of Negroes Book, No. 1, New York City, 23 Apr–13 Sep 1783,* Miscellaneous Papers of the Continental Congress, 1774–89, National Archives. Quoted in Ball, p. 240.
"nearly worn out": quoted in Quarles 1, p. 172.
"I surely be mad": quoted in Wilson 3, p. 62.

8. "I QUESTIONED WHETHER . . . GET OUT ALIVE"

106 *"commonplace in 1830":* Tilly, p. 142.
"Humanity and Freedom": Minutes, 7 June 1787.
109 *"time to enter":* n.s., quoted in Roy Porter, p. 165.
"bedside of the dying": Georg Christoph Lichtenberg, n.s., quoted in Roy Porter, p. 183.
110 *"uplifted towards Heaven":* quoted in Lascelles, p. 71.
"property of the planters": Clarkson 1, vol. 1, p. 286.
112 *"tasted in my Life":* Clarkson, journal, 26 June 1787.

"get out of it alive": Clarkson 1, vol. 1, pp. 293–294.

113 *"nearer to its end":* Clarkson 1, vol. 1, p. 319.

"scarred and mutilated back": Clarkson 1, vol. 1, pp. 298–300.

114 *"beginning to the end":* Clarkson 1, vol. 1, pp. 311–312, 325–326.

"an agitated state": Clarkson 1, vol. 1, pp. 323–324, 345–346.

115 *"in the enemy's camp":* Clarkson 1, vol. 1, pp. 338, 343, 344.

"remainder of the day": Clarkson 1, vol. 1, p. 353.

"of African productions": Clarkson 1, vol. 1, pp. 303, 425.

116 *"and go with us":* Clarkson 1, vol. 1, pp. 354, 357–358.

"beast of prey": Clarkson 1, vol. 1, pp. 428, 364.

"temper and moderation": Hoare to Clarkson, 25 July 1787, in Minutes, 7 August 1787.

117 *"had become of each":* Clarkson 1, vol. 1, pp. 416, 412 n.

eighty-one slave ships: Bean, p. 269.

more than 300,000 Africans: Trepp, p. 265.

"with an African's blood": Ramsay Muir, *A History of Liverpool* (London: Williams & Norgate, 1907), p. 204, quoted in Trepp, p. 265 n.

118 *"pervade the whole town":* quoted in Trepp, p. 266.

an angry letter: Times, 22 November 1787.

"brutalize their nature": Clarkson 1, vol. 1, pp. 386, 395–396.

"lower class of seamen": Currie to Wilberforce, 31 December 1787, quoted in Hunt, p. 179.

119 *"when I awoke":* Clarkson 1, vol. 1, p. 408.

"imprecations and abuse": Clarkson 1, vol. 1, pp. 388, 409–410.

"caution and prudence": Barton to Roscoe, 15 August 1787, quoted in Sanderson 1, p. 207.

some £200,000 worth: Hunt, p. 89.

120 *"get to my place":* Clarkson 1, vol. 1, pp. 417–418.

121 *"town of the uprooted":* Drescher 1, p. 72. He makes a strong case for the "city of strangers" argument.

"forty or fifty of them": Clarkson 1, vol. 1, p. 418.

9. AM I NOT A MAN AND A BROTHER?

122 *"men in the kingdom":* Sir William Jones, quoted in Pat Rogers, *The Samuel Johnson Encyclopedia* (Westport, CT: Greenwood Press, 1996), p. 222.

"standing on one leg": Henry Beste, *Personal and Literary Memorials* (London: H. Colburn, 1829), p. 62, quoted in Charles N. Fifer, ed., *The Correspondence of James Boswell with Certain Members of the Club* (New York: McGraw-Hill, 1976), p. lxxv.

"made a deep impression": Clarkson 1, vol. 1, p. 220.

123 *"all soul and no body":* Mary Bird, quoted in Furneaux, p. 33.

"natural eloquence in England": quoted in Ford Brown, p. 3.

123 *"may be occupied by another":* quoted in Furneaux, p. 72.
think about slavery: Harford, p. 138.
"informing him of my errand": Clarkson 1, vol. 1, p. 251.
124 *"happy against their will":* Clarkson 1, vol. 1, pp. 252–253.
"could be found": Clarkson 1, vol. 1, p. 254.
"towards her husband": Wilberforce to——?, 3 November 1804, in R. and S. Wilberforce 2, vol. 1, p. 337.
"theatre most pernicious": 26 November 1787, in R. and S. Wilberforce 2, vol. 1, p. 50.
"greatest of all causes": R. and S. Wilberforce 1, vol. 4, p. 126.
125 *"by helping him":* quoted in Ellen Gibson Wilson, "The Great Yorkshire Election," unpublished speech to the Friends of the Wisbech Museum, 30 September 1995, p. 6.
a mere seventy-six pounds: Wilson 1, p. 193, n. 8.
"shrimp became a whale": quoted in R. and S. Wilberforce 1, vol. 1, p. 54.
"wittiest man in England": quoted in R. and S. Wilberforce 1, vol. 4, p. 167.
"laughter of childhood": James Stephen, Jr., in *Edinburgh Review,* April 1838, quoted in Pollock, p. 185.
126 *"my God and Saviour":* quoted in R. and S. Wilberforce 1, vol. 1, p. 89.
fifty-six illegitimate children: Hibbert, p. 352 n.
127 *"heat and stench":* William Darton, *Little Truths better than great Fables; containing information for the instruction of children* (London: W. Darton, 1787), pp. 69–70, quoted in Oldfield 2, p. 46.
"kept almost constantly going": Clarkson 1, vol. 1, p. 459.
128 *"state of the Business":* Minutes, 19 March 1793, for example. This was one of several occasions on which a bulletin was sent to supporters.
the committee agreed: Minutes, 7 October 1788.
129 *"best written Pamphlet":* Franklin to Wedgwood, 15 May 1788, quoted in Honour, p. 62.
"pins for their hair": Clarkson 1, vol. 2, p. 192.
"inconstancy of the Ladies": quoted in Andrew, pp. 7, 149.
130 *"been struck upon it":* Woods to William Matthews, January 1788, quoted in Jennings, p. 43.
feel morally superior: See chap. 7 of Christopher L. Brown's forthcoming book on British abolition.
"throughout Great Britain": Manchester Mercury, 1 January 1788, quoted in Hunt, p. 79.
to place notices: See Hunt, p. 80, and Drescher 1, p. 70 ff.
131 *"my heart now shudders":* Newton 2, p. 98.
"traitor to the cause . . . patriots": Newton 2, pp. 103–104.
"I am a white man?": Newton 2, p. 107.
132 *"their irons together":* Falconbridge, pp. 27–28.
"a situation more dreadful": Falconbridge, pp. 20–21, 25.

133 *"caught fire": The Musical Tour of Mr. [Charles] Dibdin, in which—previous to his Embarcation for India—he finished his Career as a Public Character* (Sheffield: J. Gales, 1788), Letter LIV, 2 April 1788, p. 223.

"headlong into ruin": 10 July 1788, quoted in Hunt, p. 242.

134 *"laws permitted them":* "Candid Reflections" (1772), in James Walvin, *The Black Presence: A Documentary History of the Negro in England* (London, 1971), p. 68, quoted in Edwards and Walvin, p. 42.

"prolifick in their nature": Clarkson 3, in Bewell, p. 148.

135 *"head men of the ship":* Cugoano, pp. 16, 14, 15.

136 *"slaves should begin":* Cugoano, p. 98.

"pity and resentment": Cugoano, p. 62.

"is a Predominant Prejudice": Cugoano to Sharp [1791?], Cugoano, p. 196.

"information on the subject": quoted in Andrew, pp. 221, 220.

137 *"or to any cause": County Chronicle and Weekly Advertiser for Essex, Herts., Kent, Surrey, Middlesex, &c.,* 19 February 1788, quoted in Equiano, p. 238.

"with her sentiments": quoted in Andrew, p. 221.

"the context of religion": Midgley 1, p. 25.

"ferment in the public mind": Clarkson 1, vol. 1, p. 470.

between 60,000 and 100,000: Drescher 1, p. 82.

138 *approach 100 percent:* Drescher 1, p. 74. However, Oldfield 1, pp. 106–107, tabulates these petitions somewhat differently.

"sons of lowest labour": quoted in Drescher 1, p. 75.

"much may depend": [William Bell Crafton], *A Short Sketch of the Evidence Delivered Before a Committee of the House of Commons for the Abolition of the Slave Trade: To Which Is Added, A Recommendation of the Subject to the Serious Attention of People in General* (Tewkesbury: Dyde and Son, [1792]), n.p., quoted in Jennings, p. 68.

139 *"all the vital functions":* R. and S. Wilberforce 1, vol. 1, pp. 167–169.

140 *"but had been abused":* Joseph Woods, quoted in Jennings, p. 47.

"all the whites in Jamaica": Fuller to Lord Sydney, 25 June 1788, quoted in Carrington, p. 212.

"fit of philanthropy": quoted in Furneaux, p. 77.

"proofs of happiness": PH, vol. 27, cols. 581–582.

"in time Slaves themselves": letter to the editor, *Bonner and Middleton's Bristol Journal,* 1788 n.d., quoted in Dresser, p. 154.

141 *"runs against us":* Stephen Fuller, Letter Book I, 30 January 1788, Duke University Library, quoted in Sanderson 2, p. 59, and Drescher 1, p. 222 n. 77.

"the business themselves": Fuller to Lord Sydney, 29 January 1788, quoted in Furneaux, pp. 104–105.

142 *"Hypochondriac and Hysteric": Public Advertiser,* 27 March 1771, quoted in Rudé, p. 84.

"howling of a dog": John Willett Payne, quoted in Hibbert, p. 266.

10. A PLACE BEYOND THE SEAS

143 *at least five thousand:* Myers, p. 35, has the most careful modern estimate. There was no accurate census of blacks in England at this time. Almost all historians today feel that figures cited in the eighteenth century itself—which ranged up to forty thousand—greatly overstated the numbers.

144 *"livery are in rags":* [James Tobin], *Cursory Remarks upon the Reverend Mr. Ramsay's Essay* (London, 1785), p. 117, quoted in Braidwood, p. 31.

"Poverty, Want & Wretchedness": quoted in Braidwood, p. 30.

"my Own Country again": Peter Anderson, quoted in Wilson 3, p. 139.

"there is a committee": Sir James Stephen, p. 581.

145 *"happiest of my life":* Smeathman to Lettsom, 19 October 1782, quoted in Braidwood, p. 7.

"the riches of the East": Smeathman to John Hunter, 15 October 1785, quoted in Braidwood, p. 9.

"that of the west": Smeathman to Dr. Knowles, n.d., in Wadstrom, vol. 2, p. 197.

"plan for civilising Africa": Cumberland to Highman, 14 October 1783, quoted in Braidwood, p. 7.

"a bird and a bat": Smeathman to Lettsom, 7 February 1784, quoted in Braidwood, p. 38.

"African Plan": Smeathman to Cumberland, 17 April 1784, quoted in Wilson 3, p. 141.

"the cold fit": Smeathman to Lettsom, 16 July 1784, quoted in Braidwood, p. 11.

146 *"about the proposal":* Sharp to his brother, January 1788, in Hoare, p. 260.

"government of any kind": Sharp to Lettsom, 13 October 1788, in Hoare, p. 320.

one scholar observes: Anstey, p. 161 n.

147 *"own situation and affairs":* Sharp, p. v.

"the native inhabitants*":* Sharp memorandum of 1 August 1783, in Hoare, pp. 265–267.

"every Black in Distress": Public Advertiser, 5 January 1786, quoted in Braidwood, p. 63.

"derided but dry": Treasure, p. 233.

"worse than doing nothing": quoted in Mintz, pp. 248–249.

148 *one newspaper reported: Public Advertiser,* 6 January 1787.

"sent forth from the land": Acts of the Privy Council, XXVI (1596–1597), pp. 16, 20–21, quoted in Edwards and Walvin, p. 12.

"black persons and white": John Pugh, *Remarkable Occurrences in the Life of Jonas Hanway,* 2nd edition (London, 1788), p. 169, quoted in Hecht, p. 47.

"be thought best": quoted in Braidwood, p. 83.

149 *"any kind of grain":* Smeathman, *Substance of a Plan of a Settlement, to be made near Sierra Leone, on the Grain Coast of Africa, intended more particularly for the service and happy establishment of Blacks and People of colour to be shipped as freemen, under the direction of the Committee for relieving the*

Black poor, and under the protection of the British Government (London, 1786), in Asiegbu, p. 161.

"pay for their redemption": Smeathman to Dr. Knowles, n.d., in Wadstrom, vol. 2, p. 206.

"to deceive them": quoted in Braidwood, pp. 88–89.

"in about three days": Hoare, p. 268.

150 "Mohametans, Infidels &c": Sharp to Wilberforce, 1 March 1797, quoted in Braidwood, p. 15.

"gate-house, or watchtower": Sharp, p. 9.

151 *may have been true:* the conclusion reached by Norton, p. 419.

not willing to tolerate: A MS Volume, Entirely in Ramsay's Hand, Mainly Concerned with His Activities towards the Abolition of the Slave Trade (Phillips Ms. 17780, Rhodes House, Oxford), quoted in Shyllon 3, p. 450.

"to conduct this business": Thompson to Navy Commissioners, 21 March 1787, quoted in Braidwood, p. 152.

"regular in his information": Navy Commissioners to Treasury, 22 March 1787, quoted in Braidwood, p. 153.

11. "RAMSAY IS DEAD—I HAVE KILLED HIM"

152 *"at the same time"*: quoted in Hibbert, p. 291.

153 *"to be well served"*: Hamilton to Banks, quoted in Hibbert, p. 299.

154 *when the serfs . . . were freed:* Dale H. Porter, pp. 34–36.

"their capital to France": *Representations to the Committee for Trade by the Committee of Merchants Trading to Africa* (1788), in Harlow and Madden, p. 526.

"falling into our Hands": Richard Miles, quoted in Sanderson 2, p. 68.

"go to Games of Chance": quoted in Sanderson 2, p. 71.

"history of human depravity": Bryan Edwards, *A Speech Delivered at a Free Conference Between the Honourable the Council and Assembly of Jamaica . . . on the Subject of Mr. Wilberforce's Propositions in the House of Commons, Concerning the Slave Trade* (Kingston, Jamaica, 1789), quoted in Davis 2, p. 192.

155 *"embarrassed and frightened"*: Clarkson 1, vol. 2, p. 9.

"filled with love and gratitude": 7 February 1789, reprinted in *Public Advertiser,* 14 February 1789, and in Equiano, p. 347.

anywhere from 609 to 740: Eltis et al. database, where the ship's name is spelled *Brooks.*

156 *"upon all who saw it"*: Clarkson 1, vol. 2, p. 111.

"walls of our dining room": S. and H. Hoare, *Memoirs of the Hoare Family,* p. 17, quoted in Jennings, p. 54.

animals in Noah's Ark: Wood, p. 30.

"right to be the same": James Bruce to Grenville, 8 September 1789, quoted in Scott, pp. 192–193.

"any man I ever knew": Clarkson to Chapman, 3 October 1845, quoted in Wilson 3, p. 36.

157 *"a land of slavery":* Clarkson to Chapman, 3 October 1845, quoted in Quarles 1, p. 186.
"breakfasted—slave business": quoted in R. and S. Wilberforce, vol. 1, p. 202.
"but Mr. Arnold": Clarkson 1, vol. 2, p. 19.
158 *"accommodate us in the Sale":* Board of Trade, *Report of the Lords of the Committee . . .*, Part I, unpaginated.
"almost all conversations": Romilly to Dumont, 9 June 1789, in Romilly, vol. 1, p. 351.
"sung as a ballad": Clarkson 1, vol. 2, pp. 190–191.
160 *dispensed more than £10,000:* R. and S. Wilberforce 1, vol. 1, p. 345.
paid £4,400 to a single lobbyist: Ragatz 1, p. 271.
footnote: Stephen 2, vol. 2, p. 360.
"short-sighted politicians": "NO PLANTER" writing to *Gentleman's Magazine,* 23 April 1789, vol. 59, p. 334.
"obliged to hear him": T. Barnes, *Parliamentary Portraits* (London, 1816), p. 72, quoted in Pollock, p. 31.
"met with in Demosthenes": PH, vol. 28, col. 68.
161 *"with the British trader":* William Wilberforce 1, pp. 5, 12–13, 7.
"abolition of the Slave Trade": William Wilberforce 1, p. 28.
"parts of the House": PH, vol. 28, col. 54.
"if we did not": William Wilberforce 1, pp. 44–45.
162 *"deferred to another year":* Clarkson 1, vol. 2, p. 108.
footnote: "are previously strangled": [James Tobin], quoted in Joseph Wood, *Thoughts on the Slavery of the Negroes,* 2nd edition (London, 1785), p. 34.
slaves under his care: PH 28, col. 98, has a garbled and truncated version of Molyneux's speech, with Ramsay's name mistranscribed as "Frazer." Shyllon 2, pp. 102–104, quotes a much fuller account from the *Diary,* 22 May 1789.
"I know to be true": Public Advertiser, 5 February 1788, in Equiano, pp. 333–334.
"not to be a pig": 19 August 1788, quoted in Equiano, p. xv.
"our common nature": quoted in Clarkson 1, vol. 2, pp. 116–117.
"I have killed him": quoted in R. and S. Wilberforce 1, vol. 1, p. 235.

12. AN EIGHTEENTH-CENTURY BOOK TOUR

167 *"obliged and obedient Servant":* Clarkson to Jones, 9 July 1789, Cambridgeshire County Record Office, Vassa 132/B 1–17.
168 *"(not Gustavus Vassa)": Times,* 7 May 1789, quoted in Andrew, pp. 258–259.
"colour of a skin": Public Advertiser, 28 January 1788, in Equiano, pp. 331–332.
was quickly translated: Green, p. 368.
169 *"I could be so":* Equiano to Rev. G. Walker and Family, 27 February 1792, in Equiano, p. 358.
"moderate advance of price": quoted in Carretta 2, p. 132.
"Virtues of my Guests": quoted in John Alfred Langford, *A Century of Birming-*

ham Life: or a Chronicle of Local Events, from 1741 to 1841, vol. 1 (Birmingham: E. C. Osborne, 1868), pp. 440–441.

"assembled on the occasion": General Evening Post, 19–21 April 1792, quoted in Drescher 1, p. 190.

whom he may have met: Shyllon 3, p. 443, asserts this as fact, but gives no source.

170 *"and sell my 5th. Editions":* Equiano to Walker, 27 February 1792, in Equiano, p. 358.

"is at Edinburgh": Gazetteer and New Daily Advertiser, 30 May 1792, quoted in Equiano, p. 371, n. 27.

"Dunde[e], Perth & Aberdeen": Equiano to Hardy, 28 May 1792, in Equiano, p. 361.

"Narrative is to be had": Edinburgh Evening Courant, 26 May 1792, in Equiano, p. 361.

footnote: John Morgan, *A Complete History of Algiers,* vol. 1 (1728), preface; vol. 2 (1729), p. 5, quoted in "Politicians, Peers, and Publication by Subscription, 1700–1750" by W. A. Speck, in Isabel Rivers, ed., *Books and Their Readers in Eighteenth-Century England* (New York: St. Martin's Press, 1982), pp. 48–49.

172 *"What villany is this":* 24 February 1791, in Sollors, p. 282.

In Ireland: see Rodgers.

"repeal of the Slave-Act": Digges to O'Brien, 25 December 1791, in Equiano, p. 10.

Wedgwood promised to contact: Farrer, pp. 216–218.

173 *"thumb-screws, iron-muzzles . . . ":* Equiano, p. 234.

"treasured up in my memory": Equiano, p. 78.

"all things I saw": Equiano, p. 68.

175 *"front is a noble bay":* Sharp to Dr. J. Sharp, 31 October 1787, in Hoare, p. 313.

"tax on pride and indolence": Sharp, p. 67.

"fluxes and bilious complaints": Thompson to Admiralty, 23 July 1787, quoted in Braidwood, p. 187.

"reign here among us": Elliot to Sharp, 20 July 1787, in Hoare, pp. 320–321.

"away ever since": Weaver to Sharp, 23 April 1788, in Hoare, p. 321.

"beat the tents down": Reid to Sharp, September 1788, in Hoare, p. 322.

176 *"the same at Charing Cross":* Philip Beaver, *African Memoranda* (London, 1805), p. 305 n., quoted in Curtin, p. 127.

"the woods impenetrable": John Clarkson diary, 29 March 1792, in Ingham, p. 32.

"they were known before": Bowie to Anderson, 18 July 1788, quoted in Wilson 3, p. 164.

177 *"over their brethren":* 4 September 1788, in Hoare, p. 329.

"danger of eternal slavery*":* Sharp to the Worthy Inhabitants, 11 November 1789, in Hoare p. 345.

"whole coast of Africa": Sharp to Steele, 4 May 1789, in Hoare, p. 337.
"service of the Slave Trade": Sharp to Hopkins, 25 July 1789, in Hoare, p. 343.
178 *"for the night-watch":* Sharp to the worthy Passengers, 20 May 1788, in Hoare, Appendix XI, p. xxix.
179 *"you can imagine":* Coleman, pp. 67, 54, 53.
one occasion on record: House of Commons, *Parliamentary Papers,* 1821, vol. 23, "Second Annual Report of Sir G[eorge] R. Collier, Bt.," in "Further Papers Relating to the Suppression of the Slave Trade," p. 55.
"mouldy, rotten biscuits": Coleman, pp. 58, 68.
"an acre of land": Coleman, p. 93.
180 *"I did not inform him":* Coleman, p. 68.

13. THE BLOOD-SWEETENED BEVERAGE

181 *"anguish of his heart":* Clarkson journal, quoted in Wilson 1, pp. 55–56.
182 *"traffic in a night":* Clarkson to ——?, n.d., quoted in R. and S. Wilberforce 1, vol. 1, p. 229.
dispatched an agent: For some excerpts from his error-ridden report, see J. Philippe Garran, ed., *Rapport sur les Troubles de Saint-Domingue, Fait au nom de la Commission des Colonies, des Comités de Salut Public, de Législation et de la Marine* (Paris: Imprimerie Nationale, Year Five of the Republic), pp. 103–105.
"mild and placid man": Clarkson to Joseph Arnould, 20 August 1828, in Mackenzie, vol. 2, p. 304.
"as those in France": Clarkson to Arnould, 13 August 1828, in Mackenzie, vol. 2, pp. 248–249.
183 *"could scarcely speak":* Clarkson 1, vol. 2, p. 153.
"neighbour to be filled": Samuel Derrick, n.s., quoted in Martin, pp. 156–157.
184 *"contents to be distributed":* n.s., quoted in Bass, p. 290.
"Amidst the smoke of war": Bass, pp. 290–291.
"anybody else in the army": quoted in Bass, pp. 294, 9.
185 *"cows might be fed":* James Allanson Picton, *Memorials of Liverpool, historical and topographical, including a history of the dock estate.* (London: Longmans, Green, 1875), p. 230, quoted in Trepp, p. 266.
186 *"to the Citadel Hill":* Dyott, vol. 1, p. 51 (17 August 1788).
"dissipation and expense": quoted in Hibbert, p. 362.
"his Royal Highness": 3 April 1787.
187 *"best interests of society": PH,* vol. 35, col. 227.
"the rising of the curtain": [Joseph Knight], "Jordan, Dorothea or Dorothy, 1762–1816," in *Dictionary of National Biography on CD-ROM* (Oxford: Oxford University Press, 1997).
"state of humble happiness": PH, vol. 29, col. 1349.
188 *"is a mere hotel":* quoted in R. and S. Wilberforce 1, vol. 1, p. 255.

"he is to be found": Anne Clarkson to Phillips, 3 October 1791, quoted in Jennings, p. 66.

"the slave of slaves": Wilkinson to Robinson, 28 November 1790, quoted in Wilson 1, p. 61.

"inexpressible joy": Clarkson 1, vol. 2, p. 177.

189 *sent it to all of them:* It is not completely clear from the record just what this document or documents were. Clarkson's account of the compiling (Clarkson 1, vol. 2, pp. 207–208) implies that this was a single volume, on which William Dickson did most of the work. The committee's minutes in early 1791 repeatedly speak of Dickson working on this task, helped by Clarkson, but they also make clear there were at least two volumes printed in these months. The *Abridgment of the minutes of the evidence, taken before a committee of the whole House, to whom it was referred to consider of the slave-trade,* found in libraries today, was published in four volumes, totaling 648 pages, dated 1789 to 1791. It seems likely that Clarkson's description of the intensive editing session, which has made its way into a few history books, refers to the compilation of the last two volumes. For the far more widely distributed and reprinted *Abstract of the Evidence* of 1791, Clarkson drew on all four of these volumes, plus material from the Privy Council hearings. (Confusingly, however, both the minutes and other sources, such as Clarkson 1, vol. 2, p. 350, sometimes speak of the *Abridgment* when they apparently mean the *Abstract,* and vice versa.)

"respecting the Slave Trade": Memorial to Grenville, 5 April 1791, quoted in Craton 1, p. 225.

"fire arms and ammunition": Edwards 2, p. 91.

190 *"for no other consumption": PH,* vol. 29, cols. 279, 335, 343.

"stinking fish of Brook Watson": Plymley diary, Book 25, pp. 2–3 (28 January 1794), quoted in Braidwood, p. 247.

"commerce clinked its purse": quoted in Furneaux, p. 102.

"feelings of their hearts": Clarkson 1, vol. 2, p. 339.

"by any human Power": Clarkson to Mme. Lafayette, 17 June 1791, quoted in Wilson 1, p. 63.

191 *"affairs have been recorded":* Romilly to Mme. G——, 15 May 1792, in Romilly, vol. 2, p. 2.

"until Despotism is extinct": Morning Chronicle, 15 July 1791.

"Crown and Anchor last Thursday": Dundas to Wilberforce, 18 July 1791, quoted in R. and S. Wilberforce 1, vol. 1, pp. 343–344.

"I hope you will": quoted in Wilson 1, p. 71.

"might become known": Clarkson to Joseph Arnould, 15 August 1828, in Mackenzie, vol. 2, pp. 251, 253.

192 *"by so doing":* Plymley diary, 21–22 October 1791, quoted in Wilson 1, p. 69.

"should he be seen there": Plymley diary, 21–22 October 1791, quoted in Oldfield 1, p. 94 n. 55.

192 *footnote:* Anon., *No Rum!* . . . , p. 3.
193 *"abandoned the use of sugar":* Clarkson 1, vol. 2, pp. 349–350.
a careful modern scholar: Drescher 1, p. 79.
"off sugar on principle": Morning Chronicle, 23 March 1792.
"without sugar than drinks with": Lydia Hardy to Thomas Hardy, 2 April 1792, Public Record Office, Kew, PRO TS 24/12/1.
194 *"by the labour of* FREEMEN*": The Diary; or, Woodfall's Register,* 27 December 1791.
"the blood-sweetened beverage": "The British Slave," quoted in Sussman, p. 57.
"stroke with the cartwhip": To Everyone who uses Sugar (London, n.d.), quoted in Sussman, p. 57.
footnote: A Second Address to the People of Great Britain: Containing a New, and Most Powerful Argument to Abstain from the Use of West India Sugar (Rochester, 1792), p. 6, quoted in Ragatz 1, p. 263.
195 *"he read Fox's tract":* Dickson diary, 16 and 24 January 1792.
"totally abstaining from it": Strictures on an Address to the People of Great Britain on the Propriety of Abstaining from West India Sugar and Rum (London, 1792), p. 6, quoted in Sussman, p. 49.
"necessarily called on": Fox, p. 2.
196 *"banished it from the tea table":* "Humanus" in *Newcastle Courant,* 7 January 1792, quoted in Midgley 1, p. 37.
"all the wrongs they bear": A Poem on the African Slave Trade, quoted in Midgley 1, p. 36.
"prejudices which brutalize them": (Harmondsworth, U.K., 1975), p. 257, quoted in Sussman, p. 60.
"to an abundant harvest": Burgh to Wilberforce, 10 December 1791, quoted in Wilson 1, p. 68.
"night and day": Clarkson 1, vol. 2, p. 350.
197 *"free people of colour":* Governor's Council to Fuller, 5 November 1792, quoted in Mullin, p. 218.
"depriving slaves of their ears": [Society for Effecting the Abolition of the Slave Trade], *An Abstract* . . . , pp. vi–vii.
198 "let out the congealed blood": [Society for Effecting the Abolition of the Slave Trade], *An Abstract* . . . , p. 71.

14. PROMISED LAND

200 *"because they labour cheaper":* Benjamin Marston journal, 26 July 1784, quoted in Kirk-Green, p. 100.
"negro dances and frolicks": quoted in Wilson 3, p. 95.
"die upon the spot": King, pp. 359–360.
"with rocks and swamps": quoted in John Clarkson, p. 59 (31 October 1791).
"cause of his distressed countrymen": Thomas Clarkson, "Some account of the

new colony at Sierra Leona," *American Museum; or, Universal Magazine* 11 (April 1792), p. 230, quoted in Wilson 3, p. 178.

201 *"Which We have not Received":* Peters and Still to Parr, n.d., quoted in Wilson 3, p. 109.

"got clare of them all": Sharp to Beaufoy, 24 March 1791, quoted in Wilson 3, p. 112.

"deformity the Slave Trade": Falconbridge to Sharp, 18 April 1791, quoted in Wilson 3, p. 185.

202 *"useful subjects to his Majesty":* CO 217/63, fol. 63, in Fyfe 3, p. 119.

"Honesty, Sobriety, and Industry": handbill of 2 August 1791, in Wilson 3, p. 188.

"cultivation and encouragement": Orders and Regulations from the Directors of the Sierra Leone Company to the Superintendent and Council for the Settlement (1791), in Harlow and Madden, pp. 460–461.

"Nova Scotia to Sierra Leone": The Diary; or, Woodfall's Register, 2 December 1791.

203 *"the Slave-Trade ever received":* Clarkson to Mme. Lafayette, 17 June 1791, quoted in Wilson 1, p. 64.

204 *"make their own noses":* Plymley diary, Book 64, quoted in Wilson 2, p. 50.

"violent people": John Clarkson, p. 52 (25 October 1791).

"line of life in England": Clarkson to Thornton, 28 November 1791, in John Clarkson, pp. 81–82.

205 *"waving of hats and handkerchiefs":* John Clarkson, p. 160 (15 January 1792).

"such a storm before": King, p. 364.

"and very much bruised": John Clarkson, pp. 164–165 (18 February 1792).

206 *"all hopes of my recovery":* John Clarkson, p. 165 (22 February 1792).

"blessed time, under a sail": An Account of the Life of Mr. DAVID GEORGE, *from Sierra Leone in Africa; given by himself in a Conversation with Brother* RIPPON *of London, and Brother* PEARCE *of Birmingham* (London, 1793), in Carretta 3, p. 340.

"he vexed me extremely": John Clarkson, p. 115 (22 December 1791).

"Head of the People": quoted in Wilson 2, p. 93.

"so young a king before": Clarkson diary, n.d., in Ingham, p. 24.

207 *"sweets of free government":* 2 July 1792, in Ingham, p. 93.

"make [the settlers] miserable": J. Clarkson to T. Clarkson, 28 March 1792, quoted in Wilson 2, p. 90.

"prevails through the Colony": Coleman, p. 99 and 99 n.

208 *"you must have Rank":* T. Clarkson to J. Clarkson, January 1792, quoted in Wilson 2, pp. 79–80.

"to be his own mother": Sierra Leone Company 1794 Report, p. 108, quoted in Wilson 3, p. 242.

"I now know God and Christ": Macaulay journal, 5 and 26 July 1796, quoted in Wilson 3, p. 242.

"ran off into the woods": Clarkson diary, 27 March 1792, in Ingham, p. 26.

209 *"laid aside useless":* Clarkson diary, 1 April 1792, in Ingham, p. 36.
"how many died last night": Coleman, p. 102.
"not to know who I was": quoted in Wilson 3, p. 244.
"yet occurred among us": Coleman, pp. 110, 129–130.
210 *"in need of mutual assistance":* Clarkson journal, 21 December 1792, quoted in Wilson 2, p. 100.
"I ever had for him": Coleman, p. 110.
211 *"return to us again":* 28 November 1792, in Fyfe 2, pp. 30–31.
"have had in the Colony": Coleman, p. 117.
212 *"when they embarked":* Coleman, pp. 133–134.
"Blacks shew in Africa": Coleman, p. 135.

15. THE SWEETS OF LIBERTY

215 *"brilliant cavalcade is gone": City Press,* n.d. The description of the street is as it was in 1805. In Harvey, pp. 124–125.
216 *"affection of the brain":* Mrs. Hardcastle (Mary Scarlett Campbell), *Life of John, Lord Campbell, Lord High Chancellor of Great Britain* (London: J. Murray, 1881), vol. 1, p. 29, quoted in Harvey Robinson, p. 140.
"as a person of importance": quoted in Christopher Browne, p. 39.
217 *"seats of English liberty":* quoted in Roy Porter, pp. 170–171.
"small villages as well": Letters of a Russian Traveller, 1789–90, ed. Florence Jonas (New York, 1957), p. 329, quoted in McKendrick, Brewer, and Plumb, p. 80.
more than half . . . were literate: Judging exactly how literate people are at any time in history is a very approximate business, but a guess becomes easier after the Marriage Act of 1753, which required both bride and groom to sign the parish register, either by writing their names or making a mark. A study of a random sample of all English parishes in the years immediately after 1753 found that 40 percent of the women were able to sign their names, and slightly more than 60 percent of the men. This was, moreover, the first generation where an apparent majority of English people were literate; it is estimated that only 45 percent of men and 25 percent of women could read in 1714. See Laslett, p. 233, and Brewer, p. 167.
twenty printers and twelve booksellers: Brewer, pp. 137, 174.
218 *"a remedy for Warts":* quoted in Brewer, p. 174.
there were thirty-five: Andrew, p. ix.
"politicians and mechanics": quoted in Andrew, p. xi.
"will be thrown at him": quoted in Roy Porter, p. 182.
As the historian: see Colley 2, pp. 44, 56, 99, 179, 276.
220 *A French traveler:* [de la Coste], *Voyage Philosophique d'Angleterre fait en 1783 et 1784* (London, 1787), vol. 1, pp. 180–182.
221 *"Comparisons of different Situations":* Sir John Fielding, *Extracts from Such of*

the Laws, as Particularly Relate to the Peace and Good Order of this Metropolis (London, 1768), pp. 143–145, quoted in Equiano, p. 269 n.

"they would stand by me": Equiano, p. 93.

"a West India climate": Equiano, p. 108.

223 *"To keep him from her company":* quoted in Ennis, p. 166.

224 *five hundred violent brawls:* Rogers 2, p. 93.

"and some broken Ribbs": quoted in Rogers 1, p. 96.

"was very much beat": quoted in Rogers 1, pp. 97, 106.

225 *the town's mayor:* Public Record Office, Kew, PRO ADM 3681. Found guilty of illegal imprisonment, Pascal and several other officers were ordered to pay court costs and damages.

"some large drawers": Letter to unknown correspondent, n.d., quoted in Woods 1, p. 120.

"legality of pressing seamen": 20 May 1779, quoted in Hoare, p. 168.

"cryed out for mercy": Sharp to Oglethorpe, 18 June 1777, quoted in Woods 1, p. 122.

for her husband: Wilson 2, p. 53.

"Liberty really Slaves": R.M.S. Pasley, ed., *Private Sea Journals, 1778–1782* (London, 1931), quoted in Rogers 1, p. 85.

16. HIGH NOON IN PARLIAMENT

226 *"impossible to stem it":* Clarkson 1, vol. 2, pp. 352–353.

"psalm singing meeting": Jesse Foot, *A Defence of the Planters in the West Indies* (London, 1792), p. 72, quoted in Drescher 1, p. 213 n.

"passport out of hell": quoted in Baum, p. 11.

"crying with one voice": The Prelude, Book 10, line 213.

"progress of our cause": Dickson diary, 11 January 1792.

227 *"launched into eternity":* Dickson diary, 14 January 1792.

"must not be injured": Dickson, p. 173.

"between emancipation and abolition": Dickson diary, endpapers.

"by getting counter-petitions": Dickson diary, endpapers.

228 *"advises me to say nothing":* Dickson diary, 25 February 1792.

"this abominable trade": Newcastle Courant, 3 March 1792, quoted in Midgley 1, p. 24.

"this was their duty": Dickson diary, 6 March 1792.

229 *"but hearty otherwise":* Dickson diary, 25 February 1792.

"till next year": Wilberforce to Babington, March? 1792, quoted in R. and S. Wilberforce, vol. 1, p. 340.

"the Newspapers and otherwise": minutes of the organization, 19 January 1792, quoted in Ragatz 1, p. 268.

"Favourers of the Abolition": subcommittee minutes of 22 March 1792, quoted in Ragatz 1, p. 270.

229 *"paragraphs from this Committee":* subcommittee minutes of 22 March 1792, quoted in Ragatz 1, p. 270.

230 *"Interests of the Sugar Colonies":* subcommittee minutes of 4 April 1792, quoted in Ragatz 1, p. 271.

"particularly at Cambridge": subcommittee minutes of 1 March 1792, quoted in Ragatz 1, p. 269.

"plenty of pigs and poultry": The True State of the Question, Addressed to the Petitioners for the Abolition of the Slave Trade, by "A Plain Man" (London, 1792), quoted in Ragatz 1, p. 269.

"free use of animal food": Clutterbuck, p. 20.

leaving English ports each week: Behrendt 2, pp. 194, 199.

"anything ever known": quoted in Drescher 2, p. 117.

at least 390,000 names: Drescher 1, p. 82.

231 *some 250,000 people:* James Bradley, p. ix.

"their perpetual introduction": Diary, 12 April 1792, quoted in Drescher 1, p. 218 n. 55.

"can never be over rated": The Debate on a Motion, p. 15.

"no language impart": PH, vol. 29, col. 1065.

232 *a negligible 4½ percent: The Debate on a Motion,* pp. 81, 84, 87.

"short-hand men have furnished": Wilberforce to Gisborne, 10 April 1792, quoted in R. and S. Wilberforce 1, vol. 1, pp. 347–348.

233 *"rise to civilization":* Pitt, pp. 1, 24, 29–30. The speech is also in Williams 2, p. 14.

234 *"left alone with":* quoted in Rogers 1, p. 197.

235 *"free and happy":* confiscated broadsheet, Home Office Papers, in Hampton, p. 364.

"preparing to become so": London Corresponding Society, *Joint Address to the French National Convention, 27 September 1792,* quoted in Goodwin, p. 502.

"despotism & arbitrary Power": Elihu Robinson diary, 13 November 1792, quoted in Wilson 1, p. 79.

"tyranny of Equalization": 10 September 1792.

"connais à ses cheveux": quoted in Bass, p. 322.

236 *"savages of Paris":* 25 January 1795.

"from the above date": quoted in Bass, p. 328.

"aggression upon property": PH, vol. 30, col. 1442.

"journeys in the night": Clarkson 1, vol. 2, pp. 469–470.

237 *"also on the Decline":* Clarkson to Archdeacon Plymley, 27 August 1793, quoted in Wilson 2, p. 145.

238 *"off the next morning":* quoted in Wilson 1, p. 86.

"I sometimes fell": Clarkson 1, vol. 2, p. 469.

"Keep cool and say little": Thomas Cropper to James Cropper, 17 December 1792, quoted in Charlton, p. 57.

17. BLEAK DECADE

241 *"evil can be remedied":* De Lancey to Dundas, 13 June 1792, quoted in Black, p. 229.

modern scholars have found: Marianne Elliott, "French Subversion in Britain in the French Revolution," in Jones, p. 50.

"Abuse of Government": quoted in Thale, p. 64.

242 *"of the present time":* quoted in Mitchell, p. 58.

"to discover the disaffected": Leeds Mercury, 12 January 1793, quoted in Mitchell, p. 64.

"much deserves your pity": quoted in Black, p. 270.

243 *"same quantity of beer": Tom Paine's Jests: Being an Entirely New and Select Collection of Patriotic Bon Mots, Repartees &c on Political Subjects* (London, 1794), p. 35, quoted in Rogers 1, p. 213.

"seized the kingdom": Roscoe to Landsdowne, December 1792, quoted in Mitchell, p. 57.

"associates in London": Edwards 2, p. xvii.

"devastation and ruin": PH, vol. 31, col. 467.

"the Rights of Men": Clarkson 4, p. 3.

"liberty and equality": Wilberforce to Hey, quoted in R. and S. Wilberforce 1, vol. 2, p. 4.

244 *"Abolition of the Slave Trade":* Clarke to Wilberforce, n.d., quoted in R. and S. Wilberforce 1, vol. 2, p. 18.

footnote: quoted in Linebaugh and Rediker, p. 110.

"broad basis of the RIGHTS OF MAN": Hardy to Rev. Bryant, 8 March 1792, in Hardy, p. 15.

245 *"could lay hands on":* Joyce to Tooke, 12 May 1794, quoted in Graham, p. 608.

"no one was safe": Plymley diary, Book 29, quoted in Wilson 1, p. 87.

"abolition of negro slavery": T. Howell, *A Complete Collection of State Trials and Proceedings for High Treason and Other Crimes and Misdemeanors,* vol. 24, p. 614.

"our Negro Brethren": Proceedings of the Public Meeting, held at Sheffield, in the open air, On the Seventh of April, 1794 (Sheffield: Sheffield Constitutional Society, 1794), pp. 22–25, quoted in Fryer, pp. 211–212.

"expire in agonies": Reason Urged against Precedent in a Letter to the People of Derby (1793), quoted in Lasky, p. 79.

246 *"I have been shot at":* quoted in Furneaux, p. 136.

"constitution of this realm": quoted in Thale, p. 71.

"civil war or embroilment": quoted in R. and S. Wilberforce 1, vol. 2, pp. 114–115.

247 *"had lost his cows":* Thomas Wilkinson, quoted in Wilson 1, p. 89.

"whatever she learned": Henry Crabb Robinson, vol. 1, p. 19.

A vivacious woman: Wilson 1, pp. 92–93, vividly brings Catherine to life.

"their way of thinking": speaking to Tsar Alexander I of Russia, quoted in Wilson 1, p. 145.

248 "a prose translation": quoted in Wilson 1, p. 219 n. 43.

"his soul were saved": Thomas Allsop, *Letters, Conversations and Recollections of Samuel Taylor Coleridge* (1836), vol. 1, pp. 48–49, quoted in Wilson 1, p. 102. Wilson points out that the various attributions of this statement to Clarkson are incorrect.

"a degree of imprudence": Catherine Clarkson to Robinson, 2 May 1838, quoted in Wilson 2, p. 142.

249 *"tract on Maple Sugar":* Sharp to Dawes, 13 November 1800, in Hoare, p. 373.

"could only whisper": Sharp to Jemima Sharp, 27 February 1811, quoted in Walvin 1, p. 188.

250 *"bawling for hours":* (Oxford: Oxford University Press, 1995), pp. 20–21.

251 *"a company of ladies":* n.s., quoted in McCalman, p. 430.

"impulse of appetite": quoted in Furneaux, pp. 161–164.

252 *"disease in our society": Parliamentary Register,* 9 April 1799, quoted in Furneaux, p. 193.

"were in their places": Plymley diary, Book 43, quoted in Wilson 1, p. 95.

majority of his cabinet: see Rees.

253 *"sight of it alone":* George Stephen, p. 51.

"all their aggravations": Macaulay to Selina Mills, February 1797, quoted in Richard West, *Back to Africa: A History of Sierra Leone and Liberia* (New York: Holt, Rinehart and Winston, 1971), pp. 66–67.

"damning proof": quoted in Howse, p. 48.

254 *"weeks I was on board": Christian Observer,* June 1804, pp. 347–356. Macaulay disguised or changed a few names and dates, but the authenticity of the diary is vouched for by the editors of the magazine in his obituary, December 1839, p. 764. Further information about the voyage is contained in the Eltis et al. CD-ROM database, file 80291. After the stop at Barbados, the ship went on to sell its slaves at Kingston, Jamaica, with several more slaves dying along the way. Six of twenty-three crewmen died during the triangle voyage. Macaulay's memorable account of this journey was plagiarized, in large portions verbatim, in Reverend John Riland's *Memoirs of a West-India Planter Published from an Original Ms.* (London: Hamilton, Adams, 1827), whose preface acknowledges only unspecified "additions made by the Editor to the original papers."

more than 150 slave ships: Bean, p. 269; Anstey, p. 47; Behrendt 2, p. 194.

255 *"his hypocritical allies":* J. W. Bready, *England Before and After Wesley—the Evangelical Revival and Social Reform* (London, 1938), p. 341, quoted in Shyllon 1, p. 139.

"hear no more of": 1795 n.d., quoted in Davis 2, p. 429 n.

18. AT THE FOOT OF VESUVIUS

257 *"hearts of all of us":* Boukman Dutty, quoted in Fick, p. 93.
"houses of the town": Carteau, pp. 87–88.
"troop of cannibals": Parham, p. 28.

258 *slave owner himself:* It would be more fitting if the leader of history's greatest slave rebellion were a slave, and he is often described as such, but in fact he had been free for more than fifteen years. See Debien, Fouchard, and Menier, and the introduction by Pierre Pluchon to de Lacroix, p. 17.
Bayon de Libertat: Variant spellings include Libertas and Libertad, and, for his first name, Baillon.
"their bloody remains": Parham, p. 32.
"administered in five minutes": St. Foäche, *Instructions,* p. 119, excerpted in Debien, *Plantations et esclaves à Saint-Domingue,* no. 3 (Dakar, 1962), quoted in Fick, p. 37.

259 *"goods of the earth":* quoted in Geggus 1, p. 38.
"waiting man behind him": Rev. John Lindsay to Dr. William Robertson, 6 August 1776, quoted in Craton 1, p. 172.
"strength with numbers": De Wimpffen, p. 336.
"tree of Peace": Scott, pp. 2–3.
"printed in France": Parham, p. 34.

260 *"strangled him in mercy":* Edwards 2, pp. 83–84 n.
"coals and broken tiles": Parham, p. 60.
"wild beasts let loose": anonymous letter dated 31 December 1794, supplement (1794), p. 1167.

261 *St. Domingue's annual production:* Geggus 1, p. 7.
"the Eden of the Western world": quoted in Martin Ros, *Night of Fire: The Black Napoleon and the Battle for Haiti* (New York: Sarpedon, 1994), p. 55.
Some half million of them: The actual slave population of St. Domingue is hard to calculate. Official census reports placed it just under a half million. But given that many planters understated the number of their slaves to avoid taxes, some historians place the total as high as 700,000. Fick, p. 278, gives a good summary of various estimates.

262 *"The farce is played out":* Moreau de Saint-Méry, p. 134.
"the young and dissipated": Perkins, p. 5.
"sailed immediately for France": Hassal, pp. 25, 77, 18–19.
"merchants at a fair": Abbé Raynal, n.s., quoted in Korngold, p. 14.

263 *"divulgers of false news":* Scott, p. 209.
on the alert: Williamson to Dundas, 12 February 1792, quoted in Scott, p. 214.
"John Paine": Scott, p. 232.

264 *"they will rise":* quoted in Geggus 2, p. 277.
"Obedience to their Masters": Berkeley to Grenville, 18 November 1791. British Library, Add. Ms. 58906.

264 *"owners were against it":* quoted in Mullin, p. 222.
265 *"Secrecy to each other":* Thomas Barritt to Nathaniel Phillips, 8 December 1791, quoted in Taylor, p. 248.
267 *"world lay smouldering":* Perkins, p. 59.
268 *footnote:* Jefferson to Monroe, 14 July 1795, quoted in Garry Wills, *"Negro President": Jefferson and the Slave Power* (Boston: Houghton Mifflin, 2003), pp. 38–39.
"one year's purchase [i.e., rent]": Times, 19 May 1797, quoted in Ott, p. 76.
"a war for security": PH, vol. 32, col. 752.
"Liberty and Equality": Vaughan and Caldwell to Station Commanders, n.d. [1795], quoted in Claudius Fergus, "War, Revolution and Abolitionism, 1793–1806," in Cateau and Carrington, p. 180.
"a true loyal joy": Bartholemew James, quoted in Duffy, p. 67.
"joy and fidelity": Capt. John Ford, R.N., quoted in Heinl, p. 63.
269 *"there are countless etceteras":* Parham, pp. 145–146.
"small, frail, very ugly": Dantès Bellegarde, quoted in Heinl, p. 65.
"for the same cause": Tyson, p. 28.
270 *"while he galloped":* de Lacroix, pp. 243–245.
"over his subordinates": de Lacroix, pp. 244–245.
"a cowardly assassin": Parham, p. 31.
"naked as earthworms": quoted in Geggus 7, p. 37.
271 *"in proportion to you":* de Lacroix, p. 245.
"the honor of my country": Toussaint to Brigadier General John White, quoted in Korngold, pp. 144–145.
272 *"killed them off":* J. Fergusson, ed., *Notes and Recollections of a Professional Life, by the Late William Fergusson* (London, 1846), pp. 62–63, quoted in Duffy, p. 361.
"buried without one": Ross-Lewin, p. 33.
273 *"medicines and flannel shirts":* Ross-Lewin, p. 17.
a detailed journal: It was published for the first time only in 1985, in an excellent scholarly edition edited by Roger Norman Buckley, from which I quote here.
"extremely sulky . . . Obstinacy": Howard, p. 106.
"some trifling dispute": Howard, p. 119.
274 *"Unfortunate Men by bleeding":* Howard, pp. 39, 42, 83–84.
"the others desponding": Howard, pp. 49–51.
"own woods & Mountains": Howard, pp. 79–80.
"as the vessel passed": Edwards 1, vol. 4, p. 227.
275 *"four were Corporals":* Howard, p. 80.
purchased some 13,400 slaves: Buckley 1, p. 55.
276 *"coming across the ocean":* Buckley 1, pp. 54–55.
"the terms now offered": Sir Adam Williamson, quoted in Heinl, p. 69.
277 *"ignorant and negligent men":* John Moore, quoted in Buckley 1, p. 35.

"to furnish such Recruits": Governor Valentine Morris of St. Vincent, 11 February 1777, quoted in Ragatz 1, pp. 31–32.
carrying 19,284 soldiers: Duffy, p. 206.
one thousand soldiers died: Geggus 1, p. 362.
"becomes sour and fetid": Pinckard, vol. 2, pp. 155–156.
to Britain's ally, Russia: Duffy, p. 298.
278 *"may not perish":* quoted in Korngold, p. 143.
279 *"incumbrance in this Island":* Maitland to Liston, 29 August 1798, quoted in Duffy, p. 309.
over 60 percent: Geggus 1, p. 362.
"independent of exterior color": 12 December 1798, quoted in James, p. 226.

19. REDCOATS' GRAVEYARD

281 *"horrid system":* Stephen to Wilberforce, 24 June 1796, quoted in Pollock, p. 144.
"entirely melted away": Moore to Abercromby, 2 September 1796, in Beatrice Brownrigg, *The Life and Letters of Sir John Moore* (New York: D. Appleton, 1923), p. 66.
"kind treatment and good feeling": Major-General Sir J. F. Maurice, ed., *The Diary of Sir John Moore* (London: Edward Arnold, 1904), vol. 2, p. 224.
more than 3,000 deserted: Duffy, p. 333.
estimated as at least 19,000: Duffy, p. 334.
283 *"make all the Negroes free":* quoted in Craton 1, p. 218.
footnote: Portland to Balcarres, 3 March 1796, quoted in Campbell, p. 230.
284 *"perpetuated by years":* Walpole to Balcarres, 24 and 26 December 1795, quoted in Campbell, p. 234.
"decrease their numbers": Walpole to Balcarres, 24 December 1795, quoted in Campbell, p. 239.
"you have entered into": Balcarres to Walpole, 24 December 1795, quoted in Kup, p. 343.
285 *"facts to the world":* Walpole to Balcarres, 11 March 1796, quoted in Campbell, p. 237.
"more in affection than fear": Pinckard, vol. 1, pp. 229, 233.
"same home of captivity": Pinckard, vol. 2, pp. 217–218.
286 "maggots out of her sores": Pinckard, vol. 3, pp. 66, 72.
"for the use of the mess": Pinckard, vol. 3, p. 267.
and even cartoons: by, for example, Lieutenant Abraham James; see Buckley 3, p. 178.
"misery and hard labour": Rough Sketches of the Life of an Old Soldier (London: Longman, Rees, Orme, Brown, and Green, 1831), p. 20.
"no business on that Island": Maitland to the Earl of Lauderdale, 15 July 1796, quoted in Howard, p. xxxv.
287 *"follow her example": PH,* vol. 33, col. 1399.

20. "THESE GILDED AFRICANS"

288 *"able to reduce them":* Rainsford, p. 360.
he had learned war: Jean-Baptiste, pp. 83–84.
290 *"deviate from them":* Toussaint to the Directory, 28 October 1797, in Tyson, p. 43.
"formed his equipment": Rainsford, p. 252.
291 *"he confided to no one":* Pascal, in J. de Norvins, *Souvenirs d'un historien de Napoléon* (Paris, 1896), vol. 2, pp. 362–363, quoted in Tyson, pp. 74–75.
"first of the whites": J. de Norvins, *Souvenirs d'un historien de Napoléon* (Paris, 1896), vol. 2, pp. 362–363, quoted in Tyson p. 75. The letter has never been found.
"nothing more to wish": quoted in Heinl, pp. 96–97.
"prevent its Annihilation": Hobart to Nugent, n.d., quoted in Nugent, p. xx.
"corpses and dead horses": quoted in Heinl, pp. 97, 99, 100.
292 *"hiding in the thickets":* Moreau de Jonnès, vol. 2, pp. 129, 131, 134.
"they are deep and plentiful": quoted in Pluchon, p. 498.
"husband is not content": Hassal, pp. 7–8, 10.
293 *"taken away Toussaint":* 9 and 25 August 1802, quoted in James, pp. 345–346.
"St. Domingue is lost forever": quoted in Heinl, p. 107.
294 *"true dignity of character": Annual Register,* 1802, pp. 210 ff., quoted in Beckles 2, p. 874.
more than fifty thousand soldiers: Auguste and Auguste, p. 316.
296 *"from Britain's defeat":* Davis 5, p. 6.
"what must *it all lead to":* Nugent, p. 198 (4 March 1804).

21. A SIDE WIND

299 *"use of their weapons":* Henry Richard Lord Holland, *Memoirs of the Whig Party During My Time* (London: Longman, Brown, Green, and Longmans, 1852), vol. 1, p. 141.
"shocked than almost ever": quoted in R. and S. Wilberforce 1, vol. 2, p. 280.
300 *"we all lie begging":* quoted in Walker, p. 342.
more than 30 percent: Drescher 2, p. 19.
to the New World each year: Behrendt 2, p. 194.
301 *"and wholly presumptuous":* Stephen to Wilberforce, 20 September 1797, quoted in R. and S. Wilberforce 1, vol. 2, p. 257.
302 *"to his* prudence *alone":* Stephen 3, p. 165.
303 *"sidewind on the planters": PD,* Series 1, vol. 6, col. 919.
304 *footnote:* quoted in Bass, p. 390.
"tenderness and care": PD, Series 1, vol. 7, col. 228.
circulate a counter-petition: Drescher 4, pp. 141–144, gives a good summary of this usually overlooked episode.

305 *"traffick in human flesh": Felix Farley's Bristol Journal,* 22 November 1806, quoted in Drescher 5, p. 145.
"against the Slave Trade": PD, Series 1, vol. 8, cols. 718–719.
"the hearts of men": 12 February 1807, quoted in Furneaux, p. 251.
306 *"so infamous a trade": PD,* Series 1, vol. 9, cols. 60, 64.
"gentlemen on the road": Substance of the Debates, pp. 95–99. Doyle's speech was in Commons on 23 February 1807.
307 *"abolition upon our rulers":* vol. 10 (1807), pp. 205–206, quoted in Walvin 5, p. 122.
308 *"The Lottery, I think":* quoted in Gratus, p. 127.
"our national character": PD, Series 1, vol. 8, col. 977.
"any Legislature in the world": quoted in Davis 2, p. 449.

22. AM I NOT A WOMAN AND A SISTER?

310 *more than fifty thousand:* Jakobsson, pp. 171–172, summarizes different estimates, some of which range much higher.
"than his former owner": Fyfe 2, p. 18.
311 *"waiting for the post":* quoted in Martin, pp. 354, 357.
"the most abandoned of slaves": quoted in Gomer Williams, p. 519 n.
312 *"bound in wedlock's tie":* Peter Pindar, n.s., quoted in Tomalin, p. 248.
313 *"visible in every feature":* Catherine Majolier Alsop, quoted in Wilson 1, p. 121.
"Napoleon and Alexander": Coleridge to Southey, February 1808, quoted in Wilson 1, p. 118.
"entered a person's house": Clarkson to Macaulay, 19 November 1822, quoted in Wilson 1, p. 151.
314 *"of unstained reputation":* Wilberforce to King Henry, 27 November 1819, in R. and S. Wilberforce 2, vol. 1, pp. 389–391.
"a grateful peasantry": William Wilberforce 2, pp. 53–54.
"after the day's work": Wilberforce to Macaulay, 13 November 1823, quoted in R. and S. Wilberforce 1, vol. 5, p. 202.
"greatness of our country": Report of the Committee on the Woollen Trade (1806), quoted in Hammond, p. 213.
"bear its inconveniences": Practical View of the System of Christianity, p. 314, quoted in Hammond, pp. 231–232.
"along the public roads": quoted in R. and S. Wilberforce 1, vol. 5, p. 214.
315 *"than there was room for":* Lord Teignmouth, *Reminiscences of Many Years* (Edinburgh: David Douglas, 1878), p. 255.
316 *"which nobody answers":* Forster, pp. 143–144.
"Abolition of the Slave Trade": PD, Series 1, vol. 17, col. 678.
"appeared in it next day": Leslie Stephen, pp. 17–18.
317 *"see our Work going on":* Clarkson to Catherine Clarkson, 1814 n.d., quoted in Wilson 1, p. 126.

317 *"let loose against you":* Clarkson to Vansittart, 7 September 1814, quoted in Drescher 5, p. 162.

"more sick than the sea": quoted in Wilson 1, p. 125.

318 *"face of the earth":* Clarkson, *Account of Efforts,* pp. 18–19.

"as one of them": quoted in Wilson 1, p. 145.

319 *"with a White Female":* Codd to Leith, 25 April 1816, quoted in Craton 1, p. 372 n. 33.

"have them all freed": Daniel, in *The Report from a Select Committee of the House of Assembly appointed to inquire into the Origin, Causes, and Progress of the Late Insurrection* (Bridgetown, Barbados, 1818), p. 26, quoted in Beckles 1, p. 108.

"did in St Domingo": Robert, in *The Report from a Select Committee . . .* (Bridgetown, Barbados, 1818), pp. 29–31, quoted in Beckles 4, p. 172.

"justice on the guilty": Governor John Murray of Demerara, in the *Barbados Mercury and Bridgetown Gazette,* 14 May 1816, quoted in Beckles 1, p. 89.

320 *"Take force by force":* quoted in Brathwaite, p. 211.

"among the Slaves": John Beckles in the Barbados Assembly, 6 August 1816, quoted in Craton 1, p. 266.

"and cannot forgive": The Axe Laid to the Root, or a Fatal Blow to Oppressors, being an address to the Planters and Negroes of the Island of Jamaica, no. 1 [1817], col. 12, quoted in Fryer, p. 221.

"as soon as they please": quoted in Linebaugh and Rediker, p. 319.

"against the Maroons": The Axe Laid to the Root, or a Fatal Blow to Oppressors, being an address to the Planters and Negroes of the Island of Jamaica, no. 1 [1817], col. 12, quoted in Fryer, p. 225.

321 *"is familiar to me":* Davidson to Sarah Davidson, 7 May 1820, quoted in Fryer, p. 405.

322 *"misfortune to be connected":* William Wilberforce 2, p. 55.

"abolition of the Slave-trade": Clarkson 1, vol. 2, p. 586.

"encourage healthy propagation": Roughley, p. 77.

323 *"delighted to work":* Allen to Clarkson, n.d., quoted in Clarkson, *Account of Efforts,* p. 110.

324 *"members of the community":* Clarkson, *Speech Used at Forming of Committees, 1823–24,* quoted in Walvin 5, p. 151.

"leave off West India sugar": Diary of Travels, 2 October 1824.

325 *bold and simple majesty":* Heyrick 1, pp. 24, 20, 23.

"plead for the oppressed": Heyrick 2, p. 1.

"heroic and meritorious": Heyrick 1, pp. 31, 32.

"which impoverish . . . millions": Exposition of One Principal Cause of the National Distress, Particularly in Manufacturing Districts, With Some Suggestions for its Removal (London, 1817), p. 3; *Enquiry into the Consequences of the Present Depreciated Value of Human Labour. In Letters to Thos.*

Fowell Buxton, Esq., M.P. (London, 1819), n.p., both quoted in Corfield, p. 53.

"my plague or my darling": n.s., 1802 n.d., quoted in Corfield, p. 42.

"effectually for ourselves": Heyrick 1, pp. 4, 8, 16–17.

326 *"cup of adversity": No British Slavery; or, an Invitation to the People to Put a Speedy End to It* (London, 1824), p. 6, quoted in Corfield, p. 43.

"without limitation, without delay": Fifth Report of the Sheffield Female Anti-slavery Society (Sheffield, 1830), p. 11, and *Minute Book,* p. 46, quoted in Corfield, p. 45.

"words attached to it": [Mrs. Grundy], quoted in Heyrick 3, p. 164.

"final emancipation there": Clarkson to Townsend, 30 March 1825, Rhodes House Library, Oxford.

327 *embraced the revived sugar boycott:* Clarkson to Townsend, August 1825, Rylands English Ms. 741 (20), University of Manchester.

"finish the great work": Clarkson to Townsend, 3 August 1825, Rhodes House Library, Oxford.

"paid to their opinions": quoted in Wilson 1, p. 91.

"in their title": The resolution was passed on 8 April 1830. Corfield, p. 46.

"delineated in Scripture": Wilberforce to Babington, 31 January 1826, quoted in R. and S. Wilberforce 1, vol. 5, p. 264.

"should have kept standing": George Stephen to Anne Knight, 14 November 1834, Anne Knight Papers, Ms. Box W2/2/37, Friends House Library, London. Midgely 1, p. 44, mistakenly attributes this letter to George Thompson.

"for many months past": Heyrick to Townsend, 28 December 1826, quoted in Halbersleben, p. 183.

328 *"far advanced in pregnancy":* Smith to Burder, 21 August 1823, quoted in Craton 1, p. 269.

"vengeance of a merciful God": diary, 14 September 1817, quoted in da Costa, p. 153.

"taught to read": Smith to the LMS, 4 March 1817, quoted in da Costa, p. 137.

"with his dying wife": diary, 16 October 1822, quoted in Craton 1, p. 269.

329 *"with their station":* quoted in Craton 1, p. 246.

"been in this country": diary, 18 March 1818, quoted in da Costa, p. 146.

330 *"Our rights":* quoted in da Costa, p. 216.

"hung frightfully open": quoted in Northcott, p. 75.

331 *"West Indian slavery":* [Lord Brougham], preface to Thomas Clarkson, *The History of the Rise, Progress, and Accomplishment of the Abolition of the African Slave-Trade by the British Parliament* (London, 1839 edition), n.p., quoted in Northcott, p. 22.

"not live to see": Stephen 2, vol. 2, p. 413.

two million whip lashes: Davis 3, p. 351 n. 173.

332 *"things should still be":* quoted in Wilson 2, p. 183.

23. "COME, SHOUT O'ER THE GRAVE"

335 *"inaudible at equal distance":* George Stephen, pp. 121–122.

336 *"200 could not get in":* Agency Committee of the Antislavery Society, pp. 14, 12.

"lofty but useless resolutions": Gratus, p. 221.

"the slumber of the daddies": Knight to Abby Kelly, 17 August 1841, quoted in Tyrrell 2, p. 225.

337 *"lava bursts forth":* Wilberforce to Samuel Wilberforce, 31 October 1831, in A. M. Wilberforce, pp. 271–272.

338 *hear them preach:* see Mary Turner 1, pp. 84–85.

"only for a free one": Waddell, p. 68.

339 *"a memorable occasion":* Mary Turner 1, p. 84.

"inquire the home news": Waddell, p. 68.

"burn massa house": Waddell, p. 57.

340 *"shoot them like pigeons":* Bleby, pp. 111–112.

341 *"children shall be free":* John Clarke, *Memorials of Baptist Missionaries in Jamaica* (London, 1869), p. 103, quoted in Mullin, p. 257.

"streets of Montego Bay": quoted in Hart, p. 279.

"by Captain Burnett": Cotton to Belmore, 4 January 1832, quoted in Hart, p. 297.

died in the fighting: Hart, pp. 327–329.

342 *"free men in the struggle":* Bleby, pp. 119–120.

"distance out of the town": Bleby, pp. 25–27.

"this part of the world": quoted in Wright, p. 111.

343 *"than live in slavery":* Bleby, pp. 115–117.

paid £16, 10 shillings: Reid, p. 10.

"I'll have slavery down": Hinton, p. 139.

344 *"may take place":* Howick to Mulgrave, 7 July 1832, quoted in Wright, p. 120.

"possession of the negroes": 9 July 1832, quoted in Wright, p. 121.

"reading English newspapers": House of Commons, *Report from Select Committee . . . ,* pp. 196, 29–30.

345 *"was not healed":* Hinton, pp. 147–148.

346 *"before abolition occurs":* Stephen to Suffield, 18 January 1833, quoted in Davis 3, pp. 206–207.

"is almost run down": quoted in R. and S. Wilberforce 1, vol. 5, p. 368.

"in time & for Eternity": Wilberforce to Clarkson, 19 January 1833, quoted in Wilson 1, p. 165.

347 *"earthquake on this continent":* Charles Francis Adams, ed., *Memoirs of John Quincy Adams, Comprising Portions of His Diary from 1795 to 1848* (Philadelphia, 1877), vol. 8, p. 269, quoted in Fladeland 1, p. 208.

"*first made to the* slave": Heyrick 1, p. 22.

348 *"termination of their bondage": Times,* 23 September 1833, quoted in Turley, p. 41.

"soon he will lie": Catherine Hall, "William Knibb and the constitution of the new Black subject," in Daunton and Halpern, p. 317.

349 *"strange yet sacred joy":* Hinton, p. 257.

"almost equally wretched": Sharp to Henry Douglas, 21 December 1772, quoted in Fladeland 2, p. 6.

350 *children's board game:* Walvin 5, p. 175.

351 *"by faith and prayer":* Reginald Coupland, *The Empire in These Days: An Interpretation* (London: Macmillan, 1935), p. 264.

"vestige of oppression": Report of the Proceedings at Birmingham on the 1st and 2nd of August in commemoration of the Abolition of Negro Apprenticeship in the British Colonies (Birmingham, 1838), n.p., quoted in Turley, p. 43.

352 *full scholarly biography:* Wilson 1. From this and the two other books by Ellen Gibson Wilson listed in the Bibliography, much in this volume is drawn.

"earned their father's gold": quoted in Lascelles, p. 79.

353 *"at home and abroad":* quoted in Drescher 4, pp. 8, 12; McCalman, p. 145.

354 *"ever meet again":* in *Life of William Allen, with Selections from His Correspondence* (Philadelphia: Henry Longstreth, 1847), p. 517 (3 September 1841).

free labor or slaves: PD, 3rd Series, vol. 88, cols. 4–5, 13, 17.

"given to the same cause": quoted in Wilson 1, p. 189.

removed their hats: Illustrated London News, 10 October 1846, p. 228; Wilson 1, p. 191.

EPILOGUE: "TO FEEL A JUST INDIGNATION"

358 *"illustrious among all the days of the year":* speech at Canandaigua, New York, 3 August 1857, quoted in Mitch Kachun, "'Our Platform Is as Broad as Humanity': Transatlantic Freedom Movements and the Idea of Progress in Nineteenth-Century African American Thought and Activism," in *Slavery and Abolition* 24, no. 3 (December 2003), p. 10.

"I saw the monster die": Liberator, 6 August 1858, quoted in Quarles 2, p. 126.

"shop upon his estate": H. Breen, quoted in O. Nigel Bolland, "The Politics of Freedom in the British Caribbean," in McGlynn and Drescher, p. 123.

359 *"sorrows and sufferings":* Buxton to Mrs. Rawson, 6 October 1833, quoted in Williams 1, p. 192.

360 *"under another name":* William Morris, *A Dream of John Ball* (London: Longmans, Green, 1896), p. 31.

361 *in the same forts:* Patience Essah, "Slavery, Heritage and Tourism in Ghana," in Dann and Seaton, p. 44.

362 *was a merchant's home:* see Emmanuel de Roux, "Le Mythe de la maison des esclaves qui résiste à la réalité," in *Le Monde,* 27 December 1996; Philip Curtin, "Gorée and the Atlantic Slave Trade," H-NET List for African History, 31 July 1995; Carolyn J. Mooney, "Where History Meets Memory: A Debate about Slavery on Senegal's Gorée Island," *Chronicle of Higher*

Education, 23 May 1997; and James F. Searing, *West African Slavery and Atlantic Commerce: The Senegal River Valley, 1700–1860* (Cambridge: Cambridge University Press, 1993), pp. 1–2. The lack of any documentation that the "House of Slaves" was used as a transatlantic slave ship depot has not deterred dozens of journalists, myself some years ago included, from believing the vivid descriptions given by the building's charismatic curator.

362 *"embedded along the top":* Reader, p. 390.

"for five or six weeks": Dr. Collins, *Practical Rules for the Management and Medical Treatment of Negro Slaves in the Sugar Colonies* (London, 1803), p. 209, quoted in Stephen 2, vol. 2, p. 367.

"supine, idle, propensities": Roughley, pp. 94–95.

364 *"tears and blood":* Waddell, pp. 54–55.

366 *"known to be detested":* Sharp to Cartwright, 3 November 1787, in F. D. Cartwright, ed., *The Life and Correspondence of Major Cartwright* (London: Henry Colburn, 1826), vol. 1, p. 171.

"indignation against it": Clarkson 1, vol. 1, p. 321.

APPENDIX: WHERE WAS EQUIANO BORN?

369 *"named Essaka":* Equiano, p. 32.

Equiano's capture: Catherine Obianuju Acholonu, *The Igbo Roots of Olaudah Equiano: An Anthropological Research* (Owerri, Nigeria: Afa Publications, 1989).

"Elese, in Africa": Public Advertiser, 19 June 1788, in Equiano, p. 340.

"born in Carolina": Equiano, p. 261, n. 198.

370 *"verifiable and impressively accurate":* Carretta 1, p. 102.

"but that of Africa": Equiano, p. 5 and pp. 238–239 n.

"the sale of my Books": Equiano to Hardy, 28 May 1792, in Equiano, p. 361.

371 *"in the African mode":* Edward Long, *The History of Jamaica* (London, 1774), vol. 2, pp. 447–448, quoted in Craton 1, p. 127.

list African birthplaces: Carretta 4, p. 233.

372 *"by external evidence":* Carretta 1, pp. 99–100.

BIBLIOGRAPHY

THIS BOOK COULD NOT have been written without the great wave of new scholarship about slavery and abolition that began in the 1960s and continues unabated today. In terms of new information discovered, I cannot claim to have added to it significantly. My reliance on scholars in the field is still greater than it may appear, because even when I have drawn on a primary source, it often is one I would not have been aware of without the work of some sharp-eyed researcher long before me.

Of the dozens of writers who have devoted much of their lives to the study of slavery, the work of several was particularly helpful to me. Whenever I thought I had discovered some previously unnoticed antislavery voice, I almost always found that David Brion Davis, the dean of the field, had already looked at the writer involved with his customary subtle brilliance and noticed all sorts of things I had missed. I relied greatly on Seymour Drescher's fine scholarship, filled with new insights about the unfolding of British abolitionism as a powerful popular movement. When writers about the era of the Haitian Revolution took divergent views of what had happened and what it meant, I usually found myself turning to David Geggus's work for the most authoritative word on the subject. Hugh Thomas's history of the slave trade is a mine of useful information and steered me to many sources. Ellen Gibson Wilson's excellent biographies of the Clarkson brothers stand as proof that meticulous scholarship can also be gracefully written.

The literature on slavery is a vast one. Joseph C. Miller's bibliography on the subject lists works by nearly 5,900 scholars in its first volume (1900–1991) alone; by the 1990s Miller found that between 700 and 800 scholarly books, articles, conference papers, and the like having to do with slavery were appearing each year. Even just for British Empire slavery and abolition, anyone with access to a good university library can find a decade's worth of reading. The list that follows is far from comprehensive. In a few cases, usually when the source I have drawn from does not primarily concern abolition, slavery, or Britain, I have listed it only in the source notes and not here.

BOOKS AND ARTICLES

Adams, Capt. Scarritt, U.S.N. "The Loss of the Royal George 1782." *History Today* 9, no. 12, (1959).

Afzelius, Adam. *Sierra Leone Journal, 1795–1796,* ed. Alexander Kup. Uppsala, Sweden: Studia Ethnographica Upsaliensia, 1967.

Agency Committee of the Antislavery Society. *Report of the Agency Committee of the Antislavery Society, established in June, 1831, for the purpose of disseminating information by lectures on colonial slavery.* London: S. Bagster, 1832.

Altick, Richard D. *The English Common Reader: A Social History of the Mass Reading Public, 1800–1900.* Chicago: University of Chicago Press, 1957.

Andrew, Donna T. *London Debating Societies, 1776–1799.* London: London Record Society, 1994.

Anonymous. *No Rum!—No Sugar! or, The Voice of Blood, Being Half an Hour's Conversation between a Negro and an English Gentleman Shewing the Horrible Nature of the Slave Trade and pointing Out an Easy and Effectual Method of Terminating It by An Act of the People.* London: L. Wayland, 1792.

Anstey, Roger. *The Atlantic Slave Trade and British Abolition, 1760–1810.* London: Macmillan, 1975.

Anstey, Roger, and P.E.H. Hair. *Liverpool, the African Slave Trade, and Abolition: Essays to Illustrate Current Knowledge and Research.* [Liverpool]: Historic Society of Lancashire and Cheshire, 1976.

Asiegbu, Johnson U. J. *Slavery and the Politics of Liberation, 1787–1861: A Study of Liberated African Emigration and British Antislavery Policy.* Harlow, U.K.: Longmans, 1969.

Auguste, Claude B., and Marcel B. Auguste. *L'Expédition Leclerc 1801–1803.* Port-au-Prince, Haiti: Imprimerie Henri Deschamps, 1985.

Ball, Edward. *Slaves in the Family.* New York: Farrar, Straus and Giroux, 1998.

Barker, Anthony J. *Captain Charles Stuart: Anglo-American Abolitionist.* Baton Rouge: Louisiana State University Press, 1986.

Bass, Robert D. *The Green Dragoon: The Lives of Banastre Tarleton and Mary Robinson.* New York: Henry Holt, 1957.

Baum, Joan. *Mind-Forg'd Manacles: Slavery and the English Romantic Poets.* North Haven, CT: Archon Books, 1994.

Bean, Richard Nelson. *The British Trans-Atlantic Slave Trade, 1650–1775.* New York: Arno Press, 1975.

Beckles, Hilary McD.

1. *Black Rebellion in Barbados: The Struggle Against Slavery, 1627–1838.* Bridgetown, Barbados: Antilles Publications, 1984.
2. "Caribbean Antislavery: The Self-Liberation Ethos of Enslaved Blacks," in Beckles and Shepherd, below.
3. *Bussa: The 1816 Revolution in Barbados.* Barbados: University of the West Indies, 1998.

4. *Natural Rebels: A Social History of Enslaved Black Women in Barbados.* New Brunswick, NJ: Rutgers University Press, 1989.

Beckles, Hilary McD., and Verene Shepherd, eds. *Caribbean Slavery in the Atlantic World: A Student Reader.* Kingston, Jamaica: Ian Randle, 2000.

Behrendt, Stephen D.

1. "Crew Mortality in the Atlantic Slave Trade." *Slavery and Abolition* 18, no. 1 (April 1997).
2. "The Annual Volume and Regional Distribution of the British Slave Trade, 1780–1807." *Journal of African History* 38, no. 2 (1997).

Bennett, J. Harry, Jr. *Bondsmen and Bishops: Slavery and Apprenticeship on the Codrington Plantations of Barbados, 1710–1838.* Berkeley: University of California Press, 1958.

Bewell, Alan, ed. *Medicine and the West Indian Slave Trade.* Vol. 7 of Kitson, Peter J., and Debbie Lee, eds., *Slavery, Abolition and Emancipation: Writings in the British Romantic Period.* London: Pickering & Chatto, 1999.

Black, Eugene Charlton. *The Association: British Extraparliamentary Political Organization, 1769–1793.* Cambridge, MA: Harvard University Press, 1963.

Blackburn, Robin. *The Overthrow of Colonial Slavery, 1776–1848.* London: Verso, 1988.

Blakeley, Phyllis R. "Boston King: A Negro Loyalist Who Sought Refuge in Nova Scotia." *Dalhousie Review* 48 (1968).

Bleby, Henry. *Death Struggles of Slavery: being a Narrative of Facts and Incidents which occurred in a British Colony, during the two years immediately preceding Negro Emancipation.* London: Hamilton, Adams, 1853.

Bradley, Ian. "James Ramsay and the Slave Trade." *History Today* 22, no. 12 (1972).

Bradley, James E. *Popular Politics and the American Revolution in England: Petitions, the Crown, and Public Opinion.* Macon, GA: Mercer, 1986.

Braidwood, Stephen J. *Black Poor and White Philanthropists: London's Blacks and the Foundation of the Sierra Leone Settlement, 1786–1791.* Liverpool: Liverpool University Press, 1994.

Brathwaite, Edward. *The Development of Creole Society in Jamaica, 1770–1820.* Oxford: Clarendon Press, 1971.

Brewer, John. *The Pleasures of the Imagination: English Culture in the Eighteenth Century.* New York: Farrar, Straus and Giroux, 1997.

Briggs, Asa. *How They Lived: An Anthology of Original Documents Written Between 1700 and 1815.* New York: Barnes & Noble, 1969.

Brown, Christopher L. "Empire Without Slaves: British Concepts of Emancipation in the Age of the American Revolution." *William and Mary Quarterly,* 3rd series, vol. 61, no. 2 (April 1999).

Brown, Ford K. *Fathers of the Victorians: The Age of Wilberforce.* Cambridge: Cambridge University Press, 1961.

Browne, Christopher. *Getting the Message: The Story of the British Post Office.* Dover, NH: Alan Sutton, 1993.

Buckley, Roger N.

1. *Slaves in Red Coats: The British West India Regiments, 1795–1815*. New Haven: Yale University Press, 1979.
2. "'Black Man'—The Mutiny of the 8th (British) West India Regiment: A Microcosm of War and Slavery in the Caribbean." *Jamaican Historical Review* 12 (1980).
3. *The British Army in the West Indies: Society and the Military in the Revolutionary Age*. Gainsville: University Press of Florida, 1998.

Burton, Ann M. "British Evangelicals, Economic Warfare and the Abolition of the Atlantic Slave Trade, 1794–1810." *Anglican and Episcopal History* 65, no. 2, (1996).

Campbell, Mavis C. *The Maroons of Jamaica, 1655–1796: A History of Resistance, Collaboration and Betrayal.* Granby, MA: Bergin & Garvey, 1988.

Carretta, Vincent.

1. "Olaudah Equiano or Gustavus Vassa? New Light on an Eighteenth-Century Question of Identity." *Slavery and Abolition* 20, no. 3 (December 1999).
2. "'Property of Author': Olaudah Equiano's Place in the History of the Book," in Carretta and Gould, below.
3. Ed. *Unchained Voices: An Anthology of Black Authors in the English-Speaking World of the Eighteenth Century.* Lexington: University Press of Kentucky, 1996.
4. "Questioning the Identity of Olaudah Equiano, or Gustavus Vassa, the African" (a revised and updated version of 1), in Nussbaum, below.

Carretta, Vincent, and Philip Gould, eds. *Genius in Bondage: Literature of the Early Black Atlantic.* Lexington: University Press of Kentucky, 2001.

Carrington, Selwyn H. H. *The Sugar Industry and the Abolition of the Slave Trade, 1775–1810.* Gainesville: University Press of Florida, 2002.

Carteau, F. *Soirées Bermudiennes: ou Entretiens sur les Événements qui ont opérés la Ruine de la Partie Française de l'Isle Saint-Domingue.* Bordeaux: Pellier-Lawalle, 1802.

Cateau, Heather, and S.H.H. Carrington, eds. *Capitalism and Slavery Fifty Years Later: Eric Eustace Williams—a Reassessment of the Man and His Work.* New York: Peter Lang, 2000.

Charlton, K. "James Cropper and Liverpool's Contribution to the Antislavery Movement." *Transactions of the Historic Society of Lancashire and Cheshire* 123 (1972).

Clarkson, John. *Clarkson's Mission to America, 1791–1792,* ed. Charles Bruce Fergusson. Halifax: Public Archives of Nova Scotia, 1971.

Clarkson, Thomas.

1. *The History of the Rise, Progress, and Accomplishment of the Abolition of the African Slave-Trade by the British Parliament.* 2 vols. London: Longman, Hurst, Rees, and Orme, 1808.
2. *An Essay on the Slavery and Commerce of the Human Species, particularly the African, translated from a Latin Dissertation, which was honoured with the First Prize in the University of Cambridge for the year 1785, with Additions.* Reprint, Miami: Mnemosyne, 1969.

3. *An Essay on the Impolicy of the African Slave Trade.* London: J. Phillips, 1788.

4. *The True State of the Case respecting the Insurrection at St. Domingo.* Ipswich, U.K.: J. Rush, 1792.

[Clutterbuck, ——?]. *A Vindication of the Use of Sugar, the Produce of the West-India Islands. In Answer to a Pamphlet entitled Remarkable Extracts, &c. &c.* London: T. Boosey, 1792.

Coleman, Deirdre, ed. *Maiden Voyages and Infant Colonies: Two Women's Travel Narratives of the 1790s.* London: Leicester University Press, 1999 (contains Anna Maria Falconbridge's *Two Voyages to Sierra Leone,* 1794).

Colley, Linda.

1. *Britons: Forging the Nation, 1707–1837.* New Haven: Yale University Press, 1992.

2. *Captives.* New York: Pantheon, 2002.

Corfield, Kenneth. "Elizabeth Heyrick: Radical Quaker," in *Religion in the Lives of English Women, 1760–1930,* ed. Gail Malmgreen. London: Croom Helm, 1986.

Cotter, William R. "The Somerset Case and the Abolition of Slavery in England." *History* 79, no. 255 (February 1994).

Craton, Michael.

1. *Testing the Chains: Resistance to Slavery in the British West Indies.* Ithaca, NY: Cornell University Press, 1982.

2. *Sinews of Empire: A Short History of British Slavery.* Garden City, NY: Anchor Press/Doubleday, 1974.

3. "Continuity Not Change: The Incidence of Unrest Among Ex-Slaves in the British West Indies, 1838–1876." *Slavery and Abolition* 9, no. 2 (September 1988).

Craton, Michael, James Walvin, and David Wright, eds. *Slavery, Abolition and Emancipation: Black Slaves and the British Empire.* London: Longman, 1976.

Cugoano, Quobna Ottobah. *Thoughts and Sentiments on the Evil of Slavery and Other Writings,* ed. Vincent Carretta. New York: Penguin, 1999.

Curtin, Philip D. *The Image of Africa: British Ideas and Action, 1780–1850.* Madison: University of Wisconsin Press, 1964.

Da Costa, Emilia Viotti. *Crowns of Glory, Tears of Blood: The Demerara Slave Rebellion of 1823.* New York: Oxford University Press, 1994.

Dann, Graham M. S., and A. V. Seaton. *Slavery, Contested Heritage and Thanotourism.* Binghamton, NY: Haworth Hospitality Press, 2001.

Daunton, Martin, and Rick Halpern, eds. *Empire and Others: British Encounters with Indigenous Peoples, 1600–1850.* Philadelphia: University of Pennsylvania Press, 1999.

Davis, David Brion.

1. *The Problem of Slavery in Western Culture.* Ithaca, NY: Cornell University Press, 1966.

2. *The Problem of Slavery in the Age of Revolution, 1770–1823.* Ithaca, NY: Cornell University Press, 1975.

3. *Slavery and Human Progress.* New York: Oxford University Press, 1984.

4. *In the Image of God: Religion, Moral Values, and Our Heritage of Slavery.* New Haven: Yale University Press, 2001.
5. "Impact of the French and Haitian Revolutions," in Geggus 5, below.
6. "New Sidelights on Early Antislavery Radicalism." *William and Mary Quarterly,* 3rd series, vol. 28, no. 4 (October 1971).

Debien, Gabriel, Jean Fouchard, and Marie Antoinette Menier, "Toussaint Louverture avant 1789: légendes et réalités." *Conjonction* 134 (June–July 1977).

de Lacroix, Pamphile. *La Révolution de Haïti,* ed. Pierre Pluchon. Paris: Éditions Karthala, 1995 (reissue of *Mémoires pour servir à l'histoire de la Révolution de Saint-Domingue,* 1819).

De Wimpffen, François Alexandre Stanislaus, Baron. *A Voyage to Saint Domingo, in the years 1788, 1789, and 1790.* London: T. Cadell and W. Davies, 1797.

Dickson, William. *Letters on Slavery, to which are added, Addresses to the Whites, and to the Free Negroes of Barbadoes; and Accounts of some Negroes eminent for their virtues and abilities.* London: J. Phillips, 1789.

Diène, Doudou. *From Chains to Bonds: The Slave Trade Revisited.* New York: Berghahn Books/UNESCO, 2001.

Donnan, Elizabeth. *Documents Illustrative of the History of the Slave Trade to America.* 4 vols. Washington, DC: Carnegie Institution, 1930–1935.

Drescher, Seymour.

1. *Capitalism and Antislavery: British Mobilization in Comparative Perspective.* New York: Oxford University Press, 1987.
2. *Econocide: British Slavery in the Era of Abolition.* Pittsburgh: University of Pittsburgh Press, 1977.
3. *From Slavery to Freedom: Comparative Studies in the Rise and Fall of Atlantic Slavery.* New York: New York University Press, 1999.
4. "Cart Whip and Billy Roller: Antislavery and Reform Symbolism in Industrializing Britain." *Journal of Social History* 15, no. 1 (Fall 1981).
5. "Whose Abolition? Popular Pressure and the Ending of the British Slave Trade." *Past and Present,* no. 143 (May 1994).
6. "The Historical Context of British Abolition," in Richardson 3, below.
7. "Public Opinion and the Destruction of British Colonial Slavery," in Walvin 4, below.
8. *The Mighty Experiment: Free Labor Versus Slavery in British Emancipation.* New York: Oxford University Press, 2002.
9. "Manumission in a Society Without Slave Law: Eighteenth-Century England." *Slavery and Abolition* 10, no. 3 (December 1989).

Dresser, Madge. *Slavery Obscured: The Social History of the Slave Trade in an English Provincial Port.* London: Continuum, 2001.

Dubois, Laurent. *Avengers of the New World: The Story of the Haitian Revolution.* Cambridge, MA: Belknap Press of Harvard University Press, 2004.

Duffy, Michael. *Soldiers, Sugar and Seapower: The British Expeditions to the West Indies and the War Against Revolutionary France.* Oxford: Clarendon Press, 1987.

Dyott, William. *Dyott's Diary, 1781–1845: A Selection from the Journal of William Dyott, Sometime General in the British Army and Aide-de-Camp to His Majesty King George III,* ed. Reginald W. Jeffrey. 2 vols. London: Archibald Constable, 1907.

Edwards, Bryan.

1. *The History, Civil and Commercial, of the British Colonies in the West Indies.* 4 vols. Philadelphia: James Humphreys, 1806.
2. *An Historical Survey of the French Colony in the Island of St. Domingo: Comprehending an Account of the Revolt of the Negroes in the Year 1791, and a Detail of the Military Transactions of the British Army in that Island, in the Years 1793 & 1794.* London: John Stockdale, 1801. (Versions of this volume appear as the third or fourth volume in various editions of Edwards's *History.*)

Edwards, Paul, and James Walvin. *Black Personalities in the Era of the Slave Trade.* Baton Rouge: Louisiana State University Press, 1983.

Eltis, David. "The Volume and Structure of the Transatlantic Slave Trade: A Reassessment." *William and Mary Quarterly* 58, no. 1 (January 2001).

Ennis, Daniel James. *Enter the Press-Gang: Naval Impressment in Eighteenth-Century Literature.* Newark: University of Delaware Press, 2002.

Equiano, Olaudah. *The Interesting Narrative and Other Writings,* ed. Vincent Carretta. Revised edition. New York: Penguin Books, 2003.

Falconbridge, Alexander. *An Account of the Slave Trade on the Coast of Africa.* London: J. Phillips, 1788.

Farrer, Katherine Eufemia, ed. *Correspondence of Josiah Wedgwood, 1781–1794.* London: Women's Printing Society, 1906.

Ferguson, Moira. *Subject to Others: British Women Writers and Colonial Slavery, 1670–1834.* New York: Routledge, 1992.

Fick, Carolyn E. *The Making of Haiti: The Saint Domingue Revolution from Below.* Knoxville: University of Tennessee Press, 1990.

Finkelman, Paul, and Joseph C. Miller. *Macmillan Encyclopedia of World Slavery.* 2 vols. New York: Simon & Schuster/Macmillan, 1998.

Fladeland, Betty.

1. *Men and Brothers: Anglo-American Antislavery Cooperation.* Urbana: University of Illinois Press, 1972.
2. *Abolitionists and Working-Class Problems in the Age of Industrialization.* Baton Rouge: Louisiana State University Press, 1984.
3. "Abolitionist Pressures on the Concert of Europe, 1814–1822." *Journal of Modern History* 38, no. 4 (December 1966).

Forster, E. M. *Marianne Thornton: A Domestic Biography.* New York: Harcourt, Brace, 1956.

Fox, William. *An Address to the People of Great-Britain, on the Propriety of Abstaining from West-India Sugar and Rum.* London, 1791. Reprint, Boston: Samuel Hall, 1792.

Fryer, Peter. *Staying Power: The History of Black People in Britain.* London: Pluto Press, 1984.

Furneaux, Robin. *William Wilberforce.* London: Hamish Hamilton, 1974.

Fyfe, Christopher.

1. *A History of Sierra Leone.* London: Oxford University Press, 1963.
2. Ed. *"Our Children Free and Happy": Letters from Black Settlers in Africa in the 1790s.* Edinburgh: Edinburgh University Press, 1991.
3. Ed. *Sierra Leone Inheritance.* London: Oxford University Press, 1964.

Gaspar, David Barry. *Bondsmen and Rebels: A Study of Master-Slave Relations in Antigua.* Durham, NC: Duke University Press, 1985.

Gaspar, David Barry, and David Patrick Geggus, eds. *A Turbulent Time: The French Revolution and the Greater Caribbean.* Bloomington: Indiana University Press, 1997.

Geggus, David Patrick.

1. *Slavery, War, and Revolution: The British Occupation of Saint Domingue, 1793–1798.* Oxford: Clarendon Press, 1982.
2. "The Enigma of Jamaica in the 1790s: New Light on the Causes of Slave Rebellions." *William and Mary Quarterly,* 3rd series, vol. 44, no. 2 (April 1987).
3. "The British Government and the Saint Domingue Slave Revolt, 1791–1793." *English Historical Review* 96, no. 379 (April 1981).
4. "The Bois Caïman Ceremony." *Journal of Caribbean History* 25, nos. 1 and 2 (1991).
5. Ed. *The Impact of the Haitian Revolution in the Atlantic World.* Columbia: University of South Carolina Press, 2001.
6. "British Opinion and the Emergence of Haiti, 1791–1805," in Walvin 4, below.
7. "The Haitian Revolution," in *The Modern Caribbean,* ed. Franklin W. Knight and Colin A. Palmer. Chapel Hill: University of North Carolina Press, 1989.
8. *Haitian Revolutionary Studies.* Bloomington: Indiana University Press, 2002.

Gerzina, Gretchen. *Black London: Life Before Emancipation.* New Brunswick, NJ: Rutgers University Press, 1995.

Gifford, Zerbanoo. *Thomas Clarkson and the Campaign Against Slavery.* London: Antislavery International, 1996.

Goodwin, Albert. *The Friends of Liberty: The English Democratic Movement in the Age of the French Revolution.* Cambridge, MA: Harvard University Press, 1979.

Graham, Jenny. *The Nation, the Law and the King: Reform Politics in England, 1789–1799.* 2 vols. Lanham, MD: University Press of America, 2000.

Gratus, Jack. *The Great White Lie: Slavery, Emancipation and Changing Racial Attitudes.* New York: Monthly Review Press, 1973.

Green, James. "The Publishing History of Olaudah Equiano's *Interesting Narrative.*" *Slavery and Abolition* 16, no. 3 (December 1995).

Halbersleben, Karen. *Women's Participation in the British Antislavery Movement, 1824–1865.* Lewiston, NY: Edwin Mellen Press, 1993.

Hall, Douglas. *In Miserable Slavery: Thomas Thistlewood in Jamaica, 1750–86.* London: Macmillan, 1989.

Hammond, J. L., and Barbara Hammond. *The Town Labourer, 1760–1832: The New Civilization.* London: Longmans, Green, 1917.

Hampton, Christopher, ed. *A Radical Reader: The Struggle for Change in England, 1381–1914.* Harmondsworth, U.K.: Penguin, 1984.

Hancock, David. *Citizens of the World: London Merchants and the Integration of the British Atlantic Community, 1735–1785.* Cambridge: Cambridge University Press, 1995.

[Hardy, Thomas]. *Memoir of Thomas Hardy, Founder of, and Secretary to, the London Corresponding Society, for Diffusing Useful Political Knowledge among the People of Great Britain & Ireland, and for Promoting Parliamentary Reform, from its Establishment, in Jan. 1792, until his arrest, on a False Charge of High Treason, on the 12th of May, 1794. Written by Himself.* London: James Ridgway, 1832.

Harford, John S. *Recollections of William Wilberforce, Esq., M.P. for the County of York During Nearly Thirty Years: with Brief Notices of some of his personal friends and contemporaries.* London: Longman, Green, Longman, Roberts & Green, 1865.

Harlow, Vincent, and Frederick Madden, eds. *British Colonial Developments, 1774–1834: Select Documents.* Oxford: Clarendon Press, 1953.

Hart, Richard. *Slaves Who Abolished Slavery.* Vol. 2, *Blacks in Rebellion.* Kingston, Jamaica: University of the West Indies, 1985.

[Harvey, William]. *London Scenes and London People: Anecdotes, Reminiscences, and Sketches of Places, Personages, Events, Customs, and Curiosities of London City, Past and Present.* London: W. H. Collingridge, 1863.

[Hassal, Mary]. *Secret History; or, The Horrors of St. Domingo, in a Series of Letters written by A Lady at Cape François to Colonel Burr, late Vice-President of the United States, principally during the command of General Rochambeau.* Philadelphia: Bradford & Inskeep, 1808.

Hayward, Jack, ed. *Out of Slavery: Abolition and After.* London: Frank Cass, 1985.

Hecht, J. Jean. *Continental and Colonial Servants in Eighteenth Century England.* Northampton, MA: Smith College Studies in History, vol. 40, 1954.

Heinl, Robert Debs, Jr., and Nancy Gordon Heinl; revised and expanded by Michael Heinl. *Written in Blood: The Story of the Haitian People, 1492–1995.* Lanham, MD: University Press of America, 1996.

Heward, Edmund. *Lord Mansfield.* London: Barry Rose, 1979.

Heyrick, Elizabeth.

1. *Immediate, not Gradual Abolition: or, an Inquiry into the Shortest, Safest, and Most Effectual Means of Getting Rid of West Indian Slavery.* Boston: Isaac Knapp, 1838.
2. *Appeal to the Hearts and Consciences of British Women.* Leicester, U.K.: A. Cokshaw, 1828.
3. *Letters on the Necessity of a Prompt Extinction of British Colonial Slavery; chiefly addressed to the More Influential Classes, to which are added Thoughts on Compensation.* London: Hatchard and Son, 1826.

Hibbert, Christopher. *George III: A Personal History.* New York: Basic Books, 1998.

Hinton, John Howard. *Memoir of William Knibb, Missionary in Jamaica.* London: Houlston and Stoneman, 1847.

Hoare, Prince. *Memoirs of Granville Sharp, Esq.* London: Henry Colburn, 1820.

Honour, Hugh. *The Image of the Black in Western Art.* Vol. 4, *From the American Revolution to World War I. Part 1: Slaves and Liberators.* Cambridge, MA: Harvard University Press, 1989.

Howard, Thomas Phipps. *The Haitian Journal of Lieutenant Howard, York Hussars, 1796–1798,* ed. Roger Norman Buckley. Knoxville: University of Tennessee Press, 1985.

Howell, Colin, and Richard J. Twomey, eds. *Jack Tar in History: Essays in the History of Maritime Life and Labor.* Fredericton, New Brunswick: Acadiensis Press, 1991.

Howse, Ernest Marshall. *Saints in Politics: The "Clapham Sect" and the Growth of Freedom.* Toronto: University of Toronto Press, 1952.

Ingham, E. G. *Sierra Leone after a Hundred Years.* London: Seeley, 1894.

Jakobsson, Stiv. *Am I Not a Man and a Brother?: British Missions and the Abolition of the Slave Trade and Slavery in West Africa and the West Indies, 1786–1838.* Uppsala, Sweden: Almqvist & Wiksells, 1972.

James, C.L.R. *The Black Jacobins: Toussaint L'Ouverture and the San Domingo Revolution,* 2nd edition, revised. New York: Vintage, 1969.

Jean-Baptiste, St. Victor. *Haïti: Sa Lutte pour l'Émancipation.* Paris: La Nef, 1957.

Jennings, Judith. *The Business of Abolishing the British Slave Trade, 1783–1807.* London: Frank Cass, 1997.

Jones, Colin, ed. *Britain and Revolutionary France: Conflict, Subversion and Propaganda.* Exeter, U.K.: University of Exeter, 1983.

Kaufmann, Chaim D., and Robert A. Pape. "Explaining Costly International Moral Action: Britain's Sixty-Year Campaign Against the Atlantic Slave Trade." *International Organization* 53, no. 4 (Autumn 1999).

Kemp, Peter. *The British Sailor: A Social History of the Lower Deck.* London: J. M. Dent, 1970.

King, Boston. *MEMOIRS of the LIFE of BOSTON KING, a Black Preacher, Written by Himself, during his Residence at Kingswood-School.* London, 1798. Reprinted in Carretta 3, above.

Kirk-Green, Anthony. "David George: The Nova Scotian Experience." *Sierra Leone Studies,* new series, no. 14 (December 1960).

Korngold, Ralph. *Citizen Toussaint.* Boston: Little, Brown, 1945.

Kup, A. P. "Alexander Lindsay, 6th Earl of Balcarres, Lieutenant Governor of Jamaica, 1794–1801." *Bulletin of the John Rylands University Library of Manchester* 57, no. 2 (1975).

Lamb, D. P. "Volume and Tonnage of the Liverpool Slave Trade, 1772–1807," in Anstey and Hair, above.

Landau, Norma. *Law, Crime and English Society, 1660–1830.* Cambridge: Cambridge University Press, 2002.

Lascelles, E.C.P. *Granville Sharp and the Freedom of Slaves in England.* London: Humphrey Milford/Oxford University Press, 1928.

Lasky, Melvin J. "The Recantation of Henry Redhead Yorke: A Forgotten English Ideologist." *Encounter* 41, no. 4 (October 1973).

Laslett, Peter. *The World We Have Lost, Further Explored.* New York: Scribner's, 1984.

Lewis, Andrew. "'An Incendiary Press': British West Indian Newspapers During the Struggle for Abolition." *Slavery and Abolition* 16, no. 3 (December 1995).

Lindsay, Lord. *Lives of the Lindsays; or, a Memoir of the Houses of Crawford and Balcarres.* 3 vols. London: John Murray, 1849.

Linebaugh, Peter, and Marcus Rediker. *The Many-Headed Hydra: Sailors, Slaves, Commoners, and the Hidden History of the Revolutionary Atlantic.* Boston: Beacon Press, 2000.

Lokke, Carl Ludwig. "London Merchant Interest in the St. Domingue Plantations of the Émigrés, 1793–1798." *American Historical Review* 43, no. 4 (July 1938).

Mackenzie, Charles. *Notes on Haiti made during a Residence in that Republic.* 2 vols. London: Henry Colburn and Richard Bentley, 1830.

Mackey, Howard. "'The Complexion of the Accused': William Davidson, the Black Revolutionary in the Cato Street Conspiracy of 1820." *Negro Educational Review* 23, no. 4 (October 1972).

Marshall, P. J., ed. *The Oxford History of the British Empire.* Vol. 2, *The Eighteenth Century.* Oxford: Oxford University Press, 1998.

Martin, Bernard. *John Newton: A Biography.* London: William Heinemann, 1950.

McCalman, Iain, ed. *An Oxford Companion to the Romantic Age: British Culture, 1776–1832.* New York: Oxford University Press, 1999.

McGlynn, Frank, and Seymour Drescher, eds. *The Meaning of Freedom: Economics, Politics, and Culture after Slavery.* Pittsburgh: University of Pittsburgh Press, 1992.

McKendrick, Neil, John Brewer, and J. H. Plumb. *The Birth of a Consumer Society: The Commercialization of Eighteenth-Century England.* Bloomington: Indiana University Press, 1982.

Midgley, Clare.

1. *Women Against Slavery: The British Campaigns, 1780–1870.* London: Routledge, 1992.
2. "Slave Sugar Boycotts, Female Activism and the Domestic Base of British Antislavery Culture." *Slavery and Abolition* 17, no. 3 (December 1996).

Miller, Joseph C., ed. *Slavery and Slaving in World History: A Bibliography.* 2 vols. Armonk, NY: M. E. Sharp, 1999.

Mintz, Sidney W. *Sweetness and Power: The Place of Sugar in Modern History.* New York: Viking, 1985.

Mitchell, Austin. "The Association Movement of 1792–3." *Historical Journal* 4, no. 1 (1961).

Moreau de Jonnès, M. A. *Aventures de Guerre au temps de la République et du Consulat.* Paris: Pagnerre, 1858.

Moreau de Saint-Méry, Médéric-Louis-Elie. *A Civilization That Perished: The Last Years of White Colonial Rule in Haiti.* Lanham, MD: University Press of America, 1985.

Morgan, Kenneth. *Edward Colston and Bristol.* Bristol, U.K.: Bristol Branch of the Historical Association, 1999.

Morgan, Philip D. "The Black Experience in the British Empire," in Marshall, above.

Mullin, Michael. *Africa in America: Slave Acculturation and Resistance in the American South and the British Caribbean, 1736–1831.* Urbana: University of Illinois Press, 1992.

Myers, Norma. *Reconstructing the Black Past: Blacks in Britain, 1780–1830.* London: Frank Cass, 1996.

Newton, John.

1. *Memoirs of the Rev. John Newton, Some Time a Slave in Africa; Afterwards Curate of Olney, Bucks; and Rector of St. Mary Woolnoth, London: in a Series of Letters Written by Himself, to the Rev. Dr. Haweis, Rector of Aldwinckle, Northamptonshire.* London: A. Maxwell, 1813.
2. *The Journal of a Slave Trader (John Newton), 1750–1754: With Newton's Thoughts on the African Slave Trade,* ed. Bernard Martin and Mark Spurrell. London: Epworth Press, 1962.
3. *Works.* 6 vols. New York: Williams and Whiting, 1810–11.
4. *Letters and Sermons.* 9 vols. Edinburgh: J. Guthrie, 1798.

Northcott, Cecil. *Slavery's Martyr: John Smith of Demerara and the Emancipation Movement, 1817–24.* London: Epworth Press, 1976.

Norton, Mary Beth. "The Fate of Some Black Loyalists of the American Revolution." *Journal of Negro History* 58, no. 4 (October 1973).

Nugent, Maria. *Lady Nugent's Journal of her residence in Jamaica from 1801 to 1805,* ed. Philip Wright. Kingston: Institute of Jamaica, 1966.

Nussbaum, Felicity A. *The Global Eighteenth Century.* Baltimore: Johns Hopkins University Press, 2003.

Oldfield, J. R.

1. *Popular Politics and British Antislavery: The Mobilization of Public Opinion Against the Slave Trade, 1787–1807.* Manchester, U.K.: Manchester University Press, 1995.
2. "Antislavery Sentiment in Children's Literature, 1750–1850." *Slavery and Abolition* 10, no. 1 (May 1989).

Oldham, James. "New Light on Mansfield and Slavery." *Journal of British Studies* 27, no. 1 (January 1988).

Opala, Joseph A. *The Gullah: Rice, Slavery and the Sierra Leone–American Connection.* Freetown, Sierra Leone: U.S. Information Service, [1987?].

Ott, Thomas O. *The Haitian Revolution, 1789–1804.* Knoxville: University of Tennessee Press, 1973.

Paley, Ruth. "After *Somerset:* Mansfield, Slavery and the Law in England, 1772–1830," in Landau, above.

Pares, Richard. *A West-India Fortune.* London: Longmans, Green, 1950.

Parham, Althéa de Puech, ed. and trans. *My Odyssey: Experiences of a Young Refugee from Two Revolutions, by a Creole of Saint Domingue.* Baton Rouge: Louisiana State University Press, 1959.

Pauléus Sannon, H. *Histoire de Toussaint-Louverture.* Port-au-Prince, Haiti: A. Heraux, 1938.

Perkins, Samuel G. *"On the Margin of Vesuvius": Sketches of St. Domingo, 1785–1793.* Lawrence, KS: Institute of Haitian Studies, 1995.

Phipps, William E. *Amazing Grace in John Newton: Slave-Ship Captain, Hymnwriter, and Abolitionist.* Macon, GA: Mercer University Press, 2001.

Pinckard, George. *Notes on the West Indies: Written during the Expedition under the Command of the late General Sir Ralph Abercromby; including Observations on the Island of Barbadoes, and the Settlements captured by the British troops, upon the Coast of Guiana; likewise Remarks relating to the Creoles and Slaves of the Western Colonies, and the Indians of South America; with occasional Hints, regarding the Seasoning, or Yellow Fever of hot Climates.* 3 vols. London: Longman, Hurst, Rees, and Orme, 1806.

Pluchon, Pierre. *Toussaint Louverture: Un Révolutionnaire noir d'Ancien Régime.* Paris: Fayard, 1989.

Pollock, John. *Wilberforce.* London: Constable, 1977.

Porter, Dale H. *The Abolition of the Slave Trade in England, 1784–1807.* Hamden, CT: Archon Books, 1970.

Porter, Roy. *London: A Social History.* London: Hamish Hamilton, 1994.

Quarles, Benjamin.

1. *The Negro in the American Revolution.* Chapel Hill: University of North Carolina Press, 1961.
2. *Black Abolitionists.* New York: Oxford University Press, 1969.

Ragatz, Lowell Joseph.

1. *The Fall of the Planter Class in the British Caribbean, 1763–1833: A Study in Social and Economic History.* New York: Century, 1928.
2. *The Old Plantation System in the British West Indies.* London: Bryan Edwards Press, 1953.

Rainsford, Marcus. *An Historical Account of the Black Empire of Hayti: comprehending a view of the Principal Transactions in the Revolution of Saint Domingo with its Antient and Modern State.* London: James Cundee, 1805.

Reader, John. *Africa: A Biography of the Continent.* New York: Knopf, 1998.

Reckord, Mary. "The Jamaica Slave Rebellion of 1831." *Past and Present,* no. 40 (July 1968).

Rees, Alan M. "Pitt and the Achievement of Abolition." *Journal of Negro History* 39, no. 3 (July 1954).

Reid, C. S. *Samuel Sharpe: From Slave to Jamaican National Hero.* Kingston, Jamaica: Bustamante Institute of Public and International Affairs, 1988.

Rice, C. Duncan. "Archibald Dalzel, the Scottish Intelligentsia, and the Problem of Slavery." *Scottish Historical Review* 62, no. 174 (October 1983).

Richardson, David.

1. "Profits in the Liverpool Slave Trade: The Accounts of William Davenport, 1757–1784," in Anstey and Hair, above.
2. "The British Empire and the Atlantic Slave Trade, 1660–1807," in Marshall, above.
3. Ed. *Abolition and Its Aftermath: The Historical Context, 1790–1916.* London: Frank Cass, 1985.

Richardson, Ronald Kent. *Moral Imperium: Afro-Caribbeans and the Transformation of British Rule, 1776–1838.* New York: Greenwood Press, 1987.

Robinson, Carey. *The Fighting Maroons of Jamaica.* Kingston, Jamaica: William Collins and Sangster, 1969.

Robinson, Harvey. *The British Post Office: A History.* Princeton, NJ: Princeton University Press, 1948.

Robinson, Henry Crabb. *Diary, Reminiscences and Correspondence,* ed. Thomas Sadler. 2 vols. New York: Hurd and Houghton, 1877.

Rodgers, Nini. "Equiano in Belfast: A Study of the Antislavery Ethos in a Northern Town." *Slavery and Abolition* 18, no. 2 (August 1997).

Rogers, Nicholas.

1. *Crowds, Culture, and Politics in Georgian Britain.* Oxford: Clarendon Press, 1998.
2. "Impressment and the Law in Eighteenth-Century Britain," in Landau, above.

Romilly, Samuel. *Memoirs of the Life of Sir Samuel Romilly, written by Himself, with a Selection from his Correspondence, edited by his Sons.* 3 vols. London: John Murray, 1840.

Ross-Lewin, Harry. *With "the Thirty-second" in the Peninsular and Other Campaigns,* ed. John Wardell. Dublin: Hodges, Figgis, 1904.

Roughley, Thomas. *The Jamaica Planter's Guide; or, a System for Planting and Managing a Sugar Estate, or Other Plantations in that Island, and throughout the British West Indies in General.* London: Longman, Hurst, Rees, Orme, and Brown, 1823.

Rudé, George. *Hanoverian London.* London: Secker & Warburg, 1971.

Sanderson, F. E.

1. "The Liverpool Abolitionists," in Anstey and Hair, above.
2. "The Liverpool Delegates and Sir William Dolben's Bill." *Transactions of the Historic Society of Lancashire and Cheshire* 124 (1973).
3. "The Structure of Politics in Liverpool, 1780–1807." *Transactions of the Historic Society of Lancashire and Cheshire* 127 (1977).

Sharp, Granville. *A Short Sketch of Temporary Regulations (Until Better Shall Be Proposed) for the Intended Settlement on the Grain Coast of Africa, near Sierra Leona.* 3rd edition. London: H. Baldwin, 1788. Reprint, Westport, CT: Negro Universities Press, 1970.

Sheridan, Richard B. *Doctors and Slaves: A Medical and Demographic History of Slavery in the British West Indies, 1680–1834.* New York: Cambridge University Press, 1985.

Shyllon, Folarin O.

1. *Black Slaves in Britain.* London: Institute of Race Relations/Oxford University Press, 1974.
2. *James Ramsay: The Unknown Abolitionist.* Edinburgh: Canongate, 1977.
3. "Olaudah Equiano: Nigerian Abolitionist and First National Leader of Africans in Britain." *Journal of African Studies* 4, no. 4 (Winter 1977).

[Society for Effecting the Abolition of the Slave Trade]. *An Abstract of the Evidence Delivered Before a Select Committee of the House of Commons in the Years 1790 and 1791, on the Part of the Petitioners for the Abolition of the Slave Trade.* London, 1791. Reprint, Cincinnati: American Reform Tract and Book Society, 1855.

Sollors, Werner, ed. *The Interesting Narrative of the Life of Olaudah Equiano, or Gustavus Vassa, The African, Written by Himself.* Norton Critical Edition. New York: Norton, 2001.

Solow, Barbara, and Stanley L. Engerman, eds. *British Capitalism and Caribbean Slavery: The Legacy of Eric Williams.* New York: Cambridge University Press, 1987.

Stedman, John Gabriel. *Narrative of a Five Years Expedition against the Revolted Negroes of Surinam. Transcribed for the First Time from the Original 1790 Manuscript,* ed. Richard Price and Sally Price. Baltimore: Johns Hopkins University Press, 1988.

Stephen, George. *Antislavery Recollections: in a Series of Letters addressed to Mrs. Beecher Stowe.* 2nd edition. London: Frank Cass, 1971.

Stephen, James.

1. *The Memoirs of James Stephen: Written by Himself for the Use of his Children,* ed. Merle M. Bevington. London: Hogarth Press, 1954.
2. *The Slavery of the British West India Colonies Delineated, as it Exists Both in Law and Practice and Compared with the Slavery of Other Countries, Antient and Modern.* 2 vols. London: Saunders and Benning, 1830.
3. *The Crisis of the Sugar Colonies; or, an Enquiry into the Objects and Probable Effects of the French Expedition to the West Indies; and their Connection with the Colonial Interests of the British Empire. To which are Subjoined a Plan for Settling the Vacant Lands of Trinidada. In Four Letters to the Right Hon. Henry Addington, Chancellor of the Exchequer, &c.* London, 1802.

Stephen, Sir James. *Essays in Ecclesiastical Biography.* London: Longman, Green, Longman and Roberts, 1860.

Stephen, Leslie. *The Life of Sir James Fitzjames Stephen Bart., K.C.S.I., a Judge of the High Court of Justice.* London: Smith, Elder, 1895.

Sussman, Charlotte. "Women and the Politics of Sugar, 1792." *Representations,* no. 48 (Fall 1994).

Sypher, Wylie. *Guinea's Captive Kings: British Antislavery Literature of the XVIIIth Century.* Reprint, New York: Octagon Books, 1969.

Tattersfield, Nigel. *The Forgotten Trade: Comprising the Log of the Daniel and Henry of 1700 and Accounts of the Slave Trade from the Minor Ports of England, 1698–1725.* London: Jonathan Cape, 1991.

Taylor, Clare. "Planter Comment upon Slave Revolts in 18th-Century Jamaica." *Slavery and Abolition* 3, no. 3 (December 1982).

Temperley, Howard.

1. "Antislavery," in Patricia Hollis, ed., *Pressure from Without in Early Victorian England.* London: Edward Arnold, 1974.
2. *British Antislavery, 1833–1870.* London: Longman, 1972.

Thale, Mary. "London Debating Societies in the 1790s." *Historical Journal* 32, no. 1 (1989).

Thomas, Hugh. *The Slave Trade: The Story of the Atlantic Slave Trade, 1440–1870.* New York: Simon & Schuster, 1997.

Thompson, E. P. *The Making of the English Working Class.* New York: Vintage, 1966.

Thornton, John K. "African Soldiers in the Haitian Revolution," in Beckles and Shepherd, above.

Tilly, Charles. *Popular Contention in Great Britain, 1758–1834.* Cambridge, MA: Harvard University Press, 1995.

Tomalin, Claire. *Mrs. Jordan's Profession: The Actress and the Prince.* New York: Knopf, 1995.

Treasure, Geoffrey. *Who's Who in Early Hanoverian Britain, 1714–1789.* London: Shepheard-Walwyn, 1991.

Trepp, Jean. "The Liverpool Movement for the Abolition of the English Slave Trade." *Journal of Negro History* 13, no. 3 (July 1928).

Turley, David. *The Culture of English Antislavery, 1780–1860.* London: Routledge, 1991.

Turner, Mary.

1. *Slaves and Missionaries: The Disintegration of Jamaican Slave Society, 1787–1834.* Urbana: University of Illinois Press, 1982.
2. "The Baptist War and Abolition." *Jamaican Historical Review* 13 (1982).

Turner, Steve. *Amazing Grace: The Story of America's Most Beloved Song.* New York: Harper Collins, 2002.

Tyrrell, Alex.

1. "A House Divided Against Itself: The British Abolitionists Revisited." *Journal of Caribbean History* 22, nos. 1 and 2 (1988).
2. "'Woman's Mission' and Pressure Group Politics in Britain, 1825–60." *Bulletin of the John Rylands University Library of Manchester* 63, no. 1 (Autumn 1980).

Tyson, George F., ed. *Toussaint L'Ouverture.* Englewood Cliffs, NJ: Prentice-Hall, 1973.

Waddell, Hope Masterton. *Twenty-nine Years in the West Indies and Central Africa: A Review of Missionary Work and Adventure, 1829–1858.* London: T. Nelson and Sons, 1863.

Wadstrom, C. B. *An Essay on Colonization particularly applied to the West Coast of Africa with some free thoughts on Cultivation and Commerce.* 2 vols. London: Darton and Harvey, 1794. Reprint, New York: Augustus M. Kelley, 1968.

Walker, James W. St. G. *The Black Loyalists: The Search for a Promised Land in Nova Scotia and Sierra Leone, 1783–1870.* New York: Africana, 1976.

Walvin, James.

1. *An African's Life: The Life and Times of Olaudah Equiano, 1745–1797.* London: Cassell, 1998.
2. "The Impact of Slavery on British Radical Politics, 1787–1838." *Annals of the New York Academy of Sciences* 292 (1977).
3. *Black and White: The Negro and English Society, 1555–1945.* London: Allen Lane/Penguin Press, 1973.
4. Ed. *Slavery and British Society, 1776–1846.* Baton Rouge: Louisiana State University Press, 1982.
5. *England, Slaves and Freedom, 1776–1838.* Jackson: University Press of Mississippi, 1968.

Ward, J. R. "The British West Indies, 1748–1815," in Marshall, above.

Washington, George. *The Writings of George Washington from the Original Manuscript Sources, 1745–1799.* 39 vols. Ed. John C. Fitzpatrick and David Matteson. Washington, DC: Government Printing Office, 1931–44.

Watt, Sir James. "James Ramsay, 1733–1789: Naval Surgeon, Naval Chaplain and Morning Star of the Antislavery Movement." *Mariner's Mirror* 81, no. 2 (May 1995).

Wilberforce, A. M., ed. *Private Papers of William Wilberforce.* London: T. Fisher Unwin, 1897.

Wilberforce, Robert and Samuel.

1. *The Life of William Wilberforce.* 5 vols. London: John Murray, 1838.
2. Ed. *Correspondence of William Wilberforce.* 2 vols. London: John Murray, 1840.

Wilberforce, William.

1. *The Speech of William Wilberforce, Esq. Representative of the County of York, on Wednesday the 13th of May, 1789, on the Question of the Abolition of the Slave Trade. To which are added, the Resolutions then Moved, and a short Sketch of the Speeches of Other Members.* London: Geographic Press, 1789.
2. *An Appeal to the Religion, Justice, and Humanity of the Inhabitants of the British Empire in behalf of the Negro Slaves in the West Indies.* London, 1823. Reprint, New York: Negro Universities Press, 1969.

Williams, Eric.

1. *Capitalism and Slavery.* Chapel Hill: University of North Carolina Press, 1994.
2. Ed. *The British West Indies at Westminster, 1789–1823: Extracts from the Debates in Parliament.* Westport, CT: Negro Universities Press, 1970.

Williams, Gomer. *History of the Liverpool Privateers and Letters of Marque, with an Account of the Liverpool Slave Trade.* London: William Heinemann, 1897.

Wilson, Ellen Gibson.

1. *Thomas Clarkson: A Biography.* London: Macmillan, 1989.
2. *John Clarkson and the African Adventure.* London: Macmillan, 1980.
3. *The Loyal Blacks.* New York: G. P. Putnam's Sons, 1976.

Wood, Marcus. *Blind Memory: Visual Representations of Slavery in England and America, 1780–1865.* New York: Routledge, 2000.

Woods, John A.

1. "The City of London and Impressment, 1776–1777." *Proceedings of the Leeds Philosophical and Literary Society, Literary and Historical Section* 8, part 2 (December 1956).
2. "James Sharp: Common Councillor of London in the Time of Wilkes," in Anne Whiteman, J. S. Bromley, and P.G.M. Dickson, eds., *Statesmen, Scholars and Merchants: Essays in Eighteenth-Century History Presented to Dame Lucy Sutherland.* Oxford: Clarendon Press, 1973.

Wright, Philip. *Knibb "the Notorious": Slaves' Missionary, 1803–1845.* London: Sidgwick & Jackson, 1973.

Ziegler, Philip. *King William IV.* London: Collins, 1971.

Zips, Werner. *Black Rebels: African-Caribbean Freedom Fighters in Jamaica.* Princeton, NJ: Markus Wiener, 1999.

THESES, MANUSCRIPTS, AND OTHER DOCUMENTS

Clarkson, Thomas.

- *Journal,* 1787. Quoted by permission of the Master and Fellows of St. John's College, Cambridge. Slavery box 1, folder 2.
- *Account of Efforts, 1807–1824, to abolish Slavery* [1838]. Mss., Clarkson Papers, Huntington Library, microfilm reel 1A.
- *Diary of Travels, 30 June 1823 to 26 February 1824, and 28 June 1824 to 11 November 1824.* National Library of Wales, N.L.W. 14984A.

Dickson, William. *Diary of a Visit to Scotland, 5th January–19th March 1792 on behalf of the Committee for the Abolition of the Slave Trade.* Temp. mss. box 10/14, Friends House Library, London.

DuBois, Laurent. *A Colony of Citizens: Revolution and Slave Emancipation in the French Caribbean, 1789–1802.* Ph.D. thesis, University of Michigan, 1998.

Eltis, David, Stephen D. Behrendt, David Richardson, and Herbert S. Klein, eds. *The Transatlantic Slave Trade: A Database on CD-ROM.* Cambridge: Cambridge University Press, 1999.

Hunt, E. M. *The North of England Agitation for the Abolition of the Slave Trade, 1780–1800.* M.A. thesis, University of Manchester, 1959.

Minute Book of the Committee of the Society for Effecting the Abolition of the Slave Trade. British Library Additional Mss. 21,254, 21,255, and 21,256. Cited in notes as "Minutes."

Scott, Julius Sherrard, III. *The Common Wind: Currents of Afro-American Communication in the Era of the Haitian Revolution.* Ph.D. thesis, Duke University, 1986.

Smith, William. *Historical Memoirs from 26 August 1778 to 12 November 1783 of William Smith: Historian of the Province of New York; Member of the Governor's Council, and Last Chief Justice of that Province under the Crown; Chief Justice of Quebec,* ed. William H. W. Sabine. Typescript, New York Public Library.

PARLIAMENTARY DEBATES AND GOVERNMENT DOCUMENTS

Board of Trade. *Report of the Lords of the Committee of Council appointed for the Consideration of all Matters relating to Trade and Foreign Plantations.* London, 1789.

The Debate on a Motion for the Abolition of the Slave-Trade, in the House of Commons, on Monday the Second of April, 1792, reported in Detail. London: W. Woodfall, 1792.

House of Commons. *Report from Select Committee on the Extinction of Slavery Throughout the British Dominions with the Minutes of Evidence, Appendix and Index.* London, 1832.

The Parliamentary Debates from the Year 1803 to the Present Time. London: T. C. Hansard, 1812 and later years. Cited in notes as "*PD.*"

The Parliamentary History of England, from the Earliest Period to the Year 1803. London: T. C. Hansard, 1814. Cited in notes as "*PH.*"

[Pitt, William]. *The Speech of the Right Honourable William Pitt, on a Motion for the Abolition of the Slave Trade in the House of Commons, on Monday the Second of April, 1792.* London: James Phillips, 1792.

Substance of the Debates on the Bill for Abolishing the Slave Trade which was brought into the House of Lords on the 2nd January, 1807, and into the House of Commons on the 10th February, 1807, and which was Finally Passed into a Law on the 26th March, 1807. London: W. Phillips, 1808.

Also see Wilberforce 1 and Williams 2, above.

ACKNOWLEDGMENTS

DURING THE YEARS I worked on this book, many people on four continents showed me much kindness and gave indispensable aid. By now my friends and family should have learned to flee when I have a draft manuscript ready, but some did not escape in time. The chance for me to hear and to talk over with them their reactions to what they read was more help to me than they can know. For thoughtful feedback and suggestions, I am deeply grateful for readings by Ayi Kwei Armah, Harriet Barlow, Mary Felstiner, Frank Fried, Hermann Hatzfeldt, David Hochschild, Elinor Langer, Robert Levering, Cynthia Li, Jacques Marchand, Mike Meyer, Samantha Power, Deborah Russell, Paul Solman, Adrian Wadsworth, Allen Wheelis, and Francis Wilson. The occupations of many of these readers—political activist, journalist, historian, farmer—were at one time or another practiced by Thomas Clarkson, who would have also felt at home with the several Quakers among them.

I also benefited from careful readings by my literary agent, Georges Borchardt, and my editor at Macmillan in London, Georgina Morley. Eric Chinski, my editor at Houghton Mifflin for most of the four years I was working on the book, not only wrote me a valuable critique, but when I was searching for a subject, he seemed to have an almost uncanny sense of what topics might attract me. After Eric left Houghton Mifflin for another job, Eamon Dolan helped greatly with perceptive comments on a later draft. Larry Cooper skillfully removed unnecessary adverbs and other superfluities with his manuscript editor's scalpel.

No one was more essential to this book than the country's best freelance editor, Tom Engelhardt. Having had his help before, I knew how valuable it would be, but I've sometimes wondered what the experience of editing by Tom would be for someone who did not know this in advance. It would perhaps be like working with a friend who you thought was merely going to help you put the final coat of paint on a house you had built. Instead, he starts asking questions: Is the kitchen in the right place? Look, your chimney's not drawing properly! Are you sure you need that room over there? And we need to jack the whole thing up and work on the foundation. From cellar to rooftop, this book reflects Tom's skills; without him, it would have been an immeasurably leakier, draftier, and shoddier piece of construction.

My wife, Arlie, read the manuscript closely with her own writer's eye, and with me walked around London and traveled to where Clarkson got off his horse in Hertfordshire. She also came to know the people in these pages so well that she made me the most imaginative birthday present I've ever received: a game in which players throw dice and advance along a board, using little figures of all the principal characters in this book. There's even a figure for Lord Gardenstone's pig and a ship for John Newton, complete with sails of seashells. An elaborate set of rules guides your progress along squares for each chapter, towards a final square representing completion of the manuscript. You may unluckily land on one of the squares marked "Writer's Block." From there you can escape by spinning an arrow that directs you to take a card telling you what to write, from one of several piles marked Work, Activism, Adventure, or Romance. With Arlie, for more than forty years my arrow has landed on the last, and always will.

I owe a special debt to the scholars of slavery and its era who read the manuscript and made many suggestions: Vincent Carretta, David Brion Davis, Seymour Drescher, Ellen Gibson Wilson, and David Geggus, who read the chapters on St. Domingue. I am deeply grateful for their generosity towards an interloping newcomer on territory they have been working in for most of their lives. I learned much from talking and corresponding with them, and several steered me to sources I otherwise would have missed. Their help allowed me to correct dozens of mistakes of fact and interpretation, large and small, but they are not responsible for those that may remain. I cannot thank them enough. I am also grateful to Christopher L. Brown for letting me read the manuscript of his immensely informative forthcoming book on the origins of British antislavery.

For all sorts of additional help, my gratitude goes to many others. Horace Campbell was my traveling companion in Jamaica; having the benefit of his eyes as a professional scholar of Africa on the country where he grew up greatly enriched the experience for me. Mike Schwartz of the Windsor Research Centre helped us out when we were there, as did George C. Thomas, Esq., of Montego Bay. Phyllis Bischoff and David Anthony pointed me to books I otherwise might have missed, and Roger Buckley, Ann Burton, Bruce Hindmarsh, Jeff Howarth, Susan Jacoby, Suzanne Schwartz, and Werner Zips answered queries or helped in other ways. My cousin Patricia Labalme, to whom this book is dedicated, always inspired me with her passion for the historian's craft. She once told me that if you love history, it doesn't matter whether you teach it to high school, college, or graduate students. She herself had done all three, and was at work on her scholarly edition of the great Venetian diarist Marino Sanudo until just weeks before her death from cancer.

A great library always seems a place that allows miracles of time travel, and so a special bow to the one I used most, at the University of California at Berkeley. Its copy of the 1808 edition of Thomas Clarkson's history of abolition, with pages almost the texture of linen, has sat on my desk these past four years. And what a pleasure it was to check out Moreau de Jonnès's memoirs from Berkeley and find that the due date stamped on the inside back cover for the previous borrower was exactly one week before I was born. At Friends House Library in London, I saw someone walk out of the Quaker meeting room next door wearing one of the old high-crowned black hats and for a moment thought I had jumped back two centuries to an antislavery meeting. On the other side of Euston Road, the British Library's wealth of books and manuscripts, courteous staff, and attractive reading rooms are almost enough to make you believe in the empire after all. My thanks also to the other libraries I spent time in: at Antislavery International and the British Museum in London and, in the United States, at Georgetown University, Stanford University, Bates College, Bowdoin College, the Graduate Theological Union at Berkeley, and the Library of Congress. A thank-you as well to the other libraries that sent copies of microfilms and manuscripts, sometimes without charge: the National Library of Wales, the John Rylands Library at the University of Manchester, the Gloucestershire and the Cambridgeshire Record Office, the Public Record Office at Kew, and the libraries at Uppsala University, St. John's College at Cambridge, Rhodes House at Oxford, and Washington State University.

ILLUSTRATION CREDITS

Newton: Cowper and Newton Museum. *Equiano:* Anti-Slavery International. *Yoked slaves:* David and Charles Livingstone, *Narrative of an Expedition to the Zambesi and its tributaries; and of the Discovery of the Lakes Shirwa and Nyassa, 1858–1864;* from http://hitchcock.itc.virginia.edu/slavery, "The Atlantic Slave Trade and Slave Life in the Americas: A Visual Record," compiled by Jerome S. Handler and Michael L. Tuite, Jr. *Castle:* Courtesy of Merrick Posnansky; from "The Atlantic Slave Trade and Slave Life in the Americas." *Below decks:* British Library, 649.c.237. *Sharp:* Anti-Slavery International. *Cane cutters:* British Library, 1786.c.9. *Boiling house:* British Library, 1786.c.9. *Furnace:* Library of Congress. *Thatch hut and hut under palms:* A. Duperly & Sons, *Picturesque Jamaica. Thrown overboard:* Musée National de la Marine, Paris. *Clarkson:* Bridgeman Art Library. *Poster:* Library of Congress. *Restraints:* Thomas Clarkson, *The History of the Rise, Progress, and Accomplishment of the Abolition of the African Slave-Trade by the British Parliament. Wilberforce:* Anti-Slavery International. *Medallion:* British Museum. *Ship diagram:* Library of Congress. *Currency:* Granville Sharp, *A Short Sketch of Temporary Regulations (Until Better Shall Be Proposed) for the Intended Settlement on the Grain Coast of Africa, near Sierra Leona. Ship model:* Bridgeman Art Library. *House of Commons:* British Library, 190.e.1. *1791 cartoon:* Bridgeman Art Library. *1796 cartoon:* Library of Congress. *French officer fighting slave:* Library of Congress. *Blacks hanging white officer:* Library of Congress. *Toussaint L'Ouverture:* Library of Congress. *Parkinson:* Library Company of Philadelphia. *Rowe:* Werner Zips. *Treadmill:* Library of Congress. *Trap:* Adam Hochschild. *Broadside:* Public Record Office. *Britannia:* Wilberforce House, Hull City Museums and Art Galleries. *Slave hospital:* Horace Campbell.

INDEX

ABOUT THE AUTHOR

ADAM HOCHSCHILD was born in New York City in 1942. His first book, *Half the Way Home: A Memoir of Father and Son,* was published in 1986. Michiko Kakutani of the *New York Times* called it "an extraordinarily moving portrait of the complexities and confusions of familial love . . . firmly grounded in the specifics of a particular time and place, conjuring them up with Proustian detail and affection." It was followed by *The Mirror at Midnight: A South African Journey* and *The Unquiet Ghost: Russians Remember Stalin.* His collection, *Finding the Trapdoor: Essays, Portraits, Travels,* won the PEN/Spielvogel-Diamonstein Award for the Art of the Essay. *King Leopold's Ghost: A Story of Greed, Terror, and Heroism in Colonial Africa* was a finalist for the National Book Critics Circle Award. His books have been translated into eleven languages.

Besides his books, Hochschild has also written for *The New Yorker, Harper's Magazine,* the *New York Review of Books, Granta,* the *New York Times Magazine,* and many other newspapers and magazines. His articles have won prizes from the Overseas Press Club, the Society of Professional Journalists, and the Society of American Travel Writers. A cofounder of *Mother Jones* magazine, he has also been a commentator on National Public Radio's *All Things Considered.* He teaches writing at the Graduate School of Journalism at the University of California at Berkeley and has been a Fulbright lecturer in India. He lives in San Francisco with his wife, the sociologist and author Arlie Russell Hochschild. They have two sons.